The Bloomsbury Research Handbook of Indian Philosophy and Gender

Bloomsbury Research Handbooks in Asian Philosophy

Series Editors

Chakravarthi Ram-Prasad, Lancaster University, UK
Sor-hoon Tan, National University of Singapore

Editorial Advisory Board

Bringing together established academics and rising stars, *Bloomsbury Research Handbooks in Asian Philosophy* survey philosophical topics across all the main schools of Asian thought. Each volume focuses on the history and development of a core subject in a single tradition, asking how the field has changed, highlighting current disputes, anticipating new directions of study, illustrating the Western philosophical significance of a subject, and demonstrating why a topic is important for understanding Asian thought.

From knowledge, being, gender, and ethics to methodology, language, and art, these research handbooks provide up-to-date and authoritative overviews of Asian philosophy in the twenty-first century.

Available Titles

The Bloomsbury Research Handbook of Chinese Philosophy and Gender, edited by Ann A. Pang White

The Bloomsbury Research Handbook of Chinese Philosophy Methodologies, edited by Sor-hoon Tan

The Bloomsbury Research Handbook of Contemporary Japanese Philosophy, edited by Michiko Yusa

The Bloomsbury Research Handbook of Early Chinese Ethics and Political Philosophy, edited by Alexus McLeod

The Bloomsbury Research Handbook of Indian Aesthetics and the Philosophy of Art, edited by Arindam Chakrabarti

The Bloomsbury Research Handbook of Indian Ethics, edited by Shyam Ranganathan

The Bloomsbury Research Handbook of Indian Philosophy and Gender

Edited by

Veena R. Howard

BLOOMSBURY
NEW DELHI • LONDON • OXFORD • NEW YORK • SYDNEY

BLOOMSBURY INDIA
Bloomsbury Publishing India Pvt. Ltd
Second Floor, LSC Building No. 4, DDA Complex, Pocket C–6&7,
Vasant Kunj, New Delhi 110070

BLOOMSBURY, BLOOMSBURY ACADEMIC INDIA and the Diana logo are
trademarks of Bloomsbury Publishing Plc

First published in India 2024
First published in Great Britain 2020

Cover image: Three Maidens Under a Willow. Attributed to Baijnath c. A.D. 1810,
copied by Sumahendra, Jaipur. Wall painting, Deogarh Fort

This edition published with permission from Bloomsbury Publishing Plc,
50 Bedford Square, London, WC1B3DP, UK

A catalogue record for this book is available from the British Library.
A catalogue record for this book is available from the Library of Congress.

ISBN: 978-93-61310-54-6

Series: Bloomsbury Research Handbooks in Asian Philosophy

Typeset by Newgen KnowledgeWorks Pvt. Ltd., Chennai, India
Printed and bound in India by Replika Press Pvt. Ltd.

To find out more about our authors and books
visit www.bloomsbury.com and sign up for our newsletters

Contents

Notes on Contributors

Carol S. Anderson is Professor of Religion at Kalamazoo College. Her research focuses on religions of South Asia and feminist/queer approaches to the study of religions. She is author of *Pain and Its Ending: The Four Noble Truths in Theravāda Buddhism*, and her recent projects explore the range of sexualities found in the commentaries of the Pāli Buddhist canon.

Geoff Ashton, PhD, is Assistant Professor of Philosophy at the University of San Francisco. He specializes in Asian philosophies, has twice served as a Fulbright scholar in Asia, and has authored several publications on Asian and comparative philosophies. His current book project, *Whose Suffering? Whose Freedom? A Phenomenological Reconstruction of the Philosophy of the Sāṃkhya Kārikā*, offers a new interpretation of Classical Sāṃkhya philosophy.

Dr Raj Balkaran is an expert in Indian Goddess Traditions and Instructor at the University of Toronto School of Continuing Studies. His recent book, *The Goddess and the King in Indian Myth* (2019) charts the narrative structure of Devī Māhāmtya ("The Greatness of the Goddess," the first Sanskrit work advancing a Great Goddess), along with the ideological impact of that structure. You can find out more at rajbalkaran.com.

Ana Laura Funes Maderey is Assistant Professor of Philosophy at Eastern Connecticut State University where she teaches Asian Philosophies, East-West Comparative topics in Philosophy, and Feminist Philosophies. Her research focuses on comparative philosophy of the body, phenomenology, feminism, and notions of bodily self-awareness in the Indian philosophical schools of Sāṃkhya and Yoga.

Gopal Gupta is Associate Professor at the University of Evansville. His book, *Illusion and Identity, Maya in the Bhāgavata Purāṇa*, is forthcoming from Oxford University Press. Some of his recent publications include "The World as Illusion: Environmental Implications of the Doctrine of Māyā" (*Journal of Vaiṣṇava Studies*, 2015) and "'May Calamities Befall Us at Every Step': The Bhāgavata's Response to the Problem of Evil" in *The Bhāgavata Purāṇa, Sacred Text and Living Tradition* (2013). Gupta is the editor for the *Journal of Hindu Christian Studies*.

Veena R. Howard, PhD, is Associate Professor of Asian Religious Traditions in the Department of Philosophy at California State University, Fresno. She is also a Coordinator of Peace and Conflict studies. Her research focuses on Gandhi's philosophy, gender, animal ethics, the Sant traditions of India, and interreligious dialogue. Her publications include the books, *Dharma: Hindu, Jain, Buddhist, and Sikh Traditions of India* (2017), *Gandhi's Ascetic Activism: Renunciation and Social Action* (2013), and several peer-reviewed articles and chapters, including an Oxford Bibliography article on M. K. Gandhi (2019). She has served on multiple boards, including the Board of Trustees of the Parliament of the World's Religions.

Nikky-Guninder Kaur Singh is the Crawford Family Professor at Colby College in Maine. She received her BA in Philosophy and Religion from Wellesley College, her MA from the University of Pennsylvania, and her PhD from Temple University. Her interests focus on poetics and feminist issues. She has published extensively in the field of Sikhism, including *The Feminine Principle in the Sikh Vision of the Transcendent* (1993), *The Name of My Beloved: Verses of the Sikh Gurus*, and *Metaphysics and Physics of the Guru Granth Sahib*.

Jeffery D. Long is Professor of Religion and Asian Studies at Elizabethtown College in Elizabethtown, Pennsylvania, where he has taught since receiving his PhD from the University of Chicago Divinity School in the area of Philosophy of Religions in the year 2000. His interests range from modern Vedanta and its reception in the contemporary world to classical Jain philosophy and its relevance to religious pluralism. He is the author of *A Vision for Hinduism*, *Jainism: An Introduction* and the *Historical Dictionary of Hinduism* as well as a wide range of articles in both journal and online formats. His forthcoming works include an introduction to Indian philosophy (along with a reader of primary sources), a textbook on Hinduism in America, and a monograph on the teachings of Swami Vivekananda. He is also the series editor for the "Explorations in Indic Traditions: Ethical, Philosophical, and Theological" book series.

Nancy M. Martin is Associate Professor and Chair of Religious Studies and Director of the Schweitzer Institute at Chapman University and a Life Member of Clare Hall, Cambridge University. Her research and publications focus primarily on Hinduism with an emphasis on *bhakti*, women's religious lives, oral traditions, and the saints Mirabai and Kabir. In addition, she has directed multiple conferences and edited a book series in comparative religious ethics.

Chakravarthi Ram-Prasad is Fellow of the British Academy and Distinguished Professor of Comparative Philosophy and Religion at Lancaster University. His many publications include *Advaita Epistemology and Metaphysics*; *Human Self, Divine Self: The Philosophy of Being in Two Gītā Commentaries*; and *Human Being, Bodily Being: Phenomenology from Classical India*.

Rita D. Sherma holds an MA in Women's Studies in Religion and a PhD in Theology & Ethics (Claremont Graduate University, CA). The founding Director and Associate Professor at Graduate Theological Union's *Mira and Ajay Shingal Center for Dharma Studies*, she is also Co-Chair of Sustainability 360 and Core Doctoral Faculty at GTU, Berkeley, California. Formerly, she was the Swami Vivekananda Visiting Professor in Hindu Studies, at USC, Los Angeles. Among her published and pending volumes are *Hermeneutics and Hindu Thought: Toward a Fusion of Horizons* (2008); *Woman and Goddess in Hinduism: Reinterpretations and Re-envisioning* (2010); and *Sustainable Societies: Interreligious, Interdisciplinary Responses* (2019). She is founding editor-in-chief of the *Journal of Dharma Studies.*

Ruth Vanita, professor at the University of Montana, former reader at Delhi University and co-founder of *Manushi*, India's first nationwide feminist journal, is the author of many books and over sixty scholarly articles. She has published widely on a variety of topics, ranging from Shakespeare to Urdu poetry to sexuality in Indian literature and is now working on a book on gender and Hindu philosophy. Her novel, *Among Fairies*, set in an eighteenth-century courtesan household, will appear next year from Penguin, and in Hindi from Rajkamal.

Editor's Note

This project was supported by Fresno State's 2016-17 Provost's Research and Creative Activity Award and a generous grant from the Uberoi Foundation of Religious Studies, dedicated to the study and development of Dharmic traditions originated in India. I am grateful for their support that helped me with needed time for writing, editing, and preparing the manuscript for publication. I am indebted to Dean Saúl Jiménez-Sandoval and Associate Dean Honora Chapman (College of Arts and Humanities, California State University, Fresno) for their sustained support with this project. I deeply appreciate the consistent encouragement of Chakravarthi Ram-Prasad (Distinguished Professor, Department of Politics, Philosophy, and Religion, Lancaster University, UK), the series editor of the *Bloomsbury Handbook in Gender and Philosophy*. This volume would not have been possible without his guidance and support. I am also grateful to Colleen Coalter, Philosophy Senior Commissioning Editor at the Bloomsbury Publishing, for her patience and providing assistance whenever I needed. I want to extend my thanks to many colleagues, students, and friends for their help in various ways. Above all, I am thankful to the authors of this volume for their conversations, time, and effort in producing groundbreaking scholarship in this first of its kind project. I dedicate this volume to these fellow scholars who plumb the depths of ancient and modern Indian philosophical texts to envision new realities in the realm of gender studies and to create a better and more just world.

1

Introduction: Gender Conceptions in Indian Thought: Identity, Hybridity, Fluidity, Androgyny, and Transcendence

Veena R. Howard

Throughout human history, stories have shaped our reality as gendered beings, which is expressed through rituals, symbolism, and philosophical arguments.[1] Not surprisingly, feminist thinkers seek to create a new understanding of the self through dialogue with oral narratives, religious rituals, metaphors, and religious and philosophical texts. This volume develops that dialogue by considering selected texts from the philosophical traditions originated on the Indian subcontinent to widen the scope of stories to further deepen our knowledge of nuanced expressions of gender.[2] As scholars have noted, "gender" in much South Asian scholarship is largely restricted to a study of women (Pokazanyeva 2015). With the richly textured lives and stories in Indian philosophical texts and traditions, this volume provides a broader exploration of gender in terms of femininity, masculinity, androgyny, and other forms of gendered living.

Significantly, the Sanskrit term *darśana*, derived from the root verb *dṛś* meaning "to see" or a "way of seeing," is used for "philosophy." Indian philosophical thoughts, including Jain and Buddhist, are multifarious. Any one of several orthodox and heterodox positions in the classical texts of Indian philosophy and its living traditions we consider to be a *darśana*. Each philosophy represents a worldview and way of evaluating questions of metaphysics, ontology, cosmology, epistemology, ethics, embodiment, and social order, including questions of gender.[3] In the present context, we use the philosophical signifier, *darśana*, in the sense of illuminating the multiple constructions of gender articulated in Indic texts—ancient and modern—which themselves are composed in both classical languages and local vernaculars.

A consideration of gender in any philosophical texts or schools of *darśana* entails drawing on multiple sources and approaches. R. K. Narayan comments on how in India's context, philosophical truths and questions are considered by taking into account different disciplines and genres:

> Everything is interrelated. Stories, scriptures, ethics, philosophy, grammar, astrology, astronomy, semantics, mysticism, and moral codes—each forms part and parcel of total life and is indispensable for a four-square understanding of existence. (Narayan 1964: 4)

For evaluating questions about gender, this volume highlights the value of utilizing different literary genres that convey philosophical insights. This study reveals that no one essential approach, although certain orthodox conventions dominate, conceptualizes either gender or sexual identity within India's astonishingly vast array of philosophical and religious views.

Various classical and vernacular theological and philosophical viewpoints problematize any single construction of gender and sexual identity despite heteronormative cultural conventions. Thus, any attempts to retrieve any one prevailing philosophical analysis or essentialized approach prove fruitless. However, a close attention to language compositions, narrative structures, and multiple voices gives rise to a richer understanding of the complexity of gender constructions in Indian thought. Additionally, with such a prolific availability of narratives and perspectives, the authors of this volume also broaden theories—for example, gender as biological, social or linguistic construct—expressed in the works of eminent Western thinkers including Judith Butler, Julia Kristeva, Donna Haraway, Luce Irigaray, and so forth.

As the issue of gender intersects with questions about equality, justice, disability, race, ethnicity, and social class, there exists no one way to answer the compound question: What is gender, and how does it determine us as human beings? Such questions have been addressed in various ways in Indian thought and articulated in many philosophical views, each of which has nuanced interpretations of what is meant by the term "human being"—an embodied being that is simultaneously an entity beyond flesh and blood. Often in the Indian context, the question has been reversed from the outset, not beginning from the bodily reality but from the reality of the self (constructed both in universal and individual terms), which precedes the present physical body. Various texts have posed a more basic question long before any discussions resembling those of contemporary gender debates surfaced, and it remains: Can gender be self-determined or is it always connected to the bodily existence, and how do we determine the gender of our being beyond the constraints of one body, one life, or one practice?

The largely pan-Indian notion that an individual might have experienced numerous genders, or can experience them across lifetimes, is informed by key presuppositions (depending on the school of philosophy): *saṃsāra* (or rebirth); the relation between Divine Reality, the self, and the cosmos (this includes the affirmation or denial of God and the self/non-self); the empirical self and the body; and the individual's relationship with society. These factors implicitly intertwine with gender, creating a context for conventional truth claims. Therefore, any inquiry into issues regarding gender must always be contextualized. Hence, we must begin with philosophical texts, narratives, and traditions that have guided the conduct of a people over two millennia, along with a recognition of the historicized bias of the contemporary context, which propels our current inquiry into gender.

The scholarly project of analyzing gender constructs using contemporary gender theories can potentially create new practical insights, but it simultaneously may challenge established positions, prompting inevitable counterexamples. Therefore, we must be attentive to the perspectives set out in these texts (which are living corpora that guide their practitioners), whether they are from the point of view of an individual or social norms and expectations. The authors widen the discussion about the relationship between sex and gender, considering masculinities and femininities as plural and fluid. They variously analyze dynamics of both gender and sex by exploring whether biological sex is alterable by way of a kind of practice (ritual or meditation), the extent to which ambiguity is recognized, and whether gender can be rejected, altered, or amended by the individual themselves and on what basis. These questions arise out of essential concern for the subject of experience and gender autonomy. Both of these are impacted by the initial socially determined gender of an individual as well as social class and status, religious piety, allegiance to a tradition, or the personal power of an individual to deviate from the culture itself. Questions about gender are not absolute; they always require qualification.

Expanding Concepts of Gender from a Set of Interrelated Philosophies

While Western scholarly discourse has highly conceptualized the use of the term "gender," scholars of Indian thought have only recently begun mining the textual resources of the traditions and determining the implications of critical gender analyses for real lives.[4] Despite the availability of an abundance of Indian philosophical source materials, there is a glaring lacuna in the discussion on gender. Authors of the chapters in this volume utilize insights from Western gender and feminist theorists; and, at the same time, they offer new acumens that have the potential to broaden existing gender theoretical frameworks.[5]

For this project, we choose only a select number of texts and traditions from Indian thought that offer dynamic and complex constructions of gender. In order to simultaneously read questions of gender creatively and also construct theories that engage with the wide spectrum of contemporary and critical gender issues, this volume primarily employs a cross-disciplinary approach that negotiates multiple languages, perspectives, and periods. This project embraces sources that range from Sanskrit, Pāli, and Prākṛta texts and narratives to vernacular poetry. Such a variety of texts enables us to expand various theoretical concepts, specifically with respect to historical, hermeneutical, religious, and linguistic understandings of gender in relation to self and society.

While this volume approaches the study of gender with nuanced inquiries, it engages with the largely established discourses about gender within Indian thought. Scholars creatively analyze Indian texts and traditions, which have shaped the identity of Indian thought, to develop new insights into feminist perspectives, racial perceptions, same-sex relationships, and transgender identities. The authors of this volume engage with the texts to gain insight into contemporary concerns about gender equality vis-à-vis human dignity as well as to deepen our understanding of gender through the multivalent reflections on religiosity, epistemology, and ethics made available through ancient and modern resources. In India's cultural context, philosophical and mythical assessments with respect to gender continue to be manipulated, appropriated, and expanded in the domestic realms (e.g., women's rights) and in the domains of national politics and spiritual authority.

For example, the recent (2018) controversy of women's entry into South Indian Sabarimala temple, open to men of all ages but restricting women of menstruating age, elicited a debate on the masculine fear of fertile female bodies and the tension between the mythical god's anxiety of facing young women and its effect on the treatment of real women. Furthermore, a legal recognition of the third gender/transgender as a valid identifying marker of persons by the Indian Supreme Court is corroborated through various examples found in the Indian philosophical and religious texts. In response to a perceived need to widen the discourse, this study gestures toward a comprehensive unfurling of gender dynamics in Indian philosophical texts and traditions. It aims to expand the conversation on emerging understandings of gender in academia. But more importantly, such a cross-cultural and interdisciplinary examination has the potential to broaden our ethical awareness, methods of knowledge, and sensibilities in social relations and policymaking. Presently, no similar single volume in Indian thought encompasses philosophical viewpoints on gender as they have emerged and evolved in history. Through analyses of a broad range of texts from the Vedānta, Sāṃkhhya, Itihāsa and *Purāṇa* to the Jain, Buddhist, Sikh and Bhakti traditions, the authors in the volume aim to address this lacuna.

To situate this volume within the broader discourse on gender, we first begin with a brief overview of those debates in academic circles that are particularly relevant to this project. For this, we provide a brief survey of taxonomies of gender to familiarize the readers with the intersecting themes that emerge in this volume. These themes include grammar, language, and gender; the essentialized roles of women in Indian traditions; and wide-ranging portrayals of gender, with a primary concern for modes of androgyny, gender fluidity, and gender hybridity.

Grammar, Symbolism, and Gender Issues

Over the past several years in Western academic circles, theories of gender underwent a major conceptual shift. They generally present a revised understanding of gender as a social rather than a biological construct. Some theorists opt to analyze language structures as an informant in investigating misogynist tendencies. Others, most notably Judith Butler, show us how we appropriate language, culture, and practices to perform gender. While we accept the social construction of gender as an open question, we examine how varieties of gender in Indian philosophical traditions follow from linguistic composition, ontological presuppositions, and in what ways gender dynamics mesh with religious myths and symbolism.

Significantly, scholars in India have not been debating gender in an intellectual vacuum: feminist activists and scholars—both in and outside India and in diaspora—have been in dialogue to understand gender dynamics and hegemonies. One important question involves the relationship and intersectionality between language and gender. In her book, *Women, Men and Language*, Jennifer Coates engages in sociolinguistic studies and examines multiple factors, including linguistic strategies used by men, that can be attributed to sustaining gender inequality. Further, various linguistic theories suggest a connection between thought and language. Benjamin Lee Whorf's observation that unique grammatical structures of language shape the worldview of a people has received attention from contemporary linguists. Here we briefly provide analysis of Sanskrit language's grammatical structure, as an example, for understanding such assumptions about gender and point out some unique insights into the question of the relationship between gender and language.

Classical Sanskrit texts (*śāstra*) and literature have historically guided the Indian conceptions of gender, but Jain and Buddhist canons composed in Prākṛta and Pāli have also influenced the questions of gender. But, importantly, Indian philosophical thought arises out of a variety of linguistic structures. Hence, it must not be assumed that we will find any ultimate grammatical clues by taking recourse to Sanskrit language alone. Even though Sanskrit is not the only vehicle of discourse, it is the language of many texts analyzed in this volume's chapters. Therefore, Sanskrit demands attention from the outset, not merely for its gender-rich terminology but also for its influence on Indian thought. Furthermore, this language comprises complex grammatical structure and lexical, which provide valuable insights into any relationship between language and gender.

The *Ṛg Veda*, the ancient sacred Hindu text, identifies *Vāc* (a Sanskrit term for speech, discourse, language) as a female deity. As Sally Sutherland Goldman has claimed, *Vāc* is arguably central to the Vedas, ancient Hindu sacred texts—the repository of all forms of rituals, arts, philosophy, and sciences—and it has been "culturally marked as positive, or valorized" (2000: 60). Grammatically a feminine noun, *vāc* is the source of linguistic and ritual expressions. Traditionally, only *Brahmins* (male priests) studied the Vedas and performed rituals. The *Ṛg Veda* ascribes to *Vāc* the qualities of mother and wife. Dedicated to Vedic learning, chanting, and performing sacrifices, male *Brahmins* sought to control every aspect of speech—sound, meter, meaning, and so forth. Sutherland Goldman sees the *Brahmins*' control of Vāc (personified as the Goddess) as indicative of sexual anxiety and control. She construes the meticulous attention to speech as "fundamental to the construction of brahminic patriarchy" (2000: 60). Indeed, the male *Brahmins* protected Vedic learning and ritual performance; they prohibited women and men of other castes from having any contact with the sacred speech (Vedic ritual formulas), *Vāc*. Not surprisingly, Sutherland Goldman connects *Brahmins*' control of the feminine speech with their patriarchal worldview.

However, the perceived relationship between *vāc* and patriarchal mindset raises two contradictory issues: On the one hand, by feminizing the most essential source of Vedic learning and ritual (i.e., speech/language), the Vedic authors provide a model for the superior female power. On the other, despite the valorization of language as feminine, they have perpetuated patriarchy barring women from accessing the wisdom of the Vedas. This apparent contradiction requires further examination. First, the male scholars' will to command a language, personified as a female deity, does not necessarily imply a devaluation of women. We must be careful in projecting implicit assumptions of gender inequity on the basis of language structures revealed through a sort of textual psychoanalysis, as in the case of the relationship between the feminine speech and male *Brahmins*. As a way of meaning-making, gendered language is not necessarily an instrumental cause of patriarchal views, nor should a mastery of language mean female subjugation.

Second, besides the symbolic representation of Vāc as a goddess, scholars have considered other factors for the feminization of speech, that is, a stylistic embellishment of the language's beauty. Simon Brodbeck and Brian Black do not see any significant relationship between gendered symbolism and social reality; they rather consider poets' and philosophers' artful mixing of feminine and masculine genders as a linguistic device to "enrich the ideas of opposition and complementarity." To underscore their point of opposition, they provide examples of the specific gendering of philosophical principles in the Sāṃkhya philosophy, namely *puruṣa* (a masculine principle representing consciousness) and *prakṛti* (a feminine principle representing primordial nature) (Brodbeck and Black 2007: 14). Although the authors do not consider any impact of such gendered constructions on real women, recent scholars have analyzed the relationship between the two gendered principles with a feminist lens, as we see in Ana Funes' chapter in this volume.

Undoubtedly, there is an aesthetic dimension to the interplay of gender with philosophical ideas in a living language, but we must not overlook how language produces meaning. It may help to pay attention to the following:

1. Personifying Vāc as a female deity suggests authors' unique awareness toward the feminine gender from the very inception of the philosophical thought and religious ritual articulated in the *Ṛg Veda*.
2. Conceiving Vāc as Goddess connected to sacred formulas, rhetoric, and speech can also be alternatively construed as a way to honor the Divine Feminine principle and create a space for female voices, despite domination of male voices, in Indian philosophical and narrative texts. Chad Bower argues that language "reproduces ways of thinking" and

connects linguistic patterns and conceptual frameworks. When studying Indian philosophical narratives, one notices how female voices sway authority when they speak. Interestingly, *uvāca* (past tense verb of *vac*, "spoke") forms an always gender-neutral verb conjugation (neither feminine nor masculine); such grammatical construction levels the playing field with regard to speeches uttered by female or male characters. In dialogue, both female and male voice deserve equal attention, notwithstanding their different gender.

3. Finally, concerning the debates on women's role or their agency, female voices resound loud and logical in the narrative texts. Female protagonists unveil the ontological truths and prevailing oppressive patriarchal structures. For example, Draupadī's conversations with Kṛṣṇa and Ambā's dialogue with the ascetics in the *Mahābhārata* (see Chapter 10) shed light on the male oppression of women; and, the dialogues of female interlocutors Gārgi, Maitreyī, and Sage Yājñavalkya in the *Bṛhadāraṇyaka Upaniṣad* reveal truths about the reality of *Ātman* and *Brahman*. In each instance, these women are praised for their wisdom, clarity, and diction. In the *Mahābhārata*'s dialogue between King Janaka and a female ascetic Sulabhā, the genderlessness of the self is emphasized, opening a new understanding for the essentialized categories of male and female.

Notwithstanding historical and mythical models, the work of reconstructing relations of gender and power is ongoing, and context is never purely historical. New interpretations on the topic of gender continue to emerge through dialogue and interactions between philosophical concepts, symbolism, and modern challenges of inequality, injustice, and environmental degradation. For example, female theologians, ecofeminists, and environmental activists embrace these precise linguistic constructions and feminine symbolism for confronting prevalent patriarchal subjugation and environmental degradation. Ecofeminists, for example, often organize their arguments around feminine images and concepts, some of which stem from Yoga, Bhakti, and Tantra philosophies. Scholars and activists utilize feminine symbols of *Pṛthivī* (Mother Earth), *prakṛti* (essence/substance/nature), and the creative forces *māyā* and *śakti* (energy; power) as counter models of nurturing versus consuming. In her chapter, Ana Funes provides a fresh look at the field of feminine semantics and its implications for the worldview of many of those who experience "thought" and "consciousness" in the Sanskrit language and other vernaculars in which these Sanskrit words have been adopted. Evidently, by gendering the term *vāc* as feminine and degendering its verb form, *uvāca*, early Indian authors have offered a paradigm that potentially can be developed to create a framework for confronting gender biases.

Sex/Gender Taxonomies and Indian Philosophical Literature

As we segue into the discussion of gender in the Indian tradition, it is important to emphasize at the outset that India's systems do not offer a clear answer to the question of where sex and gender diverge, nor do we provide a single definition of these terms. In general, *liṅga* can often be used to signify gender or sex. *Liṅga* means a mark, sexual organ, gender, characteristic, or component of an inference qua being a "sign."[6] Although a distinction between sex and gender has been made in the works of various feminist scholars, some such as Brodbeck and Black have "questioned the neat divide between sex and gender."[7] Intriguingly, the term "mark" or "sign" conveys a complex construction of gender identity.

The Indian texts and traditions that routinely use the term *liṅga* display a wide array of terminology descriptive of different genders and sexuality. The Sanskrit language encompasses three grammatical genders: *puṃliṅga*, *strīliṅga*, and *napuṃsakaliṅga*. They signify the common categories of male sex and female sex—that is, *puṃs-prakṛti* (male nature) and *strī-prakṛti* (female nature), respectively—but also, as Leonard Zwilling and Michael Sweet inform us, a third category *tṛtīya-prakṛti* (referring to a "third sex") or literally, "third basic form" (Zwilling and Sweet 1996: 363). Amara Das Wilhelm comments that the term *tṛtīya-prakṛti* refers to a "natural mixing or combination of the male and female natures to the point in which they can no longer be categorized as male or female in the traditional sense of the word" (Wilhelm 2010: 16). The third category can also be referred to as "neuter gender"—*napuṃsaka-liṅga*. In addition to this, *within* the third gender we find not only individuals we would refer to as androgynous but also effeminate males and masculine women. So, the term *tṛtīya-prakṛti* can refer not only to individuals who are not, biologically speaking, male or female but also individuals whose *gender* (informed by multiple factors) does not neatly fit into the category of masculine or feminine. The term *tṛtīya-prakṛti* can refer to ambiguity in *both* sex *and* gender.

In general, Indian literature depicts a wide range of individuals as falling under the umbrella term "third gender." As Zwilling and Sweet, for instance, tell us,

> The acceptance of the category a third sex has been a part of the Indian worldview for nearly three thousand years ... Men who were impotent, did not impregnate women, were effeminate, or transvestite, were regarded as *napuṃsaka*, literally "not-a-male," that is, un-male (1996: 362).

The third gender also can refer to gender ambiguity. We find another example in the *Mahābhārata*, when Ambā/Śikhaṇḍinī who transforms into male Śikhaṇḍin is characterized as a "male-female" child of Drupada. Jain philosophy provides a theoretical framework on sex/gender that allows the possibility of having a gender orientation different from a biological sex.

Ambiguous or neuter gender has the capacity to disrupt the dualistic ways of thinking and power of negotiating gender binaries familiar in the normative culture. The power of the ambiguously gendered person is considered both dangerous and auspicious in various narratives. For instance, Mahatma Gandhi sought to identify with both genders while struggling to be asexual through his practice of celibacy. In the Vedic philosophy, *Brahman* (the ground of being), beyond both male and female categories yet encompassing both, is linguistically characterized in *napuṃsaka-liṅga*, a neuter gender. Here a neuter gender does not imply lifelessness but a state beyond gender binaries, which is hallmark of sages much like Śukadeva (the main narrator of the *Bhāgavata*). According to a mythical lore, his purity was so immersive that he was not aware of sexual differentiation, and the bathing *gopīs* felt no shame in his presence.[8]

In an altogether different modality of disrupting heteronormativity in medieval *bhakti* literature, male poets imagine themselves as women and long for their beloved, Kṛṣṇa. "Gender roles and divisions are fundamental to many aspects of social, ritual, and narrative order," as Anna Pokazanyeva observes in her Oxford Bibiography article of gender and sexuality in Hinduism. Simultaneously, she adds, "They serve as sites of tension, negotiation, conflict, and even transformation" (Pokazanyeva 2015). In many instances, negotiation of gendered identities leads the way for confronting other forms of dualistic structures of class, caste, and race. For the last four decades, feminist scholars have critiqued the dualistic structures of black/white, reason/emotion, and male/female. They have drawn attention to the relationship between racial and sexual oppression. The eminent African-American scholar Patricia Hill-Collins, known for her groundbreaking work in Black feminist thought, shows the connection between dual structures and oppression:

> Either/or dualistic thinking, or what I will refer to as the construct of dichotomous oppositional difference, may be a philosophical lynchpin in systems of race, class, and gender oppression. One fundamental characteristic of this construct is the categorization of people, things, and ideas in terms of their difference from one another. For example, the terms in dichotomies such as black/white, male/female, reason/emotion, fact/opinion, and subject/object gain their meaning only in *relation* to their difference to their oppositional counterparts. Another fundamental characteristic of this construct is that difference is not complimentary in that the halves of the dichotomy do not enhance each other. Rather, the dichotomous halves are different and inherently opposed to one another. A third and more important characteristic is that these oppositional relationships are inherently unstable. Since such dualities rarely represent different but equal relationships, the inherently unstable relationship is resolved by subordinating one half of each pair to the other. Thus, white rules black, males dominate females, reason is touted as superior to emotion in ascertaining truth, facts supersede opinion in evaluating knowledge, and subjects rule objects. (Hill-Collins 1986: 20)

Hill-Collins aptly demonstrates how dualistic categories have routinely resulted in unequal relationships. She shows that dichotomous categories often do not organize our social, economic, and intellectual realities into halves complementing one another. In general, dualistic categories result in dominant and subjugated halves and an imbalanced social reality. Consequently, Hill-Collins develops the notion of *intersectionality*, underscoring the systemic interconnectedness of gender, racial, social, and economic oppression. However, in the Indian binary mythological model of Śiva and Śakti, the two deities mutually enhance one another in an eternal codependence. The Indian philosophical traditions' mythic symbolism of mutually dependent male (Śiva) and female (Śakti), linguistic degendering of the Absolute Reality *Brahman*, and illustrations of mythical and modern characters seeking the highest state beyond gender, caste, and class differences offer model alternatives to dualistic thinking leading to unequal power systems.

Ontological Conceptions: The Interplay of Gender, Transcendence, and Androgyny

While some scholars consider dualistic categories of gender as culprit for unequal power dynamics, others attribute female subordination to male-centered conceptions of God in the Judeo-Christian traditions. Critical feminist thinkers, including Mary Daly, Rosemary Radford Ruether, Naomi Goldenberg, Julia Kristeva, and Luce Irigaray confront sex-biased language in religion. "Freud and feminists," writes Naomi Ruth Goldenberg,

> have two important ideas in common about religion. Both insist that the God of the Jewish and Christian religions is predominantly imaged as Father and both insist that this image is responsible for a large measure of oppressiveness in human society. (1982: 1)

Many feminist theologians have noted that androcentric language and symbolism in religion have historically impacted the lives of women and led to subjugation of both women and nature. When God is construed as male and women are conferred subordinate status, the real lives of women are damaged in terms of equality and dignity. Some scholars, including Radford Ruether, Merlin Stone, and Neela Bhattacharya Saxena chronologically backtrack through the traditions to recover the "Divine Feminine" and more inclusive ontological models. Others, such as Mary Daly, are inclined "to promote alternative images of the divine in powerful, gynomorphic guise" as a means of claiming female subjectivity, says feminist scholar Victoria Barker (Barker 2008: 315). However, Barker herself proposes a movement toward a more positive and inclusive model, a world-affirming ethical model distanced from transcendence:

> What feminist theology is now entitled to address is the best that our theological traditions have to bequeath. And this includes a God whose radical transcendence is traversed—and, paradoxically, underscored—by an equally radical immanence (2008: 326).

Intriguingly, Barker's vision of theology can be found in India's traditions, one that presents the Divine as both transcendent and immanent. Further, despite an articulation of polarized and gendered ontological realities, instances of challenging gender binaries abound. For the purpose of our project, I provide a brief overview of Indian philosophical notions of reality. In Indian thought, when one takes a broader view of the nature of Divine Reality (we refrain from using the term "God" due to its polemic connotations in Judeo-Christian traditions) things are not so simple. Theoretically, androcentric conceptions cannot be attributed to the ultimate nature of *God*; therefore, the "Divine Reality" has been variously construed in Indian thought. Some schools of philosophy even reject the idea of God altogether and simply focus on existential reality. In the most ancient recorded text, the *Ṛg Veda*—a record of Indian philosophy's first ruminations on the creation of the universe—the cosmic creation is conceived as the *desire* (the heat of *kāma*) of a mysterious source. The imagery of arising *desire* out of *nothingness* connects transcendence and immanence and privileges immanence.

The Divine Reality is generally conceptualized in one of the three genders encoded in the Sanskrit grammatical structure. In another of the *Ṛg Veda's* visions, the universe is created from the body of Puruṣa or Man. Seemingly, a masculine primal deity causes the universe. However, the Ṛg Vedic cosmos is also populated by a number of female deities (*Devī*), who are equally powerful as the male deities, as we saw earlier in the discussion on Vāc. Furthermore, the power dynamics shift from deity to deity; the power is neither consistent nor absolute. In one instance, the *Ṛg Veda's Devī Sūkta* uniquely ascribes ultimate power to the female divine principle. Despite ascribing to nontheist worldviews, Jain and Buddhist traditions include the principle of the feminine divine in the form of various deities or *bodhisattvas* (liberated beings of the Buddhist tradition).

Irigaray laments the lack of a "woman God" in the Judeo-Christian system of thought and ponders its consequences: "There is no *woman* God, nor a female trinity that would express the perfection of the female subjectivity" (Roy 2003: 14). However, in Judeo-Christianity's Indian philosophical and religious counterparts, female deities abound. But such an understanding of God or Being does not necessarily result in an equitable ground of reality for all genders and races. One witnesses the conspicuous prevailing of patriarchal structures undergirded in Indian philosophical texts. Thus, modern feminists have questioned any rash judgment concerning the relationship between the existence of female gods and the actual lived lives of women.

Furthermore, despite the existence of both female and male gods, power differentials operate immediately below the surface of this arrangement: among gods there is often power struggle, just as there is among humans. Such differential power relations have been shown, as we observed earlier in Sutherland Goldman's analysis, by way of the hegemonic relationship between the goddess of speech (Vāc) and the *Brahmins*. The same goddess, later identified as Bhāratī or Sarasvatī, is closely associated with poetic genius and wisdom. Creative genius and wisdom can guide us to identify and disrupt the biases that so naturally arise. Nevertheless, the fact that India's philosophical and religious texts conceptualize the nature of God in seemingly inexhaustible and nuanced ways represents reluctance toward endorsing the simplistic dichotomous categories of male/female. A quest to improve, analyze, deconstruct, and reconstruct has been a hallmark feature in the long history of Indian traditions. No single interpretation is sufficient.

The various schools and systems of philosophy define the nature of reality in different ways—with theistic, nontheistic, or materialistic language. All theistic understandings include a female *principle* in the framework of creation, but not all include male and female *gods*. We convey this point through briefly explaining the idea of *Brahman* (bearing in mind that this is only as an example and certainly not the dominant view in Indian philosophical traditions). *Brahman* becomes central to the philosophical discourse of the *Upaniṣads* and Vedāntic thought. The unity of the Self and the Universe is codified in the following Great Sayings (*mahāvākyas*): *tat tvam asi* (You are That) and *sarvam khalvidam brahman* (All this indeed is *Brahman*). These statements do away with all hierarchal ordering, both human and natural. *Brahman*, as mentioned earlier, is grammatically referred to in the neuter, with the neuter pronoun *tad*, underscoring that it is neither masculine nor feminine. According to Heinrich Zimmer, *Brahman* is "beyond the differentiating qualifications of sex, beyond all limiting, individualizing characteristics whatsoever" (Zimmer 1972: 123). *Brahman* can only be indirectly pointed at by way of negative expressions that allude to what it is *not*, as for instance, demonstrated through the provocative passage from the *Bṛhadāraṇyaka Upaniṣad* (3.8.8):

> It is neither gross nor atomic, neither short nor long, neither red nor oily, neither shadow nor dark, neither air nor space, it is unattached, neither taste nor odor, it is without eyes or ears, without the speech or mind, not-luminous, devoid of the vital force of *prāṇa* and without mouth, it is not a unit of measure, and is without both interior or exterior. It does not consume anything, nor is it consumed by anybody. (Mādhavānanda 1950: 517)[9]

Defining *Brahman via negativa*—without any human characteristics that have often been a source of human divisions and oppression—leads to an epistemic shift in our understanding of God and the universe. According to this *apophatic* line of reasoning, *Brahman* must also be without markers of sex insofar as such constructions are only *provisional* rather than *ultimate* truths of reality. The famous phrase *neti neti*—literally meaning, "not this, not this"—has been used to (indirectly) describe *Brahman*. The meaning behind this expression is that *Brahman* is never "this or that"—that is, never an empirical, describable, classifiable, propertied thing, much as the Christian apophatic theologians such as Dionysius and Meister Eckhart often referred to the Highest God only by using the so-called *via negativa*.

The idea of an unqualified Being extends beyond the *āstika* (orthodox) schools of Indian philosophy. Divine Reality in the Sikh worldview is genderless and formless. In the Sikh tradition, "reality" is described as *Ikk Onkar*—it is "the One" (the term for Supreme Being)—and it is also described through negatives. In general, Jain and Buddhist heterodox philosophical schools reject the idea of a creator God, or even God *simpliciter*, perhaps due to their contention that any conceptions of Ultimate Reality have the potential to create misinterpretations. Such *nāstika* (heterodox) and nuanced views of Ultimate Reality can be construed as hermeneutics employed to circumvent any power structures arising out of more traditional conceptions of reality, which are typically informed by polarized dyads such as feminine/masculine and emotion/reason.

However, other *darśanas* counterbalance the genderless reality of the Sikh and Upaniṣadic philosophies by including masculine and feminine divine principles and deities in their worldviews. In the Sāṃkhya system, *Prakṛti* (feminine) is the source the material world, and *Māyā* (also a feminine principle) is the force of creation in most of the theistic schools. *Śakti* (the Feminine Divine power) is the Primordial Principle in the *Devī Māhātmya* and the Āgama literature. In general, in many Indic traditions, the term *Śakti* can be used for any of the goddesses—Durgā, Kālī, Lakṣmī, or any local female deity. The goddess holds supreme status in the Tantric traditions of Hindus, Jains, and Buddhists.

But the dual-gendered figure Ardhanārīśvara provides the most intricate and ingenious conception of reality. One of the most profound alternatives to the male/female dyad is the figure of Śiva as *both* male *and* female, the form of Ardhanārīśvara—"the lord who is half woman." The androgynous Ardhanārīśvara, worshipped in this particular form, represents a fusion or perfect integration of the gender characteristics of Śiva and Pārvatī in "perfect symmetry" (Goldberg 2012: 3).

These unique attempts to understand reality through either genderless, female, male, or bi-gendered lenses collectively result in a particular language and symbolism that can be employed to both approach issues of gender bias and confront other oppressive structures that feminist and gender studies critique. In all these instances, the category of gender is unstable and experienced dynamically.

Overview of the Volume

The following section provides an overview of gender taxonomies, gender constructions, and creative interpretations that emerge from the thirteen chapters in this volume. As we discussed earlier, feminist scholars and gender theorists have confronted gender essentialism and stability by deconstructing inherently volatile conceptions of gender, and they envision alternative identities that challenge the binaries of male/female, emotional/rational, and self/divine. The analyses in this volume cultivate an idea of the self—a self that can be identified as male or female, neither male nor female, or both female and male—which is always in relation with the Other, both human and natural. By deconstructing traditional philosophical assumptions and constructing new paradigms through textual analyses of Indian materials, the authors reveal an intricate view of gender that may not neatly fit in the Western gender theoretical framework, but their analyses hold the promise to advance theoretical and lived understanding of gender.

The authors engage with the question of gender stability—and also the larger subject of *subjectivity*—through exploring various philosophical systems, gendered rules, narrative models, and modern examples. The chapters are organized in five broad categories: (1) Gender Essentialism, (2) Gender Negotiation, (3) Androgyny, Gender Hybridity, and Fluidity, (4) Gender and the Divine Feminine, and (5) Gender Transcendence. These chapters include pedagogical approaches and textual material that are seldom included in the field of gender studies, narrowly confined as generally it is to Western academies. Because the chapters deal with the issues that concern our human condition and engage (explicitly or implicitly) with the same questions that feminist and gender studies scholars have been asking, we frame each section with the introductory remarks from the modern feminist/gender studies scholars. A brief analysis of each of these gender subclassifications and how the chapters engage with them will help orient the reader in navigating through the book.

Gender Essentialism

Many feminist scholars have observed a conspicuous lack of connection between the divine representation of female deities (in Hindu, Jain, and Buddhist texts) and the real lives of ordinary women. "The fact," writes Morny Joy, "that they [women] are regarded not just as representations of the divine, but as embodiments of it, has not been of benefit to women" (2003: 59). However, such analysis overlooks the many instances in which such representations are used to assert agency and power. In Tantra and devotional sects, the principle of the Divine Feminine has been used to subvert gender essentialized roles. Tantric traditions subscribe to the Goddess as supreme and consider both female and male to equally participate in the rituals.

As we saw earlier, each of the philosophical traditions under discussion hold inclusive views of ontological reality and of the human being, and both-gendered or gender-neutral theological representations. However, the philosophical texts and religious traditions simultaneously lay out a litany of essentialized rules and regulations—whether these are commands prescribed for a wife in epics or the rules for monks and nuns in Buddhist and Jain texts. Scholars draw attention to these perplexing contradictions in texts that, on the one hand, maintain a subject position for women on the basis of inclusive theologies and, on the other hand, deprive them of their subjectivity and individual/independent self on the basis of subjugating gender rules and customs. According to Naomi Appleton, in the "Majjhima Nikāya, the Buddha is recorded as saying that it is impossible for a woman to be a fully awakened one—a *sammāsambuddha*" (Appleton 2010: 95). This is problematic because the Buddha seemingly was egalitarian and taught the path to both men and women.

Joy identifies *strīdharma* (the duties for women) in the *Manusmṛti* as methods to deny selfhood of the woman: "whatever realisation of self is allowed to a woman comes to her only as a reflection of the spiritual stature of her husband" (Joy 2003: 60). Some scholars construe the ideal of the devoted wife (*pativratā*) as a ploy for oppressive behavior, while others interpret the wife's duties as a form of *karma yoga* (the path of selfless action) and a way to attain *mokṣa* (spiritual liberation). A devoted wife attains high spiritual achievement by dedicating herself to her husband as a deity deserving complete devotion. While elaborating *pativratā dharma* (duties of a wife) as a form of *karma yoga* Arti Dhand writes, "The dedication to *dharma* is then both empowering and liberating" (Dhand 2008: 178). The narratives of devoted wives, such as Sāvitri, Sītā, and Draupadī, have been considered, by some scholars, as examples of oppressive gendered patriarchal norms but, by others, they have been presented as the tales of self-determining powerful women who (female divinity) co-create the world with their husbands (lords). Intriguingly, Irigaray presents the Hindu notions of theology and women's roles in a positive light. In particular, Joy draws attention to Irigaray's attraction toward the notion of relationship between gods and goddesses: "In India, men and women are gods together, and together they create the world, including its cosmic dimension" (In Joy 2003: 54).

However, an idealistic interpretation of the Indian myths and principles of classical philosophical systems can potentially prove dangerous for real women, subjecting them to difficult challenges. Idealistic interpretations have also been responsible for essentialized gender norms. Notably, the texts and related traditions are simultaneously self-aware of the pitfalls of such essentialist systems, and authors in this volume highlight this through close readings of select texts. The three essays in this section by Ana Funes, Veena Howard, and Gopal Gupta provide a fresh look at the select texts of Sāṃkhya philosophy, Jain thought, and the *Purāṇas*, and they problematize the obvious gender essentialist interpretations as a way of creating more constructive views on gender. These chapters also point to examples and provide creative readings that seek to subvert gender essentialism regarding female representations.

In her chapter, "The Unbearability of the Male Gaze: A Phenomenological Exposition of Sāṃkhyan Philosophy of the Body through Feminine Eyes," Ana Funes challenges Sāṃkhyan philosophy's metaphysical dualism expressed in the polarity between a pure conscious principle (*Puruṣa*, male) and an unconscious material one (*Prakṛti*, female). The relation between *Puruṣa* and *Prakṛti* in Sāṃkhya is often expressed as the interactions between a male and a female, *puruṣa* representing the male and *prakṛti* the female. Funes argues against any justification for essentializing the binary of the masculine cosmic principle and the feminine material principle since both principles are present in all humans and all aspects of creation. Nevertheless, gendered metaphors are often used in the Sāṃkhya tradition to express the metaphysical functions of the two principles. Conceptualizations of the masculine and the feminine have traditionally had—and still have—an impact on the composition of female and male subjectivities. Using Merleau-Ponty's phenomenological notion of "flesh" and Irigaray's notion of the "maternal feminine," she creatively recovers the notion of body in Sāṃkhya philosophy and highlights the interrelation between *puruṣa* (consciousness) and *prakṛti* (materiality) as it is played out in the realm of the body.

Veena Howard's chapter, "Women's Liberation in Jainism: Understanding Philosophical Debates and Cultural Dialectics," focuses on the issue of women's spiritual liberation (*strī-mokṣa* or *strī-mukti*), which has been a source of contention between the two major sects of Jainism, the Digambaras (Sky-clad) and the Śvetāmbaras (White-clad). She examines the controversies that have arisen between these two sects, especially the counter-debates. The issue of gender becomes complicated in Jainism because the Digambara sect historically emphasized the impossibility of attaining the ultimate spiritual goal of liberation (*mokṣa*) in the female body, while other sects persuasively defend women's right to take up a spiritual life.

Howard's analysis highlights various Jain attempts that take women's liberation seriously and offers a glimpse into Jain dialectics on gender, sex, female anatomy, and female nature, which have been utilized by both camps for their arguments and counterarguments. Through close reading of the Jain texts, Howard identifies the sources of the distinctive views of gender and sexuality and debates surrounding these issues. By drawing on the historical narratives and current lives of Jain nuns and laywomen, she argues that the persistent and robust female monastic movement and sustained laywomen's religiosity can be understood as resistance modes to misogynist tendencies.

In his essay "Woman as Māyā: Gendered Narrative in the *Bhāgavata Purāṇa*," Gopal offers a new, innovative reading of the prominent Vaiṣṇava text's characterization of women as *māyā*, which is commonly understood to mean illusive power, illusion, or deception. He argues that the *Bhāgavata* portrays women and traditional feminine nature (of gentleness, beauty, sensuality, sensitivity, caring, sweetness, devotion, tolerance, and nurturance) in ways similar to *māyā* (with its two functions of obscuring and revealing). In the worldly realm, female nature entangles the soul—it makes the soul more attached to the persons, places, and things of this world. But in the context of the divine, the feminine nature reveals the divine—it becomes a channel through which the divine can be accessed. Women are described in the *Dharmaśāstras* and the *Mahābhārata* as a "dangerous sorceress," but in the *Bhāgavata* they are most exalted devotees of Kṛṣṇa, who are far more advanced than their husbands. In fact, the *Bhāgavata Purāṇa* affirms that simply hearing about the divine play of the *gopīs* (the cowherd maidens) with Kṛṣṇa cures humans' worldly lust. Gupta concludes that the *Bhāgavata*'s views on *māyā* and female spirituality are radical, given the time period and cultural context in which it was composed.

Gender Negotiation

If we understand gender, along with Joan Scott, to be "a constitutive element of social relationships based on perceived differences between the sexes, and gender is a primary way of signifying relationship of power" (In Castelli 2001: 3), as has been generally accepted by the scholarly community, then gender can be negotiated. Elizabeth Castelli further draws attention to the fact that feminists focus on the "troubling category" of "women" and "gender" and battle with religious traditions, institutions, and "over-zealous identifications" (Castelli 2001: 3). Indian philosophical texts and traditions provide examples of how women and men have been negotiating and crossing over the categories of "men," "women," "body," and "soul" in creative ways.

Various devotional sects present a rich site where normative gendered roles are transformed for higher purposes. Jessica Frazier points out that "India has a long history of men identifying with female exemplars" (Frazier 2010: 199). In the poetry of many *bhakti* saints, gender binaries are subverted, and gendered social norms are shattered, when male poets express their love for the male god in erotic and passionate language. Furthermore, in the Vaiṣṇava traditions, male devotees often deliberately adopt the so-called female *bhāva* (emotion) to bring themselves closer to the male Viṣṇu or Kṛṣṇa. There is a glaring paradox of condemning women as temptresses while glorifying femaleness as the highest ideal on the path of devotion. Maleness is negotiated for femaleness, assuring expeditious success on the path of devotion.

The three essays by Nancy Martin, Ram-Prasad, and Jeffery Long explore how essentialized gender norms have been negotiated and subverted, highlighting select historical Indian saints' unique ways of disrupting gendered identities, either through a male using female voices or through males centralizing the female divinity. In her chapter, "The Gendering of Voice in the Medieval Hindu Literature," Martin examines the nuanced understandings of gender in medieval Hindu devotional literature and theology. She argues that the stories of saints and songs in their voices, particularly those of female saints, serve to expose, challenge, and subvert patriarchal norms and offer rich resources for dismantling gender oppression and for crafting a much wider and more fluid array of gendered identities and relations. These voices offer a vehicle to publicly articulate and reject patriarchal norms (especially in the voices of female saints) and to explore alternatives. They open up an intersubjective space to experiment with gendered identities and cultivate empathy (particularly as male saints and singers speak in female voices), thereby fostering spiritual and/or psychological wholeness and transformation, and even potentially, though not necessarily, inspiring positive social change.

In his essay, "Given, Taken, Performed: Gender in a Tamil Theopoetics," C. Ram-Prasad engages with feminist and gender scholarship on the question of sex and gender, and he focuses especially on the works of the Tamil poets Nammāḻvār and Āṇṭāl in order to retrieve a richer understanding of gender. Nammāḻvār writes in the voice of "the young woman" and Āṇṭāl keeps her female voice. The argument of the chapter is centered on the question how performativity affects both what one expresses as one's gender and what one expresses as the meaning of that gender. Ram-Prasad shows, through the contours of some of Nammāḻvār's poetry, that the conventional givenness of the man–woman binary is shown to be labile in the performance of emotion, while Āṇṭāl enables exploration of new limits to the givenness of being a woman. He concludes that these examples make us think about how gender may be negotiated between what is given/taken and performed, how boundaries may be acknowledged only to be crossed, and how norms can be symbolically deployed only to reconfigure their meaning. Through teasing apart the contrasting intuitions we may have about Nammāḻvār's and Āṇṭāḷ's literary expression of womanhood, he provides theoretical insights into the relationship between the self-expression and reception of gender identities in light of assumptions about what we take to already know about men and women, adding the cautionary remark that we should try to neither conflate sex and gender nor ontologize a difference.

In his chapter, "Gender in the Tradition of Sri Ramakrishna," Long focuses on how the Ramakrishna tradition's understanding of gender is shaped by its approach to transcendence as available equally to women and to men, its orientation toward the Mother Goddess, and the prominent roles played by women early in its history. He presents the Ramakrishna tradition, originated in the nineteenth century with the leadership of Sri Ramakrishna, as a case of an Indic tradition in which, according to its own ideals, femininity is something to be affirmed, while at the same time, institutionally male domination tends to be the norm. Long draws attention to the abundant resources available for affirming female equality within the tradition but contends that they represent a potential that has yet to be fully realized.

The icon of Goddess Kālī standing on the body of Śiva is enshrined at Dakshineshwar, where Ramakrishna practiced his *sādhana*s. This powerful icon symbolizes Ramakrishna's views on gender: the divine feminine, embodied devotion, and his emphasis on a personal realization of nonduality (beyond gender) cuts through the patriarchal structures of his time and reveals his feminine sensibilities. This becomes even more evident in his relationship with his wife, Mother Sarada Devi. Long chronicles the importance women had in Sri Ramakrishna's life and the formation of his tradition, arguing that the egalitarian potential posed by the gynocentric view of its founder should find its way into current practices of the tradition, which is still male dominated.

Androgyny, Gender Hybridity, and Fluidity

"The dyads male-female and their mapping to masculine-feminine are constitutive exclusions that feminist philosophy of religion can no longer presume," writes Nancy Frankenberry, foreboding the end of not so stable categories and opening a space for creative practice (Frankenberry 2004: 22). The binary of the two-sex model has long been put into question. As we look at India's social, philosophical, and religious contexts, that model is breached in many instances, despite a strong emphasis on gender normativity in social roles. As an example, Frazier draws attention to psychoanalytic observation of Indian patients' by Sudhir Kakar, which revealed a "striking 'fluidity of the patients' cross-sexual and generational identifications'" (Frazier 2010: 200).

In addition to reading the religious imagery in deeply philosophical ways, there are also examples of men and women who negotiate gender relationships and conceptions in other creative ways. Indeed, we encounter many Indian texts and narratives that see beyond this dyad. As Wilhelm as well as Zwilling and Sweet inform us, terms are also found describing women who do not fit traditional categories, for instance, the term *svairiṇī*, "independent woman," used in the Vedic literature to refer to a lesbian woman (Wilhelm 2010: 17). Zwilling and Sweet bring attention to the terms *ṣaṇḍha*, a man who behaves like a woman; *keśavān*, a "long haired man"; and *paṇḍaka* and *klība*—both connoting a man who is impotent with women or a "sexually defective man" (i.e., in at least some instances, a homosexual man) (1996: 365, 363–4). The many expressions for many shades and grades of sex and gender in Indian philosophical texts suggest that the tradition exhibited a greater sensitivity in envisioning a complex ecosystem of gendered beings in Indian philosophical texts compared to our modern sensibilities.

We see this in the case of three examples provided below in the chapters by Geoffrey Ashton, Carol Anderson, and Veena Howard. The authors focus on of the imagery of Ardhanārīśvara, philosophical discourses in the Buddhist Pāli canon, and Ambā's narrative in the *Mahābhārata*, respectively. Each chapter offers examples of nuanced configurations of gender and the implications these patterns have for the broader gender discourse.

In iconography, the classic representation of Ardhanārīśvara (Lord Śiva's androgynous image) challenges gender essentialism through envisaging an embodied being constituted of both male and female natures. Such an image leads one to inquire, "What is the gender of Ardhanārīśvara? What does this convey to those who take it as a symbol for philosophical contemplation?" In his chapter, "Divine Androgyny and the Play of Self-Recognition: Revisiting Some Issues in Gender Theory through an Un-Orthodox Interpretation of Ardhanārīśvara," Ashton explores a philosophical interpretation of the Ardhanārīśvara motif through the lens of the Pratyabhijñā system, a medieval school of thought that reformulates the binaries noted above in order to disclose the nature of the god Śiva. Using Ellen Goldberg's feminist critique, *The Lord Who Is Half-Woman*, he argues that the Ardhanārīśvara mythology is a guide to enacting a play of self-recognition whereby one realizes the divine in all manifestations beyond dualities, a sentiment that echoes the concerns of contemporary gender theorists. Far from repeating the gender biases of India's religious law texts and philosophies, the Ardhanārīśvara image can be read as resisting them in ways that might push existing debates on gender in new directions. Ardhanārīśvara and more specifically, Ardhanārīnaṭeśvara, or "The Lord of Dance Who Is Half-Woman," the androgynous god can be seen as a direct expression of resistance toward normative systems of gender—something adhered to not just by Pratyabhijñā thinkers but also by Kashmir Śaivas generally.

Through a creative hermeneutic of Śiva's image as half-male and half-female, Ashton concludes that the liberated agent is a kind of theatrical actor-dancer who imaginatively explores alternative identities in and through powers of cognition ("I am Rāma," "I am Hamlet") and action (the actor's performing the role of Rāma, Hamlet, etc.). Moreover, this mode of performativity enacts a deep identification with the Other (i.e., one's audience) in order to spawn new relations in terms of a kind of transpersonal consciousness. The goal of the Pratyabhijñā system is not the realization of disembodiment, gender neutrality, or escape from the "prison of gender" but unending investigation of the self through its countless manifestations—including its variegated masculinities and femininities as well as from a "queer" perspective that opposes gender binarism.

Scholars and religious people often conceive of the Buddhist system as being rooted in essentialist gender binaries, especially scholars studying *vinaya* (Pāli discipline rules for the Buddhist monastics). However, the *vinaya* texts catalog numerous forms of gender and sexual orientation. In her essay, "Gender in Pāli Buddhist Traditions," Anderson challenges the common view of scholars who have suggested that the Pāli Buddhist sources reflect an essentialist binary system in which biologically sexed bodies are mapped directly onto culturally gendered living beings. Through a close study of the texts, she shows that this model is not as accurate as has been suggested. On the contrary, texts routinely exhibit instances of gender fluidity, such as sex change by monks and nuns. Anderson questions scholarship that sees only binary gender categories in the Pāli Buddhist tradition and argues that gender fluidity exists within the Buddhist tradition, which needs to be extensively examined.

The Pāli *imaginaire*—the world shaped by the ideas, teachings, and practices of Pāli Buddhism—recognizes four different genders: females, males, *ubhatobyañjanakas* (intersex), and *paṇḍakas* (generally referring to an impotent person). These four exist among humans, nonhumans (gods as well as beings in the hells), and animals. The relationship between biologically sexed bodies and the performance of gender is rather complicated in the early periods of Pāli Buddhism. In Pāli Buddhism, Anderson identifies two different explanations for the relationship between the faculties (*indriyāṇi*) that are present in womb-born beings from the moment of conception and biological sex and gender. The first explanation says that the faculties are displayed and manifested in one's biological sex and gender, as evidenced in such ways as one's deportment, occupation, fashion, and so on. The second explanation, however, argues that the male and female faculties are ultimately the cause of one's biological sex and also the basis for the gender that one performs. The intricacy of these analyses demonstrates that Pāli Buddhism is more complex than an essentialist, sexually dimorphic system.

One example of gender hybridity is found in the *Mahābhārata*'s narrative of Ambā. In her essay, "Narrative of Ambā in the *Mahābhārata*: Female Body, Gender, and the Namesake of the Divine Feminine," Veena Howard carefully analyzes the text to show an extraordinary example of a woman defying conventional gender norms and roles. When Ambā is abducted by the patriarch Bhīṣma and consequently rejected by her lover Śālva, she emerges as a fierce independent woman and, with her words and actions, exposes oppressive patriarchal marriage laws.

The chapter provides a fresh reading of Ambā's tale and draws attention to her defiance of conventional gender and sexual norms, which have been overlooked by scholars. Ambā argues her case with powerful men and ascetics; she rejects the comfortable life of a princess and undertakes fierce austerities to kill her wrongdoer, the mighty Bhīṣma; and she resorts to unconventional means to change her sex to confront Bhīṣma in battle. Howard concludes that Ambā's character is strikingly different from that typifying the women of the Indian epics, women who are traditionally bound by normative patriarchal laws. Last, she shows how Ambā negotiates her female sex to face Bhīṣma in battle. Although she changes sex from a female to a male, she is perceived as having hybrid sexual identity—that is, both male and female. Ambā's story is not simply a tale of the victimization of a woman trapped by patriarchal customs nor a tale of scintillating sexual themes, but, rather, it is an attempt to shed light on the *Mahābhārata*'s theme of *dharma*—restoring justice to those who are on the side of right. The tale reveals oppressions arising out of patriarchal *dharma* laws and normative gender roles. Howard argues that such misogyny must be confronted by an equally powerful feminine force, which is not constrained by Ambā's biological sex. A close literary and feminist reading of the text offers new insights into Ambā's choice to sacrifice her initially female body—the body that was violated, rejected, and humiliated—for a hybrid identity to challenge patriarchal structures.

Gender and the Divine Feminine

As noted, feminist scholars have critiqued androcentric language and masculine representations of God and seek to recover the divine feminine models. Irigaray sees the value of feminine religious symbols and representations in disrupting structures of oppression and providing positive images for women. She appreciates the goddess traditions and symbolism that celebrate female body and power. Merlin Stone, in her seminal book, *When God Was a Woman* (1976), traces historically prevalent representations of the Divine as feminine in various cultures and connects the decline of the Divine Feminine models with the current subjugated status of women. In their groundbreaking scholarship, Alf Hiltebeitel and Kathleen Erndl (2000) ask the pertinent question, "Is the Goddess a feminist?" and, by tracing various goddess traditions, explore the issue of the impact of goddess traditions on the social and psychological lives of women in South Asia. The models of the Divine Feminine are being explored beyond India's traditions. For example, Rabbi Rami Shapiro's collection (2005) of biblical literature creatively traces the tradition of "Wisdom" (known as *Chochma* in Hebrew and *Sophia* in Greek), the Divine Feminine, the Mother of Life. Such scholarship demonstrates the significance of female divinities to empower women.

Two chapters by Rita D. Sherma and Raj Balkaran focus on two essential issues concerning the feminine and Divine, respectively: (1) philosophical principles embedded in the Divine Feminine articulation and representation of the *Devī Māhātmya*, which have been overlooked by scholars, and (2) the uniqueness of the Divine Feminine who engenders, supports, and governs phenomenal reality, compelled through compassion toward cosmic preservation.

In her essay, "God the Mother and Her Sacred Text: A Hindu Vision of Divine Immanence," Sherma shows that the conceptualization of feminine deity in the Hindu traditions of the Mahādevī/Śakti offers Her ultimate divine status as God, the Mother. She argues that Hindu texts offer arguably the only extant, widely accepted, systematic theological vision of God the Mother as the Supreme Divine—transcendent and immanent, the efficient and material cause, sustenance and destination of all existence. By focusing on the *Devī Māhātmya*, she argues that most scholars of Hinduism's Divine Feminine have focused on liturgical, ritual, festive, and pilgrimage aspects. That is, in general, it is elements of religious practice that are associated with Her.

Sherma notes that some scholars also analyze the impact of the strong presence of the Divine Feminine in the India's traditions on the lives and liberties of actual women. Sherma, however, draws attention to what is an overlooked problematic: how foundational philosophical categories play an important part in the vision and definition of the theology of the Mahādevī (the Great Goddess), a fact that is evident in the conceptualization of divine nature presented by the *Devī Māhātmya*. She argues that the modern (eighteenth century onward) conventional disjunctive bipolarity of philosophy and theology has not been the traditional norm for Hindu thought in which the two categories often interpenetrate and inform each other. In this vein, she shows how philosophical principles such as *prakṛti* (matter/components of the physical world); the *guṇas* (the three foundational characteristics/tendencies of matter); *mūlapradhāna* (the root material cause of creation); *māyā* (the cosmological power of veiling the Ultimate Reality); and conceptual paradigms such as *satkāryavāda* (postulating the presence of the cause *within* the effect) and *pariṇāmavāda* (positing transformation of the cause *into* the effect), are deeply imbued in the structure of the Śākta theology advanced by this seminal essay.

Balkaran's essay, "The Story of Saṃjñā, Mother of Manu: Shadow and Light in the *Mārkaṇḍeya Purāṇa*," revisits the famous story of Saṃjñā, wife of the sun. Balkaran critiques the dominant interpretation of this myth, expounded by Wendy Doniger, as one harkening to the "wicked stepmother" motif prevalent in Western religious and mythlogical traditions. Balkaran addresses some significant overarching issues—such as dichotomies of good and evil, male and female—through a close analysis of the story. He argues that rather than presenting us with a flawed feminine figure, the Saṃjñā story presents us with a resilient feminine figure who succeeds in softening overbearing masculinity. This chapter sheds light not only on the inner workings of the myth cycle but also why it is dovetailed with the *Devī Māhātmya* (the Glory of the Goddess), anchored in the *Mārkaṇḍeya Purāṇa*.

From the perspective of the *Devī Māhātmya*, which glorifies the Hindu Great Goddess whose might surpasses even the creator's and whose grace is responsible for installing the next Manu, the story of Saṃjñā ornaments and echoes the Goddess' grandeur. Through a careful analysis of Indian thought, Balkaran shows that in the *Purāṇic* discourse, lines between good and evil are incredibly (and intentionally) blurred. In various narratives, gods behave nefariously (typically for a greater good) and demons may exhibit extraordinary piety (particularly in devotional milieus) for the sake of acquiring power. Only from a limited perspective do these forces appear to oppose each other, like hands intent upon opposing directions, obstinately pressed together. From a grander perspective, one sees that they are pressed together in *añjali mudrā*, stemming from the same ground of being, producing a unified gesture. Balkaran concludes that the *Devī Māhātmya*, bolstered by its Puranic context, affirms that the diversity of this phenomenal world, along with the myriad of life forms finding homes there, is as supreme as that dynamic feminine mystery. The Divine Feminine engenders, supports, and governs the phenomenal reality, compelled through compassion toward colossal acts of cosmic preservation.

Gender Transcendence

As we saw earlier, Daly argues that "the women's revolution ... is an ontological, spiritual revolution, pointing beyond the idolatries of sexist society and sparking creative action in and toward transcendence" (1973: 6). The move to realize gender transcendence requires cultivating symbols and metaphors that are inclusive and relational. All language is symbolic when describing Reality, God/Goddess, or Self. To Clifford Geertz, religious symbols are "historically created vehicles of reasoning, perception, feeling, and understanding" (1986: 9). Geertz's idea can be interpreted in the context of gender as a *socially created vehicle* that creates a relational self through which feelings and understanding are processed. The goal of attaining gender transcendence—along with its soteriological telos (realization of the unity of the self and the divine)—can also mean freedom from gender-based social and religious rules. In Indic philosophy and theology, gender transcendence also implies rising above constraints of race, caste, gender, and so forth.

The chapters authored by Ruth Vanita and Nikky-G. Kaur Singh highlight the philosophical and theological emphasis on gender transcendence on the basis of the philosophical conceptions of the Self/Divine as *one* (*ek*; *ikk*) or *none* (*neti*, void). They simultaneously emphasize the positive engagement with the world as real not illusory. Further, through a close textual analysis of the Hindu epic narratives and the Sikh scripture, the authors show how feminist hermeneutics can help to highlight the philosophical principles that challenge the prevailing gender-based inequality.

Vanita's essay, "Male–Female Dialogues on Gender, Sexuality and Dharma in the Hindu Epics," examines the paradoxes that arise in the course of two dialogues between male and female sages in the *Mahābhārata*. One dialogue focuses on the ontology and epistemology of gender. The other dialogue brings bodily pleasure and sexual desire into picture, questioning the philosophical concept of nondifference with regard to both gender and age. From different perspectives, both dialogues demonstrate the invalidity of the dictum that a woman must always be under a father's, husband's, or son's protection. In both dialogues, the woman interlocutor ends up instructing the man. Through a comparative analysis, Vanita explores the complex ways in which Hindu texts frame and interrogate gender difference, likeness, and equality in relation to *dharma*.

In her essay, "The Vision of the Transcendent One: Feminist Hermeneutics and Feminine Symbolism in the Sikh Scripture," Nikky-G. Kaur Singh seeks to challenge the hold of masculine assumptions in the perception of the Divine that have been shaped by exegetes, scholars, and translators of the *Guru Granth Sahib* (GGS).[10] The fundamental Sikh theological expression is *Ikk Onkar*—stated at the very outset of the volume and reiterated throughout its 1,430 portfolio pages. This unique and all-embracing configuration by the first Guru spells out the infinity of the singular Divine beyond any dyads. Although this expression does not leave room for any gender specification, Kaur Singh laments that it has been structured and shaped into a male god—its vastness reduced to an exclusionary concept and an intimidating male symbol. She contends that the colonial machine reinforced an omnipotent lordly "God" that ruptured the intimate relationship between humans and the divine at the heart of the Sikh scripture. Since male subjectivity produced Sikh scriptural hermeneutics, it has resulted in male-dominated identity formations, social relations, and power structures. Because of this one-sided approach, the transcendent, egalitarian, and liberating theological, ethical, and aesthetic currents of the sacred text have neither been fully understood nor are they put in practice.

Kaur Singh argues that a change of lens—from androcentric to the feminist approach—engages the Sikh theological construct with the potential for the radical "metapatriarchal journey" proposed by the feminist philosopher Mary Daly, exorcizing an internalized father—for example, God in his various manifestations and incarnations. As the inclusive numeral "One" shatters the dominance of male imagery, it creates a space for the Divine to be experienced in other new and important ways. Logically, the One is totally transcendent and beyond all categories. But in the poetry of the Gurus, both female and male dimensions run parallel. The Divine is identified in both genders: "Itself male, Itself is female" (GGS, 1020). She concludes that it is essential to retrieve both the transcendent model of the Divine and the feminine imagery that is embedded in the text in order to create a balanced perspective that is crucial for mental and spiritual health.

Concluding Insights

The wide-ranging chapters in this volume encourage fresh inquiry into classic questions by offering critical analyses that have relevance to the disciplines of gender, literary, cultural, theological, Asian, and religious studies as well as philosophy. Within the general topic of gender, the contributors have worked within their areas of expertise providing close and constructive readings of various texts. We remain cognizant of the multiplicity of texts and traditions; therefore, to ensure plurality of viewpoints (*darśana*), selected texts encompass a broad range of traditions: ancient and modern, orthodox and heterodox, classical languages, and local vernaculars. The subcategories and taxonomies outlined above emerged organically, creating a complex mosaic of gender constructions in Indian thought and beyond. As is evident, these chapters focus only on select texts and traditions, and therefore many have been left out. Thus, there is a great need and scope to expand this project that will include a broad range of texts and traditions, including Islam. There are many texts that could be of service in broadening the scope of the above-outlined theoretical approaches to explore the ever-changing landscape of gender more broadly—for example, the issues of the genderless Self and women sages in the *Upaniṣads*, the implication of female Bodhisattvas in Mahāyāna Buddhism, gender transcendence in the Jain Siddha state and its implication for gendered female subjects, understanding the deep meaning of the feminine symbolism in Vajrayāna, and the gendered mandates for women in the *Dharmaśāstra*. Any new insights offered through analyzing the cultural past will also prove helpful in dealing with questions regarding self, nature, and society.

Notes

1 We acknowledge the limitations of this volume. Despite a wide variety of philosophical traditions included in this volume, many texts and traditions are not represented. The chapters in this volume focus only on the select philosophical texts and traditions originated on the Indian subcontinent.

2 Alasdair MacIntyr (2007) elaborates on the teleological character of the narratives:

> He [She] is not essentially, but becomes through his [her] history, a teller of stories that aspire to truth. But the key question for [wo]men is not about their own authorship; I can only answer the question 'What am I to do?' if

I can answer the prior question "Of what story or stories do I find myself a part?" 216.

3 In the Indian context, *darśana* conventionally refers to the six orthodox (*āstika*) schools of philosophy: Nyāya, Vaiśeṣika, Sāṃkhya, Yoga, Mīmāṃsā, and Vedānta. Jain and Buddhist philosophies are termed as heterodox (*nāstika*) systems.

4 In answer to the question, *What is gender?* Simon Brodbeck and Brian Black—in their edited anthology *Gender and Narrative in the Mahābhārata*—take up a linguistic question about the changing distinction between the term "sex" and that of "gender." They comment on the changing meanings of the term: "David Glover and Cora Kaplan have commented upon the ubiquitous use of the word 'gender' in scholarly discourse: 'Gender' is now one of the busiest, most restless terms in the English language, a word that crops up everywhere, yet whose uses seem to be forever changing, always on the move, producing new and often surprising inflections of meaning" (2000: ix).

5 There are a few exceptions. *Gender and Narrative in the Mahābhārata* (2007) initiates this project of exploring gender in Indian thought. This offers a first of its kind analysis of gender in the context of the largest Indian epic, the *Mahābhārata*, composed around third century BCE. An earlier volume, *Invented Identities: Interplay of Gender, Religion, and Politics in India* (2000), explores how gender identities are formalized through ritual, language, and narrative.

6 Allowing the term "gender" to remain fluid while "sex" is the more universal of the two in our English vocabulary works to the advantage of understanding gendered narratives. Markers of "sex," which are the stable determinations of an individual, serve as a medium on which to construct expressions of gender. Sex may be altered in theory, or not, but gender is seen as a creative, performative act.

7 "Where as 'sex' is understood as a biological identity, 'gender' has been employed to refer to social identity; 'sex' is what makes a human being male or female, but 'gender' is what makes a someone masculine or feminine" (2007: 11).

8 Gandhi invoked the mythical lore of the Sage Śukadeva's purity in defense of his views on miraculous power and idiosyncratic practices of celibacy (Howard 2013).

9 Some changes have been made to the original translation for the sake of clarification.

10 An online version of the GGS can be accessed at http://www.srigranth.org/servlet/gurbani.gurbani?S=y

References

Appleton, N. (2010). *Jātaka Stories in Theravāda Buddhism: Narrating the Bodhisatta Path*. Burlington, VT: Ashgate Pub.

Barker, V. (2008). "Feminism and the Deconstruction of God's Death." *Sydney Open Journals Online*, 312–28. Accessed July 18, 2018.

Brodbeck, S., and Black, B. (eds.) (2007). *Gender and Narrative in the Mahābhārata*. NewYork: Routledge.

Bynum, Caroline W. (1986). *Gender and Religion: On the Complexity of Symbols*. Boston, MA: Beacon Press.

Castelli, E. (2001). "Women, Gender, Religion: Troubling Categories and Transforming Knowledge." In Rosamond Rodman and Elizabeth Castelli (eds.), *Women, Gender, Religion: A Reader* (pp. 3–28). New York: Palgrave.

Daly, M. (1973). *Beyond God the Father*. Boston, MA: Beacon Press.

Das Wilhelm, A. (2010). *Tritiya-Prakriti: People of the Third Sex: Understanding Homosexuality, Transgender Identity, and Intersex Conditions through Hinduism*. Philadelphia, PA: Xilbris.

Dhand, A. (2008). *Woman as Fire, Woman as Sage: Sexual Ideology in the Mahābhārata*. Albany: State University of New York Press.

Frankenberry, N. (2004). "Feminist Approaches." In Pamela Sue Anderson and Beverley Clack (eds.), *Feminist Philosophy of Religion: Critical Readings* (pp. 3–28). London: Routledge.

Frazier, J. (2010). "Becoming the Goddess: Female Subjectivity and the Passion of the Goddess Radha." In Pamela Sue Anderson (ed.), *New Topics in Feminist Philosophy of Religion: Contestations and Transcendence Incarnate* (pp. 199–216). Dordrecht: Springer.

Goldberg, E. (2002). *The Lord Who Is Half Woman: Ardhanārīśvara in Indian and Feminist Perspectives*. Albany: State University of New York Press.

Goldenberg, N. (1982). *The End of God: Important Directions for a Feminist Critique of Religion in the Works of Sigmund Freud and Carl Jung*. Canada: University of Ottawa Press.

Hill-Collins, P. (1986). "Learning from the Outsider Within: The Sociological Significance of Black Feminist Thought." *Social Problems* 33(6): s14–s32.

Hiltebeitel, A., and K. Erndl (eds.) (2000). *Is the Goddess a Feminist? The Politics of South Asian Goddesses*. New York: New York University Press.

Howard, V. (2013). "Rethinking Gandhi's Celibacy: Ascetic Power and Women's Empower." *Journal of the American Academy of Religion* 81(1): 130–161.

Joy, M. (2003). "Irigaray's Eastern Explorations." In Morny Joy, Kathleen O'Grady, and Judith L. Poxon (eds.), *Religion in French Feminist Thought: Critical Perspectives* (pp. 51–67). London: Routledge.

MacIntyre, A. (2007). *After Virtue: A Study in Moral Theory*. Notre Dame, IN: University of Notre Dame Press.

Mādhavānanda, Swāmi (trans.) (1950). *The Bṛhadāraṇyaka Upaniṣad with the Commentary of Śaṅkarācārya*. Almora: Advaita Ashrama.

Narayan, R. K. (1964). *God, Demons, and Others*. Chicago, IL: University of Chicago.

Pokazanyeva, A. (2015, August). "Gender and Sexuality." Oxford Bibliographies. Accessed July 2018 from https://www.oxfordbibliographies.com/view/document/obo-9780195399318/obo-9780195399318-0157.xml.

Roy, M. (2003). "Women and Spirituality in the Writings of Luce Irigaray." In Morny Joy, Kathleen O'Grady, and Judith L. Poxon (eds.), *Religion in French Feminist Thought: Critical Perspectives* (pp. 13–28). London: Routledge.

Shapiro, Rabbi R. (2005). *The Divine Feminine in Biblical Wisdom Literature: Selections Annotated & Explained.* Woodstock, VT: SkyLight Paths.

Stone, M. (1976). *When God Was a Woman: The Landmark Exploration of the Ancient Worship of the Great Goddess and the Eventual Suppression of Women's Rights.* New York: Houghton Mifflin Harcourt.

Sutherland-Goldman, S. (2000). "Speaking Gender: *Vāc* and the Vedic Construction of the Feminine." In Julia Leslie and Mary McGee (eds.), *Invented Identities: The Interplay of Gender, Religion and Politics in India* (pp. 57–83). Delhi: Oxford University Press.

Zimmer, R. (1972). *Myths and Symbols in Indian Art and Civilization.* Princeton, NJ: Princeton University Press.

Zwilling, L., and M. J. Sweet (1996). "Like a City Ablaze: The Third Sex and the Creation of Sexuality in Jain Religious Literature." *Journal of the History of Sexuality* 6(3): 359–84.

Part One

Gender Essentialism

2

The Unbearability of the Male Gaze: A Phenomenological Exposition of Sāṃkhyan Philosophy of the Body through *Feminine* Eyes

Ana Laura Funes Maderey

Introduction

The classical philosophy of Sāṃkhya, as developed in the *Sāṃkhyakārikā* (*SK*) of Īśvarakṛṣṇa (ca. 500 CE), is famous for its metaphysical dualism expressed in the polarity between a pure conscious principle (*puruṣa*) and an unconscious material one (*prakṛti*). Characterized as a passive spectator (*SK* 19), *puruṣa* observes the movements and doings of *prakṛti*, without which there is no creation or experience of the world and whose actions are initiated for the sake of *puruṣa*'s spiritual release (*SK* 58).

The relation between *puruṣa* and *prakṛti* in Sāṃkhya is often expressed as the interactions between a male and a female, with *puruṣa* representing the male and *prakṛti* the female. However, it would be simplistic to identify *puruṣa*'s gaze as that of a man and *prakṛti*'s natural power of procreation with the role of a woman (Jacobsen 1996, 2006; Natarajan 2001). Neither the use of feminine metaphors—such as that of a "female dancer" (*SK* 59), "milking cow" (*SK* 48), or "wife" (Māṭhara's commentary to *SK* 66)—to refer to *prakṛti*'s function in the universe nor the feminine gender of the Sanskrit word makes *prakṛti* a "female."[1] There is, indeed, no justification in essentializing genders in a binary between the masculine cosmic principle and the feminine material principle. Both principles are present in all genders, including men and women, and all aspects of creation. Nevertheless, gendered metaphors are often used in the Sāṃkhya tradition to express the metaphysical functions of the two principles. Conceptualizations of the masculine and the feminine have traditionally had—and still have—an impact on the way female and male subjectivities are constructed. This can be seen in the commentaries of the *SK* and in later theological, social, medical, and legal discourses of Indian culture (Natarajan 2001: 1401). Thus, the analysis of such conceptualizations becomes relevant to unearth unquestioned assumptions regarding sexual difference[2] and offer new possibilities of meaning.

This essay examines the gendered aspect of Sāṃkhyan philosophy and reveals the problematic nature of the "male gaze" as it is illustrated in various metaphors used by the tradition to explain the *puruṣa-prakṛti* (consciousness-matter, observer-observed) relationality. The purpose of this analysis is to recover the notion of body—particularly the "subtle body"—in Sāṃkhya philosophy using Merleau-Ponty's phenomenological notion of "flesh" and Luce Irigaray's notion of the "maternal feminine." The phenomenological approach brings to the fore an aspect of Sāṃkhya that is usually overlooked: that the interrelation between *puruṣa* and *prakṛti* is played out in the realm of the body, of our bodies. The feminist perspective helps to show that the recognition of the feminine aspect of embodiment in Sāṃkhya can guarantee a reciprocal and reversible interaction of both principles—consciousness and matter—within the flesh.

That Modest Delicate Lady

In verse 61 of the *Sāṃkhyakārikā* it is stated,

> It is my belief that there is no one more delicate and graceful (*sukumāra*) than *prakṛti*, who [realizing] "I have been seen" never again comes to the sight of *puruṣa*.[3]

In his commentary (*Tattvakaumudī*) on this verse, ninth-century scholar Vācaspati Miśra interprets the adjective *sukumāra* as "modest/timid/bashful." He then compares *prakṛti* to a married lady from a noble family, whose garment or veil has been accidentally blown away in public, exposing her body and head to the sight of strangers. Embarrassed and unable to bear being observed by other men, she takes extra care not to let this happen again by keeping herself—that is, her body—forever inaccessible to the eyes of other men. Vācaspati continues, "In this way *prakṛti* being the most virtuous of all wives, out of discernment, does not expose herself again."[4]

This passage perfectly expresses the gendered dimension of Sāṃkhyan metaphysics. The experience of the world is brought about by the observation of *prakṛti*'s body, but such observation is the product of an accident and a mistake. The exact cause of that mistake is unknown, as is the cause of this lady's disgraceful unclothing. Her naked body, however, is seen as an object of desire by the voyeurs—male strangers who enjoy looking at her. However, in their enjoyment they ignore that this experience is binding them to the suffering marked by continuous rounds of satisfactions and frustrations. Their desire causes them to feel attraction toward the object enjoyed and frustration for its loss. *Puruṣa*, represented by the male observers, forgets himself in what he sees and misidentifies himself in the midst of *prakṛti*'s actions. He forgets himself in the experience of happiness and sadness, virtue and vice, knowledge and ignorance, and so forth. On the other hand, the hiding lady represents *prakṛti*'s withdrawal into the unmanifested (*avyaktam*) form of reality and has as its consequence the seer's liberation, who having enjoyed the experience, separates himself from it. Consequently, the seer recognizes himself alone as pure consciousness, as an immutable seer liberated from all passion.

According to Īśvarakṛṣṇa, *prakṛti* is characterized by her multiple qualities (*guṇas*). She can move in an energetic way (*rajas*), or remain calmed and delightful (*sattva*), or become obscure and dense (*tamas*). All her movements and actions would be nothing if they were not observed by *puruṣa*. This is why it is said in the *SK* verse 60 that *prakṛti* moves for the sake of the observer without benefit for herself, for she is supposed to be unconscious. Moreover, in the classical description of this relationship, *prakṛti* assists with *puruṣa*'s liberation without him doing anything for her.[5]

However, in Vācaspati's interpretation of *SK* 61, he gives—perhaps inadvertently—a different Sāṃkhyan perspective on the nature of *prakṛti*'s actions. That modest delicate lady liberates herself from the unbearable gaze of the male lookers by hiding her body—the seen object—away from them. *Prakṛti* is the one who, in spite of being nonintelligent (for she is matter, not consciousness), discerns the difference between her and the disembodied onlooker and who resorts to hiding away from being determined as an object (of desire). She acts for her own sake by preventing repeated exposure and avoiding any further embarrassment/mistake. In doing so, her actions benefit the onlookers (*puruṣas*) with their own liberation.

But what makes the gaze of the observer (gendered as male on the Sāṃkhyan account) so unbearable? Both the feminine and the masculine principles in Sāṃkhya have the same level of importance. We could say (half-jokingly) that there is metaphysical gender equality in Sāṃkhya philosophy. They are both eternal, uncreated, independent from each other, and both are equally responsible for the manifestation of the world. However, Īśvarakṛṣṇa's classical account is marked by the lack of reciprocity between both principles, also visible in the gendered metaphors of the spectator and the dancer, the husband and the wife, as will be shown later. Lacking in the classical formulation of Sāṃkhya, as pointed out by Alfred Collins (2000), is *puruṣa*'s acknowledgement of *prakṛti* as a Self, as a subjectivity that acts for her own sake (65). However, Vācaspati's metaphor of the modest lady does show that there is an intersubjective, reciprocal aspect within Sāṃkhyan dualism that could be unveiled if the perspective of the system were assumed from *her* eyes.

Assuming *her* perspective requires a movement that can situate us within her body. The rest of this paper offers precisely such a move. In order for the feminine perspective to emerge within the reading of classical Sāṃkhyan philosophy, a phenomenological approach to the notion of "body" (*śarīra*) is necessary. As seen with Vācaspati's interpretation of *SK* 61, the interaction between *puruṣa* and *prakṛti* plays out clearly in the naked exposition of that modest lady's body.

Merleau-Ponty's understanding of "flesh" can help bring forth the phenomenological import of the Sāṃkhyan notion of body, particularly in its characterization as "subtle" (*sūkṣma* or *liṅga śarīra*). Thus, in what follows, I read the Sāṃkhyan notion of the "observer" and "the observed" through Merleau-Ponty's phenomenology and problematize it by appealing to Luce Irigaray's feminist perspective. This will allow us to recognize the role of *prakṛti* as "the other" in its own agential difference—something that is missing in Īśvarakṛṣṇa's perspective and hinted at in Vācaspati's commentary to verse 61 of the *Sāṃkhyakārikā*.

Her Subtle Body Exposed

One of the words used for "body" in the *Sāṃkhyakārikā* is *śarīra*. The root of this word refers to the body either as a support or as that which is easily destroyed or dissolved. Both of these meanings are implicit in the Sāṃkhyan articulation of the term (*SK* 39–40) that distinguishes between a body born out of parents (*mātāpitṛjā*)—the biological body—and a "subtle" body (*sūkṣma śarīra*). The biological body is considered to be a dense body because it is constituted by the predominance of the inert, stable, and dull tendency (*tamas*) of matter (*prakṛti*). This body is the product of the combination of the five material elements: earth, water, fire, air, and ether. According to Vyāsa, following the ancient healing tradition of Āyurveda, these elements conform the six main components or sheaths (*kośas*) of the physical body: hair, blood, flesh, sinews, bones, and marrow.[6]

The subtle body, on the other hand, is not considered to be transmitted by mother and father. It is constituted by the reflective mind (*buddhi*), the ego sense constructed as *I-am-ness* (*ahaṃkāra*), an operative or attentive mind (*manas*), ten capacities of sensation and action (*indriyas*), and five subtle elements or elemental qualities of the objective experience (*tanmātras*).[7] It could be said that what Sāṃkhya calls the "subtle body" is usually known as the mind in the Western philosophical tradition. However, because the mind is considered an embodiment of the self, Sāṃkhya does not fall into the same type of mind–body dualism that has marked Western philosophy since Descartes. In Sāṃkhya, "body" already encompasses the interaction with the mental at the level of the manifested matter (*vyakta prakṛti*).

Sāṃkhyan materiality is constituted by different levels of "density" or "subtlety" that follow a process of evolution in which the manifested (*vyaktam*) develops from the unmanifested (*avyaktam*), like the effect is produced by its cause (*SK* 9). The process is triggered by the constant movement and combination of three basic material cosmic forces or qualities (*guṇas*, *SK* 13). They are *sattva*—the tendency to manifest, illuminate, and make things intelligible; *rajas*—the tendency to move or change; and *tamas*—the tendency to remain stable, to obstruct, to confuse. The more *tamas* is present within a particular configuration, the more concrete, "heavy," and dense that object is (Larson 1998: 162–4). According to Sāṃkhya, that which is "dense"—manifold, visible, variable—derives from that which is "subtle"—single, invisible, permanent:

> From the intellect [arises] the ego, from the ego [arises] attention, the capacities of sensation and action, as well as the elemental qualities of objective experience, and from these [arise] the five elements.[8]

It is difficult to make sense of the Sāṃkhyan traditional derivation of the physical elements from subtle material entities if one takes a contemporary materialist perspective. It is of no help to look for a better explanation in commentaries of the tradition, for they all leave one asking exactly how something that is objective and materially "dense," such as a lump of earth, could have arisen or evolved from a mental entity such as the intellect, without making of this an idealist system.

Recently, some scholars have suggested that the term "subtle" is not an accurate translation of the Sanskrit word *sūkṣma* and suggest "minute" as a better way to convey the meaning of such derivation (Wujastyk 2009). In this way, the intellect, ego, attention, and the rest of mental capacities would be emergent faculties of the more basic minute processes that occur in the body such as neural synapsis, chemical exchanges, and neural networks that happen at the subatomic level. This interpretation, however, does not explain how Sāṃkhya can derive the physical elements that constitute the world and the rest of our body out of minute processes of the nervous system, unless we interpret it as offering a kind of virtual reality ontology, which I doubt should be the case. However, I will not argue this point further here since these types of discussions presuppose a metaphysical interpretation of the system. Instead, I think the issue of deriving something "dense" from something "minute" or "subtle" could be better understood under a phenomenological perspective.

A phenomenological reading of the "subtle" does not need to specify the kind of entity Sāṃkhya philosophy speaks of when referring to the subtle elements because it takes those elements as categories of experience and not as entities with a certain ontological status. A phenomenological reading of the Sāṃkhyan subtle body was first proposed by Mikel Burley (2007), who offered a Kantian interpretation of its cosmology. From this perspective, the intellect does not literally generate an ego, and the ego does not literally generate a mind and the sensorimotor capacities, nor do the subtle qualities create the physical elements through a material ontological causation. Rather, all objects of experience are constituted by the subtle elements in the sense that these provide the transcendental condition of possibility for objective experience to appear. For example, without the sensorial capacity of tasting, we would not be able to have the experience of sweet, salty, sour, and so forth. Since our capacity of taste is necessary for the experience of flavor, and the experience of flavor is necessary to distinguish the distinct varieties of taste, Sāṃkhya deduces that the sensorial capacity (*indriya*) and the quality of flavor (*tanmātras*) are constitutional elements, "conditions of possibility" in Kantian terminology, of our experience of sweet, salty, or sour objects.

In this way, without the elemental qualities (*tanmātras*) of sound, touch, light, flavor, or smell, there would be no experience of physical elements (space, air, fire, water, earth). Without the sensorimotor capacities (*indriyas*) of hearing, seeing, touching, or grasping, and so forth, there would not be the experience of sound, forms, tactile feelings, or solid objects. Without the possibility of directing the attention (*manas*) to each of the capacities of sensation and action, there would be no determinate cognition, coordination of actions, or distinct experiences. Without the capacity of referring each experience to oneself (*ahaṃkāra*), everything would remain as an impersonal apprehension of random sensations and actions; and without the intellectual ability to determine the world or reflect upon its meaning (*buddhi*), the personal experience would not be able to be articulated with the rest of our environment.

The Kantian reading proposed by Burley is successful in its attempt at getting rid of the dualistic, cosmogonic, and causal narrative present in the Sāṃkhyan system. This is important because the causal metaphysical interpretation of Sāṃkhya fails to explain how mind-independent entities such as the biological body of, for example, a fetus in the womb would "evolve" from mental entities such as intellect, ego, and subtle material qualities. It is very hard to understand under the metaphysical account how the elements of the perceptual system could pre-arise or predate the actual gestation of any particular life without falling into an idealism, which Sāṃkhya is not. This perplexity is avoided in the Kantian reading offered by Burley because the perceptual system or the psychosensory apparatus, which is what he calls the subtle body, is taken as a transcendental condition of possibility for experience and not as an ontological cause of denser bodily structures. As such, the subtle body distinguishes itself from the biological one in the level of experiential accessibility (Burley 2007: 122).

The hands, the legs, the eyes, the ears can be easily perceived by one's own self and by others. Even other organs such as the heart, the lungs, the stomach, and so on, are potentially perceivable from the third-person perspective given the appropriate tools to access them. However, perceiving the capacity of hearing, seeing, walking, grasping, and so forth, requires a special mode of attention—the type of phenomenological attention that Merleau-Ponty (1945/2002: 105–7) exemplifies with the touched touching hand: the left hand touching the right hand, which in turn is touching an object. Perceiving the touched hand is different from perceiving the same hand touching. The hand is the organ by which the "subtle" capacity of touching or grasping is enacted, but this capacity cannot be perceived in the same way as the hand is. The touched hand is an object, but the touching hand is the bodily awareness that arises in the midst of its own activity. Normally, this activity is transparent to one's own consciousness; that is, we do not normally pay attention to the body as it acts. This subtle aspect of our body as a condition of possibility for experience usually remains elusive, hidden, and imperceptible to a distracted and outwardly directed mind.

Yet, the subtle body should not be understood as a mere transcendental system either. The sense in which the Sāṃkhyan body is "subtle" should not be confused with that which is difficult to conceptualize or to objectify through one's reflection. The bodily capacities of sensation, action, and cognition are subtle precisely because of the difficulty in categorizing them as part of a fixed and objective perceptual system. They are instead the enactment of an embodied dynamicity that moves indefinitely (like the perception of the touched touching hand) between abstract and concrete, particular and universal, private and shared, hidden and manifest, subject and object.

Prakṛti's body exhibits (in its metaphorical shyness) its unwillingness to be fully objectified, even while representing the very objective reality whose role is to be experienced, to be seen. She—in her pure essence, her metaphysical modesty—remains invisible. But her manifested body is the site where seer and seen meet, where the mistaken association between the body and the observer happens, and where suffering, enjoyment, and liberation take place. It is precisely the dynamics of this encounter with all its gendered connotations that we are aiming to flesh out in this chapter. However, the Kantian reading of the subtle elements of the body is unable to account for this dynamic ambiguity in the Sāṃkhyan notion of the body. In what follows, I show how Merleau-Ponty's notion of "flesh" is better equipped to give us a deeper insight into Sāṃkhya's subtle body.

"I Have Been Seen," She Says

> When we speak of the flesh of the visible . . . we mean that carnal being, as a being of depths, of several leaves or several faces, a being in latency, and a presentation of a certain absence, is a prototype of Being, of which our body, the sensible sentient, is a very remarkable variant, but whose constitutive paradox already lies in every visible. (Merleau-Ponty 1968: 136)

In Merleau-Ponty's philosophy of perception, the world appears when the body in its two-dimensionality as a sensible (an object) and sentient being (a subject) turns back upon the whole of the visible, that is, upon the whole of the world of which it is a part. For Merleau-Ponty, just as for Sāṃkhya, the phenomenon of vision structurally expresses our experience of the world. To experience is to see. But for Merleau-Ponty (1968), "vision" is marked with a fundamental act of narcissism because the seer gets inevitably caught up in its own act, seeing itself (i.e., its position, spatiality, and perspective) in what it sees (139). This is also true for the Sāṃkhyan model of perception. However, for this system, the narcissistic view—expressed in the mistaken association of *puruṣa* with actions of the body as if they were its own—needs to be eradicated because it is the source of all suffering.

According to Sāṃkhya, it is through the body that consciousness sees itself as if it were affected by pleasures and pains, vices and virtues, and so forth. It is not until consciousness manages to distinguish itself from the cosmic elements and happenings of the body that it realizes itself as it is: pure awareness. Only then suffering ceases because there is no more association with sensations, conditions, or affective dispositions, all of which are localized in the body. The ultimate purpose of the body for Sāṃkhya is thus to serve as a "characteristic mark" (*liṅga*) to infer the existence of the true self and its difference from matter.

The term *liṅga* is another word for "body" in the *Sāṃkhyakārikā* and evokes a similar ambiguity found in Merleau-Ponty's notion of "flesh." Both terms refer to the body in its sensible and sentient aspects. To have a body means that one can be reduced to an object under the gaze of another, but it also means that one can experience oneself as a seer, even if mistakenly one thinks that such power comes from the body itself. Since it is through the body that the embodied self becomes aware of its unconscious materiality as well as of its sentiency (through feeling, seeing, and touching the world), the body represents a "mark" (i.e., a *liṅga*) of both principles. But as soon as the mistaken association between the conscious and unconscious principles disintegrates, the body, especially the subtle body, merges back (another meaning of *liṅga*) into the unmanifested and nonconscious material principle (*pradhāna*). The metaphor of the "modest lady" narrated above refers to this precise moment with the image of the naked lady retracting to her chambers to avoid been seen again.

From a phenomenological perspective it could be said that the "hidden," unmanifested body in Sāṃkhya amounts to a bare field of possible experience. But from this, multiple questions result: What then does it mean phenomenologically to have a subtle body? In what way does it precede or pre-arise to the physical body? And why is this relevant for a feminist philosophy of the body considering that this notion of embodiment comes from a dualistic system?

Without taking Sāṃkhyan cosmogony in its literal and metaphysical sense but keeping the dynamism of its cosmology, let us consider the gestation of a body. The distinction between the biological and the subtle body points to that which is *not given* by the mother or the father. That which is not passed down by genetics is the cosmic elements and the *modes* in which they are sensed. For example, the color of the hair, the type of blood, the thickness of the bones, the length of the marrow, the shape of the body, the genitals, and so forth, are determined by the parents' genes. But the food (earth) that the mother eats nourishing the unborn child, the liquidity (water) surrounding the fetus, the warmth (fire) from the mother's skin, the breath (air) that moves rhythmically resonating in the womb, and the space that the unborn body pervades are not given by genes, but rather they are given by the cosmic elements of the immediate environment. The way our embodied self perceives the elements and is affected by them in the womb will determine the way it perceives itself when it is born. In other words, even before there is experience of the eyes, the ears, the legs, and hands—that is, of the physical, biological body—there is, indeed, at least an intimate and determinate, affective experience of seeing, hearing, moving, and touching in relation to the cosmic elements. From a phenomenological reading of Sāṃkhya, it is in this way that "the subtle" level precedes (*pūrvotpannam*)[9] the dense.[10]

The "subtle" cannot be then conceived in the same concrete way as other bodies and objects are. Merleau-Ponty (1968) explained that ideas or the invisible "could not be detached from the sensible appearances and be erected into a second positivity" (149–50). Indeed, the subtle is not hidden like an object that will be eventually found or discovered once we have the proper tools or scientific devices. Merleau-Ponty appeals to a "hidden invisible" that needs to remain hidden so that there is "vision" (i.e., experience). As he explains, we do not see the ideas, do not hear them, not even with the mind's eye do we see them, but they are there, behind the sounds or lights (152). In this sense, the subtle body is always "behind" our experiences of the world and of our own embodied self.

Behind the sound, there is the pre-arisen capacity of hearing; behind the grasped object, there is the already existent capacity of the grasping hand. "Behind" the objective body, there is the body as subjectivity. We have here a kind of phenomenology that points to the potentiality of that which is there but is not yet born, and when it is finally born, it becomes hidden in the very mode of the appearance that it itself makes possible.

Merleau-Ponty (1968) thought that the best way to refer to the "flesh" was through the old notion of "element" in the sense that "it was used to speak of water, air, earth and fire, that is, in the sense of a general thing, midway between the spatiotemporal individual and the idea" (139–40). In his phenomenology of the flesh, the elemental body is much more than a mere physical or biological fact, not in the sense of being composed by body and spirit but rather because of the possibility of the body to make itself a seer (146).

Merleau-Ponty explains this process with the idea of reversibility: the flesh is the visible body that *can* see itself in the act of making something else visible. He exemplified this with the gesture of shaking hands. The hand "feels" itself shaking the other as it is being shaken. The reversible aspect of the flesh is subtle because it is a "hidden invisible" in the "heart of the visible." We see the hand; we might see the action of shaking, but we do not easily see the feeling, the intention, the thoughts, the dispositions that may be implicit in the act. These dispositions (*bhāvas*)[11] are thought of by the Sāṃkhyan tradition as aromas "perfuming" (*adhivāsita*) our subtle body with their pre-arisen determinations, which can be positive or negative. The *bhāva*-s leave their affective psychic traces in our sensorimotor capacities, mind, ego, and intellect and are always "impregnating" our attitudes, habits, patterns, actions, movements, and responses with their scent.

It is precisely because of the invisibility of flesh that Luce Irigaray points out the possibility of others not sharing the same "hidden invisible" disposition. Irigaray's critique of Merleau-Ponty's notion of the invisible raises the issue that the latter does not address the nonreversible characteristic of the "unborn" flesh (Irigaray 1993: 154–60). The flesh may be nonreversible particularly when it only sees what it desires to see or to imagine, without recognizing the "seer" who stands behind the body that it sees. In other words, the shaking hand, the hearing ear, or the seeing eye, and so forth, does not always perceive itself as being shaken, heard, or seen, in turn. The nonreversible character of the flesh is the aspect of ourselves that does not open up to the encounter with the other as a sentient being; it merely encounters it as a body to be objectified. In this sense, for Irigaray, Merleau-Ponty's seer is narcissistic and simulates the state of an unborn child who is unable to "see" the mother who "sees" it. It could also be said of the Sāṃkhyan seer (*puruṣa*) that it is like the "unborn" child because it perceives his mother (*prakṛti*) merely as the one who feeds him, carries him, protects him, and pleases him, in order to release him. In other words—and using again the earlier metaphor of the "modest lady"—the narcissistic onlookers (*puruṣa*) do not see the lady as an "other" that is aware of them but only as an object that is there for their pleasure alone.

The problem with Merleau-Ponty's "vision," and by extension with the Sāṃkhyan onlooker, is that the "other" invisible ends up being seen as imagined and not as it is in its own difference. What this means is that Merleau-Ponty's narcissistic seer is incapable of seeing the difference in the "hidden invisible," for he becomes oblivious to the fact that the "seen" (i.e., the other) may have a different gender, different feelings, different dispositions, different memories, and different expectations as the ones the seer is willing to recognize. In this sense, we could say that vision of the other and a true sense of reversibility and reciprocity are never really born in a narcissistic view. This is why the classical metaphysical consideration of Sāṃkhya cannot provide a reciprocal relation between the conscious observer and the observed material reality. Only a reading that takes the perspective of the "modest lady" in its agential difference could do it.

For Irigaray (1993), the "hidden invisible" is precisely the place of difference, and the recognition of this can turn it into a "tangible invisible" even while remaining beyond the graspable or sensorial experience (160). In other words, the subtle body is the aspect of our bodies that prevents them from being fully reduced to the gaze of the seer, that is, to being fully objectified. In this sense, the subtle body comprehends the affective, intellectual, and dispositional dimensions of our embodiment, which remain, last, and endure even when our biological body perishes.[12] The subtle is that which is transmitted from generation to generation (as ideas, behaviors, attitudes, feelings), lingering between the unmanifested and manifested moments, reincarnating from one body to another, reproducing dispositions of insight or ignorance, attachment or detachment, empowerment or weakness, and impressions of love, desire, greed, fear, anger, or delusion for ages. The subtle body is, thus, the place of suffering, where the human predicament begins and reproduces.

In Sāṃkhya, it is precisely the subtle body that has to be seen as something "other" and distinct to our real self. To stress the visibility of this difference, the Sāṃkhya tradition genderizes the relation between self and nature, the seer and the seen. But in doing so, it defaults into a metaphysical dualism that irreconcilably separates the subject from the object in such a way that its ultimate separation ends up being symbolized by the image of an "infertile elderly couple" (*vṛddham-samyogāt-apatyam na bhavati*). This metaphor was used by Māṭhara in his commentary (*Māṭharavṛtti*) to explain the moment in which the pure principle of consciousness (*puruṣa*) recognizes itself as distinct to the material unconscious one (*prakṛti*):

> "She has been seen by me," says the indifferent one; "I have been seen," says the other one as she stops [her dance]. Although they remain together there is no need for [further] creation.[13]

This passage implies that the only purpose for *prakṛti*'s visibility and reproduction (i.e., for the birth of embodied existence) is for the pleasing of a disembodied conscious male principle. In its role as female, her reason to express herself is centered around the male's gaze. The material unconscious principle, like a beautiful dancer (*nartakī*), displays her movements before the observer, who, satisfied by the show, fulfills himself in his own consciousness as spectator (*SK* 59). The dancer, having exhibited herself to the spectators, finishes her dance and retracts.

A relation like this lacks reversibility. The seer is not really seen back by the seen (since this one is not conscious) or vice versa; the dancer is not really seen by the spectator apart from the narcissistic pleasure that the dance causes him in the act of seeing. The modest lady is not perceived in her embarrassment but only as a naked body under objectifying eyes. And the elderly wife who has stopped being attractive does not draw the eyes of her husband back to her again, even while remaining together. *Purusa*'s liberation, expressed in the metaphor of the male's gaze, would seem to be egotistic, narcissistic, and self-absorbed.

Although Sāṃkhyan metaphysical dualism presents a metaphysical gender equality, it lacks gender reciprocity. Yet, its philosophy of embodiment presents a body that cannot be fully objectified. The lack of reversibility in the act of seeing lies in the incapability of the metaphysical eye—"the male gaze"—to transcend its own subjectivity. The other is seen as an object (of desire, of pleasure, of service, etc.) but not in its difference, which is given precisely by that which remains hidden and ungraspable, but present in the interaction, that is, the other as subjectivity. However, Vācaspati's metaphor of the modest lady makes us wonder: can there be an act of "seeing" that is not narcissistic within Sāṃkhya? Can there be a reciprocal relation in the Sāṃkhyan experience of the world? Can a reversible vision be born?

And They Both Asked, "Who Are You?"

There is only one simile within the *Sāṃkhyakārikā* that could shed light into a reciprocal relation between the two principles and into the intersubjective reversibility of the flesh in Sāṃkhyan philosophy of the body. This simile compares the association between *puruṣa* and *prakṛti* with that between a blind person and a lame man. The blind person helps the lame man by carrying him under his shoulders, while the lame man directs the way with his eyes. The commentator to this *kārikā* (21) in the *Suvarṇasaptati* narrates a background story, which is about a caravan attacked by a group of thieves. All the merchants fled, leaving behind a blind person and a lame man:

> The infirm one asked him: "Who are you?" The other replied: "I am blind from birth. Not knowing the road, I run without aim. But who are you?" The infirm

> one replied: "I am paralytic from birth. I am capable of seeing the road, but I cannot march. I propose that you take me on your shoulders and that you carry me, while I show you the road." Associating themselves in that fashion, the two men could get to their homes; by means of such a union, they could attain their goal. (Takakusu 1933: 29)

In this simile, the recognition of each other in their subjectivity is granted by the question, "Who are you?" Both see each other in their desperation, weakness, need, and possibility to help each other. They meet in their embodied "disability" and work together for the benefit of both. Only under this metaphor is the feminine principle—represented here by the figure of the blind—recognized as having a purpose (*artha*) for her own sake. While all other metaphors take *prakṛti* as working for the sake of *puruṣa*'s emancipation, this one clearly pictures a reciprocal action for the sake of the emancipation of both.

Irigaray (1993) says that in order for there to be reversibility and a non-narcissistic way of seeing, the "maternal-feminine" must not be forgotten (162). In the context of Sāṃkhya, I take this to mean that only if we turn to see the cosmic elements of the body without the metaphysics will we have a clearer, reversible vision of oneself and the other. This means that we need to recognize each other as irreducible bodies. The metaphor of disability reflects this irreducibility well. The seen body—the blind—is also a "seer" because, even if the seer (lame man) cannot see the other "seeing" back, the lame recognizes the blind as an "other" with his own needs, fears, strengths, and vulnerability. Behind the blind body there is an "other," a "subtle body" that looks back at us from its own place of difference.

"Behind" the visible elements and the visible bodies are subtle determinations that affect the embodied experience of our subjectivity and that predispose our desires, emotions, and behaviors even before these become manifest, as the phenomenological analysis of the unborn body shows. Our bodies are always possible objects of another's gaze and at the same time refrain from being fully objectifiable; they are subtle, affective, sentient.

In this sense, the subtle body analyzed under a feminist phenomenological lens can be understood as a dynamic process of awareness that precedes and determines our dispositions toward the environment and our relationship to others, dispositions that are always affective, and which may remain as a "hidden invisible" in a lifetime, migrating and reincarnating from body to body for generations. As long as the subtle body (that modest delicate lady) remains unknown, and unrecognized, our *flesh* will remain nonreversible.

The reason for this is that seeing oneself and others without recognizing the invisible determinations at the root of our differences makes our vision of the world ego-centered and conducive to the experience of affliction and suffering. A nonsuffering existence might instead be possible when the body (i.e., the "other" material being that opposes our "seeing") stops being seen merely as an object and starts being recognized as a subject in its own right. In other words, when *prakṛti* is considered not only as "the seen" but as "a seer" as well.

Conclusion

A Sāṃkhyan vision of existence could seem unable to evade metaphysics insofar as its seer (a male conscious principle), the only enjoyer of the "show," cannot recognize the dancing material reality in its self-aware and self-enjoying cosmic body. Indeed, the simile of the lame and blind men seems to contradict what Sāṃkhya clearly denies: that *puruṣa* and *prakṛti* are both conscious. Yet, only when the distinction between *puruṣa* and *prakṛti* is not taken in a metaphysical sense can the cosmic relevance of their inevitable union in the "subtle" intermediate realm of the affective modes of being (*bhāvas*) emerge. The phenomenological reading of the interrelationality between *puruṣa* and *prakṛti* yields a notion of body in Sāṃkhya philosophy that recognizes it as multidimensional, self-aware, and intersubjective. Reading the Sāṃkhyan metaphors from the feminine perspective may help us see how this is possible. Both the images of the modest delicate lady and the blind man show a Sāṃkhyan subjectivity that recognizes its dimension in the body (with the lady) and the mutual purpose of existence in liberating one another (with the blind man). The relevance of the "maternal-feminine" becomes evident in Sāṃkhya philosophy when the body is recovered in its relationality with the environment (the cosmic elements). From this perspective, the Sāṃkhyan phenomenology of embodiment can offer a productive, reversible, bearable, and non-narcissistic account of experience—or of "vision" (*darśana*) as reciprocal seeing.

Abbreviations

Gbh = *Gauḍapādabhāṣya*
MV = *Māṭharavṛtti*
SK = *Sāṃkhyakārikā*

TK = *Tattvakaumudī*
TV = *Tattvavāiśāradī*
Ybh = *Yogabhāṣya*

Notes

1 There are other metaphors in the Sāṃkhya tradition that refer to *prakṛti* as a blind person (*SK* 21), an unselfish servant (Vācaspati Miśra's commentary *(TK)* on SK 60), or a debtor (Gauḍapāda's commentary *(GBh)* on SK 66).
2 I use "sexual difference" in the same sense as Luce Irigaray in her book *An Ethics of Sexual Difference* (1993), that is, as a difference that has its origin in the natural world but that needs to be expressed in the realm of language and the symbolic, that is, in society and culture. According to Irigaray, this difference has never been expressed in the history of Western philosophy, because its cultural structures continue to represent or cultivate only a male subjectivity. To express in language and in the symbolic realm, the sexual difference of the feminine is a task that needs to be done to guarantee an ethical relation between subjects. I attempt to show in this paper that, despite the problematic nature of the notion of subject found in Sāṃkhya classical philosophy, there are important conceptual resources within this tradition that could contribute to an intercultural philosophy of sexual difference.
3 In the original, this is stated: *prakṛteḥ sukumārataram na kiñcid astīti me matir bhavati | yā dṛṣṭāsmi iti punar na darśanam upaiti puruṣasya ||* (*SK* 61). The translation is mine.
4 Originally, this is worded: *parapuruṣa-darśana-asahiṣṇuti* (*TK* 61).
5 *Prakṛti*, who is endowed with qualities, moves for the sake of him who has no qualities [and] without any benefit for herself. She assists with *puruṣa*'s liberation in a variety of ways without him returning any favor. *nānā vidhair apāyair upakāriṇi anupakāriṇaḥ puṃsaḥ |guṇavati aguṇasya satas tasyārtham apāthakam carati ||* (*SK* 60).
6 See *Gbh* 39 and *Yogabhāṣya* (*Ybh* III.29).
7 The *tanmātras* could also be understood as constituting spheres of objective experience, each of them characterized by their specific but indeterminate general quality and material potency: sound waves, movement, and contact sphere of tactile feeling (*sparśa*); color and luminosity sphere of visual appearance (*rūpa*); liquidity sphere of taste *(rasa)*; solid particles sphere of smell (*gandha*). See Vyāsa (*Ybh* III.44) and Vācaspati Miśra (*TV* I.44).
8 This is originally stated as: *prakṛteḥ mahāṃs tato'ahaṃkāras tasmād gaṇaś ca ṣoḍaśakaḥ |tasmād api ṣodaśakāt pañcabhyaḥ pañcabhūtāni ||* (*SK* 22).

9 In the original: *pūrvotpannam asaktam niyatam mahadādisūkṣmaparyantam | saṃsarati nirupabhogam bhāvair adhivāsitam liṅgam ||* (*SK* 40). The subtle body is pre-arisen, unrestricted, and enduring, comprising "the great" and the rest, down to the subtle elements; it migrates without acquiring experience and is "perfumed" with dispositions.

10 One could think about the implications of Sāṃkhya philosophy when thinking of the relation between the categories of sex and gender. If gender is the way one experiences one's own embodied subjectivity mediated by history, culture, and social environment, in so far as it has to do with self-other-world interpretation (*buddhi, ahaṃkāra*), one's performativity (*manas, indriyas*), and modes of being sensible to the environment (*tanmātras*), then it pertains to the functions of the subtle body, and in this way gender "pre-arises" and determines sex. It is relevant for this discussion to point out as well that in defining the essential functions of each of the five motor capacities (*karmendriyas*), Īśvarakṛṣṇa (*SK* 28) attributes enjoyment (*ānanda*)—and not reproduction—to the sexual organs (*utsarga*).

11 The *bhāvas* are well-disposed (*dharma*), ill-disposed (*adharma*), insightful (*jñāna*), noninsightful (*ajñāna*), nonattached (*vairagya*), attached (*avairāgya*), empowered (*aiśvarya*), and disempowered (*anaiśvarya*) (*SK* 44).

12 The realm of particulars is divided in three: subtle (bodies), bodies born out of parents, and the primordial elements. Of these, the subtle bodies endure, while the ones born out of parents perish (*SK* 39).

13 In the original: *dṛṣtā mayety upekṣaka eko dṛṣṭāhamity uparamaty anyā| sati saṃyoge'pi tayoḥ prayojanaṃ nāsti sargasya ||* (*SK* 66). See also *MV* 66 in Sarma (1922).

References

Primary sources

Sāṃkhyakārikā of Īśvarakṛṣṇa, with a commentary of Gauḍapāda (1964). T. G. Mainkar (ed. and trans.). Poona: Oriental Book Agency.

Sānkhya Kārikā by Īśwara Krishna, with a commentary of Mathara Charya (1922). Vishnu Prasad Sarma (ed.). Chowkhamba Sanskrit Series, Benares: Vidya Vilas Press.

Tattva-Kaumudī of Vāchaspati Miśra (1896). G. Jhā (ed. and trans.). Bombay: Tookaram Tatya.

Tattva-Vāiśāradī of Vāchaspati-Miśra in the Yoga System of Patañjali (1914). J. H. Woods (ed. and trans.). Cambridge, MA: Harvard University Press.

The Sāmkhya-Kārikā, Iśvara Kṛṣṇa's Memorable Verses on Sāmkhya Philosophy with the commentary of Gauḍapādācarya (1933). H. D. Sharma (ed. and trans.). Poona: Oriental Book Agency.

The Sāmkhya-Kārikā of Iśvara Kṛṣṇa (1973). S. S. Suryanarayana Sastri (ed. and trans.). Madras: University of Madras.

Vyāsa, *Yogasūtrabhāṣya* (1983). In S. Hariharānanda Āraṇya, *Yoga Philosophy of Patañjali* (trans. P. N. Mukerji). Albany, NY: SUNY Press.

Secondary sources

Burley, M. (2007). *Classical Sāmkhya and Yoga: An Indian Metaphysics of Experience.* New York: Routledge.

Collins, A. (2000). "Dancing with *Prakriti:* The Samkhyan Goddess as Pativrata and Guru." In Alf Hiltebeitel and Kathleen M. Erndl (eds.), *Is the Goddess a Feminist? The Politics of South Asian Goddesses* (pp. 52–68). Sheffield: Sheffield Academic Press.

Irigaray, Luce. (1993). *An Ethics of Sexual Difference.* Ithaca, NY: Cornell University Press.

Jacobsen, K. A. (1996). "The Female Pole of the Godhead in Tantrism and the Prakṛti of Sāṃkhya." *Numen* 43(1): 56–81.

Jacobsen, K. A. (2006). "What Similes in Sāṃkhya Do: A Comparison of the Similes in the Sāṃkhya Texts in the *Mahābhārata*, the *Sāṃkhyakārikā* and the *Sāṃkhyasūtra*." *Journal of Indian Philosophy* 34: 587–605.

Larson, G. (1998). *Classical Sāmkhya. An Interpretation of Its history and Meaning.* Delhi: Motilal Banarsidass.

Merleau-Ponty, M. (1945/2002). *Phenomenology of Perception* (C. Smith, trans.). London & New York: Routledge Classics.

Merleau-Ponty, M. (1968). *The Visible and the Invisible* (A. Lingis, trans.). Evanston, IL: Northwestern University Press.

Natarajan, K. (2001). "Gendering of Early Indian Philosophy: A study of 'Samkhyakarika.'" *Economic and Political Weekly* 36(17): 1398–404.

Takakusu, M. (trans.) (1932). *The Sāmkhya Karika Studied in the Light of Its Chinese Version.* Madras: Diocesan Press.

Wujastyk, D. (2009). "Interpreting the Human Body in Premodern India." *International Journal of Hindu Studies* 13(2): 189–228.

3

Women's Liberation in Jainism: Understanding Philosophical Debates and Cultural Dialectics

Veena R. Howard

Since the beginning of Indian philosophical thought, religious literary texts and their authors have debated and continue to debate the status of women, particularly in relation to their access to the spiritual goal of liberation (*mokṣa*). Even though earlier philosophical texts provided records of accomplished female scholars and leaders, some orthodox Vedic schools (Vedānta, Mīmāṃsā, etc.) explicitly barred women from reading religious and philosophical texts and assuming authoritative roles. Heterodox Buddhist and Jain philosophies, despite their strong female monastic traditions, have often deemed women to be subordinate to male counterparts.

The issue of gender becomes even more complicated in Jainism, however, because one of its sects, the Digambara (literally, "sky-clad"), has espoused the impossibility of women's attainment of the religious goal of liberation in the female body, while the other sects including the Śvetāmbaras (literally, "white-clad") persuasively defend women's right (as human beings) to embark on spiritual life.[1] A close reading of the Jain texts offers significant insight into Jain views on the difference between gender and sexuality, female body, and the question of *strīmokṣa* (women's liberation). This chapter will analyze how the robust female monastic movement and laywomen's religiosity—drawing strength from the scripture and spiritually accomplished Jain women exemplars—can be seen as a resistance to misogynist tendencies.

A study of Jain texts reveals a characteristically diverse attitude toward women and their bodies, ranging from one of overt misogyny to a more relaxed approval for liberation in the female body. As Manisha Sethi observes, "There is no single archetype but a heterogeneity of ideals that appear sometimes to buttress women's claim to independent spiritual life, and at other times, to erode this pursuit" (Sethi 2009: 56). While at times the Jain writings relegate women to an inferior status due to their biology and their peculiar nature, the Jain texts also contain examples of early Jain women, such as Rājīmatī, wife of the 22nd Tīrthaṅkara Nemīnātha, who by the virtue of chastity and righteousness attained liberation. Throughout the Jain history, the question of female soteriological pursuit has been taken seriously.

Thus, notwithstanding the much greater number of male authoritative figures, the Jain tradition is not entirely male-centered with respect to its theology. John Cort notes that goddess worship in Jainism has been a signifying mark of the tradition (Cort 1987: 236). There are thus two historical factors that indicate that the issues of women's right to spiritual liberation and their religiosity have been taken seriously in Jainism: (1) Historically, Jainism has institutionalized the order of female ascetics (*sādhvīs*) alongside of the male ascetics, at least since the time of 24th Tīrthaṅkara Lord Mahāvīra (ca. sixth century BCE), indicating women's right to attain spiritual goals. (2) A substantial number of Jain philosophers and leaders have debated the question of women's liberation, validating their concerns for women's spiritual liberation.

Jain philosophical literature offers significant insights regarding the biological and anatomical differences between various life forms in general and about the two sexes in particular.[2] The Jain debates on spiritual liberation uniquely and systematically deliberate on the question of whether gender is rooted in the physical nature of the human female. The question of the possibility of a woman's life as a renunciate—which according to Jain traditions is the only path to spiritual liberation—holds significance beyond any intellectual debates. This issue relates to the actual lives of women in the Jain communities; therefore, not surprisingly, many texts record the prolonged criticisms leveled by the Śvetāmbaras and other minor sects against their Digambara counterparts' views.

In *Gender and Salvation* (1991), Padmanabh Jaini compiled and translated numerous debates, pioneering research on the female body and the prospect of women's renunciation and liberation, drawing on texts spanning from the second to the eighteenth century. This question dominates intersectarian debates that continue to this day. In their outstanding studies, scholars such as Kelting (2017), Sethi (2012), Balbir (1994), and Cort (1987) have contributed to a broader, nuanced study of women's role, their right to ascetic life, and the religiosity of Jain laywomen and nuns (*sādhvīs*). This chapter builds on the previous scholarship and primarily draws attention to the fact that despite misogynist tendencies, Jain texts and Jain women—renunciate and lay—have taken the question of the women's right to renunciation and emancipation seriously.

In this chapter, after providing a brief overview of the essential principles of Jain philosophy—which are crucial for engaging with the question of women's liberation—I will focus on three essential issues. The first issue centers around the anxieties regarding the female body, that is, whether the female anatomy, which is considered inherently flawed in some Jain texts, and women's "fickle" nature render them unfit for attaining liberation.

The second issue concerns the distinctive Jain articulation of the difference between biological sex and sexual inclination and a recognition of a third gender beyond the binaries of male and female. Such a theoretical understanding has provided a framework to argue for women's right to liberation. This analysis provides an insight into the various Jain attempts that take the possibility of women's liberation seriously as well as offering a glimpse into the dialectics on gender, sex, female anatomy, and female nature that have been utilized by both camps for their arguments.

Finally, a brief survey of the examples of celebrated Jain women who have attained spiritual liberation, even the highest status of Tīrthaṅkara (a "Bridge-builder"; a realized being), substantiates the fact that Jain women pursued and have been recognized for spiritual accomplishments, despite certain counter viewpoints. In current times, a vibrant Jain female monastic movement and the prevailing tradition of deep religiosity of laywomen, which is integrally linked to the sustaining of female and male monastics, can be construed as forms of resistance toward the patriarchal misogynistic traditions.

Introducing the Debate: An Overview of the Principles of Jainism

Before providing an overview of the main tenets of Jain religious tradition, it is important to situate Jainism in the Indian social and religious context in which it was formed and flourished. In ancient India, two traditions of thought, the Brahmanical (Vedic) tradition and the Śramaṇa (literally, "striver, wandering ascetic") tradition helped develop the landscape of culture through philosophical thought and religious rituals and moral laws. Brahmanism (generally associated with the Vedic rituals and laws) also included strands of ascetic traditions. Generally, scholars view Hinduism as attached to the Brahmanical tradition and associate Buddhism and Jainism with Śramaṇa traditions.[3] The Śramaṇic traditions primarily differ from the Brahmanical traditions in their rejection of the authority of the Vedas, which are considered the foundational texts within Hinduism, as well as some other issues including specific moral codes and rituals. The two strands represent two different views about (1) the relation between human beings and the world and (2) the ultimate goal of human life.

Commonly, Vedic traditions attribute the creation of the world to a Supreme Being and religious life includes various forms of rituals and religious mandates. The Śramaṇa traditions mostly reject the idea of a creator God. The world has no beginning, and the relation of humans and the world is contingent. Liberation from *saṃsāra* (the cycle of death and rebirth) characterizes the final goal, not any union with God.[4] The *śramaṇa* (striver who attains liberation by self-effort) epitomizes the central goal of Jainism. The latter's 24 Tīrthaṅkaras represent the ideal of ascetic detachment and intense self-effort. Due to their own strict disciplines and regimens, the Tīrthaṅkaras realize liberation; therefore, Jain monastic and lay communities consider them exemplary and worthy of veneration. We will see later in the chapter how this focus on the ultimate goal of liberation through intense ascetic practices gives rise to the crucial questions of women's renunciation and their possibility of achieving liberation. The following survey of Jainism's essential principles would provide an insight into the question of gender and spiritual liberation. On the one hand, Jain philosophy presents absolute equality to all souls; and on the other hand, the tradition supports masculinized renunciation as the only way to attain the highest soteriological goal, creating an ambivalent situation for women, simply based on their physical bodies.

Three Essential Principles of Jain Tradition: Equality of Soul and Emphasis on Self-Effort

The basic thought of the Jain tradition is explained in a threefold way:

1. All *jīva*-s (souls) are equal (*sama*).
2. The final goal of human life, that is, liberation, is obtained only by self-effort (*śrama*), not by the grace of either God or a teacher.
3. Asceticism or renunciation is essential for attaining liberation.

These schemata should allow for equal access to liberation for both men and women insofar as all *jīvas* are equal. However, as we will see later, the issue of the female body obfuscates this equality of *jīvas*. Furthermore, as Jainism considers all *jīvas* equal, the observance of *ahiṃsā* (nonviolence; literally abstaining from harming any being) becomes the central value of the tradition. We will see later how this becomes an issue in proscribing liberation to women.

Jainism is historically known as a tradition of Jinas ("conqueror") or Tīrthaṅkaras ("bridge-builder"). Jinas are enlightened beings who have observed absolute nonviolence, conquered all passions, and have achieved liberation.[5] Jainism holds that there are twenty-four Tīrthaṅkaras—Ṛṣabhanātha being the first and Vardhamāna Mahāvīra considered the last in the series. The present philosophy and practices are developed out of the documentation of the teachings of the Tīrthaṅkaras, especially Lord Mahāvīra, who is the most recent one.

Central Doctrines: Gender Neutral Philosophy

Some central doctrines of Jain philosophy and religion are as follows:

1. The universe we perceive really exists (it is not illusory in the way that some philosophical schools like Vedānta postulate); it is eternal and without beginning or end.
2. Since the world is without a beginning, Jainism is atheistic in the sense that it does not accept the concept of a creator and sustainer God. The universe is considered to be an autonomous system governed by its own natural laws.
3. According to Jain philosophy, every soul possesses the potentiality for becoming a supreme being—that is, the disposition to attain liberation. By means of self-discipline, the individual soul may reach the highest form of perfection.
4. The soul (*jīva*) is regarded as an eternal principle (in contrast to Buddhist thought, which rejects the concept of a permanent soul). The soul possesses four essential characteristics: infinite knowledge, infinite faith, infinite energy, and infinite bliss. The soul is the doer and enjoyer of all actions. It cannot escape the consequences of its own actions. The soul becomes liberated when the effects of all *karma*, which obfuscate the luminous nature of soul, are completely eliminated.
5. All souls enjoy the potential to achieve liberation. This equality of souls is entwined with the doctrine of *ahiṃsā*, which is arguably the primary

principle of Jain philosophy. Because all souls are equal, no soul has the right to harm any other soul in any way. Any bodily, mental, or verbal activity is regarded as violent if it harms other living beings. Furthermore, performance of harmful activity, instigating another person to perform harmful activities, or appreciating harmful activities performed by others—all these are considered equally harmful and keep the soul in the cycle of death and rebirth. Jain philosophy upholds *ahiṃsā* as a fundamental principle, making nonviolence the foundation of its ethics. Its unique and total adherence to nonviolence (even to the minutest beings) sets the Jain worldview apart from other Śramaṇa traditions.

6. The law of *karma* is central in the Jain system. The cycle of birth and death, the course of life, and the overall working of the universe depend upon the law of *karma*—a law that operates entirely free of any divine interference. Worldly souls become impure because of their association with karmic matter. However, one can acquire purity by observing the moral code of conduct and the austerities prescribed in Jain texts. Jain life upholds a strict code of conduct, namely, the *Mahāvratas* (the great observances for ascetics) and the *Anuvratas* (the minor observances for the laity), including the vows of abstaining from killing, lying, stealing, etc. The vow of *ahiṃsā* is the backbone of all moral codes, and it is the root principle behind all other vows—for example, *satya* (truth), *asteya* (nonstealing), *brahmacarya* (celibacy or chastity), and *aparigraha* (nonpossessiveness). All moral vows are oriented toward the telos of liberation—freedom from negative *karmas* and attainment of *kaivalyam* (the pure liberated state devoid of any passions and desires).

The Goal of Final Liberation vis-à-vis *Karma*: The Issue of Gendered Bodies and Rebirth

According to Jain philosophy, the soul (*jīva*) is eternal and is independent of matter (the body). The project of life is to release the soul from the confines of the body. Due to the inflow of karmic matter (created from physical, mental, and speech acts) into the soul, the soul is in the bondage of *saṃsāra* (the cycle of death and rebirth). Both Hinduism and Buddhism subscribe to the law of *karma* and provide guidance for freedom. However, Jainism uniquely focuses on the goal of the cessation of *karma*. This cycle of bondage can be ceased by stopping all activity, and previously accumulated *karma* can be extinguished by performing austerities and observing ethical rules of conduct. When the effects of all actions are exhausted, the soul is liberated from the physical constraints of the body.

The possibility of liberation is premised upon the assumption that human beings are bound in the cycle of *saṃsāra*. Rather than claiming that bondage "began" at a specific moment in time, Jainism holds that *karma* accrued from past lives—both good and bad—is the cause of bondage. All previous *karmas*, caused by lack of discipline, harmful activity, false belief, and passion (anger, pride, etc.), bind the person to a worldly life of ignorance, suffering, and violence. The past *karma*s are the cause of our present physical birth and condition. Since an individual soul causes bondage through one's own actions, it can also achieve ultimate liberation through purifying the previous *karmas* and not creating new *karmas*. In general, adherence to three principles of the Jain tradition (Right belief, Right knowledge, Right conduct) leads to annihilation of the burden of previous *karma*. Thus, liberation can only be achieved by nonattachment, asceticism, and moral discipline, the latter defined in terms of the "five great vows" (nonviolence, truth, non-possession, celibacy/chastity, and non-stealing). In this vein, some Jain texts fault ill *karmas* for birth in a woman's body. Just as a woman can take rebirth as a man by doing good *karmas*, so can a man be reborn as a woman due to evil and harmful actions.

Before moving into the actual debates, we will briefly analyze how the above principles, which undergird Jain philosophy, also complicate the possibility of women's liberation in the Jain tradition. Jain philosophy emphasizes the equality (*sama*) of all *jīvas* (souls), and all humans are put in the same highest category of living beings. It also emphasizes absolute *ahiṃsā* on the basis of the underlying sanctity of all beings, not just human beings. Such emphasis on *ahiṃsā* plays a pivotal role in casting women as not worthy of liberation. Digambaras believe that women's bodies inherently cause harm; therefore, they are not worthy of liberation. This view partially arises from a belief that menstrual blood kills microorganisms living in the female body, and that the female body is therefore karmically inferior.

In addition, the Digambaras argue for *total* renunciation—including even shedding of one's clothes. Despite this self-imposed mandate of nakedness for liberation, the Digambara texts prohibit women's nudity because of their physical anatomy and psychological modesty, an obstacle we will look at it in detail later in the chapter. The Śvetāmbaras, however, argue for the liberation of women on the basis of the equality of all *jīvas* and do not see nudity as a necessary condition for liberation. They refer to the authoritative scripture, the *Tattvārthasūtra*, saying "the path to moksa consists of Three Jewels (*ratnatraya*)—right view (*samyak-darśana*), right knowledge (*samyak-jñāna*), and right conduct (*samyak-cāritra*)—and all of three of These Jewels are to be found together in women.

Women therefore have no deficiency in regard to the attainment of *mokṣa*" (Jaini 2000: 169). They additionally substantiate their claim with the legends of pious women throughout Jain history and especially draw attention to the fact that the nineteenth Tīrthaṅkara (Māllīnātha) was a woman.[6]

The above overview of Jain philosophy and principles demonstrates that overall Jain principles are egalitarian and gender-neutral. However, the belief in past *karmas* that determine the present condition, including the body and nature, has resulted in casting women as inferior subjects and their bodies not worthy of liberation. The following sections will focus on the debates surrounding the question of women's right and ability to attain the highest goal of emancipation.

The Jain Perspective on Women's Liberation: A Brief Analysis of Debate

In his book, *Gender and Salvation*, Jaini lays out how the spiritual liberation of women (*strīmokṣa*) has been a major point of contention between the two major sects of Jainism—the Digambaras and the Śvetāmbaras. He also highlights the work of an earlier Jain sect, known as Yāpanīya, that advocated women's liberation. This section examines the main arguments and controversies pertaining to the place of women within Jainism. The Digambaras have consistently insisted that women cannot attain liberation in the female body, while the Śvetāmbaras have refused to deny women access to the liberated state (*Arhat* or *Siddhahood*).[7] This controversy hinged on two issues: first, the Digambara insistence on the impossibility of nakedness for women, which was an essential requirement to achieve liberation, and second, the anatomy of the female body and women's nature, which are construed as being violent.

Nakedness and Women's Liberation

Jaini succinctly identifies one of the central issues dividing the Śvetāmbaras and Digambaras: whether or not ascetics, those who dedicate their lives to attaining the goal of liberation, should wear clothes. This debate represents a basic concern in Jain soteriology, especially because the Śvetāmbara male ascetics reject the practice of nudity. If nudity is the main factor in denying women liberation, then women, the Śvetāmbaras surmise, would be equally eligible for attaining liberation, because in their view nudity is *not* required for this goal.

Furthermore, Śvetāmbaras cite examples of renowned female ascetics who hold illustrious status due to their spiritual attainments.

All Jain adherents acknowledge that the last great Jain leader, "the Great Hero," Vardhamāna Mahāvīra (599–527 BCE) had renounced everything and observed harsh austerities, including discarding his clothes. Mahāvīra is portrayed as a "naked ascetic," and his nakedness signifies complete detachment from possessions, resolve, and his observance of physical and mental purity. Jaini traces the historicity of this practice saying, "some of his early adherents had been similarly 'sky-clad' (*digambara*) and came to be known as *jinakalpins* (i.e., similar to the *jina*)" (Jaini 1991: 2). However, the significance of Vardhamāna Mahāvīra's nakedness, as well as that of his immediate disciples, was differently interpreted by the two sects.

The Digambaras, who follow the naked ascetic Mahāvīra's example, claimed that a seeker of spiritual liberation observes nakedness on the basis of the Jain ethical principles of *aparigraha* (nonattachment) and renunciation of all possessions, including wearing clothes. Monks observe severe austerities and possess almost nothing. They could carry only two objects: a small whisk broom for brushing insects away and a water gourd used for sanitary purposes. They also carry a religious text. Jaini states that Digambaras "accepted only naked monks as the true mendicant adherents of the Jina, and they regarded the Śvetāmbara monks, who continued to wear white clothes (*śveta-ambara*) after ordination, as no better than celibate laymen (*brahmacāri-gṛhastha*)" (Jaini 1991: 2). Nudity thus became the fundamental mark of an ascetic in the Digambara sect and in time was ratified as a necessary condition for the attainment of liberation. Nudity is an extreme form of renunciation and its practice restrains serious seekers from the mundane interactions with householders, which would distract them from pursuing the path of liberation with single-minded focus.

The defense for women's right to liberation came not only from the Śvetāmbaras but also from minor Jain sects as early as the eighth century. For example, the ninth-century text, *Strīnirvāṇaprakaraṇa*, summarizes the views of the Digambaras: "Nudity must be considered as the prerequisite for *mokṣa*; if this were not so, it would not be obligatory for males also. Being unfit for nudity, a woman must be considered unfit for Siddhahood [a realized state], like anyone who is unfit to receive initiation" (Jaini 1991: 64). The interlocutor in the text provides various arguments to show that there is no relationship between achieving liberation and nudity.

For the Śvetāmbaras, the observance of nakedness was not a mandate but a suggested requirement, "somewhat similar to the practice of austerities such as fasting, which, although commendable, was hardly mandatory" (Jaini 1991: 2).[8] The Śvetāmbaras argued against the revival of the observance of nudity citing what was written in the canon. This is similar to the viewpoints of the schools of Theravāda and Mahāyāna Buddhism: the former focused on what the Buddha *said* and the latter on what the Buddha *did*. The Śvetāmbaras presented the practice of nudity as a heresy that was unsupported by the Jain canon, but the Digambaras refused to relinquish their position that nakedness was mandated, as evidenced by the example of nude Tīrthaṅkara Mahāvīra.[9]

These debates are significant because they continue to affect the actual lives of women, both renunciate and lay. In the Digambara sect, since nakedness was essential to attaining spiritual liberation, women were considered not worthy of attaining liberation because their female bodies were not suitable for observing nakedness. According to Balbir,

> Because the underlying idea is that a woman can by no means go naked because of her specific physiology and innate impurity due to the presence of numerous subtle microscopic beings in her body, she is not considered to be able to reach emancipation as a woman. She has to be reborn as a man first. (2005: 2)

This passage underscores the physiology of women as the reason for not being able to practice nudity insofar as her body is construed as a site of violence (against microscopic beings) during menstruation. In her introduction to *Religion and Women*, Katherine Young cites the Digamabra view on women's bodies: "The genital organs of the woman, her navel, armpits, space between her breasts are said [in the scriptures] to be breeding grounds for subtle forms of life. How can there be [full] renunciation for women?" (Sharma and Young 1994: 30). Such detailed accounts of the repulsion toward the female body do not take into account the biological fact that the male body is equally a breeding ground of microbes. The Śvetāmbara counterarguments notwithstanding, misogynist tendencies continue to exist within the tradition. The following section provides further details on the traditional attitudes highlighting not only the deficiencies of the female body but also the defect in the female nature.

Flawed Bodies and Fickle Nature: Issues in Violence and Female Subjugation

Many Indian philosophical and religious traditions express revulsion toward the female body and advise caution because of its capacity to tempt even the most restrained ascetics. The *Mahābhārata* contains examples of great sages who fall into temptation at the very sight of women. However, a close reading of the Jaina texts clearly shows that the Digambaras' principal argument against the liberation of women rests on the perception of gender differences and the profound anxieties concerning the anatomy of the human female in general and her reproductive system in particular.[10]

More specifically, the Digambaras ground this argument in their interpretation of the nature of menstruation. As Robert Goldman notes, "Meghavijaya, representing the Digambara position, remarks that, 'she has an impure body as is evident from the flow of menstrual blood each month'" (quoted in Jaini 1991: Forward, xviii–xix). Menstruation is generally considered a taboo in patriarchal societies and women, whose bodies are circumscribed by purity laws, are prohibited from performing rituals during this time. But some Jain texts casts the involuntary act of menstruation as violent and subsequently deems women as violent.

Jain arguments therefore rest distinctively on women's anatomy. "What is unique about the Jaina debates on the spiritual liberation of women," writes Goldman, "is not the attitude they display toward the female sex but rather their systematic focus on the question of gender, their extension of the general debate, and to some degree their rooting it specifically in the biophysical nature of the human female" (Jaini 1991: Forward, xvi). Jainism elevates *ahiṃsā* to the highest vow, and the female body becomes a locus of violence because of its anatomy and reproductive organs. Natural bodily secretions such as menstrual blood and sweat become sources of women's disqualification from spiritual attainments.

Many of India's ascetic traditions express misogynist attitudes, as noted by various scholars (e.g., Doniger 1976; David Gilmore 2001). The major concern surrounds the functions of female body and questions of its purity. A negative focus on menstruation has likewise been widely observed in many traditional cultures both in India and elsewhere. Judith Butler traces the lived realities of female bodies and observes the traditional restrictions posed on the female body and disgust expressed over the female biology of menstruation and armpit hair.[11] Sethi traces the roots of this "denial of soteriological agency to women" to a "kind of 'gynophobia'" in which the natural bodily process is maligned (Sethi 2009: 43). It appears, however, that some Jain texts take patriarchal anxiety and misogynistic representations of the female body's natural processes to an *extreme.* Although the Jain argument is based on the issue of violence caused by female biology, debarment of liberation can also be construed as a form of violence toward women, who are denied their human prerogative to go beyond the cycle of death and rebirth. The unintentional violence caused by the female bodies becomes the cause of the intentional exclusion of women from the path of emancipation.

Furthermore, some Jain texts also abhor female nature along with the body. Unlike other Indian traditions that celebrate female virtues such as humility and bashfulness, many Jain texts construe modesty and concern for protecting one's body as a sign of mental deficiency, which is an impediment on the path of liberation. In his *Nyāyakumudchandra*, Digambara Ācārya Prabhācandra (c. 980–1065) argues,

> The same can be said about the presence of shame. It is not proper to say that shame is compatible with freedom from desire, for it is the nature of shame to wish to cover the loathsome parts of the body when one is aroused by desire.
>
> A person who is free from desire will not feel shame;
>
> like a child;
>
> you consider nuns to be free from desire.
>
> [However, since you maintain that nuns wear clothes in order to dispel shame; they therefore cannot be free from desire.]. (Jaini 1991: 127)

Thus, in addition to disparagement of women's bodies, India's ascetic traditions, in general, demonstrate contempt toward women's nature casting it as fickle and impure. Balbir notes that "the pan-Indian prejudices against women, who are said to be weak-minded, fickle, treacherous, and impure, are shared by the Jains" (Balbir 1994: 129). In one Jain argument, a woman is compared to an incurable disease and female birth is ascribed to the results of previous bad *karmas*: "Untruth, violence, deceit, stupidity, excessive greed, impurity, and cruelty are the innate negative points of women" (Balbir 1994: 134). However, such views have been counterbalanced by opposing views stating, "The same is true of men too. They also are very often seen to be cruel, full of bad points" (Balbir 1994: 134). The fact that counterposed arguments exist in Jain texts demonstrates their concern for women's agency for attaining final emancipation.

Despite the Śvetāmbara and other sects' concern for the question of women's liberation, disparaging attitudes toward the female body and female nature prevail in the texts of the tradition. Anne Vallely, who has been engaged with studying the lives of Jain women (monastic and lay), summarizes,

> Although the Svetambar and Digambar are often depicted as opposites with respect to their views on female religiosity, the ideas they share in common

> are as important as those on which they differ. Both hold the same negative understanding of female nature as flawed and associated with sexuality and sin. (2002: 16)

The female nature has been considered flawed and therefore male birth is deemed superior. Deceitfulness is deemed dangerous and is considered as the primary reason for female birth. However, Jain texts proclaim easy transformation in female-male bodies with rebirths, unlike their Brahmanical counterparts. The tenth-century Maheśvarasūri's *Nānapañcamīkahā* decrees: "As a result of manifesting deception a man in this world becomes a woman. As for a woman, if her heart is pure, she becomes a man in this world" (Balbir 2005). Following this logic, men are also warned against not taking the male birth as a prerogative: lest they watch their minds, a female birth might be around the corner.

Even though Jain texts differentiated gender and sex as two *separate* notions, as we will see in the next section, most of the misogynistic attitudes are based on biological sex. Many Jain texts including the *Sūtrakṛtāṅga Sūtra* warn monks against temptress women. Notably, the most ascetic rules containing injunctions against violence, lying, nonpossession, etc., are addressed to both nuns and monks; however, the most rules describing sexual restraint are in the masculine language and warn male mendicants against women. For instance, the *Āchārāṅga Sūtra* warns the male ascetics:

> A Sramana engaged in penance, should not allow himself to watch the shape, beauty, coquetry, laughter, prattle, gestures, and glances of women, nor retain a recollection of them in his mind.[12]

The fact that the text only cautions male ascetics against women (as Sethi 2009 notes) implies that the female body is a dangerous distraction for those on the path of liberation. But it might also suggest that men easily succumb to distractions and female mendicants are more self-controlled. Mahatma Gandhi, who was influenced by Jainism, often construes women as naturally self-restrained. Nevertheless, such essentialized gendered assumptions are problematic and overlook the complexity of gender/sex as have been theorized by recent gender studies.

Intriguingly, notwithstanding essentialized gendered roles and rules, Jain texts distinctly recognize at various points that gender and sex are not identical. Their pioneering viewpoints in the area of gender analysis are unprecedented in Indian philosophy. A brief analysis of sex and gender in Jain texts will help us better understand contemporary debates on the relationship between sex and gender and their promise for gender equality.

A Jaina Theory of Gender/Sex and Its Implications for the Issue of Women's Liberation

Jain authors use peculiar gender theories to provide logical arguments to advance their views about renunciation and women or intersex individuals. While modern gender theorists and feminists like Butler caution against conflating biological sex and gender on the basis of a theory of performativity, Jain texts provide psychological reasons (sexual inclinations) to differentiate the two. The Sanskrit language grammar identifies three genders (as we see in Howard's introduction in this volume), but Jainism goes a step further by making a distinction between biological sex and sexual orientation. In her article, "Gender and Jainism," Balbir notes that some thinkers even "have devised a fine analysis of the notion of gender, which they see as different from sex, through a Sanskrit term (*veda*) meaning, in fact, libido, thus transcending the physiological sex distinction" (Balbir 2005: 2). Balbir is referring to the concept of *veda* (literally, sexual orientation), which is not always related to biological sex. Robert Goldman writes on this topic, explaining,

> The concept of veda, sexual orientation that is not necessarily related to biological gender, appears to be unique to the Jaina texts in traditional India and to constitute the only consistent theoretical attempt in this culture, and perhaps any premodern culture, to explain the phenomena of heterosexuality and homosexuality. The latter phenomenon [homosexuality] in particular is all but ignored in the śāstraic literature associated with the Hindu tradition. (Jaini 1991: Forward, xviii)

Indeed, heterosexuality is primarily the normative default position in the Indian texts and traditions. Despite recognition of the "third gender" in the Indian context, homosexuality is still largely a tabooed orientation.

Jaina texts refer to three biological genders: male (*puṃliṅga*), female (*strīliṅga*), and neuter (*napuṃsakaliṅga*), the latter of which roughly corresponds to intersex in that its gender sign is not strictly male or female. Leonard Zwilling and Michael Sweet note the following broad definition of neuter-gender people, which might be helpful in understanding the category of neuter gender: "Men who were impotent, did not impregnate women, were effeminate, or transvestite, were regarded as *napuṁsaka*, literally 'not-a-male,' that is, unmale" (Zwilling and Sweet 1996: 362). However, the Jain text, *Tattvārthasūtra*, defines *napuṃsakaliṅga* as intersex or bisexual, having desire for both a man and a woman. Here we provide the complete quote from Umāsvāti's *Tattvārthasūtra*:

> Linga literally means characteristic sign ... The three lingas or sexual characteristics are the masculine, the feminine, the neuter. Another name for liṅga is veda. Each of these three vedas is of two types—viz. the dravya type and the bhava type. By the dravya type of veda is understood the external sign, by the bhava type of veda the concerned [sic]specific desire. (1) That bodily sign through which a man is recognized as such in masculine veda of the dravya type, the desire of the pleasure born of intercourse with a woman is masculine veda of the bhava type. (2) That bodily sign through which a woman is recognized as such is feminine veda of the dravya type, the desire for the pleasure born of intercourse with a man is feminine veda of the bhava type. (3) The collective of bodily signs in which some constituents are characteristic of a man and some characteristic of a woman is neuter veda of the dravya type, the desire for the pleasure born of intercourse with a man as well as a woman in neuter veda of a bhava type ... The relation between the dravya and bhava types of veda is that of the means and end or that of the sustainer and sustained. (Umāsvāti 1974: 193–4)

Thus, the text uniquely differentiates the three kinds of biological sexes (*dravya*) and three kinds of sexual feelings (*bhāva*), identified as *strīveda*, *puṃveda*, and *napuṃsakaveda*—the sexual feelings appropriate to a woman, man, and an intersex. The text also recognizes that the sexual feeling may not correspond to the physical *liṅga* (mark or sex). The physical sex (intersex) was thus seen as creating mental indecision toward the objects of its sexual desire, which produced in turn an eternal insatiability of mind. Zwilling and Sweet draw further attention to the fact that the Jains believed bisexuality, or third-gender sexuality, to be the most intense because it was seen as a sexual feeling comprised of both *strīveda* and *puṃveda* (Zwilling and Sweet 1996: 372). Because the path of renunciation requires overcoming sexual desires, both Jain sects often argue that an intersex individual may not receive ordination, as their physical condition produced an incurable restlessness of mind that prevented it from the kind of concentration required for spiritual exercises. However, some scriptural references confirm that biological sex is not a factor in attaining freedom. "Jainas emphasized that in looking for hierarchy one should examine conduct, not birth ..., and one's sex or family affiliation were of no consequence in perfecting conduct" (Jaini 2001: 160). According to Jaini, both Buddhists and Jainas opened their monastic orders to women and men of lower birth, and historically a large numbers of men and women joined the monastic orders in their youth (Jaini 2001:161).[13]

What might this detailed analysis of gender mean for our contemporary context, wherein the issues of gender instability have been openly debated? The awareness of various sexual inclinations reveals that Jain thinkers recognize various sexual orientations as naturally occurring. Second, it shows that a recognition of male sexual orientation in a woman's body also can be interpreted as an argument for women's rights to liberation because, even in a woman's body, the person may have a male sexual orientation because of the past life *karmas*. The Yāpanīya in their debate with the Digambara precisely use this logic to affirm women's agency in attaining the spiritual goal.

> In one moment, [a maximum of] eight hundred men (*puruṣa*) and twenty women [*strīliṅgena*, lit., of female gender] and ten of the remaining [gender, i.e., the hermaphrodites] also attain nirvana …
>
> These and other scriptures are the authority for the [presumption that] nirvana [is possible for women. (Jaini 1991: 119)

Thus, this argument may render femaleness or maleness arbitrary categories. This scriptural example seems progressive and egalitarian: it not only argues for liberation for women but also for all irrespective of biological sex or psychological orientation. Furthermore, Jain traditions believe that a realized soul transcends sex and reaches the state beyond any bodily limitations, thus rendering both femaleness and maleness as only bodily conditions that need to be transcended.

The various arguments canvassed thus far demonstrate that Jainism takes the question of female sex and the issue of women's liberation seriously. While some texts contain arguments against women's liberation, the others present counter-debates that meticulously lay out reasons against those claims that deny women their right to renunciation and liberation. Notwithstanding arguments grounded as they are in female anatomical and psychological inclinations, female monastic traditions and laywomen's religiosity have been vital parts of the Jain tradition. In the following section, we will see how the Jain female monastic movement and devout women's examples throughout the historical tradition serve as resistance to patriarchal attitudes laid out in their traditions.

Ascetic Women's Resistance and Laywomen's Religiosity: A Way of Resistance

India's religious and ascetic traditions, in general, discourage women from embarking on the reclusive path for liberation. Most male seekers adopt a renunciant lifestyle, but women's inclination toward renunciation is often deemed as a dangerous contravention of established norms. Sethi identifies the primary reason: "Renunciation of traditional wifely roles would imply the withdrawal of the woman's reproductive capacities and the disruption of the normative order of *samsara* " (Sethi 2009: 43). Despite Jainism's emphasis on the goal of liberation from *saṃsāra*, most followers defend the tradition of family life, which is primarily upheld by women. Furthermore, the societal norms and security concerns mandated that women must be accompanied by male guardians, generating a sort of hysteria upon a young woman's wish to renounce.

Strīdharma (duties of a woman) limit the role of women to the household. For instance, Hindu law books such as the *Dharmaśāstras* prescribe *pativrata*—devotion to the husband—as the central path for women. Hindu epics elevate this ideal as the highest path by which women could attain the heavenly states, as illustrated through the narratives in the *Mahābhārata* and the *Rāmāyaṇa*. Thus, renunciation and *mokṣa* were not considered primary concerns for women. However, innumerable examples in the same epics demonstrate that women rejected the normative model and dedicated themselves to the *nivṛtti mārga* (the path of renunciation) for the highest realization. The texts hold reverential attitude toward the renunciate women.

Buddhist traditions present more complex views with regard to the question of women's roles and their right to resort to a monastic lifestyle for attaining *nirvāṇa*. Although women were not expressly beholden to ideals such as the *pativrata* vow, the tradition was, as a whole, not entirely eager to include women in the monastic order. The Buddha himself is said to have been reluctant to permit women into the *Saṅgha*. As Sethi notes, even when allowed entry, nuns were burdened with eight additional monastic rules over and above those prescribed for their male counterparts (Sethi 2009: 43). Further, misogynist tendencies are found in the Buddha's own words and in later permutations of the order.

Since the time of Lord Mahāvīra, despite misogynist attitudes toward women, Jainism stipulates two options for women: married life and the life of a nun. Conforming with the Indian cultural norms, Jain women mostly become wives, generally entering into marriage by the age of 20, most often arranged by the parents. Jainism also upholds the value of the *pativrata* ideal as Whitney Kelting states,

> It is considered most important that a *pativratā* (wife) be completely faithful to her husband sexually and produce sons by her husband for the benefit of her husband's lineage. The expectation spans the entire life span of a woman; a woman should have no other romantic involvement before, during, or after

> her marriage … [T]here is also an expectation of complete emotional fidelity, which includes not being emotionally intimate with other men, not being seen with men outside the family, and not speaking badly about one's husband. This fidelity is extended beyond a husband's death, for widows. (Kelting 2009: 16)

Such codification of women's conduct is not limited to the Jain tradition but is present across traditions. Both Hindu and Jain narratives celebrate the lives of women for their chastity, devotion, virtues, wisdom, and moral strength (Kelting 2003: 645).

Devout women are routinely revered by way of stories promulgated throughout Jainism. For instance, Sethi speaks of a long history of *satī* narratives, the "popular stories about chaste women and the miraculous powers their chastity grants them" (Sethi 2009: 45). The list of reverential female figures demonstrates a favorable view toward devout women. Some prominent women include Rājīmatī, the wife of the 22nd Tīrthaṅkara Nemīnātha, Candanabālā, who was said to be the first women ordained under the Tīrthaṅkara Mahāvīra, and Marudevī, mother of the first Tīrthaṅkara Ṛṣabhanātha. It should also be noted that the Śvetāmbaras consider the 19th Tīrthaṅkara Māllīnātha to have been a woman, while their Digambara counterparts dispute this claim.

Despite their common occurrence, Jain women do not generally rely upon the models of the figures eulogized in the *satī* narratives. On the contrary, many of them are construed as far too ascetic in character and therefore too divergent from the ideal of the Jain wife. For instance, Sethi remarks,

> Virtuous as the Jain satis are clearly accepted by the Jains to be, "their lives are not chosen … as models for the lives of the laywomen in their families." This is because the Jain sati narratives usually conclude with these glorified women becoming nuns; the tension between the demands of the family and the draw of the faith is resolved in favour of the woman renouncing the obligations of kin and family. (Sethi 2009: 46)

The traditional women extol exemplary figures, quite distinct from those canonized in the *satī* narratives, who, although devoted to Jain vows and displaying religious piety, do not become renouncers of the world. Mayna Sundari, for example, has been celebrated in Jain texts and traditions. She represents the pinnacle of Jain piety: a devoted wife who despite all her devotion, nevertheless, remained committed to her husband (e.g., does not renounce all her worldly duties).

In general, following the Jain virtues, women undertake important roles in sustaining a spiritual atmosphere within the home by serving the community of monks and nuns and observing religious vows. They frequently visit temples where they meet with other women to sing and share with one another their devotional compositions known as *stavan*. Women also engage in complex fasts to ensure auspiciousness within the home, including taking only bland foods (*Ayambil Oli*) and sometimes completely abstaining from food (*Upvas*) for up to seven days or even a month (Chapple 2017: 120). Such austere observances demonstrate their piety and participation in the Jain ideals of renunciation while remaining in the household. Furthermore, Kelting in her ethnographic studies shows how women reinterpret idealized role models, according to their lived experiences, not the mythical accounts in texts.

The laywomen are the primary source of providing cooked food for the monastics who refrain from lighting fires because of their absolute vow of nonviolence. By taking on the role of serving the monastic community, laywomen place themselves in the center of monastic life, without concerning the traditional views about the female body. Both Digambara and Śvetāmbara monastics accept alms from laywomen and impart religious wisdom in public meetings. Thus, Jain laywomen can be viewed as the very *sustainers* of the lives of monastics, figures who nurture the new generation of religious leaders and seekers of liberation.

Laywomen remain reverential to their religious traditions but resist misogyny by making themselves indispensable to the survival of monastic community. Women serve both Śvetāmbara and Digambara monastics—male and female—equally and earn the merits of good *karmas*, essential for final emancipation. Evidently, with regard to the question of women's liberation and their status, Jain tradition holds diverse views, not simply monolithic mandates. While laywomen negotiate their gendered roles to advance the spiritual goal of liberation, female ascetics defy the stereotype of female nature through their austere life, deep dedication to Jain principles, and service to the lay community.

The Jain female monastic movement continues to be vibrant despite the tide of modernity. Most nuns are in the Śvetāmbara movement, but a Digambara order of nuns also exists. Jain nuns, similar to monks, dedicate themselves to a life of great rigor: a complete renunciation of any possessions and all domestic duties, including preparing food for themselves or others. They renounce all ornamentation and fine apparels and wear only a simple white garment. They walk without shoes, despite heat and uneven grounds, and forego any artificial means of conveyance, by not accepting rides and always moving about on foot. Many nuns carry a cloth mask to cover their mouths while speaking to avoid harm to the many life forms found in the air and a broom to sweep insects safely out of harm's way. They perform harsh austerities including plucking hair twice each year as a form of penance to purify previous bad *karmas*. Just like the male monastics, it is customary for nuns to stay in one locale for only three days at a time except during the rainy season when they take shelter at a safe, friendly place provided by the lay Jain community. Each day the nuns commit themselves to the following six observances:

1. *Sāmayika* (equanimity)
2. *Caturviṃśatistava* (praise of the twenty-four Tīrthaṅkaras)
3. *Vandana* (homage to the teacher)
4. *Pratikramaṇa* (repentance of faults and negligence)
5. *Kāyotsarga* (abandonment of body)
6. *Pratikhayan* (renunciation)[14]

Such a disciplined regimen supports nuns' dedication of their lives to the path of the Jain tradition and the goal of liberation. As we have seen earlier, the issue of women's right to enter in the monastic order has been taken seriously, evidenced by the long-ongoing debate between the Śvetāmbaras, Digambaras, and other minor sects concerning *strīmokṣa*. Notwithstanding the overt denial of liberation for women by the texts of Digambaras, the Jain traditions have created a space for women's inclusion in the monastic life oriented toward attaining the ultimate liberation. Such attitudes signify a great leap forward for the women's rights movement in the Indian monastic context.

Followers of Jainism are encouraged to hold equal respect toward male and female ascetics, but women ascetics are generally sought after because of their wisdom and compassion. The women find solace in the fact that the path of liberation is available to them. They have displayed great interest in treading the harsh path of asceticism as well as confronting the stereotyped beliefs about women's nature. The female monastics, whose austerities exceed traditional mandates, defy the Jain assessment that "women are more fragile creatures" (Balbir 1994: 123). Women enter the monastic life in large numbers. Balbir compares the numbers across traditions. Śvetāmbara nuns in the late seventies and early eighties numbered 3,400, while monks totaled 1,200. Likewise, Sthānakvāsin nuns numbered 522 and monks 325. Terāpanthin nuns, in 1981, numbered 531 and monks 164. The only statistical discrepancy was found in the Digambara sect: Digambara monks totaled 125 during the same period while the population of nuns was only 50 (Balbir 1994: 124). Sethi provides the data of the late 1990s. The total number of Jain monastics numbered 11,518, and out of those 8,946 were nuns—way above half of the total monastic population

(Sethi 2009: 44). While volume alone is obviously not indisputable evidence of equality, it is nevertheless unprecedented when compared to other Indian sects. This general inclusivity of women in Jainism is codified in the Śvetāmbaras' *Chedasūtras* (concerning monastic conduct), according to which *only* pregnant women, or women with very small children, are barred from entering the order (Balbir 1994: 122). From the time of Lord Mahāvīra, the nuns' (*sādhvī*) order was institutionalized along with the monks' (*sādhu*) order.

It is worth noting that Jain women undoubtedly enjoyed a greater suite of privileges and rights in the monastic order than their Hindu and Buddhist counterparts, particularly due to the relentless debates arguing for their right to renunciation and liberation as well as the teachings of Jainism. However, scholars draw attention to the disparity between the status of nuns and monks. Balbir, for example, writes,

> I can find no record of such high titles as *ācārya* and *sūri* being used for nuns. They have their own titles such as *gaṇinī*, "head of a *gaṇa*," of a small unit of nuns, *pravartinī*, and *mahattarā*, which appears to be a special designation conferred on a restricted number of very learned nuns. In the chronicles that record the lives of Śvetāmbara orders in the middle ages (thirteen to fifteenth century), it is evident that both the decision and the act of conferring titles upon nuns always fell to male dignitaries. (Balbir 1994: 123)

However, with the shifting attitudes toward women, Jain women are taking prominent roles, both as nuns and lay followers, in India and in the diasporic communities.

Despite early misogynist attitudes, Jain female monasticism plays an integral role as a resistance movement to patriarchy and as an adhesive cohering the lay and monastic community together. The early Jain debates concerning the defects of the female body and women's right to spiritual emancipation may have been factors in energizing the female monastic movement and laywomen's religiosity. This has resulted in equality of female and male monastics and lay followers. "A class of female ascetics and pious female lay followers—sadhvis and *shravikas*, respectively—is not only distinctly identified, but is placed on an equal footing with the two male classes: sadhus (or munis) and *shravaks*, that is, male ascetics and pious male householders," observes Sethi (2009: 43–4). It appears that monastic life serves as a great equalizer between the male and female renunciates.

In her comprehensive study, *Escaping the World: Renouncers among Jainism* (2012), Sethi elaborates on some of the reasons for the great number of women choosing ascetic lifestyle. These reasons include women's desire to escape patriarchal marriage structures and subservience and seek autonomy, quietude, and education—away from the hustle-bustle of a householder life. Even though Sethi does not see the female monastic movement as a form of homegrown "feminism," I argue that nuns and laywoman are resisting patriarchy and misogyny by creatively navigating their texts and traditions. The sheer numbers of nuns suggest they are providing spiritual sustenance to the Jain community, both male and female followers, even though some scholars might construe their lack of high honors as signifying lower status. The fact is, their asceticism might be considered all the more stalwart because they remain unconcerned with such honors (which themselves signify attachment). Monastic and laywomen through religious piety, purity of conduct, dedication to the Jain principles, and service to the community embody the Jina ideal (conqueror of passions and self-centeredness), defying any bodily stereotypes.

Conclusion

We began with a short exposition of the Jain philosophy, in general, sketching its main tenets and their relevance to the question of spiritual liberation for women within the Jain soteriological framework. According to the Jain tradition, nonviolence is the highest principle and the pursuit of liberation is the highest end: the telos of human life. The goal of final liberation requires ridding the self from karmic bondage through the practice of complete nonviolence. From the time of Lord Mahāvīra, the Jain spiritual world has been classified into four categories: monks and nuns and laymen and laywomen, symbolized by the sacred swastika symbol. Many spiritually accomplished women are celebrated in the tradition. As was seen, the schism in Jainism between the two sects—the Digambaras and Śvetāmbaras—primarily pivots upon the question of whether or not nudity is a necessary condition for liberation. The issue of nudity implicates the question of women's liberation because women are prohibited from observing nudity due to their anatomy and shy nature. As articulated in its theory of *karma*, liberation is an elongated process that continues across many lifetimes until all accumulated negative *karma* has been worked off, resulting in a male birth.

In the Digambara sect, absolute nonviolence requires extreme austerity and detachment, including even shedding the last bit of material modesty: clothing. The followers of this tradition fervently upheld the ideal of nudity, emphasizing that the practice of nudity cannot be compromised by those who seek the ultimate goal of liberation (*mokṣa*). Although the Śvetāmbaras concur with the Digambaras concerning the source of the model of renunciation in the tradition—for example, the celebration of nudity exhibited by the 24th Tīrthaṅkara, Lord Mahāvīra—they dismiss the observance of nudity on the basis of those words of the Jain canon that do not mandate nudity. Nevertheless, even the Śvetāmbaras are often reluctant to contravene the strong scriptural arguments with respect to women, and women's bodies more specifically, that traditionally relegated women to a subordinate status. Their attitudes are consistent with the general Indian perceptions that have associated women with deception and considered it a woman's defining evil characteristic. Various negative attitudes toward women in the religious and philosophical literature have adversely impacted the lives of real women, lay followers or nuns.

However, the preceding discussion highlights the following specific ways through which the Jain thinkers confront the misogynist attitudes by deciphering the Jain principles and philosophy to affirm women's right to soteriological goal:

1. Jain teachings and principles are gender-neutral (all *jīvas* are equal) and form the basis of women's right to spiritual emancipation, the highest end of life.
2. Numerous debates in Jain texts and commentaries, spanning from the first century CE, engaging with the questions of female sex, female nature and aptitude, and women's liberation, validate that the issue of women's liberation was taken seriously.
3. Gender mobilization is much easier in Jainism when compared to other philosophical traditions, including Vedānta and Buddhist traditions, which scarcely offer examples—mythical or real—of gender mobility between sexes. Jain texts elaborate extensively on types of *karmas* and identify various determining factors of sex and sexual orientation in the Jain cosmology. A woman can be reborn as a man and a man as a woman because of acts of deceit and deception (*māyā*).
4. Jain differentiations of gender/sex confront the dichotomy of heterosexuality, opening a way to assert the availability of soteriological goal for all.
5. Finally, a vibrant tradition of nuns, the exemplary models of virtuous women, and the deep religiosity of laywomen of the Jain tradition continue to challenge misogynist attitudes, building on the textual traditions and religious traditions of accomplished women.

Notes

I am grateful to Professor Kamini Gogri, a Jain practitioner and scholar, for her inspiration and ideas about the topic of this chapter.

1 Whitney Kelting (2003) provides an account of the historic schism in Jainism: "Jainism divided into two sects—the Śvetāmbar and Digambar—during the first part of Jain history; this schism was solidified at the Council of Vallabhi in the fifth century CE. The Śvetāmbar sect is contemporarily the vast majority. They are concentrated in western India, with the highest densities in Gujarat, Rajasthan, and western Maharashtra, especially Bombay" (Kelting 2003: 640)

2 The Jain view of the universe is hierarchal: (1) one-sensed beings—touch (earth, water, plants, etc.); (2) two-sensed bodies—touch and taste (worms, oysters, etc.); (3) three-sensed bodies—touch, taste, smell (ants, flees, etc.); (4) four-sensed bodies—touch, taste, smell, sight (butterflies, moths, etc.); (5) five-sensed bodies—touch, taste, smell, sight, hearing (fish, birds, animals, humans, and gods).

3 In Prākṛta, the word *Śramaṇa* is pronounced as *Samana.* The scriptural texts of Jainism (and also Buddhism) are written in Prakrit languages. The Jaina texts use Ardhamāgadhī, while the Buddhists use the Pāli.

4 Both Buddhism and Jainism arose in around sixth century BCE. Historical and archaeological evidence traces Jain thought to before the sixth century BCE. However, its followers claim it is an "eternal tradition."

5 Tīrthaṅkaras are the "builders of the ford," which leads human beings across the great ocean of existence.

6 For the complete story, see Balbir's entry on Māllīnātha in *Jainpedia*.

7 Jaini provides a historical account of the split between the two sects: "Both traditions agree that the final breach between the two sects occurred around 300 BC, during the time of the venerable Bhadrabāhu, a contemporary of Emperor Candragupta, the founder of the Mauryan dynasty. Since that time, the two sects have refused to accept the validity of the other's scriptures, the Digambaras actually claiming that the original words of Mahāvīra are lost" (Jaini 1991: 1).

8 Furthermore, the Śvetāmbaras "resorted to eschatological arguments to justify their claim: the practice of nudity, while commendable during the time of Mahāvīra himself—was no longer advisable in this degenerate age. Their scriptures related that after Mahāvīra's death the practice of nudity became extinct" (Jaini 1991: 2).

9 Śvetāmbaras therefore considered the Digambaras heretics for rejecting the authenticity of their canon (*āgama*), especially for defying the canonical injunctions against nudity and for showing disrespect to the white-clad Śvetāmbara monks who were following the prescribed practice of the *Sthavirakalpa* (i.e., being clothed and being a member of the ecclesiastical community).

10 Jaini (1991) provides a comprehensive survey of the material on this issue, including various texts with their commentaries and translations.

11 Judith Butler provides "a phenomenology of the body as lived throughout the stages of a woman's life." She describes how a girl's body when it reaches puberty becomes the site of horror and disgust. "Feminist Perspectives on the Body (2.2)," in *Stanford Encyclopedia of Philosophy* (September 11, 2014). Accessed July 27, 2018, from https://plato.stanford.edu/entries/feminist-body/.

12 Sethi provides references from various texts. See Sethi (2009: 50–1).

13 P. Jaini edited and compiled his own collection of scholarly papers on Buddhist and Jaina Studies in two volumes (2000 and 2001) that had been published earlier in his career.

14 Chapple provides an analysis of women's issues in his chapter "Jain Dharma: The Eternal Law of Ahimsa" in the anthology entitled *Dharma: The Hindu, Jain, Buddhist and Sikh Traditions of India.*

References

Balbir, N. (1994). "Women in Jainism." In Arvind Sharma and Katherine Young (eds.), *Religion and Women* (pp. 121–38). New York: State University of New York Press.

Balbir, N. (2009–19). "Jainpedia: The Jain Universe Online." *Malli*. Accessed July 28, 2018, from http://www.jainpedia.org/nc/themes/people/jina/malli.html?sword_list%5B0%5D=malli&cHash=050a26b7929891e77566d1d2355f5a28.

Balbir, N. (2005). "Gender and Religion: Gender and Jainism." *Encyclopedia of Religion*. Retrieved July 27, 2018, from http://www.encyclopedia.com/environment/encyclopedias-almanacs-transcripts-and-maps/gender-and-religion-gender-and-jainism.

Chapple, C. K. (2017). "Jain Dharma: The Eternal Law of Ahimsa." In Veena R. Howard (ed.), *Dharma: The Hindu, Jain, Buddhist and Sikh Traditions of India* (pp. 103–43). London: I.B. Tauris.

Cort, J. (1987). "Medieval Jaina Goddess Tradition." *Numen* 34 (Fasc. 2): 235–55.

Jaini, P. (1991). *Gender and Salvation*, 1st ed. Berkley: University of California Press.

Jaini, P. (2001). *Collected Papers on Buddhist Studies*. Delhi: Motilal Banarasidass Publishers.

Jaini, P. (2000). *Collected Papers on Jaina Studies*. Delhi: Motilal Banarasidass Publishers.

Kelting, W. M. (2003). "Good Wives, Family Protectors: Writing Jain Laywomen's Memorials." *Journal of the American Academy of Religion* 71(3): 637–57.

Kelting, W. M. (2009). *Heroic Wives: Rituals, Stories, and the Virtues of Jain Wifehood*. New York: Oxford University Press.

Kelting, W. M. (2017). "Jainpedia: The Jain Universe Online." *Rājīmatī*. Accessed May 30, 2017, from https://archive.fo/20170530183403/http://www.jainpedia.org/themes/people/women-in-the-jain-tradition/rajimati.html.

Sethi, M. (2009). "Chastity and Desire: Representing Women in Jainism." *South Asian History and Culture* 1(1): 42–59.

Sethi, M. (2012). *Escaping the World: Women Renouncers among Jains*. London: Routledge.

Sharma, A., and Young, K. (eds.) (1994). *Religions and Women*. New York: State University of New York Press.

Umāsvāti. (1974). *Pt. Sukhlaji's Commentary on Tattvārtha Sūtra of Vācaka Umāsvāti*. Translated by Shri K. K. Dixit. Ahmedabad: L. D. Institute of Indology.

Vallely, A. (2002). *Guardians of the Transcendent: An Ethnography of a Jain Ascetic Community*. Toronto: University of Toronto Press.

Zwilling, L., and Sweet, M. J. (1996). "Like a City Ablaze: The Third Sex and the Creation of Sexuality in Jain Religious Literature." *Journal of the History of Sexuality* 6(3): 359–84.

4

Woman as Māyā: Gendered Narrative in the *Bhāgavata Purāṇa*

Gopal K. Gupta

Introduction: Issues in Gender Identity and Hegemony

Indian texts have played a crucial role in constructing, and greatly influencing, gender roles and social norms in Indian society. Scholarship on these texts has identified problems of identity and hegemony that have blossomed into several subfields such as subaltern studies.[1] Because of cultural practices such as *satī* and religious laws for widows, Hinduism and some of its prominent texts tend to have a reputation for patriarchal misogyny. However, such critiques are not limited to Hindu texts. Lisa Tuttle in her *Encyclopedia of Feminism* suggests that we ask "new questions of old texts," and in this essay we do so by examining the *Bhāgavata Purāṇa*'s (hereafter the *Bhāgavata*'s) gender discourse, focusing on the text's characterization of women as *māyā*, which is commonly understood to mean illusive power, illusion, or deception (Tuttle 1986: 184).

This essay does not carry out a comprehensive feminist reading of the *Bhāgavata*, because such a study is beyond its scope. This essay simply explores conceptions of *māyā* and female spirituality in the *Bhāgavata*, keeping in mind the time period and cultural context in which the text was composed. Through a close analysis, it becomes apparent that while the *Bhāgavata* supports patriarchal institutions and practices, at a deeper level it reveals a more prominent position for women in terms of society, soteriology, and spiritual practice than one would generally expect from a text that scholars today believe was composed from around the fourth to the ninth centuries CE.

Within Purāṇic literature,[2] the *Bhāgavata Purāṇa*, which focuses on the acts of Kṛṣṇa or Viṣṇu (who the *Bhāgavata* considers to be God) and his devotees (the Vaiṣṇavas), has been most influential, both in intellectual circles and in popular Hinduism. It has served as a scriptural foundation for several Vaiṣṇava movements and is held by them to be as authoritative as the Vedas, the foundational texts of Hinduism. While most *Purāṇas* have no commentaries, and a few only one or two, there are eighty-one extant commentaries on the *Bhāgavata* (and many more that are known only by name) (Bryant 2003: xii). Furthermore, the *Bhāgavata* is famous not only as a work of theology but also as literature and has often been characterized as the "literary Purāṇa" (Jarow 2003: 35). Edwin Bryant points out that the text has inspired "more derivative literature, poetry, drama, dance, theatre, and art than any other text in the history of Sanskrit literature, with the possible exception of the Rāmāyaṇa" (2003: lxvii). Because the *Bhāgavata* has held such a central place in Indian thought and literature, an academic study of its highly developed discussion on women and *māyā* will prove useful to a wide variety of scholars.

Given that ascetic practice was primarily a male phenomenon in ancient India, the text upholds the normative ideology present in Hindu society at the time, which considered women to be an impediment on the path to liberation for the archetypal male ascetic (Jarow 2003: 77). Women are often portrayed as temptresses or sensual disturbances on the ascetic's path. However, at the same time, the *Bhāgavata* is unorthodox insofar as it elevates female spirituality and many of its religious role models are women.

The Dual Role of *Māyā* (and Women)

Although the concept of *māyā* has a significant presence in Indian sacred literature, it has received sparse academic attention, most of which has focused on Śaṅkara's nondualistic understanding of *māyā* as "illusion" or "appearance."[3] The word *māyā*, however, has held a variety of meanings in Indian sacred literature, oldest among them belonging to its referents in the *Ṛg Veda*. *Māyā* as a concept is multivalent, foundational, and complex. Indeed, the nineteenth-century German philosopher Paul Deussen famously stated that there is no doctrine more central to Indian thought than that of *māyā* (1906: 226).[4] The eminent Sanskritist Daniel Ingalls went a step further than Deussen and chose to call *māyā* "one of the most beautiful concepts in the history of religion" (Ingalls 1984: xii).

Māyā is personified as a goddess (*Yogamāyā*) and *māyā*'s scope and role in the *Bhāgavata* is far-reaching.[5] One of *māyā*'s key functions in the *Bhāgavata* involves attracting souls toward sensual desire. *Māyā* is portrayed as the illusive power of God that entices souls away from the path of spiritual perfection and keeps them in bondage by entangling them in physical pleasures. One of the main ways *māyā* does this, according to the *Bhāgavata*, is through the form of women.

In the *Bhāgavata*, however, *māyā* is not only the agency that hides the identity of God from unworthy souls but it is also the agency that reveals God's identity to worthy souls. This divine power, which is intimately associated with the Lord, is often called *yoga-māyā*.[6] Thus, the same illusory power can work two ways—for the Lord "either obstructs or uncovers [one's] vision by his personal māyā" (Bryant 2003: 372). Since the *Bhāgavata* sees women as personifications of *māyā*, I will argue that the *Bhāgavata* portrays women and traditional feminine nature (of gentleness, beauty, sensuality, sensitivity, caring, sweetness, devotion, tolerance, and nurturance) in ways similar to *māyā*. In the worldly realm, female nature binds the soul: it makes the soul more attached to the persons, places, and things of this world. But in the context of the divine, the feminine nature reveals the divine—it becomes a channel through which the divine can be accessed.

Women as Temptresses

At the outset, the *Bhāgavata* echoes themes found in the *Dharma-Śāstras* (such as the *Laws of Manu*) and the epic *Mahābhārata*, which often depict woman as a "dangerous sorceress, a fascinating embodiment of powers which cause bewilderment (*moha*) for the masculine, ascending spirit/intellect" (Jarow 2003: 80). Richa Clements observes that although the *Bhāgavata* often holds men responsible for "participating in the world of the senses," in general the text holds a "bias against women" (2002: 121). Some passages in the *Bhāgavata* "portray women and their feminine nature in terms of passion and sexuality; and the negative aspects of a woman are constantly juxtaposed to man's weakness" (Clements 2002: 121). In the *Bhāgavata*, Kapila (who is considered an incarnation of Viṣṇu or Kṛṣṇa) declares,

> He who has attained self-realization by my service, and desires to attain the highest stage of Yoga, should never associate himself with women. For they (*yogis*) call woman as the gate of hell. A woman is the *māyā* created by God. She slowly approaches you. You should look upon her as your death, like a deep pit covered by grass.[7]

Attachment to women is seen as *māyā*'s ultimate trap; it shackles a man to this world and bars him from attaining the world of immortality. The *Bhāgavata* vividly illustrates this in some of its narratives—especially in the story of the churning of the milk ocean.[8]

This famous narrative relates how the power of *māyā* tempts through a woman's beauty: Once long ago the "demons" (*asuras*) and "gods" (*devas*) had decided to cooperate in order to produce nectar by churning the milk ocean, but when the pot of nectar finally appeared, the demons snatched it away from the gods, much to their dismay. The *asuras* did not immediately consume the nectar but instead began fighting among themselves, snatching it from one another. Meanwhile, the *devas* approached Viṣṇu for help, who agreed to retrieve the pot of nectar from the *asuras*. Viṣṇu assumed the form of Mohinī, a woman of matchless beauty, and the *asuras* became infatuated as soon as they saw her. Unable to settle their infighting, and having been overcome by Mohinī's charming words, they turned the nectar over to her and requested her to fairly distribute it. However, with clever words and enticing beauty, she distributed all the nectar to the *devas*, leaving none for the *asuras*.

The moral of this narrative is clear. The demons lose the nectar to the gods because they are bewildered by women, whereas the self-controlled gods are not. Those attached to women, therefore, lose their opportunity for immortality. Jarow points out that in the *Bhāgavata* attachment to women is considered synonymous with death. On the other hand, freedom from attachment to women leads to immortality.

According to the *Bhāgavata*, *māyā*, envisioned as woman, not only affects the demons but all living creatures. She is associated with the sexual attraction that is the shackle (*nigaḍā*) that imprisons the self and that no one in the world can break:

> With the exception of the sage Nārāyaṇa who else in this world is not attracted by māyā in the form of a woman?[9]
>
> Behold the strength of my māyā in the form of a woman! By the mere movement of her eyebrows she tramples under foot the conquerors … [of the world].[10]

What to speak of ordinary mortals when the *Bhāgavata* portrays even the gods as becoming enticed by *māyā* appearing in the form of women? For example, after creating his daughter, Brahmā became enamored by her beauty. When his beautiful daughter assumed the form of a doe, Brahmā assumed the form of a buck and ran after her to the astonishment of the other gods.[11] Thus, the text warns humans against a woman's enticing power that can lure even the gods.

As a committed Vaiṣṇava *Purāṇa*, the *Bhāgavata* describes that even Śiva, the supreme ascetic, once became overcome by Viṣṇu's manifestation of *māyā* in the form of a woman. After Mohinī enchants the demons and deprives them of nectar, Śiva, who is overconfident of his ascetic perfection, asks if he could view Viṣṇu's form as Mohinī. Viṣṇu agrees and Śiva soon becomes infatuated by her beauty. "Befooled by the māyā of God," Śiva pursues her "on the banks of the rivers and lakes on the mountains, in forests and gardens, and wherever sages lived."[12] The *Anvitārtha-prakāśikā* commentary states that Mohinī specifically took Śiva to the places where great sages lived to show them the power of his *māyā* and warn them to never feel overconfident of their ascetic perfection. The other lesser gods and sages had not fallen victim to Mohinī—Śiva did because he had become overconfident of his asceticism.[13]

The Cause of Temptation: Passion Not Women

The *Bhāgavata* often relegates women to a lower status. Women are manifestations of *māyā*, and they carry the qualities of *māyā*—they are bewildering, deceptive, and undependable. Despite this frequent identification of women with *māyā*, the *Bhāgavata* elsewhere tempers its views regarding women by pointing out that women are not *māyā* in and of themselves but only for the uncontrolled man. Regarding the danger of female sexuality in Hindu texts, Marglin has observed that "the danger resides not in the female *per se*, but in [practicing] celibacy, whether practiced by a female or male" (1985: 44).[14] Thus, men can also be tempters, and manifestations of *māyā*, for women. In the *Bhāgavata*, the situation is similar: the text warns that men can be *māyā* for women and thus women should beware of attachment to men:

> One who, due to attachment to women attains the female gender, in delusion considers my [Bhagavan's] *māyā*, in the form of a man, as her husband, the bestower of wealth, home, and children. He should recognize the illusion of the self as having the nature of husband, home and children, one that is death brought about by fate, just as the singing of the hunter is death for the deer. (Jarow 2003: 77–8)[15]

Similarly, Queen Rukmiṇī, Kṛṣṇa's principal wife in Dvārakā, rebukes those women who love worldly men as their husbands rather than loving Kṛṣṇa:

> That woman is extremely foolish who, without smelling the honey of [Kṛṣṇa's] lotus feet, picks a lover who is a living corpse covered in skin, nails, and facial, body, and head hair; and with gas, bile, phlegm, stool, bowel worms, blood, bone, and flesh inside.[16]

Although women and men can trigger passion in each other, and are therefore embodiments of *māyā* for one another, the ultimate problem lies in the uncontrolled and impure mind that is attracted to the opposite sex. The *Bhāgavata* suggests that a person whose mind is purified of the lower *guṇas* (*tamas* and *rajas*) and is firmly situated in *sattva* does not see any distinction between men and women. Śuka-deva, the speaker of the *Bhāgavata*, is regarded as the greatest ascetic because, unlike his father Vyāsa, he saw no distinction between male and female. The *Bhāgavata* states that once a group of heavenly damsels was bathing in a river. When Śuka-deva passed near them, they did not care to put on their garments, even though he was young and naked. But seeing the old and properly dressed sage Vyāsa, who was following his son Śuka-deva, they blushed and put on their garments. Observing this, the sage requested them to explain their strange behavior. They responded to Vyāsa by saying, "In your outlook there is discrimination between man and woman, but it does not exist in your son whose outlook is pure."[17]

The *Bhāgavata* believes that the self is essentially asexual, and physical bodies are simply the changing garments worn by the self. Through a host of narratives, the *Bhāgavata* attempts to persuade its readers to develop this vision. One such narrative, appearing in the ninth book, describes the life of Sudyumna, a prince who changed gender every month due to a curse but still attained *mokṣa* (liberation).[18] In this narrative, the *Bhāgavata* suggests that anyone can attain *mokṣa*, regardless of gender, be they males, females, or transgender individuals. In alternate versions of this story found in the epics, Sudyumna regains his masculinity permanently and lives happily ever after in his kingdom (*Rāmāyaṇa* 7.87.10–29; 7.90.15–20). The *Bhāgavata*'s narrator, however, allows Sudyumna to remain in the awkward situation, because thanks to this Sudyumna becomes detached and frustrated with the world and ultimately attains liberation.[19]

Women as the Highest Devotees of Kṛṣṇa

Although the *Bhāgavata* devalues women in the context of asceticism, the text elevates the feminine nature in discussions of devotional practice. Men are often portrayed as expressing characteristically feminine emotions or aspiring to gain those emotions in order to achieve the highest devotion. The overarching practice of the *Bhāgavata* is *bhakti*, which involves love, emotion, devotion, service, and attachment to Kṛṣṇa. Because the *Bhāgavata* regards women's nature as more emotional and sensual, they generally outdo the men in attaining Kṛṣṇa. One such narrative in the tenth book particularly illustrates this.[20] A summary of this narrative is as follows.

Once when Kṛṣṇa, his brother Balarāma, and his cowherd friends were playing in the forest, they became hungry. Kṛṣṇa advised his friends to go to the sacrificial arena and request the *brāhmaṇas*, who were engaged in reciting the Vedas to attain heaven (*svarga*), for some food. When the cowherd boys requested food from the *brāhmaṇas*, they ignored them without even responding "with either a 'yes' or 'no.'"[21] Dejected, the cowherd boys returned to Kṛṣṇa, who then sent them to request food from the wives of these *brāhmaṇas*. Unlike their husbands, the wives had always been eager for a glimpse of Kṛṣṇa. The *Bhāgavata* describes that their response to the request of the cowherd boys was very different from that of their husbands:

> Taking along a great variety of the four types of food in pots, they surged forth to meet their beloved, like rivers to an ocean. [Although] they were obstructed by their husbands' brothers, relatives, and sons, their hopes [of meeting Kṛṣṇa] had long been sustained by hearing about him [Kṛṣṇa's extraordinary activities and qualities].[22]

When the wives arrive with food, Kṛṣṇa praises their devotion and calls them truly learned. "There is no doubt that those who are learned and who understand their self-interest, engage in selfless, uninterrupted *bhakti* to me, because I am the one who is dear to their souls."[23] Kṛṣṇa points out that all living beings are part of him, he is the soul and source of all beings, he is the most dear object, even more than their families, so their decision to leave their husbands and serve him instead was correct.[24] However, Kṛṣṇa then tells the *brāhmaṇa* wives to return to the sacrificial arena, because their husbands cannot perform sacrifices without their participation. However, the wives respond, "You should not speak to us in such a cruel fashion, O Lord! Abide by your own doctrine [that you are the soul and most dear object of all living beings]!"[25] Nevertheless, Kṛṣṇa does not allow them to stay. He tells them that "physical contact between people in this world does not [produce] joy or affection. Therefore, fix your mind on me, and you will obtain me without delay."[26] This narrative illustrates that women are often closer to the Divine than men.

When the wives return, the *brāhmaṇas* realize their folly: while their wives had broken through the *māyā* of household life, they had been deluded by *māyā*:

> Curses on that birth which is threefold, curses on vows, curses on extensive learning, curses on our family lineage, curses on skill in rituals: we still remain

> averse to Adhokṣaja [Kṛṣṇa]. Truly the māyā of Bhagavān bewilders even the *yogīs*. Because of it, we *brāhmaṇas*, the gurus of humanity are confused about our own self interest. Aho! See the unlimited devotion of these very women for Kṛṣṇa, the guru of the world. It [their devotion] has pierced the fetters of death under the guise of household life. Neither the *samskāra* purificatory rites of the twice born, nor residence in the house of the guru, nor austerity, nor inquiry into the self, nor rites of cleanliness, nor auspicious rituals were [practiced] by these women. Nonetheless, they were constant in devotion to Kṛṣṇa, the lord of the lords of yoga, whose glories are renowned. This was not the case with us, even though we have undergone the *samskāra* and other such rites.[27]
>
> Aho! how fortunate we are to have wives such as these! Their devoutness has given rise to unwavering devotion to Hari in us.[28]

Here the archetypal *brāhmaṇas* admit that they have been deluded by Bhagavān's *māyā* in the form of their distinctly male attributes—twice-born status, ritual proficiency, and scholarship—a theme we find repeatedly in the *Bhāgavata*. The *brāhmaṇas* observe that although their wives never learned "cleanliness," "auspicious rituals," or "austerity," they were able to pierce "the fetters of death under the guise of household life." They were able to break the shackles of *māyā*'s ultimate trap—attachment to the opposite sex and the household—and liberate not only themselves but also their husbands, thus reversing the traditional role of guru that the husband is supposed to fulfill for his wife. The *brāhmaṇas* praise their own good fortune to have wives who "gave rise to unwavering devotion to Hari" in themselves. Thus, the text glorifies the life of women, the role of the wife, and feminine virtues in the context of devotion to Kṛṣṇa.

In another narrative in the tenth book of the *Bhāgavata*, Uddhava, a highly praised male devotee of Kṛṣṇa, desires to possess the same emotions as the *gopīs*, the cowherd girls of Vṛndāvana. In the *Bhāgavata*, the *gopīs* are considered the highest exemplars of devotion. Uddhava considers the *gopīs*' position so exalted that he prays for the dust of their feet:

> These *gopī* women are the highest embodied beings on the earth: their love for Govinda [Kṛṣṇa], the soul of everything, is perfected. Those who are fearful of the material world aspire to this and so do sages, and so do we ourselves. What is the use of births as Brahmā?[29]
>
> Aho! May I become any of the shrubs, creepers, or plants in Vṛndāvana that enjoy the dust of the feet of these women. They have renounced their own relatives, who are so hard to give up … and worshipped the feet of Mukunda.[30]

Indeed, because of their devotion, the *gopīs* have accomplished a task so difficult that no male devotee has accomplished it—they have renounced their spouses and children in love for Kṛṣṇa.

The *Bhāgavata* adheres to the *dharmic* norm, found in the *Dharma-śāstra*, that a woman's duty is to serve her husband, regardless of her husband's spiritual or social position. This principle is illustrated in the *Bhāgavata* in the narrative of Cyavana Muni and Sukanyā[31] in Kaśyapa's speech to his wife Diti and Kṛṣṇa's speech to the *gopīs*.[32] Yet, the *Bhāgavata* tempers this *dharmic* norm of the Dharma-śāstra when it redefines women's *dharma* of serving their husbands. A nice example is Kṛṣṇa's speech to the *gopīs* in the *rāsa-līlā* narrative (10.29.24–25). When the *gopīs* come to meet Kṛṣṇa at night in the forest, Kṛṣṇa first teases the *gopīs* by telling them that they should not dance with him but instead return to their homes to fulfill their *dharma* toward their husbands:

> The highest *dharma* [duty] of a woman is to serve her husband faithfully,[33] to ensure the well-being of her relatives, and to nourish her children. A husband who is not a sinner, even though he be of bad character, ill-fated, old, dull-headed, sick, or poor should not be abandoned by women who desire to attain heaven. Without exception, the adultery of a woman of good birth does not lead to heaven. It is scandalous, fear-laden, worthless, fraught with difficulty, and abhorrent.[34]

In words similar to those spoken by the wives of the *brāhmaṇas*, the *gopīs*, however, fearlessly and cleverly retort, "You, the knower of *dharma*, have declared that the occupational *dharma* of women consists of attending to friends, husbands, and children. Then let this be our *dharma* when it comes to you, the source of this advice, O Lord—after all, you are the soul within all."[35] The *gopīs* refute Kṛṣṇa's words using his own *dharmic* advice. They argue that since all living beings are part of Kṛṣṇa, he is the soul of their husbands, he is their true husband, and therefore associating and serving him is *dharma*. Kṛṣṇa agrees, and soon after the *rāsa-līlā* dance between the *gopīs* and Kṛṣṇa commences. The *Bhāgavata* does not deny that women's *dharma* is service to husbands, but in this passage, it redefines that *dharma*. The text believes that if a woman fulfills her *dharma* toward Kṛṣṇa, the supreme husband, she fulfills all *dharmic* obligations toward her other family members. The eleventh book expresses this sentiment, "He who with all his heart takes shelter in Mukunda [Kṛṣṇa], the shelter of all beings, has no obligations to gods, sages, creatures, relatives, and people."[36] After serving Kṛṣṇa, the *gopīs* complain that their husbands are only a source of great trouble. "You are the eternal beloved, O soul of all, and so the learned place their affection in you. What is the use of husbands and children who simply cause problems?"[37]

Far from condemning them for leaving their husbands, the *Bhāgavata* and its commentators regard the *gopīs* as exemplars of devotion, precisely because their love, unlike that of Kṛṣṇa's wives in Dvārakā, involves risk and transgression—for they leave their husbands and households in the middle of the night to dance with Kṛṣṇa. Bryant's words adequately describe this:

> The text [*Bhāgavata*] portrays the *gopīs* as prepared to surrender everything in order to attain Kṛṣṇa, and as such they are exemplars of the highest possible achievement of the human soul. Since, in the mundane world, the love of the paramour is forbidden, ostracized and dangerous, the *gopīs* exemplify the highest attainable intensity of love for God—a love that totally disregards all repercussions; that cannot be bound by any material ethical convention; that transcends regulatory institutions such as that of matrimony. (Bryant 2003: liv)

Kṛṣṇa himself praises their *bhakti* before the *rāsa-līlā* dance commences, "You have broken the enduring shackles of the household, and have served me. You are full of goodness and without fault, and I am unable to reciprocate [your love], even in the lifetime of a god. Therefore, let your reward be your own excellence."[38]

The *Bhāgavata* sticks to the "normative" *dharma* of women serving and worshiping their husbands as a general social and religious practice. But in the context of pure *bhakti*, the *Bhāgavata* sees this as a form of *māyā*. A woman who does not serve Kṛṣṇa but only her husband "in delusion considers *māyā*, in the form of a man, as her husband" (Jarow 2003: 77–8).[39] The *Bhāgavata* not only adheres to ordinary *dharma* defined in terms of human morality and gender roles but also establishes a higher *dharma* (*para-dharma*) defined in terms of spontaneous *bhakti* that supersedes and often contradicts ordinary morality. "Whatever activity is dedicated to me, the supreme, without self-interest, even if it be useless and performed out of fear or other such things, is *dharma*, O best of saintly persons."[40]

Because of their advanced vision, the *gopīs* do not see their husbands as bestowers of "wealth, home, and children" because they recognize that the true provider, source, and shelter of all beings is Kṛṣṇa. Unlike ordinary women, the *gopīs* have transcended "*māyā* in the form of man" and like ascetics have left home to attain Kṛṣṇa.

Adhering to being "a countersystem, opposed to classical and orthodox systems" (Ramanujan 1989: 10), the *Bhāgavata* even portrays prostitutes as eligible for complete liberation. These unmarried women eventually become great devotees of Kṛṣṇa. A good example is the prostitute Piṅgalā, whose story appears in the eleventh book of the *Bhāgavata*.[41] The story is narrated by a *brāhmaṇa avadhūta* (renunciate), who makes spiritual progress by observing the life of Piṅgalā, and thus considers Piṅgalā one of his gurus.[42]

One day the prostitute Piṅgalā dressed herself in very attractive clothing and ornaments and waited from sunset until midnight for a customer, but as time passed her mind became very uneasy. No man came to see her, and in disgust she finally became renounced, giving up her desire for the arrival of a customer. Thereafter, she engaged herself in thinking only of the supreme lord, Hari, and her mind achieved the supreme platform of peace. Unlike the *gopīs*, who attained liberation through attraction to Kṛṣṇa, Piṅgalā attained detachment and liberation by the frustration associated with being a prostitute.

Conclusion

The *brāhmaṇas'* wives', the *gopīs'*, and Piṅgalā's salvation was not conditional upon their fulfilling their duty as women (*strī-dharma*). Rather, desire to love Kṛṣṇa and frustration with material aspirations wins them release from the bonds of *māyā*. The love displayed in the Lord's play (*līlā*) with his devotees finds its highest expression in the relationship between the *gopīs* and Kṛṣṇa. Although the *Purāṇa* criticizes feminine beauty as dangerous in the worldly realm, particularly for the male ascetic, it celebrates feminine nature in the spiritual realm where it becomes useful to serve Kṛṣṇa.

In the *Bhāgavata*, feminine nature also works in a way similar to *māyā*. In the worldly realm, feminine nature degrades the soul. It makes the soul more attached to the persons, places, and things of this world. But in the context of the divine, feminine nature reveals the divine as it becomes a channel through which the divine can be accessed. The *Bhāgavata* sees women as personifications of *māyā*. However, neither men nor women are intrinsically evil; the self's identification with a particular body, mind, and senses is the essential human problem. Once the misidentification is in place, *māyā* creates sense objects suitable for that particular body in the forms of men and women to further entangle the soul.

The *Bhāgavata*'s views on *māyā* and female spirituality are radical, given the time period and culture context in which it was composed. Women who are described in the *Dharma-śāstras* and the *Mahābhārata* as a "dangerous sorceress" are in the *Bhāgavata* the most exalted devotees of Kṛṣṇa, who are far more advanced than their husbands. The *gopīs* and the wives of the *brāhmaṇas* break free of *māyā* in the form of attraction to the opposite sex—the very attraction that the gods Brahmā and Śiva succumb to. In fact, the *Bhāgavata Purāṇa* affirms that simply hearing about the divine play of the *gopīs* with Kṛṣṇa is the cure for worldly lust. "One who is filled with faith, who hears or describes this play, having regained the highest devotion for the beloved lord, has lust, the disease of the heart, quickly removed without delay—such a person is peaceful and wise."[43]

Notes

1 One version of the mythological antecedent for *satī* can be found in *BhP* 4.2–7.

2 The *Purāṇas* are the largest genre of Sanskrit literature. There are eighteen major *Purāṇas* and many minor *Purāṇas*. They describe a wide range of topics, including cosmologies, narratives of various gods and goddesses, and the philosophies and theologies of various traditions. Many scholars today believe these texts were most likely composed from the third to the tenth century CE.

3 Śaṅkara's use of *māyā* has been thoroughly researched by Thomas O'Neil (1980) and Satapathy (1992).

4 Like Deussen, Eliade also believes that the idea of *māyā* is at "the core of Indian sprituality" (Eliade and Trask [1989: 3]).

5 I have carried out a detailed study of the *Bhāgavata*'s conception of *māyā* in my dissertation, *Illusion and Identity: Maya in the Bhagavata Purana* (Oxford: Oxford University Press, December 2013).

6 See Figures 1 and 2 for exact references and usages.

7 *BhP* 3.31.39–40, trans. Jarow.
saṅgaṁ na kuryāt pramadāsu jātu yogasya pāraṁ param āruruksụḥ
mat-sevayā pratilabdhātma-lābho vadanti yā niraya-dvāram asya ||39||
yopayāti śanair māyā yoṣid deva-vinirmitā
tām īkṣetātmano mṛtyuṁ tṛṇaiḥ kūpam ivāvṛtam ||40||

8 *BhP* 8.6–12. The narrative of Yayāti illustrates this as well, *BhP* 9.18–19.

9 *BhP* 3.31.37, I have used Tagare's translation with minor changes.
tat-sṛṣṭa-sṛṣṭa-sṛṣṭeṣu ko nv akhaṇḍita-dhīḥ pumān
ṛṣiṁ nārāyaṇam ṛte yoṣin-mayyeha māyayā ||37||

10 *BhP* 3.31.38, I have used Tagare's translation with minor changes.
balaṁ me paśya māyāyāḥ strī-mayyā jayino diśām
yā karoti padākrāntān bhrūvi-jṛmbheṇa kevalam ||38||

11 *BhP* 3.31.36.

prajāpatiḥ svāṁ duhitaraṁ dṛṣṭvā tad-rūpa-dharṣitaḥ
rohid-bhūtāṁ so 'nvadhāvad ṛkṣa-rūpī hata-trapaḥ ||36||

12 *BhP* 8.12.34–5, I have used Tagare's translation with minor changes.

sarit-saraḥsu śaileṣu vaneṣūpavaneṣu ca
yatra kva cāsann ṛṣayas tatra sannihito haraḥ ||34||
skanne retasi so 'paśyad ātmānaṁ deva-māyayā
jaḍīkṛtaṁ nṛpa-śreṣṭha sannyavartata kaśmalāt ||35||

13 Ganga Sahaya's *Anvitārtha Prakāśikā*, commentary on verse 8.12.34.

14 See Marglin (1985).

15 *BhP* 3.31.41–42, trans. Jarow, pp. 77–8.

yāṁ manyate patiṁ mohān man-māyām ṛṣabhāyatīm
strītvaṁ strī-saṅgataḥ prāpto vittāpatya-gṛha-pradam ||41||
tām ātmano vijānīyāt paty-apatya-gṛhātmakam
daivopasāditaṁ mṛtyuṁ mṛgayor gāyanaṁ yathā ||42||

16 *BhP* 10.60.45, trans. Bryant.

tvak-śmaśru-roma-nakha-keśa-pinaddham antar
māṁsāsthi-rakta-kṛmi-viṭ-kapha-pitta-vātam
jīvac-chavaṁ bhajati kānta-matir vimūḍhā
yā te padābja-makarandam ajighratī strī ||45||

17 *BhP* 1.4.5, I have used Tagare's translation with minor changes.

dṛṣṭvānuyāntam ṛṣim ātmajam apy anagnaṁ
devyo hriyā paridadhur na sutasya citram
tad vīkṣya pṛcchati munau jagadus tavāsti
strī-pum-bhidā na tu sutasya vivikta-dṛṣṭeḥ ||5||

18 *BhP* 9.1.

19 *BhP* 9.1.40.

20 *BhP* 10.23.

21 *BhP* 10.23.12.

na te yad om iti procur na neti ca parantapa
gopā nirāśāḥ pratyetya tathocuḥ kṛṣṇa-rāmayoḥ ||12||

22 *BhP* 10.23.19–20, trans. Bryant.

catur-vidhaṁ bahu-guṇam annam ādāya bhājanaiḥ
abhisasruḥ priyaṁ sarvāḥ samudram iva nimnagāḥ ||19||
niṣidhyamānāḥ patibhir bhrātṛbhir bandhubhiḥ sutaiḥ
bhagavaty uttama-śloke dīrgha-śruta-dhṛtāśayāḥ ||20||

23 *BhP* 10.23.26, trans. Bryant.

nanv addhā mayi kurvanti kuśalāḥ svārtha-darśinaḥ
ahaituky avyavahitāṁ bhaktim ātma-priye yathā ||26||

24 *BhP* 10.23.27.

prāṇa-buddhi-manaḥ-svātma dārāpatya-dhanādayaḥ
yat-samparkāt priyā āsaṁs tataḥ ko nv aparaḥ priyaḥ ||27||

25 *BhP* 10.23.29, trans. Bryant.
maivaṁ vibho 'rhati bhavān gadituṁ nr-śaṁsaṁ
satyaṁ kuruṣva nigamaṁ tava pada-mūlam
prāptā vayaṁ tulasi-dāma padāvasṛṣṭaṁ
keśair nivoḍhum atilaṅghya samasta-bandhūn ||29||

26 *BhP* 10.23.32, trans. Bryant.
na prītaye 'nurāgāya hy aṅga-saṅgo nṛṇām iha
tan mano mayi yuñjānā acirān mām avāpsyatha ||32||

27 *BhP* 10.23.40–44, trans. Bryant.
dhig janma nas tri-vṛd yat tad dhig vrataṁ dhig bahu-jñatām
dhik kulaṁ dhik kriyā-dākṣyaṁ vimukhā ye tv adhokṣaje ||40||
nūnaṁ bhagavato māyā yoginām api mohinī
yad vayaṁ guravo nṛṇāṁ svārthe muhyāmahe dvijāḥ ||41||
aho paśyata nārīṇām api kṛṣṇe jagad-gurau
duranta-bhāvaṁ yo 'vidhyan mṛtyu-pāśān gṛhābhidhān ||42||
nāsāṁ dvijāti-saṁskāro na nivāso gurāv api
na tapo nātma-mīmāṁsā na śaucaṁ na kriyāḥ śubhāḥ ||43||
tathāpi hy uttamaḥ-śloke kṛṣṇe yogeśvareśvare
bhaktir dṛḍhā na cāsmākaṁ saṁskārādimatām api ||44||

28 *BhP* 10.23.49, trans. Bryant.
aho vayaṁ dhanyatamā yeṣāṁ nastādṛśīḥ striyaḥ
bhaktyā yāsāṁ matirjātā asmākaṁ niścalā harau ||49||

29 *BhP* 10.47.58, trans. Bryant.
etāḥ paraṁ tanu-bhṛto bhuvi gopa-vadhvo
govinda eva nikhilātmani rūḍha-bhāvāḥ
vāñchanti yad bhava-bhiyo munayo vayaṁ ca
kiṁ brahma-janmabhir ananta-kathā-rasasya ||58||

30 *BhP* 10.47.61, trans. Bryant.
āsām aho caraṇa-reṇu-juṣām ahaṁ syāṁ
vṛndāvane kim api gulma-latauṣadhīnām
yā dustyajaṁ sva-janam ārya-pathaṁ ca hitvā
bhejur mukunda-padavīṁ śrutibhir vimṛgyām ||61||

31 *BhP* 9.3.

32 *BhP* 6.18.

33 The word the *BhP* uses for "faithfully" is *amāyayā*, literally "without maya"!

34 *BhP* 10.29.24–6, trans. Bryant.
bhartuḥ śuśrūṣaṇaṁ strīṇāṁ paro dharmo hy amāyayā
tad-bandhūnāṁ ca kalyāṇaḥ prajānāṁ cānupoṣaṇam ||24||

duḥśīlo durbhago vṛddho jaḍo rogy adhano 'pi vā
patiḥ strībhir na hātavyo lokepsubhir apātakī ||25||
asvargyam ayaśasyaṁ ca phalgu kṛcchraṁ bhayāvaham
jugupsitaṁ ca sarvatra hy aupapatyaṁ kula-striyaḥ ||26||

35 *BhP* 10.29.32, trans. Bryant.
yat paty-apatya-suhṛdām anuvṛttir aṅga
strīṇāṁ sva-dharma iti dharma-vidā tvayoktam
astv evam etad upadeśa-pade tvayīśe
preṣṭho bhavāṁs tanu-bhṛtāṁ kila bandhur ātmā ||32||

36 *BhP* 11.5.41, I have used Tagare's translation with minor changes.
devarṣi-bhūtāpta-nṛṇāṁ pitṝṇāṁ na kiṅkaro nāyam ṛṇī ca rājan
sarvātmanā yaḥ śaraṇaṁ śaraṇyaṁ gato mukundaṁ parihṛtya kartam ||41||

37 *BhP* 10.29.33, trans. Bryant.
kurvanti hi tvayi ratiṃ kuśalāḥ sva ātman
nitya-priye pati-sutādibhir ārti-daiḥ kim
tan naḥ prasīda parameśvara mā sma chindyā
āśāṁ dhṛtāṁ tvayi cirād aravinda-netra ||33||

38 *BhP* 10.32.22, trans. Bryant.
na pāraye 'haṁ niravadya-saṁyujāṁ sva-sādhu-kṛtyaṁ vibudhāyuṣāpi vaḥ
yā mābhajan durjara-geha-śṛṅkhalāḥ saṁvṛścya tad vaḥ pratiyātu sādhunā ||22||

39 *BhP* 3.31.41, trans. Jarow, pp. 77–8.
yāṁ manyate patiṁ mohān man-māyām ṛṣabhāyatīm
strītvaṁ strī-saṅgataḥ prāpto vittāpatya-gṛha-pradam

40 *BhP* 11.29.21, trans. Bryant.
yo yo mayi pare dharmaḥ kalpyate niṣphalāya cet
tad-āyāso nirarthaḥ syād bhayāder iva sattama ||21||

41 *BhP* 11.8.

42 *BhP* 11.7.34–5.

43 *BhP* 10.33.39, trans. Schweig.
vikrīḍitaṁ vraja-vadhūbhir idaṁ ca viṣṇoḥ śraddhānvito 'nuśṛṇuyād atha varṇayed yaḥ
bhaktiṁ parāṁ bhagavati pratilabhya kāmaṁ hṛd-rogam āśv apahinoty acireṇa dhīraḥ ||39||

References

Bryant, E. (2003). *Krishna, the Beautiful Legend of God: Śrīmad Bhāgavata Purāṇa, Book X: With Chapters 1, 6, and 29–31 from Book Xi*. London: Penguin.

Clements, R. (2002). "Embodied Morality and Spiritual Destiny in the 'Bhagavata Purana.'" *International Journal of Hindu Studies* 6(2): 111–45.

Deussen, P. (1906). *The Philosophy of the Upanishads*. Translated by A. S. Geden. Edinburgh: T & T Clark.

Eliade, M., and W. Trask. (1989). *Yoga: Immortality and Freedom*. London: Arkana.

Ingalls, Daniel H. H. (1984). "Foreword." In Noel Sheth (ed.), *The Divinity of Krishna*. New Delhi: Munshiram Manoharlal.

Jarow, R. (2003). *Tales for the Dying: The Death Narrative of the Bhāgavata Purāṇa*. Albany: State University of New York Press.

Marglin, Frederique A. (1985). "Female Sexuality in the Hindu World." In Clarissa W. Atkinson, Constance H. Buchanan, and Margaret R. Miles (eds.), *Immaculate & Powerful: The Female in Sacred Image and Social Reality*. Boston, MA: Beacon Press.

Ramanujan, A. K. (1989). "Talking to God in the Mother Tongue." *Women Bhakti Poets: Manushi* 50–52: 9–14.

Satapathy, D. R. (1992). *The Doctrine of Māyā in Advaita Vedānta*. Calcutta: Punthi-Pustak.

Thomas O'Neil, L. (1980). *Māyā in Śaṅkara: Measuring the Immeasurable*, 1st ed. Delhi: Motilal Banarsidass.

Tuttle, Lisa (1986). *Encyclopedia of Feminism*. New York: Facts on File Publishing.

Part Two

Gender Negotiation

5

The Gendering of Voice in Medieval Hindu Literature

Nancy M. Martin

The search for women's voices from the past has led many to turn to the female saints of medieval Hindu literature, an extraordinary array of women known for the songs they composed. Their songs have been enlivened and amplified across the centuries by countless subsequent singers and composers. Selected songs have also been committed to writing in order to aid memory and featured in scribal traditions as acts of devotional piety and the institutional consolidation of devotional teaching lineages or *sampradāys*, whether their founders were Vaiṣṇava, Śaiva, or devoted to the Lord beyond form. Songs of the ninth-century Tamil Śrī Vaiṣṇava saint Āṇṭāḷ, the twelfth-century Kannada Vīraśaiva saint Mahādēviyakka, and the sixteenth-century North Indian devotee of Kṛṣṇa Mīrābāī continue to ring out, not only in religious gatherings but also from concert stages, on All India Radio, in films and television programs, and even as cell phone ringtones.

The life stories of these female saints, woven into hagiographic narratives, are as integral to their popularity as their songs are and as essential to understanding the meaning of their verses as the specific lines of poetry. Indeed, the saint is effectively a character internal to the song as its singer (Hawley 2005: 40–3). The voices therein are understood as belonging to very specific women with a known set of life experiences. Perhaps not surprisingly, their songs have been treated as if they give us direct access to female subjectivities and voices that can then be compared with those of their male saintly contemporaries. But is this really what we have? In the vast majority of cases it is definitively not, for these bodies of song belong to the improvisational realm of oral performance and most bear the marks of innumerable contributors in an ongoing process of co-creation by women and men from a vast range of social locations that cross the boundaries of language, culture, religion, and time.

What we do have, then, is a language in which many people speak, grounded in a theology in which gender plays a pivotal role and marked by a collective recognition of diverse gendered subjectivities and of the fluidity of such social constructions. These voices offer a vehicle to publicly articulate and reject patriarchal norms (especially in the voices of female saints) and to explore alternatives. They open up an intersubjective space to experiment with gendered identities and cultivate empathy (particularly as male saints speak in female voices), thereby fostering spiritual and/or psychological wholeness and transformation and even, potentially though not necessarily, inspiring positive social change. The songs sung in these voices and the stories told about their saintly initiators thus reveal a rich cultural heritage and wisdom with respect to gender and provide an immense resource for interrogating and creating alternative formulations of gendered relations and identities. In their shared singing and telling, these songs and stories provide a sanctioned arena for public conversation and debate, and in their theology, they provide a ground for action in love and for an egalitarian and holistic embrace of the masculine and feminine.

To fully grasp the implications of the gendering of voice in this literature, we must first understand the religious context that generates these voices and the life stories of the saintly figures in whose names these voices continue to be spoken. Accordingly, we will trace the origins and nature of devotional Hinduism. Theologically gender inclusive and embracing a feminine spiritual identity, the stories and songs of its saints will nevertheless reveal an ongoing bias against women and upholding of patriarchal norms that is continually challenged, particularly by women saints whose life stories follow very different trajectories than their male counterparts, and that male and female devotees alike must transcend. We will explore the nuances of male saints speaking of their love for God in female voice, in contrast to women saints doing so. Such analysis will lead us to consider the larger implications of subsequent devotees, both male and female, speaking in these gendered saints' voices. While touching on a wide range of male and female saints' stories and songs, we will focus in more detail on arguably the two most popular poet-saints—the sixteenth-century royal female devotee of Kṛṣṇa, Mīrābāī, and, by way of contrast, the fifteenth-century low-caste male devotee of the Lord beyond form, Kabīr.

Bhakti, Poet-Saints, and Their Songs

Beginning in the sixth century in South India, a new mode of devotional religiosity, *bhakti*, began to emerge in the broad flow of what is now commonly known as "Hinduism." Regional variations and teaching lineages developed across the subcontinent in the millennium that followed and continue to be widely embraced today. *Bhakti* is marked by a deeply personal relationship with the one divine reality, experienced as loving Lord, whether manifest in a particular form (*saguṇa*) or transcending the limitations of form (*nirguṇa*). The word *bhakti*, though generally translated as "devotion," is immensely richer in its implications than the English word. As A. K. Ramanujan has explained, the registers of meaning of its root *bhaj* include

> to divide, distribute, allot or apportion to, share with; to grant, bestow, furnish, supply;
> to obtain as one's share, receive as, partake of, enjoy (also carnally), possess, have;
> to turn or resort to, engage in, assume (as a form), put on (garments), experience, incur, undergo, feel, go or fall into ...
> to pursue, practise, cultivate;
> to declare for, to prefer, choose (e.g., as a servant);
> to serve, honour, revere, love, adore. (Ramanujan 1993: 104)

The relationship between the divine Beloved and devotee lover traverses the full range of possibilities embedded in this term, in "a mutual participation of the Infinite Soul and finite souls," as John Carmen and Vasudha Narayanan describe it, with the Infinite Self or God as desirous and needful of the human devotee as the devotee is of the divine (Carman and Narayanan 1989: 39). Further, in the Hindu scheme of things, though personal, God is all in all, the multiplicity of the world a manifestation thereof, so that the human lover, divine Beloved, and the love which unites them are all part of that one divine reality, manifesting and actualizing the love that is God. For some devotees, the experience will be of the One who encompasses and transcends all form, the *nirguṇ* Lord. Others will encounter the Ultimate, at least at times, in more limited and thus more graspable and notably gendered forms as Śiva, Viṣṇu (most often in his incarnations as Kṛṣṇa or Rāma), or Mahādevī, the Great Goddess in her myriad guises. In either case, they will pour out their love in song.

Extraordinary individuals appear across the centuries who follow the path of *bhakti* and enter into powerful relationships with the divine. They compose and sing songs that illuminate the terrain of those relationships—songs of praise, of love and longing, of complaint and request. These songs incorporate iconic and mythic descriptions and draw on the most intimate of human relations—between parents and children, servants and their masters, friends and lovers. Their composers utilize tropes and images from classical literary genres, as well as those of more ordinary song traditions, to craft a language of religious realization and transformation. The songs of these extraordinary devotees draw others into ever-deepening devotion through hearing and singing. Indeed, these lyrics are the principle "literature" of the *bhakti* religious stream, coupled with the stories of their saintly composers. Both songs and stories are regularly performed in communal gatherings to foster devotion. These are supplemented by *purāṇic* (mythological) compendiums of stories about divine incarnation and by works of theological and philosophical reflection.

Only vernacular languages are deemed appropriate for expressions of such intimacy, making singing and composition accessible to all, in dramatic contrast to the Sanskrit of elite Brahmanic traditions. As a corollary, religious authority is based on the publicly recognized depth of a person's devotion and his or her ability to draw others into deeper devotion, not on birth or education or institutional affiliation. Among the greatest devotees are those formerly deemed "untouchables," *brahmins*, and everyone in between—including women, men, and even children. Thus, *bhakti* traditions cut across the boundaries of caste, gender, and status, making religiosity available to all people. For our purposes, however, it is the complex understandings of gender that emerge in the devotional theology of *bhakti* and through the lives and especially the songs attributed to these male and female saints that are of particular interest.

Gender-Inclusive Theology and Saintly Gendered Voices

In Hindu traditions, gender as well as caste is recognized as a characteristic of a particular birth, not an essential or eternal aspect of the true self (*ātman*), with each of us sometimes male and sometimes female in a "serial androgyny" across rebirths (Doniger O'Flaherty 1982: 303–10). The self is, thus, at once neither male nor female and yet also both male and female. The tenth-century Vīraśaiva male saint Dēvara Dāsimayya sings,

> If they see breasts and long hair coming, they call it woman;
>
> If beard and whiskers they call it man—
>
> The self that hovers in between is neither man nor woman.[1] (Ramanujan 1973: 110)

These words reflect a deep awareness not only of the assumptions people make based on outward appearances but also of the socially constructed and superficial character of gender assignations. It is not surprising that caste and attendant designations of purity and impurity are similarly denounced. Low-caste saints from the tenth-century Śrī Vaiṣṇava Nammāḻvār to the fifteenth-century *nirguṇ* devotee Kabīr, as well as *brahmin* saints such as the fifteenth-century Gujarati Vaiṣṇava Narasī Mehtā, equally decry privilege or prejudice on the basis of caste (Hess and Singh 2002; Ramanujan 1993; Shukla-Bhatt 2015).

Theologically, the one divine reality, too—whether experienced as the transcendent *nirguṇ* Lord or taking form as Śiva, Viṣṇu, or Mahādevī—stands inclusive of all the distinctions of manifest existence, constrained by none. Divine androgyny (albeit of male deities) is vividly portrayed in the image of Ardhanārīṣvara—Śiva as half male and half female—and in the depictions of unified embrace of Kṛṣṇa and Rādhā. Such representations recognize gender as a fundamental aspect of manifestation, in its diversity, inner relationality, and wholeness. However, in contrast to such ultimate androgyny of the singular divine reality, as well as the deities and the true self across lifetimes, the bodies and most intimate relationships of the great devotee poet-saints of *bhakti* are profoundly marked by particularity. They are specific individual men and women, high caste and low, from different linguistic and cultural regions and times, who experience God in divergent ways and manifest forms, paradoxically side by side with the Lord who is all in all. As historical individuals, their lives are lived and their voices speak out of this gendered embodied experience.

As particular human beings, the saints experience varied challenges, and their lives take different trajectories. Yet distinctive patterns emerge in the hagiographies that develop around them, their immense diversity notwithstanding. David Lorenzen has examined the life stories of a number of male *nirguṇī* saints (devoted to the formless divine), identifying common elements of their lives (Lorenzen 1995). In his analysis of their narratives, he notes that lower-caste males must in some way overcome the social strictures of caste prejudice and, in certain cases, religious affiliation. Their stories also characteristically include uncommon birth stories; demonstrations of their piety, power, and/or divinity in childhood; authorizing transformative experiences mediated by a guru, celestial voice, or vision; tests by religious authorities and rulers that prove them beloved of God and immune to the temptations of wealth and power; and an "unusual death, often at a very advanced age" (Lorenzen 1995: 185–9). With regard to family and sexuality, they may be celibate or married, they may have children naturally or miraculously, or they may renounce family and social life altogether (Lorenzen 1995: 185–6). If they are married, most often their wives are fellow devotees, as is the case for Kabīr and Pīpā, though for a notable few spouses are a hindrance, as is the case for Tukārām who rails against his wife's bitter complaints about his obsession with God and resulting neglect of the family.[2] Overall, however, gender is not an impediment to these male saints' life choices.

Women Saints, Marriage, and Defiance of Normative Gender Roles

The life stories of women saints differ considerably. A. K. Ramanujan identifies five shared stages in the stories told about them—childhood devotion (without any need for the kind of transformative experience male saints typically undergo), escape from the trap of marriage, challenges to caste and gender norms, initiation by a guru, and merging/marrying God (Ramanujan 1999: 270–8). Their femaleness is front and center, and their absolute devotion to God is largely incompatible with the normative expectations for a *pativrata* (an ideal wife). According to *dharma* texts like the *Laws of Manu*, an ideal wife is enjoined to treat her husband as her god and find her salvation only through him. How women saints manage this conflict varies in the stories told about them, but they must do so, unless they are the wives of male devotees who share their absolute focus on God.

The very first saint of *bhakti* was a woman—the sixth-century Tamil devotee of Śiva, Kāraikkāl Ammaiyār. She is portrayed by her twelfth-century male hagiographer Cēkkiḻār as an ideal wife who unintentionally terrifies her husband with her miraculous powers, which arise from her devotion (Craddock 2010: 73–89). Her husband abandons her as his wife, worshipping her from afar instead as a goddess and releasing her to pursue her devotion to Śiva unimpeded. She in turn renounces her beauty and femininity, asking Śiva to give her the form and identity of one of his ghouls (*pēy*) who inhabit the cremation grounds where he practices austere meditation. In her now demonic form, the saint takes up residence there, where she might enjoy Śiva's cosmic dance. This transformation motif is found in the stories of other female saints. While the Kannada Vīraśaiva saint Tilakavve became "a male by God's grace," the Tamil saint Avvaiyar, known for her poetic skill and wisdom as well as her unwavering commitment to education and ethical engagement, was "transformed into an unmarriageable old woman" by Ganesh at her request to avoid an unwanted marriage and to be able to move about freely (Ramanujan 1999: 274).[3]

Still others refuse marriage or are freed by widowhood or simply leave. The Vīraśaiva saint Mahādēviyakka was utterly in love with Śiva but wed to a king who desired her, attracted by her beauty rather than her devotion. However, she ultimately left the king and all else behind. It is clear from her poetry that she, nevertheless, continued to be subjected to harassment by other men who still saw her only as an object of potential sexual satisfaction (Dabbe and Zydenbos 1989; Ramanujan 1973: 111–14). The fourteenth-century Kashmiri Śaiva (or some say Sufi) saint Lallā would do the same, finally leaving behind the harsh mistreatment her in-laws and husband continually meted out to her (Hoskote 2011; Kishwar and Vanita 1989b; Odin 1999). Both she and Mahādēviyakka are said to have discarded even clothes to wander naked in their ecstatic love for God and absolute repudiation of patriarchal norms for women's behavior.

Only the seventeenth-century Maharashtrian Vārkarī saint Bahiṇā Bāī remained in a bad marriage, even having a child. But in her autobiography she recounts her regret and details her husband's brutality and violent opposition to her practice of *bhakti* (Abbot 1996; Vanita 1989). Even for her, however, the situation would eventually be mitigated by his conversion. Being a devotee in a woman's body, it seems, is highly problematic—a tension also voiced in tales told by more ordinary women devotees (Gold 1994). Many songs attributed to women saints dramatically reject normative *pativrata* ideology. Indeed, both Mahādēviyakka and Mīrābāī refuse to accept their erstwhile husbands, instead affirming their "marriage" to God alone. Mahādēviyakka emphatically declares, "Take these husbands who die, decay and feed them to your kitchen fires" (Ramanujan 1973: 134).[4] In so saying, she affirms devotion while rejecting a mortal man as its proper object or the source of a woman's salvation and repudiates the ideology that credits a woman with ensuring her husband's life through her virtuous behavior, while laying the blame at her feet if he should predecease her. The saint leaves no doubt that the only one worthy of such devotion is God and thus if "marriage" is defined in this way, then God is the only "husband" she will recognize.

The voices of these women become audible in their stories, especially in the context of their defiance of gender and caste norms and in the tests they are reported to undergo before being recognized as great devotees (and sometimes also being initiated) by male gurus. In the case of Mahādēviyakka, she is challenged to defend her naked wandering by Allama Prabhu, the spiritual leader of the short-lived Vīraśaiva community established on the casteless egalitarian principles of *bhakti* in Kalyāṇa. She responds in song that nothing can be concealed "when all the world is the eye of the Lord, onlooking everywhere," but the guru counters asking why then she in fact covers herself with her long flowing hair (Ramanujan 1973: 131). She responds wisely, again in verse, that her exposed nakedness would arouse lust in men, so she does it for their protection. Sixteenth-century Kurūr Amma of Kerala wins a similar battle of words when reprimanded for chanting the name of God while in a state of menstrual impurity. She points out that death may come at any time and asks her accuser whether it is not better to die with the name of God on your lips regardless, and of course he must concur (Ramanujan 1999: 275). Also living in the sixteenth century, the poet-saint Mīrābāī challenges the male saint Jīv Goswāmī (or in some tellings Rūp or Sanātan), when he categorically refuses to meet or look upon a woman. She responds by sending him the message, "Are not all as women in the presence of the decidedly male god Kṛṣṇa?" In so saying, she upends any notion of male superiority before God, using an argument from the theology he himself espouses, and he immediately agrees to see her.

The Third Gender of *Bhakta* and Gender Bending Devotion

In dismantling the gendered assumptions of their interrogators, A. K. Ramanujan suggests that these women have transitioned into a third gender, that of *bhakta* (devotee). They are no longer "female" in its socially constructed normative embodiment, and they act in ways that are usually reserved for men, particularly by becoming wandering renouncers (Ramanujan 1999: 291). Mīrā's challenge suggests that men, too, must move beyond maleness to this third gender. The tenth-century male saint Dēvara Dāsimayya affirms the self as "neither male nor female" and his fellow Vīraśaiva saint Basavaṇṇa declares to the world openly, "I wear these men's clothes only for you. Sometimes I am man, Sometimes I am woman" (Ramanujan 1973: 110, 87).[5] Indeed, among those who enter this third gender as saints, Ramanujan observes, "The lines between male and female are crossed and recrossed in their lives" (Ramanujan 1989: 10). Whether anatomically male or female, these saints traverse the full range of socially defined femininity and masculinity in their love for God and their radical transgressions of social norms, restrictions, and expectations based on gender (Ramanujan 1999: 291).

Maleness, thus it seems, is equally an impediment to the practice of devotion but in a very different way than female embodiment is for women devotees. From the earliest strands of *bhakti* directed to the divine youth Kṛṣṇa, male poets have identified with the cowherding *gopī* women of his adopted community, who all fall completely in love with the ravishing divine youth. For devotees, the narrative of Kṛṣṇa's life (recounted in full in the *Bhāgavata Purāṇa*) simultaneously describes both his incarnation in time and the eternal drama of the human–divine love affair, in which all participate.

The ninth-century Tamil male saint Nammāḻvār was a devotee of Viṣṇu and composed songs that brought the listener into his Lord's presence in his multiple incarnations—in the midst of battle with Rāma's forces in Laṅkā, beside Viṣṇu's dwarf incarnation as Vāmana as he grew to cosmic proportions with Bali's offered boon of all the land he could command in three steps, and into the groves of Vṛndāvan to hear and feel the irresistible call of Kṛṣṇa flute (Ramanujan 1993: 4–13, 47–51). For Nammāḻvār and so many other poet-saints, the emotions and language of erotic love come closest to the impassioned desire that drives them toward God and the experience of embodied union, where the lines between one and two, self and other, become translucent and dissolve. Gendered social constructs of erotic love place the devotee (whether male or female) in the role of female to the decidedly male God. Consequently, Nammāḻvār and many other male poets at times speak from the subject position of the imagined female lover in relation to the male divine, whether in the form of Viṣṇu or his incarnations or of Śiva, or even when addressing the *nirguṇ* (transcendent) Lord.

An elaborate theology and religious discipline (or *sādhana*) was developed in later Vaiṣṇava traditions to facilitate this shedding of male identity to become spiritually female. As David Haberman has so carefully detailed in his study of Rūp Goswāmī's sixteenth-century formulation of *rāghānugā bhakti sādhana*, the stories of Kṛṣṇa's incarnation form the script for the ultimate drama, one that is in a sense more real than our transitory ordinary, individual social lives and identities (Haberman 1988). Through dramatic enjoyment and the cultivation of the emotional states (*bhāvas*) of the characters in this narrative world, the practitioner readily moves beyond imitation to identification with paradigmatic figures therein. Practitioners come to know, enjoy, and identify with these characters outwardly through story, song, and theatrical enactment and inwardly through performance and visualization practices. Individuals' identities and the world of ordinary existence and physical bodies recede in importance and are emptied of substantial reality as practitioners come to reside more and more fully in this ultimate and eternal realm, manifesting their true identity as lovers of God.

In this theology, the ideal self is decidedly feminine in its relation to the male divine, but the degree to which the physical and social being should be brought into alignment with this transforming internal identity is highly contested among later theologians. Only a limited few male practitioners actually take up *sakhī bhāv*, and others insist that such a taking on of the feminine characteristics, mannerism, and actions of Kṛṣṇa's *gopī* lovers should be restricted to visualizations and subtle bodies rather than performed outwardly by those with [male] physical bodies. Increasingly, practitioners were encouraged to identify with the male Goswāmīs (the authors of this *sādhana*) as ideal models of devotion and to enjoy the exquisite and unmatchable love of Kṛṣṇa and Rādhā from the position of observers rather than feminized participants (Haberman 1988: 53–4). Actual women, needless to say, had no place in this discourse.

Yet the degree to which normative masculinity may impede devotion is evident even when *bhakti* is directed toward the divine in the female form. According the *Devī Bhāgavata Purāṇa* (chronicling the acts of the Great Goddess), male devotees must abandon the defensive stance and dominating qualities tied to their gender identification—egoism, lust, arrogance, and pride—before intimacy with the female divine is possible (Ramanujan 1989: 10). In a famous mythological story, when the great gods Śiva, Brahmā, and Viṣṇu want to come to the Goddess' island paradise and join in attending her, they too must become women before they will be admitted to enter her intimate presence (Brown 1990: 206–12; Martin 2000b). Such stories and practices show clear awareness of the socially constructed nature and limitations of gendered identities and hierarchies, with a concomitant affirmation of valued qualities associated with the feminine.

Contradictory Attitudes toward Women and Gender Biases

Notwithstanding such poetic language, devotional theology, and mythic narratives, women are still denigrated in songs of male saints. Ironically, these saints continue to condemn actual women, even while speaking in female voice as lovers of God. The seventeenth-century Maharashtrian Varkari saint Tukārām speaks contemptuously of his wife, calling her a "shrew" and a "stupid bitch" (Chitre 1991: 40–9). Songs attributed to the fifteenth-century devotee of the *nirguṇ* Lord Kabīr speak of the temptress Māyā, who "wanders all over the world, carrying her noose" of illusion, and they make negative reference more generally to women as devouring wives, "whores," and "sluts" (Dharwadhkar 2003: 146–7; Hess and Singh 2002: 75, 119). Kabīr's voice also lauds the *satī* (the woman who ascends her husband's funeral pyre, lighting it by the inner heat of her virtue, to accompany him into the next life) as heroic and brave like the fearless warrior who rides out into battle in the attire of a renouncer to certain death (Hess 2015: 88; Martin 2002: 208).

Needless to say, such imagery is nowhere to be found in songs attributed to Mīrābāī, though in one song the saint Mīrā emphatically refuses to become a *satī* as she rejects the status of widow, acknowledging only the immortal Kṛṣṇa as her husband and Lord (Pauwels 2006: 235–7). In other songs, however, Kabīr speaks as the bride about to marry God or a young woman who must leave behind her parental home to join her in-laws, stepping out alternately into an unknown future or to meet death, as indeed we all must do alone (Dharwadhkar 2003: 133–4; Henry 1988: 174–5; Martin 2002: 209–10).[6] Still other times Kabīr identifies men and women as "nothing but [God's] forms," gender being one of so many distinctions by which we falsely judge one better than another (Dharwadhkar 2003: 130).

A number of scholars have looked at the songs attributed to *bhakti* saints, male and female, to address this contradictory attitude toward gender and identify distinct differences between male and female saints' poetry generally and, more specifically, between the "female voice" as it is employed by both men and women. Madhu Kishwar and Ruth Vanita note that in songs attributed to male saints, women are viewed as a primary temptation—along with wealth and power—that draws men away from spiritual pursuits. Such statements fuel the negative projection of sexual desire and aversion articulated in these male voices that is evident in a long-standing Indian male perception of women as spiritually eviscerating. Women, however, do not seem to view men as the same sort of temptation, though as prospective or actual husbands they may be an immense impediment. It is rather the social approbation, status, and privileges of *suhag*—the happily married state—that women saints identify as the obstacle that would keep them from embarking on the arduous path of *bhakti* (Kishwar and Vanita 1989a: 85–6).

The prevalence of patriarchal oppression can be gauged through the stories told about these female poet-saints as well as songs sung in their voices. Mīrābāī outwits a lascivious *sādhu*, who declares that Kṛṣṇa has ordered him to make love to her, by setting up a beautifully decorated bed for the tryst in the midst of the company of devotees. His lie and lust unmasked, he is mortified, and, seeing her now as saintly guru rather than as a woman to be exploited, he begs both to be forgiven and to be allowed to become her disciple. Kabīr's wife Loi agrees to prostitute herself to a rich merchant in order to get the supplies necessary for Kabīr's promised meal for fellow devotees. However, the merchant releases her from the obligation when she arrives dry-footed despite the rain because Kabīr, hearing about her bargain, carries her there himself. She is true to her word and willing to pay the price to fulfill the promise and obligation of feeding fellow devotees, as is her husband Kabīr who assists her in reaching her destination unsullied by the mud. In the face of such simple virtue and generosity, the merchant must recognize their full humanity, beside which his own pales. The same story is also told of the saint Pīpā's beautiful wife Sītā, whom he repeatedly and freely offers to other desirous men as a prostitute with her consent, both willing to share all with anyone who asks, though her virtue is such that they are unable to touch her and they instead become Pīpā's disciples (Callewaert and Sharma 2000: 11–17).[7]

Saint Mahādēviyakka leaves her royal husband, whose proposal of marriage her parents had no choice but to accept, when he takes her against her will three times, after she had warned him she would leave if he did. In her poetry, she describes all men as having "thorns in their chest" and asks "brothers" and "fathers" why they keep bothering her (Ramanujan 1973: 125, 135). It is clear that though she has shed her socially prescribed gender to enter the third gender of *bhakta*, men still look at her with sensual desire, unable to see beyond outward appearances and their own assumptions. She addresses them with familial terms, even as her own appellation as *akka* affirms her status as "older sister," though she warns of the danger of getting too close to them.

Female Voice as Bhakti Ideal

Though songs of male saints may continue to condemn actual women and employ negative female imagery and female saints may continue to undergo challenge and harassment by men (evidenced by their stories and songs), there remains a paradoxical glorification of femaleness in devotional poetry and theology, and male poet-saints readily employ female voice to speak of their love and longing for God. As Kumkum Sangari observes, "Once gender is stretched into the metaphysical realm, femaleness becomes something men can adopt in order to gain spiritual advantage … [and t]he female voice thus qualifies to be simultaneously the essence of devotion, a *patra* or vessel/medium, and the *marg* or path of bhakti" (Sangari 2006: 247). Ramanujan acknowledges that there are preexisting traditions of poets speaking as women in love, and he identifies multiple levels of possible religious and psychological meanings for male devotees who engage in speaking in female voice:

> to become bisexual, whole and androgynous like the gods themselves (Puruṣa, Śiva, and Viṣṇu); in a male-dominated society it serves also to abase and reverse oneself, rid oneself of machismo, to enter a liminal confusion, become open and receptive as a woman to god; and it is possibly also a poetic expression of the male envy and admiration of women. (Ramanujan 1999: 293)

Sangari concurs with much of this and notes further that "the explicit adoption of the female role and voice inadvertently revealed both to be cultural constructs, hinted at the limits of such construction, transformed their fixity into at once a liminal and a universal space which could be occupied by a male devotee" (Sangari 2006: 240). Such analyses explore the wide-ranging implications, both psychological and spiritual, for an individual man assuming female voice as a poet or singer or a female persona as a devotee.

For a female saint poet to speak as a woman in love requires no parallel transformation of gender identity, though when love becomes so intense that the boundary of self and other begins to dissolve, she may be as one possessed to such a degree that she "becomes" the male Beloved. Indeed in one Mīrā song the saint declares that she will dress as Kṛṣṇa, take up the flute, and herd the cows herself in his absence, and I have encountered a woman devotee in Vṛndāvan who behaves in a similar way (Alston 1980: 110–11). Widely known by the name "Bansidhāri Mīrā" (the flute-carrying Mīrā), she routinely dresses rather flamboyantly in sparkling gold as Kṛṣṇa, with trademark flute in hand, and has been observed on at least one occasion dancing amidst a group of male Bengali drummers attired as Kṛṣṇa's female *gopī* lovers, in a complete reversal of social genderings and identities in the liminal space of a temple celebration (Martin 1997: 24–6).[8] She is the exception rather than the rule, of course, as is the above-referenced Mīrābāī poem, while male adoption of female voice is a standard trope and identification with the *gopīs* a cultivated religious practice. Yet there is clearly a mutability of gender here for both men and women that *bhakti* opens up, allowing for and indeed sanctioning such gender-bending behavior.

John Stratton Hawley explores the psychological trajectory of men assuming female voice further, focusing particularly on the *virahiṇī*—the impassioned woman separated from her lover, desperate in her longing for his return—a common figure in classical and folk love songs as well as devotional songs (Hawley 2005: 165–78). Theologically, this figure corresponds to the separation between devotee and Lord required to actualize the relationship of love and to periods when, for the devotee, God feels impossibly distant and unreachable, despite the intellectual realization that the devotee is not ultimately separate from God, who is all in all and thus dwells everywhere, including in the human heart. At such times, the devotee is filled with intense and even unbearable longing for the experience of divine presence and [re]union, and the gendering of the voice that articulates such vulnerability and longing is decidedly female.

Such love longing is often described as a disease that wounds the *virahiṇī* and threatens her very existence. The only cure is her lover's return, which she is powerless to effect. Hawley offers a comparison of nearly identical songs of this nature sung in the voices of Mīrābāī and the great male Kṛṣṇa poet-saint Sūrdās. He notes "how many registers are provided for the language of female suffering in Mīrābāī poems, and how active these tend to be," reflecting the nuanced experiences of embodied women and their agency rather than mere passivity in longing (Hawley 2005: 173). In contrast, he notes that in Sūrdās poems "the persona of the *virahiṇī* [as] helpless victim of separation" predominates, and he ponders why it is "that men revel in the weakness—and specifically in the sickness—of women" and whether "a woman ... gets the same sort of buzz that a man does from the idea that Kṛṣṇa serves as a magnet for numberless, often rather faceless women" (Hawley 2005: 173).

Such imagined overt male power over women and infinite and irresistible attractiveness to them clearly has masculine appeal. In such a reading, male speech in the female voice of the *virahiṇī* serves to reinforce normative gendering and patriarchal relations but in its excess also hints at the fragility of male control and identity. Many of these songs are set in the rainy season, as Hawley observes, when separation is said to be most painful, a time also when uncontrollable goddesses are alleged to give and cure diseases like small pox and cholera at their whim. For those composing, singing, and hearing such songs, the presence of these powerful goddesses is inseparable from the generativity of the rains and stands in stark contrast to images of feminine weakness and passivity. Hawley turns to the psychogenesis of masculine gender identity through separation and opposition to, rather than continuity with, the mother by way of possible further explanation of this male fascination and characterization. He reads here:

> a man's game, a game of trying on women's clothes and women's feelings ... a game of playing God, the way God (or Goddess!) plays with us men ... [a] game [that] gives a gender to longing. (Hawley 2005: 178)

Indeed as we noted at the outset, *bhakti* does imply trying on, enjoying, partaking, possessing, and being possessed. Manifest existence, too, has this quality of *līlā* (play), both as an unfolding drama and as God's playful creative manifestation. It is also the case that the gendered language of intimacy, whether between lovers or parents and children, is emotionally laden and psychologically entangled with experiences and conflicts of its mundane counterparts and issues of control and mastery that are part and parcel of human existence and limitation. Such a trying on then may give substance to unconscious conflict and desire but equally may promote psychological integration and healing. At its best, it may serve male devotees as a "spur for discovering their own humanity," as Lorenzen suggests, and allow them to tap into the vulnerability and powerlessness that are a mark of embodied human existence, as Sangari proposes (Lorenzen 1995: 192; Sangari 2006: 248). It is in transgressing the boundaries of an oppositionally defined masculinity and embracing or at least trying on (rather than denigrating or denying) banished "feminine" aspects of self and experience that a more complete and balanced vision of humanity might arise, a humanity shared by men and women, with a concurrent loosening of gender normativity. As powerful as this analysis is, however, it remains limited, speaking primarily to the spiritual and psychological implications for individual men speaking in female voice and playing at being women. And such play and even realization does not necessarily transform men's attitudes toward actual women, if we are to judge by the continued condemnation of women in songs attributed to male saints.

Viraha in the Voice of Women Poet-Saints: Songs of Mīrābāī

Women saints also speak of *viraha*, or "love longing in separation," in "female voice" as *women*, and when they do, it seems something much different is afoot. In her own comparative study of *viraha* and "female voice," Sangari notes,

> Even as [*viraha*] emerged from a socially determined world, displayed patriarchal relations of dependence and subjugation through the female voice … and crafted a sensuous inwardness with a socially constructed vulnerability, viraha also imaged a transgressive love (un)able to transcend these barriers. Thus with Mirabai customary subjection was transformed into a matrix of rapture and agency and achieved new dislocations and contradictory spaces. (Sangari 2007: 283–4)[9]

Mīrābāī's life story infuses the meaning of ostensibly almost identical words with the choice to take God as her lover and embrace the renunciation that marks such immense longing, disavowing her marriage and the privileges of her caste and class.

From the earliest hagiographic accounts of her life found in Nābhādās's *Garland of Devotees* (c.1600), it is clear that Mīrābāī's public speech evoked violent but ultimately unsuccessful suppression (Hawley 2005: 35). Needless to say, the same words in "female voice" attributed to a male saint elicit no such response. Safely confined to the realm of imagination and subtle bodies and at least potentially reinforcing normative feminine dependence, vulnerability, and passivity, they are readily incorporated into the canons of Vaiṣṇava and *nirguṇ sampradāy*s (sectarian teaching lineages), where Mīrābāī's have not been. When a woman sings such songs, they are embodied much differently, and the psychological resonances differ starkly from those of the male singing in female voice. Sumanta Banerjee has noted the long history of Bengali women's use of images of Rādhā and Kṛṣṇa to articulate their own emotions—from the pain of abandonment or separation to the joys of erotic pleasure—as well as "women's grievances in contemporary society" (Banerjee 1989: 136–7). Indeed, Vidya Rao, finding overlapping songs of courtesans and female poet-saints, suggests,

> They encourage us to question the sharp distinctions we make between … the erotic and the devotional … [a]nd by doing so … encourage us to question the many divisions we set up—of forms, gender, place, and religion. (Rao 2011: 206)

Women singing these types of devotional songs in "female voice" no doubt do speak at many levels, their own voices and desires becoming audible, perhaps sometimes for the first time, in the "I" of the woman poet-saint's speech. Such an observation goes a long way toward explaining the complexities Hawley noted in *viraha* songs attributed to Mīrābāī in contrast to Sūrdās.

In carrying out such analysis, however, we have still been speaking largely as if poems attributed to male and female saints were composed by those particular male and female individuals. In fact, the songs that we have available to us emerge out of the intersubjective realm of improvisational oral performance and collective devotional practice. In the case of Mīrābāī, Kabīr, and Sūrdās, most certainly the vast majority of the songs sung in their names reflect the innovations and creative interventions of countless others (Callewaert 2004, 2005; Hawley 2005: 89–116; 2009: 24–8). Although some number of the songs undoubtedly were initiated and performed by these individuals, it is impossible to determine which ones, and in this milieu even they may not have always sung the songs in the same way (Callewaert and Friedlander 1992: 58–9). Manuscripts do exist that allow us to glimpse early repertoires of songs sung in the names of Kabīr and Sūrdās, but even such early manuscripts are not available for Mīrābāī. In any case, what we do have is not sufficient to verify authorship. Further, the recorded poems are only freeze-frames of a devotee's performance, with "writing ... an *aide memoir*, a mnemonic device, for materials to be rendered orally ... [s]peech l[ying] dormant on a page until it is awakened by ... voice" (Ramanujan 1999: 538–9). To treat such songs as if they give us access to the subjectivities of these individual men and women saints and as if their meaning were completely contained in a singular written artifact is therefore unwarranted. There are rare exceptions, however, where individual authorship is more certain as for the poetry attributed to the Tamil woman poet-saint Āṇṭāḷ.

Āṇṭāḷ is credited with composing two major works: the *Tiruppāvai*, still recited publicly during a month-long winter festival undertaken especially by young, unmarried women in South India, and the *Nācciyār Tirumoḻi* in which she speaks in far more intimate, erotic language of her love for her Lord (Dehejia 1990; Meenakshi 1989). Her poetry, together with that of other Āḻvār poets of the Śrī Vaiṣṇava tradition, was recorded in the tenth century (Ramanujan 1986: xiii). We might reasonably assume that these texts may actually give us access to the thoughts and feelings of this specific ninth-century woman of a *brahmin* household (Dehejia 1990: 9).

In the *Nācciyār Tirumoḻi*, we find her frank and exquisite articulation of embodied female desire.[10] However, unlike the *Tiruppāvai*, this work has been preserved but marginalized, neither widely recited nor known (with the exception of one verse that has been incorporated into Tamil marriage celebrations) (Dehejia 1990: 5–6; Meenakshi 1989: 36). This marginalization suggests that a woman's explicit expression of embodied desire is much more problematic than male expressions of women's desire, such as those found in male Bengali Vaiṣṇava poetry (Dimock and Levertov 1967). The perceived danger of such self-expression is mitigated by her life story, however. Āṇṭāḷ was reportedly found in a field and raised by her *brahmin* devotee stepfather. Her miraculous birth supported her deification, as she was equated with the earth goddess Bhūdevī. As a child she was known for shamelessly trying on the daily garland to adorn Viṣṇu before offering it, an act that ordinarily would be defiling but which her Lord affirmed he treasured, and her garlanded image can still be found in Śrī Vaiṣṇava temples today. She married and merged with her Lord at Śrīraṅkam Temple at the age of 16, making her erotic words the expression of the soon to-be-wed bride, her love ultimately uncontainable in embodied mature female form.

For the vast majority of other *bhakti* poet-saints, it is impossible to legitimately assume that "their" songs are the actual words of specific historical male or female authors. Certainly with saints like Mīrābāī as well as Kabīr, Sūrdās, and many others, the poetry we have in their names is decidedly intersubjective—co-created by men and women, high caste and low, rich and poor, sung in the improvisation milieu of performance and manifest in multiple languages and cultures across India and beyond. Aware of this intersubjectivity, scholars try to find alternate ways to write about the saints' "song traditions" or "voices" and strive to describe the nature of this "co-authorship." The songs are in some sense "impersonal," reflecting a "public consciousness," as Sangari notes, but they are not anonymous in the way that folk songs are (Sangari 2006: 251). They are understood to be the voices of very distinct individuals whose character and stories are widely known and loved.[11] Women's active participation in this collaboration across gender lines is readily apparent, for example, in the presence of women's song forms associated with weddings and *gaunā* (bride's leave-taking to the husband's house) in songs attributed to Kabīr as well as Mīrābāī (Martin 2000a). So we have both men and women co-creating the voice of a woman saint speaking in "female voice" and the voice of a male saint speaking in "female voice" as well as "male voice." And these specific gendered voices are recognizable to participants in this process, regardless of who creates or speaks them.

If these songs do not give us direct access to an individual historical gendered author's voice and people know this—singers and audiences as well as scholars—then there is an additional level of considerable complexity added to the gendering of voice in this devotional Hindu literature. How might it be different if an individual man composes and/or sings in the voice of a woman saint like Mīrābāī, speaking in what we might call a "female female voice" or in the voice of a male saint like Kabīr, speaking in what we might call "male female voice" (i.e., songs attributed to this male saint but spoken in the voice of a woman in love). Eminent Hindi literary scholar Namvar Singh will opine that even "to be able to say anything about Mīrā, the minimum requirement is that at least in the heart each man must think of himself as a woman" (Singh, N., 2008: 219). An imaginative gender fluidity appears to be an essential quality also for speaking this voice—not an abstract female voice of a faceless *gopī* embodying ideal devotion but the voice of a very specific embodied woman, who danced and sang her ecstatic love for Kṛṣṇa in wild abandon and who suffered greatly because she would not conform to the socially prescribed norms of her gender, class, and caste.

In her groundbreaking study of oral song traditions of Mīrābāī among communities designated low-caste in Rajasthan and Saurashtra, Parita Mukta makes a much stronger claim:

> When men of a society in which the male consciousness and male constructs are used as yard sticks for the whole of human experience begin to sing in the *stri vachya* [feminine gender], then a radical shift occurs in the moral order. It requires a break from and a transcendence of the world created and upheld by men. It requires the recreation of humanity in the female image. The world has to be *strimay* i.e. the world has to become female. This requires more, much more than an empathy with the female subject … [It requires a] process of becoming Mira and thereby entering the mind and heart of a woman.[12] (Mukta 1994: 87)

What Mukta is suggesting here is that something much more than a superficial appreciation of the feminine is facilitated for men speaking in this very specific "female female voice," indeed that there is a radically transformative potential in doing so, not readily accessible through "male female voice."

She goes on to try to distinguish this "becoming Mira" from what happens when a *brahmin* saint speaks in the voices of extremely low-caste people and women in his verses (as the Marathi Varkari saint Eknāth does) and when a very low-caste male saint sings in the voice of a female *gopī* (as the male Saurashtrian saint Dāsī Jīvan does). In the first case, she suggests the high-caste male saint enters into his full humanity and, in this process of merging identities, his empathy deepens to encompass a much wider realm of experience (even as Lorenzen and Sangari had affirmed of male use of "female voice"). In the second, the very low-caste saint "transcend[s] [his abject social standing] to become someone who holds a particular relationship to Krishna and Krishna alone" (Mukta 1994: 89). While "male female voice" brings the high-caste man "down" from his socially granted and internalized sense of superiority to a common humanity, the "male female voice" of the *gopīs* brings the low-caste man "up" from his socially imposed and internalized sense of inferiority into a direct relationship with the divine. For a man to sing in the "female female voice" of Mīrābāī, Mukta claims, in contrast, requires an identification and solidarity such that maleness is left behind as the feminine permeates reality and the world is seen as through a woman's eyes. Such a becoming Mīrābāī is indeed recognized as possible more widely, with particular women devotees and performers readily referred to as "incarnations" of the saint and some women and even some men taking up "Mīrā *bhāv*" in much the same way that some men fully adopt *sakhī bhāv* in Vaiṣṇava traditions (Martin 1997; Singer 1966).

In making this comparison with high- and low-caste male saints, Mukta importantly reminds us how essential it is to consider the intersectionality of caste and gender identities, though she slips back into talking about male saints as individuals rather than those who sing in their voices. The voice of each saint is tied to, but not limited to, the hagiographic/historical individual, as subsequent individuals and communities take up these voices and co-create them such that "the past is evoked and reborn anew and it returns to form a real part of the present" (Mukta 1994: 89–90). Mukta is struggling here to articulate how taking up this very distinctive "female female voice" for a man differs from taking up the "male female voices" of saints like Eknāth and Dāsī Jīvan and to identify what is so distinctive about Mīrābāī's voice, the collective singing of which seems to transform not only individuals but also people's relationships to each other.

Mukta makes audible Mīrābāī's voice as it is sung and heard among low-caste communities in this specific region, and she asserts that to understand it, we must enter into the worlds and experiences of those who sing, in this case "the veil of tears" of their poverty, oppression, and degradation (Mukta 1994: 45). Mīrā's voice, here, speaks of shared suffering and resistance to the commodification of women in arranged marriage; the strictures of widowhood; the seclusion, silencing, and suppression of women; exile, the itinerant life, and displacement; and caste oppression. In story and song, Mīrā rejects the rights of her class and caste gained through patriarchal and feudal violence and exploitation, standing in solidarity with those of low-caste, living as they live and taking the leatherworker Raidās as her guru. For these communities to sing in Mīrā's voice and for us to truly hear that voice or to sing their Mīrā repertoires is to enter into this solidarity.

Building on Mukta's work, Rashmi Dube Bhatnagar, Renu Dube, and Reena Dube also wrestle with the co-authoring of Mīrā's voice, and they choose to treat "her" songs as "a social text of patriarchal critique" and boldly assert that "a Meera lyric is always an oppositional argument explicitly opposing the Rajput patriarchal values," including female infanticide (Bhatnagar, Dube, and Dube 2005: 174, 184). They read and hear in poems in Mīrā's name predominantly the voices of Rajput women (the warrior/ruling caste to which Mīrā herself belongs), though they acknowledge others. They importantly highlight Rajput women's contributions, though Mukta wants to claim this voice exclusively for low-caste communities. In elite Indian nationalist circles and among Hindi literary scholars, both were largely excluded, with any Mīrā songs mentioning Raidās as her guru or seemingly critical of her husband or not conforming to *pativrata* and Rajput ideals deemed inauthentic and excluded.[13]

Yet many have spoken and contributed to Mīrā's voice, from all walks of life, so hers is neither the voice of a single historical individual nor exclusively the voice of women or of the oppressed any more than of a conforming elite wife. There is much more that can and is said in this voice, as there is in the voices of other saints such as Kabīr. Defining the boundaries of these vast territories of song is no easy task, as the songs of one saint's voice overlap in content and even precise wording with those of others as we have noted (Hess 2015: 91–4; Martin 2000a). But the meaning of the song texts is dramatically impacted by whose voice is singing them, both which saint and which individuals and communities enliven them as song.

It is not just anything that is said in these voices, however, and they are understood as decidedly gendered. As we have noted, the very popular male *nirguṇ* low-caste saint Kabīr speaks in female voice of his love for God, yet his voice also denigrates women at other times. Purushottam Agrawal ponders this contradiction in Kabīr, particularly given that his voice speaks so stridently against all prejudice based on false distinctions of birth and continually proclaims the divine dwelling equally in all, eliciting the outflowing of love that motivates his social critique (Agrawal 2011). Others have claimed that love songs in female voice do not belong authentically to Kabīr's voice, but Agrawal will argue emphatically that they do:

> For Kabīr, femininity is a metaphor for the agency of love, for the capacity to be able to love. In order to attain the capacity to love, he takes the form of a female in his poetry and makes the object of his love, "loving" Ram, not the avatar Ram. Kabir is not a theorist of abstract love; he is a poet of the heart and knows that without being absorbed in some kind of "form," one cannot be a lover or a poet. (Agrawal 2011: 65–6)

And that form of love is female. Kabīr's love for God (Ram), his social outrage, and his spiritual realization are all of a piece such that body and mind, self and other, internal and external worlds are not walled off from each other but rather are the loving God manifest. And Kabīr "assays all things on the touchstone of love" (Agrawal 2011: 56). Yet Agrawal will also affirm that given his outspoken opposition to social hierarchies of caste and religious squabbling, Kabīr should have spoken out also against gender oppression, noting that just because the saint failed to do so does not mean we should.

Agrawal takes recourse to language approaching that of Mukta in speaking about the "eternal feminine" and the need for the world to become female (rather than man-made) so that a man might truly be "able look at himself and society through the eyes of women in the realm of society, outside the limited scope of spiritual practice" (Agrawal 2011: 75). For those who collectively sing and co-author Kabīr's voice, it seems, his voice may be employed not only as "male female voice" to powerfully express and generate love for God but also as strictly male voice to uphold patriarchal gender norms and to articulate condemnation of women. It is also a voice that unequivocally exposes the lack of grounds for any hierarchy between male and female and the superficiality of gender assignations with regard to the true self and God. But it is not a voice that might speak against the subjugation of women and of their suffering directly or of the linkage between caste and gender oppression (at least not yet). These realities it seems can only be spoken in a "female female voice," like Mīrābāī's.

When we step back from identifying these saintly voices with male and female individual authorial subjectivities and instead recognize them as speaking a much broader "public consciousness" (in the words of Sangari), this literature reveals a profound understanding of multiple ways of being and speaking as male and female and a radical awareness of the constructed nature and flexibility of gendering. Songs attributed to male saints in female voice are recognized as one way of speaking, a way that recognizes—among other things—that the characteristics culturally assigned to feminine gender are qualities found in all human beings and essential to fulfillment, wholeness, and liberation. Those same male saints' voices may speak in male voice about women, sometimes in very derisive ways, at other times with appreciation (though more often than not within the normative ideals of the *pativrata*). These are also recognized as male perspectives.

Their viewpoints are malleable but have real consequences for actual women, and such patriarchal conditioning is deeply embedded and extremely hard to shake. The emergence of a whole range of female saints and the continued speaking of their "female female voices" suggests a recognition and affirmation of all kinds of other ways of being female, even as there are of being male. And many of these female saints' voices speak directly to unmask male prejudice and violence and offer alternate sets of values and ways of being in the world. In the preservation and continued speaking of these voices, the validity of their perspectives is affirmed, shared, and extended, even as the flourishing of independent and powerful women is instantiated in the social imaginary. The immense diversity of gendered voices and the people who speak in them offer men and women alternate possibilities to taste, try on, assume, play with, and enjoy, with the potential for transformation, both spiritual and social, embedded therein.

Even so, we know all too well that potentiality does not guarantee actuality, a point made poignantly by Mallika Sarabhai in her multimedia dance drama "An Idea Called Mira," which debuted in Los Angeles in 2002 and which she has since performed around the world. For Sarabhai, Mīrā is "a feminist rabble rouser of the most wonderful kind" in her own time and ours—one of those rare women who "dig deep into themselves to find one's personal truth" and inspire others to do the same and then to act on it (Roy 2005).[14] Yet though the saint might be beloved and embraced as a national cultural heroine in India, women who would follow in her footsteps, speak in their own voices, and pursue a life of their own choosing might not yet find themselves embraced in the same way. They are still misunderstood and condemned as other stories say the saint was, by intimates as well as the larger society, and subject to violence. Even Sarabhai herself has been harassed and placed under house arrest for her extraordinary nonviolent work for social justice through the arts (Sarabhai 2009). The acceptance and domestication of *bhakti* saints like Mīrābāī can readily close down their disruptive and transformative potential, and there are those who would have it be so (Martin 2000c). This is why A. K. Ramanujan insists, "They have to be constantly renewed, reinterpreted, and rescued from the domestication that they suffer. But they do offer alternatives, humane and creative ways of being and acting, to both men and women" (Ramanujan 2009: 14). Those who continue to speak their voices and tell and perform new and yet familiar stories of their lives—devotees, artists, and scholars—contribute to this process of renewal and keep alive the alternatives offered by these gendered voices, initiated by saintly women and men in centuries past. In this regard, Mīrābāī and Kabīr together with other Hindu medieval devotional poet-saints remain alive and relevant for the modern era.

Notes

1 This poem by Dēvara Dāsimayya is also discussed in the context of gender by Ramanujan (1989: 11).
2 See Dilip Chitre (1991: 42–9) for a series of poems by Tukārām under the title of "Advice to an Angry Wife."
3 See Uma Chakravarty (1989) for details of Avvaiyar's life.
4 Ramanujan (1989: 11) highlights this particular line from Mahādēviyakka's poetry in a discussion of women bhakti saints.
5 Ramanujan (1999: 290) cites this full poem by Basavaṇṇa in his discussion of "Men, Women and Saints" and the third gender of *bhakta*.
6 Linda Hess (1987) notes that the songs attributed to Kabīr in which he speaks in woman's voice appear in the more Vaiṣṇava western *Panchvani* collections of the Dadupanth, as indeed all those translated by Dharwadhkar do. G. N. Das has

translated 101 love songs of Kabīr drawn from diverse sources, with Kabīr speaking in "female voice" in most, in his *Love Songs of Kabir* (1992).

7 This all happens after she has been asked by Pīpā's guru Rāmānanda to dance naked in the public square to show she has indeed entered the third gender of *bhakta*, which she does without hesitation, in Rāmānandī Anantadās's sixteenth-century hagiographic telling.

8 When I first met her in 1993 she was living in small temple known for the immense *śālagrām* (aniconic stones identified with Viṣṇu/Kṛṣṇa) it housed in Loi Bazaar. She has since then built her own small ashram and is now widely known by the name "Bansīdhārī Mīrā," and when I last saw her in 2011, she had started a tradition of delivering annual month-long public *kathās* or teachings on the *Bhāgavata Purāṇa*.

9 Sangari discusses the patriarchal forces that generated and are reinforced by *viraha* and other dimensions of female voice in *bhakti* in further detail in "Mirabai: The Female Voice and Oral Composition" (2006: 242–51).

10 The fourteen poems of the *Nācciyār Tirumoḻi* are translated in full with notes by in Dehejia (1990: 73–159).

11 The stories told about these saints are also multiple and contested, particularly in the cases of Mīrābāī and Kabīr.

12 Rashmi Dube Bhatnagar, Renu Dube, and Reena Dube quote and expand on Mukta's statement in their own discussion of the cocreation of Mira's voice (2005: 210).

13 For an example of such Hindi literary analysis, see Alston (1980).

14 Mallika Sarabhai is responsible for the concept, script, and artistic direction of the project as well as choreographing the dance in collaboration with Daksha Mashruwala, and she incorporates elements from Rajasthani folk traditions as well as a range of other sources on the saint. Excerpts from the "An Idea Named Meera" can be viewed at https://www.youtube.com/watch?v=jljABROoIRk.

References

Abbot, A. (1996). *Bahina Bai: A Translation of Her Autobiography and Verses*. Delhi: Motilal Banarsidass.

Agrawal, P. (2011). "The Erotic to the Divine: Kabir's Notion of Love and Femininity." In K. Panjabi (ed.), *Poetics and Politics of Sufism and Bhakti in South Asia: Love, Loss and Liberation* (pp. 55–82). Kolkata: Orient BlackSwan.

Alston, A. (trans.) (1980). *The Devotional Poems of Mīrābāī*. Delhi: Motilal Banarsidass.

Banerjee, S. (1989). "Marginalization of Women's Popular Culture in Nineteenth Century Bengal." In K. Sangari and S. Vaid (eds.), *Recasting Women: Essays in Indian Colonial History* (pp. 127–79). New Brunswick: Rutgers University Press.

Bhatnagar, R., R. Dube, and R. Dube (2005). *Female Infanticide in India: A Feminist Cultural History*. Albany: State University of New York Press.

Brown, C. M. (1990). *The Triumph of the Goddess: The Canonical Models and Theological Visions of the Devi-Bhagavata Purana*. Albany, NY: SUNY Press.

Callewaert, W. (2004). "Bhakti Literature: An 'Oral-Scribal' Archetype." In R. Modiano, L. Searle, and P. Shillingsburg (eds.), *Voice, Text, Hypertext: Emerging Practices in Textual Study* (pp. 121–30). Seattle: University of Washington Press.

Callewaert, W. (2005). "Kabir: Do We Sing His Songs or Someone Else's?" In A. King and J. Brockington (eds.), *The Intimate Other: Love Divine in Indic Religions* (pp. 129–52). Hyderabad: Orient Longman.

Callewaert, W., and P. Friedlander (1992). *The Life and Works of Raidas*. Delhi: Manohar Press.

Callewaert, W., and S. Sharma (2000). *The Hagiographies of Anantadās: The Bhakta Poets of North India*. Richmond: Curzon.

Carman, J., and V. Narayanan (1989). *The Tamil Veda: Piḷḷāṉ's Interpretation of the Tiruvāymoḻi*. Chicago, IL: University of Chicago Press.

Chakravarty, U. (1989). "The World of the Bhaktin in South Indian Traditions: The Body and Beyond." *Women Bhakta Poets, Manushi* 50–52: 18–29.

Chitre, D. (trans.) (1991). *Says Tuka*. New Delhi: Penguin.

Craddock, E. (2010). *Śiva's Demon Devotee: Kāraikkāl Ammaiyār*. Albany, NY: SUNY Press.

Dabbe, V., and R. Zydenbos (1989). "Akka Mahadevi." *Women Bhakta Poets, Manushi* 50–52: 39–44.

Das, G. N. (1992). *Love Songs of Kabir*. New Delhi: Abhinav.

Dehejia, V. (1990). *Āṇṭāḷ and Her Path of Love: Poems of a Woman Saint from South India*. Albany: State University of New York Press.

Dharwadhkar, V. (trans.) (2003). *Kabir: The Weaver's Songs*. New Delhi: Penguin.

Dimock, E., and D. Levertov (trans.) (1967). *In Praise of Krishna: Songs from the Bengali*. Chicago, IL: University of Chicago Press.

Doniger O'Flaherty, W. (1982). *Women, Androgynes and Other Mythical Beasts*. Chicago, IL: University of Chicago Press.

Gold, A. (1994). "Devotional Power or Dangerous Magic?" In G. Raheja and A. Gold (eds.), *Listen to the Heron's Words: Reimagining Gender and Kinship in North India* (pp. 149–63). Berkeley: University of California Press.

Haberman, D. (1988). *Acting as a Way of Salvation: A Study of Rāgājugā Bhakti Sādhana*. New York: Oxford University Press.

Hawley, J. (2005). *Three Bhakti Voices: Mirabai, Surdas, and Kabir in Their Time and Ours*. New Delhi: Oxford University Press.

Hawley, J. (2009). *The Memory of Love: Sūrdās Sings to Krishna*. New York: Oxford University Press.

Henry, E. (1988). *Chant the Names of God: Music and Culture in Bhojpuri-Speaking India*. San Diego, CA: San Diego State University Press.

Hess, L. (1987). "Three Kabir Collections: A Comparative Study." In Karine Schomer and W. H. McLeod (eds.), *The Sants: Studies in a Devotional Tradition of India* (pp. 111–42). Delhi: Motilal Banarsidass.

Hess, L. (2015). *Bodies of Song: Kabir Oral Traditions and Performative Worlds in North India*. New York: Oxford University Press.

Hess, L., and S. Singh (trans.) (2002). *The Bījak of Kabir*. New York: Oxford University Press.

Hoskote, R. (trans.) (2011). *I, Lalla: The Poems of Lal Ded*. New Delhi: Penguin.

Kishwar, M., and R. Vanita (1989a). "Poison to Nectar: The Life and Work of Mirabai." *Women Bhakta Poets, Manushi* 50–52: 75–93.

Kishwar, M., and R. Vanita (1989b). "A Second Rabia: Lal Ded of Kashmir." *Women Bhakta Poets, Manushi* 50–52: 103–6.

Lorenzen, D. (1995). "The Lives of *Nirguṇī* Saints." In D. Lorenzen (ed.), *Bhakti Religion in North India: Community Identity and Political Action* (pp. 181–211). Albany: State University of New York Press.

Martin, N. (1997). "Mīrābāī: Inscribed in Text, Embodied in Life." In S. Rosen (ed.), *Vaiṣṇavī: Women and the Worship of Krishna* (pp. 7–46). Delhi: Motilal Banarsidass.

Martin, N. (2000a). "Kabīr and Mīrābāī in Folk Traditions of Western Rajasthan: Meghwāl and Mānganiyār Repertoires." In M. Offredi (ed.), *The Banyan Tree: Essays on Early Literature in New Indo-Aryan Languages* (pp. 391–418). Delhi: Manohar Press.

Martin, N. (2000b). "Loving the Goddess in Hinduism." In J. Runzo and N. M. Martin (eds.), *Love, Sex and Gender in the World Religions* (pp. 88–111). Oxford: Oneworld.

Martin, N. (2000c). "Mirabai in the Academy and the Politics of Identity." In M. Bose (ed.) *Faces of the Feminine from Ancient, Medieval and Modern India* (pp. 162–82). New York: Oxford University Press.

Martin, N. (2002). "Homespun Threads of Dignity and Protest: Songs of Kabīr in Rural Rajasthan." In M. Horstmann (ed.), *Images of Kabīr* (pp. 199–214). New Delhi: Manohar Press.

Meenakshi, K. (1989). "Andal: She Who Rules." *Women Bhakta Poets, Manushi* 50–52: 34–8.

Mukta, P. (1994). *Upholding the Common Life: The Community of Mirabai*. New Delhi: Oxford University Press.

Odin, J. (1999). *To the Other Shore: Lalla's Life and Poetry*. New Delhi: Vitastā.

Pauwels, H. (2006). "Hagiography and Reception History: The Case of Mīrā's *Padas* in Nāgridās's *Pada-prasaṅga-mālā*." In M. Horstmann (ed.), *Bhakti in Current Research, 2001–2003* (pp. 221–44). New Delhi: Manohar Press.

Ramanujan, A. (1973). *Speaking of Śiva*. New York: Penguin.

Ramanujan, A. (1989). "Talking to God in the Mother Tongue." *Women Bhakti Poets: Manushi* 50–52: 9–14.

Ramanujan, A. (trans.) (1993). *Hymns for the Drowning: Poems for Viṣṇu by Nammālvār*. New Delhi: Penguin.

Ramanujan, A. (1999). *The Collected Essays of A. K. Ramanujan*. Edited by V. Dharwadker. New Delhi: Oxford University Press.

Rao, V. (2011). "The Voices of Bhaktas and Courtesans: Gender, Love and Renunciation in Thumri and Bhakti Poetry." In K. Panjabi (ed.), *Poetics and Politics of Sufism and Bhakti in South Asia: Love, Loss and Liberation* (pp. 181–209). Kolkata: Orient BlackSwan.

Roy, S. (2005). "An Idea Named Mallika." *Little India* 5. Accessed January 15, 2018, from https://littleindia.com/an-idea-named-mallika/.

Sangari, K. (2006). "Mirabai: The Female Voice and Oral Composition." In J. Grewal (ed.), *Religious Movements and Institutions in Medieval India* (pp. 228–60). New Delhi: Oxford University Press.

Sangari, K. (2007). "Love's Repertoire: Qurratulain Hyder's River of Fire." In F. Orsini (ed.), *Love in South Asia: A Cultural History* (pp. 259–85). New Delhi: Cambridge University Press.

Sarabhai, M. (2009). "Performing Ecstasy, Performing Agony." In P. Chakravorty and S. Kugle (eds.), *Performing Ecstasy: The Poetics and Politics of Religion in India* (pp. 17–23). New Delhi: Manohar Press.

Shukla-Bhatt, N. (2015). *Narsinha Mehta of Gujarat: A Legacy of Bhakti in Songs and Stories*. New York: Oxford University Press.

Singer, M. (1966). "The Radha-Krishna Bhajanas of Madras City." In Singer (ed.), *Krishna: Myths, Rites, and Attitudes* (pp. 90–138). Chicago, IL: University of Chicago Press.

Singh, N. (2008). "Mīrā, the Ocean of Love and Devotion." In A. Singh (ed.), *The Voice of Women: Gārgī to Gaṅgāsatī* (pp. 219–27). New Delhi: D.K. Printworld.

Vanita, R. (1989). "Three Women Saints of Maharashtra: Muktabai, Janabai, Bahinibai." *Women Bhakta Poets, Manushi* 50–52: 58–61.

6

Given, Taken, Performed: Gender in a Tamil Theopoetics

Chakravarthi Ram-Prasad

There are many challenges to doing philosophy of gender through historical materials. Feminist sensibilities—in whatever manner we interpret them—are a mark of recent modernity, and we would be misguided if we sought to find them in any self-conscious way in premodern texts. This presents a particularly acute problem in cultures of thought, such as the Indic, that experienced a hermeneutic rupture in the course of modernity, where we must rethink their native resources in order to contribute to an intercultural, global philosophy that is not merely Western philosophy gone global. In such cultures of thought, interpreting the ideas of the past becomes necessary to establish what might be original and what might bring fresh perspectives to the project of thinking globally. The past is therefore critical to the constitution of a present philosophy if it is not to be merely presentist. But as many thoughtful explorations of the historical materials of the West from a feminist perspective have shown,[1] we have to be careful to foreground our distinctly contemporary reading of these complex materials rather than read into their historical context ideas that are not the primary concern of those materials themselves.

I will begin by outlining the theological context in which we find the poetry of two related figures in a Hindu tradition. I will then pose some framing questions arising from contemporary feminist discussions about gender and self-representation, for example from those like Judith Butler. In the second part of the essay, I will explore some of the work of these two devotional poets, Nammāḻvār and Āṇṭāl, and from that try and tease out implications for contemporary ideas on gender from their very different, literary-historical milieu, one that contributes modes of conceiving of gender to a contemporary debate shaped almost entirely through the ideas of the modern West.

Two Lovers of God

The distinctive genre of intensely emotional writing on the love of God—*bhakti*, the togetherness wrought by devotion—spreads into most languages and regions of India over a period of a thousand years, but it is generally identified as having begun in the Tamil country around the sixth to seventh century. In Tamil, it crystallizes around two conceptions of the personal God, Śiva and Viṣṇu; I shall look at two key figures who belonged and contributed to the constitution of a community of worship around the latter. This community, due to its later, distinctive theological conception of the divine as Viṣṇu-with-his-consort Śrī (or Lakṣmī), is called Śrīvaiṣṇavism and traces its originary sacred material to the compositions attributed to twelve figures—the *Āḻvār*s—who are dated by historical scholarship to between the seventh and tenth century.

I compare here some words of two of these Āḻvārs[2] who have remained major figures even in the contemporary reading practices and temple rituals of the community, Nammāḻvār and Āṇṭāl. Āṇṭāl—"the Lady who Rules [the Lord, but also the devotees of the Lord]"—has always been represented as a woman and writes of herself as Koṭai—"daughter of Viṣṇucittan"—which the tradition explains as her being the adoptive daughter of the Āḻvār Periyāḻvār. It must be noted that the complex process by which the corpus of the Āḻvārs was canonized[3] elides independent evidence for who they really were historically. There are, of course, other reasons why we may agree with David Shulman's wry remark that the speaker of the poems is "Āṇṭāl herself, or an assumed persona—it hardly matters" (2016: 118). Nammāḻvār is perhaps the most significant of the Āḻvārs, given the centrality of his compositions to the sacred corpus. In several poems that are celebrated by the community to this day, he writes in the ancient Tamil voice of "the young woman,"[4] in the symbolic context of *akattiṇai*, the modes of the *akam*, or so-called "inner" genre of love in Caṇkam Tamil poetry (see Hardy 1983: 354, 364). I suggest that we think of the two categories of *akam* and *puram* as "inward" and "outward" rather than "inner" and "outer." The distinction is not metaphysical; rather, it pertains to the intentional direction of the emotions expressed in each genre—the former toward love and longing, the latter toward war and social norms, with frequent mingling of metaphors, sexual desire, and martial prowess, for example.[5] One might even think of them as a possible framing of the private/public distinction.

The poet-saints write passionately about missing their beloved Lord, including in terms that are both erotic in mood and occasionally sensuous in their specificity—drawing on the tropes of Caṇkam compositions and on the persona of the heroine (*talaivi*) but also moving sharply away from its conventions, in naming the unnamed hero, by naming their God as their hero, and in never having the hero speak.[6] Their revised theopoetics lead us to reflect on the hermeneutic of gendered self-expression.

Gender and Bodiliness: Reconciling Meaning and Performativity

Let me begin with the tension that has informed critical feminist thought between (1) the apparently pregiven and hence "naturalized" intuitions about the norms for what counts as men and women and (2) the instability of the concepts that inform those intuitions, once they are subject to analysis. [7] This, of course, has taken the form of the discussion over "sex versus gender."

In the 1960s and 1970s, feminists sought to use the distinction between biological features and expectations about conduct or capacity to challenge the notion that biology determines what men and woman can do and who, consequently, they are. Kate Millet (1979: 29), for example, articulated the point that gender is "overwhelmingly cultural," pointing to how aggression in boys is not some inbuilt biological orientation but a pattern of behavior that is encouraged by society. But this idea of using the sex/gender distinction for feminist purposes was subsequently challenged because it was argued that "sex" does not come free of interpretation since it is already loaded with and coded by the very gender norms that feminists want to challenge. However, there is a continued line of thought that maintains that the sex/gender distinction is an analytic one that allows us to think more carefully and precisely about the concepts that inform the relationship between people.[8]

One key aspect of the retention of the sex/gender distinction is that it is *analytic*—it merely draws attention to such things as the cluster of sex properties that do play a role in medical health, for example, and also engages with ordinary language practices that need to be made sense of and not discarded altogether at the cost of radical unintelligibility. That is to say, retention of this distinction is not a commitment to an *existential* difference between what persons experience as being about their sex and as being about their gender. It is not that one recognizes size as a bare fact and then separately decides whether "size matters" or not, for meaning (whatever its implications) is already there in the adult's noticing of oneself or another. At the same time, it is not as if it is impossible to have a physical measurement of body parts as such. It is the same with "race." On the one hand, we cannot deny that people have skin or hair of different colors, but that is not noticed independently of what being that person of color means in any context (including in the company of the mirror alone). Compare acceptance of this analytic link with the existential one in biological determinism, the latter of which might hold that having a vagina simply is indicative of being "hysterical" or "less able to work successfully at large software companies."

What is notable about the consequence of understanding sex and gender analytically but not existentially is that it permits us to look at the human being whole. Although disagreeing on its implications, many feminists have sought to move around the tension between sex and gender by talking about the "lived body"—that is, bodily subjectivity (what I call here "bodiliness") as always already suffused with meaning from the time reflexivity dawns on the subject. At the same time, this meaning can also be seen as capable of being reworked creatively. To take an example of a feminist philosopher of the lived body, Toril Moi has eloquently argued for the need to describe the meaning that one finds in such bodiliness through phenomenology.[9]

The meaning found in reflexive attention to the structures of one's experience is nevertheless not fixed. By the time a person seeks to find meaning in her experience of herself in her environment, she already finds herself with a repertoire of concepts—ideas, expectations, patterns of conduct directed at her, and so on—which are an ineliminable part of her capacity for self-understanding. But not only does this repertoire change through the life course, many of the changes are wrought by her creative agency as much as circumstances. There is a constant percolation of meaning-making of experience and selfhood between what one finds oneself already to be and what one finds oneself becoming through events and effort.[10] In short, phenomenology is not an abstract determination of subjectivity but the constant re/location of that subjectivity in an ecology of action, emotion, affect, and interaction. This "ecological" reading of phenomenology comes most naturally out of a consideration of classical Indian materials that have a very different orientation to questions of subject, body, identity, gender, and experience than the modern West.[11]

Within such an approach, I suggest that we can still benefit from Judith Butler's application of the philosophical concept of "performativity" to gender, although clearly I am not following her here into her larger theory that all statements about sex are nothing other than gender norms.[12] As Butler puts it,

> Acts, gestures, and desire produce the effect of an internal core or substance, but produce this on the surface of the body ... Such acts, gestures, enactments, generally construed, are performative in the sense that the essence or identity that they otherwise purport to express are fabrications manufactured and sustained

> through corporeal signs and other discursive means. That the gendered body is performative suggests that it has no ontological status apart from the various acts which constitute its reality. (1990a: 186)

To state my position bluntly: it is insightful to argue that people constantly act themselves into being in a variety of ways—in speech, gesture, expressions, comportment, clothing, ritual, projection, and reception of the erotic, short-term conduct and longer-term self-narratives. These actions are in constant interaction with whom they are given to themselves and take themselves to be from the dawn of self-consciousness. To recognize how what is given/taken configures people is humane; to acknowledge that people seek creative agency to reconfigure themselves is a profound form of hope. Philosophically, the important point is that this is a description of how people's lives work out and an ethical guide to how we must try to work out life. The assertion that people have psychological essences—which is the denial of performativity—goes beyond that to a mysterious metaphysical claim. But equally, it seems as if the Butlerian contention that all of a person's sense of being is a "fabrication" goes beyond observation of oneself and others to a competing metaphysical claim.

Without therefore taking a view on Butler's fundamental, metaphysical claim that gender "is *real only to the extent* that it is performed" (1990a: 411), we may nonetheless accept her point that although people cannot simply ignore gender norms in one's society, we may, as Alison Stone puts it, "reflect critically on our own behaviour, to assess and modify it" (2007: 65). This leads Butler to advocate "a proliferation of styles of individual bodily behaviour" that is not constrained by whether one is supposed to be a "man" or "woman" (Butler 1990a: 65). Despite my caution over the radical Butlerian claim, it is worth emphasizing that by no means do I want to say that there is an essence, let alone that that is given by "sex." If we are sensitive to how performativity points to the continuous construction of identity, then we will spot that "sex" itself comes with conceptual weight, with social meaning. Instead, I want only to say that the assignment of meaning to sex properties is a characteristic part of what is given/taken at the start of one's lifelong project of performativity. To call someone a man or a woman is an important part of the analytic of communication; it is what makes sense (to us and to others) of what we perform with or against. What it means to be called thus, it should be clear to our anthropological imagination, is acutely conditioned by cultural time and place.

Now, Butler's main objective in developing performativity as a means of generating genres is to challenge the man-woman binary and what she argues against is the dominance of the heterosexual matrix. I should acknowledge straightaway that the world of the Āḻvārs that my study explores is one that is unquestioningly founded in just that binary, as is the case throughout the classical world. I will not engage with the objection that Butler's challenge to the gender binary itself reinscribes it, regardless of its worth. Instead, I focus on a perhaps more manageable matter, which is how performativity affects both what one expresses as one's gender and what one expresses as the meaning of that gender. To anticipate the course of this chapter, with some of Nammāḻvār's poetry, we see that the conventional givenness of the man-woman binary is shown to be labile in the performance of emotion, while in Āṇṭāl we see the exploration of new limits to the givenness of being a woman.

The notion of performative genres of comportment suggests that it is the critical mode by which a person uses creative agency to refashion phenomenology as it is already given. The percolation of subjectivity, as in the performance of the repertoire of emotions we find in the Āḻvārs, can also be seen as the movement of self-experience from what is given to what one does with it.[13]

Let me sum up the main points of the somewhat short line I have taken through aspects of contemporary feminist philosophy. While rejecting the pernicious assumption that sex determines gender, it is possible to retain an analytic distinction between sex and gender and point out that sex characteristics are always found laden with meaning. Given the constant and inescapable meaning-making of human beings, we must respond to the way gender norms have constrained and restricted people by seeing human beings whole, in terms of their lived body or bodily subjectivity. It can easily become question-begging to talk of the particular human being as masculine or feminine, as if normative presuppositions did not already inform our talk. We need to understand the lived body as constituting an ecological phenomenology, in which there is a continual flow of meaning into and out of experience due to the dynamic environment of such subjective responses as emotions. Given that the human being is in possession of concepts about herself that include normative requirements of how to be herself, there must be—given revisionary ways of dealing with the power of social norms—creative, agentive responses to the gendered situation in which that human finds herself. Here, I take agency to be expressed in the literary performance of gendered emotion, either to question what gender one is or how one takes a gender to be.

We have now created a constellation of concepts with which to turn to a closer examination of poems from Nammāḻvār and Āṇṭāl. The idea that there are men and women is analytically available when making sense of how meaning is found in reflexive understanding of selfhood. At the same time, it is never found without norms constructed around it. But the constructed nature of these norms suggests that there can be creative responses to them, directed at what one *takes* oneself to be. This taking oneself to be is a form of creativity. When looking at the distant past, we are perforce required to seek such creativity in the formalized expression of it in literary production (and its reception: when we look at our poems, we begin to see how the tradition has received them through its own reception of gender). We can point to ways in which these traditional texts can contribute to a richer understanding of gender, even while recognizing their limitations and lacunae.

A Bodily Theopoetics

For anyone working through various *bhakti* texts, it is surprising to realize how recent and provocative it has been in Christian theology to think that the infinite desire for God is tied to an irreducible bodily subjectivity. As Rowan Williams had to point out as recently as the early 1990s, "For Gregory [of Nyssa] … we could say, there is no such thing as the soul in itself; it is always implicated in contingent matter, and even its final liberation … depends … upon the deployment and integration of bodiliness and animality" (Williams 1992: 244).[14] The Āḻvārs in their expression of the love of God, by contrast, demonstrate a Tamil sensibility that treats the inner as simply part of the topology of lived reality. As a way of indicating this very different configuration of selfhood, I will use "bodiliness" precisely not to mean just a material entity with which subjectivity can be related in some way but rather as the very way subjectivity is expressed, to itself and others. That is to say, "bodiliness" in my usage indicates that, from the start, we are dealing with the human whole that is enmeshed and constantly reformed within its environment. Such a fluid ecology is manifest in Āṇṭāḷ's expression of longing:

> Cool clouds, water-laden—
> rise high and spread yourself,
> pour down on Vēṇkaṭam,
> home of the one who took the world from the great demon king.
> Tell him, the lord of men, of my terrible love-sickness:
> For he entered me,
> consumed me,
> took my all,
> Like a worm that has entered a wood-apple. (*Nācciyār Tirumoḻi* [NT] 8.6, *viṇ nīla mēlāppu*)[15]

Given our previous considerations about the ecological (and therefore bodily) nature of phenomenology, we can see how natural it is for the Āḻvārs to formulate their theopoetics in terms of intense bodily affect suffused with divine presence and emotional richness. While it is true that if we read a particular ontology—of human subject located within an objective world—into the dense phenomenology of existence, then the rain clouds are a "mere" metaphor for a woman's torrential thoughts of God; the analytic components of our experience—for there is no denial that there are clouds and hills and human beings—do not themselves constitute a rigid distinction between things and people. They inform what it is to experience, and for Āṇṭāl here, there is a phenomenological field in which what it is to be her shifts and changes with her love of the personal yet pervasive Kṛṣṇa. Her bodiliness ranges over her environment, her feelings shape and are shaped by what she knows, senses, imagines, relocates, and immerses her sense of self in. In this, she is exemplary of a much-valued poetic sensibility most evident in Tamil and "Southern" Sanskrit literature, as Steven Hopkins (2004) has shown.

I would therefore like to say, programmatically, that we must always keep in mind this larger picture of what the poet expresses of her body's ecological livedness. But within it, we cannot think of bodily being without its markers and here—in particular—gender. The relationship between a sense of transcendence and the gendered body is one that has only recently become thematized in contemporary Western thought. As Amy Hollywood says,

> The transcendental conditions of subjectivity are bodily ... Whether as sensorially experienced or psychically configured, the body is the very site and support of human transcendence and subjectivity ... As women take on subjectivity as embodied beings, what Irigaray calls the sensible transcendental ... radically reconfigures the conditions and possibilities of subjectivity itself. (2002: 189–90)

This is already the case with the Āḻvārs, for the bodily subjectivity that attends forms of *bhakti* is not only not ignored—it forms the self-evident locus of expression. Fred Hardy (1983) long ago talked of Nammāḻvār as "a mystic of the cosmos of the senses" (371). We need, therefore, to keep our attention on the role of bodiliness in its generality as well as the way bodiliness is keyed to gender.

Now, bodiliness in the love of God is not always keyed to gender, yet gender gradually emerges in the richly detailed expression of emotion that is the key signifier of the Āḻvārs' poetry. I will delineate this emergence by looking at the particular salience the notion of "speaking as a young woman" has in the devotional love of Kṛṣṇa.

Emotion and Bracketing Gender

To reiterate, what characterizes the genre of *bhakti* poetry is an intensity of emotional expression that may not always be keyed to gender. That is to say, the poet-devotees often present loving God as something that is not inflected by the gender of the devotee even while bodily self-awareness is central to that love. We can see this in the case of another celebrated Tamil woman poet saint, from the Śaiva rather than Vaiṣṇava tradition, Kāraikkāl Ammaiyār. Her poems are among the oldest of the *bhakti* writings, dating back to the sixth century in all likelihood. Karen Pechilis (2016: 201) has argued eloquently that Karaikkāl Ammaiyār "only obliquely thematizes the human body, in contrast to the three major male poet-saints of the Tamil Śaiva bhakti tradition." Although her "devotional subjectivity" is sometimes expressed through her body, "the poet chooses not 'to body' beyond assuming characteristics common to all human bodies" (Pechilis 2016: 203).

Birth in this body
enabled me to express
my overflowing love
through speech,
and I reached
your sacred henna red feet. (*Aṟputat Tiruvantāti* v. 1)

Pechilis points out that the poet-saint "describes the intersubjectivity of emotion" in a way that "decenters the individuality of the body" (2016: 204). That is to say, while emotions are inescapably expressive of bodily presence, she strives to express them as what anybody could express.

At the same time, the poet-saint implicitly expresses the fact that even the emotion she expresses for the sake of all (devotees of Śiva) nevertheless arises from what she has made of herself. The hagiographies have it that she was a beautiful, married woman but already devout. When her errant husband returned to her only to fall at her feet in respect, she asked Śiva to rid her of her beauty and make her ghoul-like so that she might wander the world singing his praise without drawing the male gaze upon her. This narrative doubtless takes its inspiration from such words as in her signature verse in another composition, which refers to the fearsome location of one of Śiva's dances: "The ghoul, Kāraikkāl of the blazing mouth and teeth, thrives at this burning ground" (*Tiruvālaṅāṭṭut Tiruppatikam* 2. v. 11). Karen Pechilis argues that

> her use of the third person may provide a protective distance from the controversy of training a detailed descriptive gaze on a body that is human, female, and her own. But the larger point is that Kāraikkāl Ammaiyār does not train a descriptive gaze on her own body in her poetic corpus; she speaks generally of the human body as that which allows the experience of both painful afflictions and sublime love. (Pechilis 2016: 209–10)

As we will see, by contrast, Āṇṭāl offers exactly a "detailed descriptive gaze on a body that is human, female, and her own" and yet with the same emotional focus on her beloved God. So, we are likely to be persuaded by Pechilis's argument that the reason why Karaikkāl Ammaiyār deflects attention from her bodily intensity of devotion is because she wants her emotional expression to be available intersubjectively for other devotees regardless of gender. Nevertheless, I want to draw attention here to how—especially in light of the hagiographic narrative's exegesis of her words—she has performed a shift—through literal, miraculous bodily reconfiguration—in how her gender is to be interpreted. For, notoriously, the human norms of the gender binary are suspended when it comes to ghouls, even more so of those that then invert their liminality by centering themselves on the presence of God. So, she makes herself a ghoul, observes the ghoul, and has the ghoul's vivid and very particular bodily self-expression speak nonetheless for the intensity of devotion quite generally.

Nammāl̲vār, being given as a man, does not seem to require a comparably elaborate performance of reconfiguration, of blurring the meaning of gender and then coming to speak for all devotees (although we will later see that he too has his own performance of crossing back and forth). He can often express intense love of God that is not keyed to gender, even while suggesting an erotic intensity. For who, in feeling that way about God, would think there to be a gender that did not permit mingling with the lover?

> In truth he mingled with me.
> Mingling with my spirit,
> the Lord took it as well. (*Tiruvāymol̲i* 1.8.5–6)[16]

In short, while *bhakti* is an expression of sensible transcendence and is richly bodied in its language, it is not always a performance of gender, even if the deflection of gendered language requires a complex reconfiguration on the part of the (woman) poet. Having acknowledged this, we can turn to increasingly precise ways in which the performance of devotional emotion can be revealed as gendered in thought-provoking ways.

Engendering Emotion within Norms of Perspective

In the *Tiruppāvai*, the poet writes primarily in the first-person plural of a group of questing cowherd girls (*gopīs*) as they wake up and prepare to find their way to the house of their beloved Lord, where he is asleep with his Tamil̲ consort, Nappin̲n̲ai. Sometimes, a group of them address one of their friends, who has not woken up yet. Very occasionally, the poet's perspective implicitly looks upon the group from the outside. The commentarial tradition interprets this as Āṇṭāl locating herself as one of the *gopīs*. This often-choral voice of women, expressing a sometimes demanding but always well-mannered and respectful love and longing for their beloved God, is received by the tradition as speaking for all devotees. To this day, it is recited by men as well as women, quite generally, even though it is clearly keyed by gender.[17] Worshippers today, men and women, take on the persona of the *gopī* and read that as taking on Āṇṭāl's persona as a *gopī* so that a man may sing as a woman singing as another woman.

It would be a different undertaking to trace the reception, history, and contemporary dynamics of Āṇṭāl's figuration in the liturgical imagination of Śrīvaiṣṇava men. The (after) life of a gendered text may have its own implications for performativity, for the situation with the *Tiruppāvai*'s reception is more than a little unusual in religious history. For this essay, however, I only want to draw attention to the fact that the issue of gendered performance may lie not only within the textual expressivity of the poet but also in its reception by the community (of liturgical rather than merely literary readers). It is an open question as to what exactly happens in the liturgical rendition of Āṇṭāl, for it is not merely acting when it comes to the existential tug of devotion. At the least, we can say that the taking on of the *persona* of a poet-saint-goddess for profound spiritual activity does something to conceptions of masculinity, even if it does not make for the shifting of gender binaries.

Returning, then, to what is given within text, this sense that performance is not about a shift in gendered selfhood but a taking on (for howsoever profound a motivation) of a *persona* is conveyed well in the artful experimentation of another Āl̲vār, Tirumankai.[18] The tradition itself recognizes this: the hagiography has him chasing after women before his transformation.[19] As Archana Venkatesan has said, he is thought of as the "poet's poet," who "experiments with genres, metres and poetic situations" and uses "poetic virtuosity" in "molding his women (*talaivi*s) and their maddening predicament" of loving a God who is absent (Venkatesan 2007a: 19). I mention Tirumankai only in order to clarify that not all poetic voices are equally existential in the import of their performance of gender. But we have to be cautious about drawing any hard and fast lines between "mere" *persona* and something more transfigurative. Depending on our criteria, we may read the implications of these theopoetic voices differently.

From a literary perspective, Venkatesan offers this reading:

> In contrast to Andal, our two male poets, Tirumankai and Nammāḻvār, do not juxtapose the material and mythic worlds ... Rather, they employ the full complement of female characters of the *akam* genre to construct and comment on the interior world of their *talaivi* [heroine]. (2007a: 21)

This might indicate that, if we use as criterion the choice of literary *topoi*—which offers one perspective on the ecology of the poet's phenomenology—we can find a difference in expressiveness between those we already take to be the male poets and their female counterpart.[20]

If we shift our attention to the dimensions of emotional expression in that bodily intense way that characterizes many of Nammāḻvār's composition, and suspend the presupposition of what it means to say that he is a male poet, other aspects of his poetry come to the fore. So, let us look at Nammāḻvār's expression of love as a woman for the male God and ask if the surface differences in literary tropes that Venkatesan points out overlie a deeper similarity with Āṇṭāl. Here, the distinction between *persona* and character, between literary style and existential performativity, is blurred. For example, consider these verses:

> I had not consented, but He came and consumed my life,
> Day after day He came and consumed me
> altogether.
> Except for serving my Lord in southern
> Kātkarai with its dark rain clouds
> Is there anything else that my dear life
> could enjoy? (*Tiruvāymoḻi* 9.5.8)[21]

> ... The disease of my desire climaxes, deep
> going, melting in a torrent.
> It seemed He would just rule over me,
> But instead He consumed my life, that
> amazing one, and
> Just a little is left after He consumed my
> dear life.

> I had not consented, but He came and
> consumed my life. (*Tiruvāymoḻi* 9.6.7–8)
> ... He is my Lord Krishna,
> And to Him I have surrendered my
> womanhood.
> So what's the use of getting angry, women? (*Tiruvāymoḻi* 7.3.5)

Nammāḻvār does appear to juxtapose the mythic and the local (the reference is to the temple in Thirukatkarai, near present-day Eranakulam, Kerala). But the important point is that, in doing so, he expresses here an urgency of emotion that goes beyond the literary donning of a *persona*—instead entering into—performing—a gendered genre of being. The woman's voice here follows cultural and literary norms, and we are not to overstate the case and think that nonbinary genders are being imagined into being. Nonetheless, at this point, in this way, Nammāḻvār is performing the conception of womanhood available to him, not as literary ventriloquism but as existential reconfiguration of the phenomenology of *bhakti*. The poet here feels in a way that can, necessarily, only be articulated through his conceptual repertoire—but there is more to it than mimesis.

Here we need to find a fine balance. When we are exploring what it might mean to understand a classical Indian reworking of gender, we cannot afford to help ourselves to the sexual identity of the poet, as if the culturally given category closes off the agency to perform outside of that identity. We learn nothing about the phenomenology of gender if we say that here is a man writing "as" a woman and leave it at that. But neither can we afford to lose our footing in the culturally given identity altogether, for then it makes no sense at all to say that the young woman's voice here is Nammāḻvār's. We will be left with no purchase on the thought that gender can be performed, if we do not start with how performers construe their own bodily self-presence while essaying their performance.

This is why I want to say that here a man is performing womanhood. By which I mean to say that we should try to neither conflate sex and gender nor ontologize a difference. We can gain a sense of what is expressively similar in the performance of gender if we compare Nammāḻvār with Āṇṭāl, even as the comparison can function hermeneutically only through the terms of thinking of the former's verses as a reconfiguration and the latter's as a figuration of certain (theopoetically transformed) norms of "womanhood." So let us consider Āṇṭāl's invocation of "womanhood" (*peṇmai*).

> My tears gather and spill between my breasts
> like waterfalls.

He has destroyed my womanhood.
How does this bring him pride? (*Nācciyār Tirumoḻi* 8.1, *viṇ nīla mēlāppu*)

Similar too is the invocation of the familiar Tamil tropes of being entered, of being consumed, of being tortured—all of it secret or a secret that, once proclaimed, has the added force of revelation.

My clever and perfect lord
whose mighty arms easily wield the *śārṅga* bow
between him and me
a secret has passed
that only he and I know. (*Nācciyār Tirumoḻi* [*Maṉṉu perum pukaḻ Mātavan*] 5.8)

I confess I find it mostly difficult to say how the emotional presentation is different in the two cases. But because of the inescapable knowledge that the latter examples are from Āṇṭāl, it seems as if she is impatient of her fate, more ready to quarrel with her beloved, prepared to complain rather than endure. Perhaps here, we see traces of the aetiology of Nammāḻvār's imagination of himself into womanhood—namely, his normative understanding of what it is to become woman—whereas Āṇṭāl just is, and we need to follow her into an understanding of whatever it is to be woman because she says so. (Better to be hesitant here about drawing hard and fast conclusions about one's own suppositions about gender.) Once we are made sensitive to her readiness to be herself rather than an idea of herself, we see that violent intensity that is as far away as one could get from a demure rendition of masculinist norms of being "woman."

My perfect lord
who holds the spotless white conch in his left hand
refuses to reveal himself to me.
Instead he enters me, tortures me all day,
toys with my life,
and leads me a merry dance. (*Nācciyār Tirumoḻi* [*Maṉṉu perum pukaḻ Mātavan*] 5.2)

In between: A Note on Nammāḻvār's Gender Crossings

If we are to press on and ask if there is any noncircular way of asking how Nammāḻvār and Āṇṭāl express womanhood, we should look more carefully at the role of body morphology in their language, for the greatest trouble for reading around the gender/sex problem is the idea of sex-specific properties. But before that, it is worth looking at a particularly provocative yet much celebrated poem of Nammāḻvār's. I think it shows that performance works on many levels of signification at the same time, and to be comfortable rather than uncomfortable with the changes implied by performance is an important requirement for those who would wish to be sensitive to gender play in devotional love. These are the two relevant verses from the poem:

> Lifting my modesty, stealing my heart,
> The Lord of the deities reaches the highest heavens.
> I swear, my friend!
> I shall shock all the earth,
> Do weird things—ride the palmyra stem like a horse.
> With no sense of shame, I shall ride
> the palmyra stem through every street in town,
> and women from all the lands will cheer me on.
> And I shall demand from the Lord
> a cool blossom from the *tuḻai* plant
> and adorn my head with it. (*Tiruvāymoḻi* 5.3.9–10)[22]

The reference is to the practice of *maṭal ūrtal*, a version of which is traceable to the Caṇkam literature and which is performed in some parts of the Tamil country to this day. In it, a man who has been spurned by a woman sits in acute discomfort on the sharp fronds of a palmyra stem and pretends to ride it like a horse around town, declaiming his love for her. His public humiliation shows the depth of his love and is meant to convince her to agree to his suit in order to stop the display.

As can be seen straightaway, here Nammāḻvār writes as a woman who threatens to act as a man and that in a spectacularly mortifying way.[23] Is it a return to his self-understanding as a man, or is it a further move from imagining how a woman may think it properly provocative to be "weird" in order to draw God's attention? And let us think too: if the ritual is for a man to force a woman to put him out of his misery, does the woman performing as a man—through an act forbidden for women—imply that the beloved is a man or a woman (given the expectation that heterosexual norms apply)? Here we see how heteronormativity and the gender binary themselves become a powerful frame for performative engendering of emotion.

This particular passage from Nammāḻvār should make us think carefully of the existential force of performativity, especially when it is for the sake of divine love, understood in *bhakti* as the very furthest a human being can go in meaningful emotion.

Morphology and the Performance of Gendered Emotion

It is true that, apart from a very few instances of invoking symbolic tropes from *akattinam*, Nammāḻvār does not offer a morphologically keyed view of the woman devotee in a way that might be seen as merely reducing gender to biological sex. Nammāḻvār does use the emotional registers and, of course, the psychogeography of the symbolic Tamil landscape. But when it comes to writing as the young woman, his imaginative location is only occasionally—if tellingly—reliant on bodily morphology and much more on these other markers of his sensorium. So, we are made sensitive to the construction of gender within the context of what the tradition takes to be the givenness of his male body.

> This is no compassion, no compassion
> at all, Kṛṣṇa.
> Every time You touch my full breasts
> There swells inside me a vast flood of joy
> That crests not even in heaven, it surrounds
> and submerges all I know—
> And yet it ends like a dream.
> Desire reaches deep deep inside me—
> but, alas, not that a life can bear,
> oh!
> Yet separating from You right now is still
> worse,
> When You go out to herd the cows:
> It is my ruin. (*Tiruvāymoḻi* 10.3.2)

> Our life like wax melting away in fire,
> Our bright bracelets and cloth slack and
> slipping down,
> Tears like pearls trickle from our flower
> eyes, our breasts are pale, shoulders
> frail. (*Tiruvāymoḻi* 10.3.7)

Intense love courses through the entirety of the Āḻvār's phenomenology. What is shown here is not a universal mode of devotion to God but the particularity of feeling lovelorn, the whole of oneself brought into an emotional state that is naturally described by the available resources of one's cultural repertoire. By now, surely, it seems otiose even for the critic—let alone the devotee—to seek judgment of whether a man has imagined what it would be like to feel something in breasts that he does not have or whether there is just a field of complex, gendered subjectivity within which the poetic voice has found itself.

The particular use of bodily materiality to express lovelorn (*virāha*) devotion in Āṇṭāl too is accompanied by the symbolic tropes of Caṇkam poetry. She too deploys the symbols of that cultural repertoire. So, for example, in the famous opening song of the *Nācciyār Tirumoḻi*, she says,

> O, Ancient God of Love
> I painted your name upon the wall—
> the black sugarcane bow, the banner bearing the shark, the horses,
> and the maidens with their fly-whisks.
> Have you even noticed?
> From childhood
> I adored the Lord of Dvaraka,
> Pledged my swelling breasts to him. Quickly.
> Unite me with him. (*Nācciyār Tirumoḻi* [*tai oru tiṇkaḷ*] 1.4)

The intense love is communicated through sensual experience of the body. Fred Hardy says in this regard,

> One only has to look … at the recurring references to her breasts, to realise how much she is a person "of flesh and blood," how strongly aware she is of, and accepts positively, her physical nature. No other Āḻvār is so definite about it. … Though I think it is legitimate to regard many songs of Āṇṭāl as personal expressions, as belonging to the level of mysticism, we must not overlook the close similarities to the symbolic language typical of the girl poems. In other words, even when Āṇṭāl speaks directly about her personal emotions, she does it by resorting to certain typical symbols: her breasts and her abdomen. (Hardy 1983: 427–8)

But by now, we know that it cannot be the mere occurrence of these material symbols of a whole-body phenomenology of love that marks the song of the "woman" (or "girl," as Hardy has it in the language of a generation ago). Yet it is not entirely out of our aesthetic reach to focus on the poetry while bracketing the poet and ask if perhaps in Āṇṭāl there is a morphological frankness that is peculiarly hers, which is evident in her plea.

> Tormented by that Hṛṣikeśa
> who is exalted by the gods of every direction
> I lost the luster of my pearly white smile
> the redness of my full lips,

and my young breasts surrendered their beauty. (*Nācciyār Tirumoḻi* [*Maṉṉu perum pukaḻ Mātavaṉ*] 5.6)

That frankness is not just the way she returns to gendered symbols but how specific, how frankly aware of the mirror, they appear in the poetry. And it is not just the appearance but other modes of her sensorium.

Are they fragrant as camphor? Are they fragrant as the lotus?
Or do those coral lips taste sweet?
I ache to know the taste, the fragrance of the lips
of Mādhava, who broke the tusk of the elephant. (*Nācciyār Tirumoḻi* [*Karuppūram Nāṟumō*] 7.1)

Here, the freshness and immediacy of her language seems less focused on gendering performance and more a recreation of the significance of a gender she takes as given. Of course, there is nothing sensorily "bare" about the "given," for as soon as any of us speaks of how we feel and what we take our emotions to be, we cannot but take recourse in the lexicon available to us. And, Āṇṭāl is a poet of skill and sophistication who is totally in command of her literary inheritance. But what I think is that the primary lesson about gender we get here is that creative agency in Āṇṭāl is about asserting what the person who takes herself as woman may tell of her emotions rather than about asserting that she is a woman as her culture would have it. Perhaps it is only in Nammāḻvār's desperate threat to behave like a lovesick man that we find in him this challenge to what a woman may be in classical Tamil culture.

Āṇṭāl, Erotic Theopoetics, and Writing "as" a Woman

We have now found our way through how there is a subtle relationship between a given/taken gender that turns on assumptions about sex identity and the performative nature of gender (as found in the textual expression of theopoetics). On the one hand, if we trace all our literary and existential responses to the nature of the poetry back to a simple assumption of which poet is a man and which one is a woman, then we lose sight of the significance of how gender is performed in these works. On the other hand, both the literary skill and the existential urgency of performing gender make little sense if we do not set the poetry against the background of the cultural knowledge of who is given/taken as whom (here, in the hagiographies of the poet-saints).

With that balance in mind, we should also be aware that the salience of gendered performance might vary, and we notice that within and outside the poetic compositions. Inside the poem, we see the literary qualities that may distinguish as well as unite Nammāḻvār and Āṇṭāl, while outside it, we may ask similarly about what it means that both write "as" young women in love with a personal male God. Not just in the cultured expression of raw emotion but also in the use of symbolic tropes, many things unite the two Āḻvārs. But Āṇṭāl has what I call a "morphological frankness" in her *Nācciyār Tirumoḻi* that is unparalleled. I suggest that this is because she is "starting" with a gendered identity she does not construct, and therefore her creative agency is directed toward exploring how that identity may be expressed against the limits of cultural norms. This is important. When we talk about what it is to be gendered, we should also mean how we should so. With this consideration in mind, I will finish my study of Āṇṭāl's work with a look at how the erotic dimension of her theopoetics points to the subversive nature of her interpretation of her gender.

We should, of course, recognize the literary relationship of dependence between her employment of, on the one hand, the older *akam* topoi that hold between people and, on the other, her new mythopoetic reformulation of them in her relationship with God. But we should not therefore take the *eros* of the latter as an emotional derivative of the former. Too often, we take "the erotic" to be first a relationship understood between humans that only subsequently gets theologized as a model of a relationship with God. We should not take the desire for God as something parasitic on a secular reality but, instead, as a fundamental expression of *eros*. When Āṇṭāl talks of being married to no man, it is not like, say, her preferring King Ranga to Priest Śekhara but rather a distinction between two orders of being.

She cries out:

Lord of Desire! My ripening breasts swell
For that Lord who holds the conch and flaming discus
I could not live,
If there is even mention of offering my body to men.
That would be as terrible as a forest-roaming jackal coming in
and sniffing the offering,
That the learned Brahmins who uphold the Vedas,
Have given up to the gods in heaven. (*Nācciyār Tirumoḻi* [*tai oru tiṉkaḷ*] 1.7)

Notice the elegant simplicity with which the completely conventional trope of maidenly modesty in front of the male (human) gaze is startlingly inverted by the claim of arousal—that is to say, the yearning to gaze toward the face of the absent God, the God who will not look at her. Here, the very performance of her given/taken gender is an assertion of its changed (albeit theopoetic) meaning. So, we see that creative performance is about what it means to be gendered as much as what it means to engender oneself.

My breasts seek the gaze of the one
whose beautiful hand lifts the discus.
Bound tightly in a red cloth, their eyes
shy away from the gaze of mere mortals
desiring none other than Govinda.
I cannot live here a moment longer
Please take me to the shore of the Yamunā. (*Nācciyār Tirumoḻi* 12.4)

Learning from the Tradition

Despite this way of thinking about the erotic and gender, we still have a fundamental question: if we are to guard ourselves against the essentialism of taking gender to be what is always and already given/taken even as self-consciousness dawns on the individual with the emergence of personhood, what do we do about the intuition within community and academy that we have here the writings of older-man-as-young-woman and young-woman-as-young woman? I think an answer that imputes a wholesale false consciousness, in which everyone is trapped in ignorance of gender construction, is not only morally bleak but also epistemologically unviable. So, we must ask what is going on in the reception of Āṇṭāl as herself, the one woman among the Āḻvārs and thus "the lady who rules." Of course, there are the purely poetic characteristics of Āṇṭāl: the unwavering first personalism, the blending of the mythic into the personal, the weight of repeated focusing on bodily morphology, and the community's own recognition of her use of sexual relationality: as it is clear in Periyavāccāṉ Piḷḷai's medieval commentary, there is a straightforward acceptance of her use of sexual metaphors.[24] Her assured frankness and intimate detail takes many forms. This may be in tenderness:

The master of the cowherds,
tends his calves, staff in hand.
He danced too with the waterpots in sacred Kuṭantai.
Bring me the cool blue basil leaf
And place it on my soft, tangled curls. (*Nācciyār Tirumoḻi* [*Kaṇṇaṉ eṉṉum*] 13. 2)

Or it may be in agonistic ferocity that skillfully evokes and radically reworks the imagery of the Caṅkam heroine Kaṇṇaki (who, upon hearing of the unfair execution of her unfaithful husband by the king, in fury tore off her breast and flung it at his city, and set it afire):

> I melt, anguished.
> But he does not care if I live or die.
> If I see that thief,
> that looting lord of Govardhana,
> I shall pluck these useless breasts of mine
> from their roots,
> Will fling them at his chest,
> And stop that raging fire in me. (*Nācciyār Tirumoḻi* 13. 8)

The trouble I have been talking about is the impossibility of disentangling intuitions about the given/taken nature of gender from performative re/construction of it, even when we know that gendered power is encoded in that givenness. But let us think of the significance the tradition attaches to the conflation of the devotee's poetic "I" and the personal "I" in Āṇṭāl, simply by virtue of treating the author of the *Tiruppāvai* and the *Nācciyār Tirumoḻi* "as" a woman. The tradition and scholarship tends to think that because she is a woman, she writes in a particular way that men do not. (As per Fred Hardy, mystical ecstasy for Nammāḻvār, "in the girl and *gopī* songs" is "clearly connected with eroticism. Āṇṭāl, who was herself a girl, was uniquely able to integrate the erotic and the mystical planes" [1983: 369]). This makes sense when we hold normative gender identities for granted and ask only about literary representation and think of such poems as talk about women as—in Martha Selby's words—"representations of male attempts to aesthetically capture and portray female sexuality" (Selby 2000: 104). But from the perspective of this essay and its concern about the question of how gender is re/constructed, this can seem circular as a general statement. Obviously, if there is a context that invites the reader to see the stylized, literary expression as a self-conscious replication of a different gendered perspective—as in the case of Tirumankai, whose coming to devotion includes an extravagantly heterosexual male identity, as a man who used to chase women—then it is fair enough to accept the poet's word. But absent such a context—and in the case of Nammāḻvār, there is no second-order hagiographic guidance apart from the giveness of an identity as a man—then we must let the poetic voice that emerges in the text to remain immersed in its gendered performance.

Instead, we should see—through looking at how the tradition takes it that this is a woman while Nammāḻvār is a man—that the imaginative gender location in theopoetics (at least) is on a continuum between different modes of gender construction: from where the person strives agentively to express identity, all the way to where some self-formation has always already been there, especially through a morphology that is used in different and fluid cultural contexts to affirm a view of one's gender. We have to make sense of our intuition that we can talk of a man writing as a woman and a woman writing as a woman, but we must understand that this is inescapably circular; for what we are looking at is how a human being is being gendered, always already and yet also by choice. We can neither start with a contrast between the given and the constructed nor can we claim to see a pure act of construction with nothing given left over.

So, we must see the use of morphological characteristics as lying at the point where always already given constructions are taken up and used in creative agency, not always of "a gender" but what it might mean in the ecology of one's experience of being oneself. In our contemporary theoretical concern to deconstruct all sense of the given, we tend to ignore the challenge of having to account for the creative bearing that materiality has for our gendered selves. There are powerful reasons why bodily morphology can be the ground of the "first construction," whose primacy lies in its appeal to an apparent essence. I want to suggest that the contemporary significance of Āṇṭāl lies in her being taken as a woman who speaks of love of God but with a voice resembling that of a man whose work she must have known, a voice, moreover, already heard in a preexisting literary sensibility.

The reception by the Śrīvaiṣṇava tradition of her as a woman of authority, appeal, and a virtually unsurpassed relevance to this day shows that even if self-expressions of essence are fundamentally constructed, that emotional power and poetic teleology can evoke in others the possibility of their own narratives through a theoaesthetics of gender: "The passion of Āṇṭāl and the surrender of Nammāḻvār are the passion and surrender of the devotee" (Narayanan 1987: 150). But, in these subtle ways, sometimes reflexive and at others lost in the sheer force of devotional belonging, the passion and surrender are also gendered and inflect what it means to be gendered when participating in the Śrīvaiṣṇava liturgy. And that participation, I want to say, is a magnifying lens through which to look at more general existential conditions by which representation feeds into the gendering of emotion. The theopoetics we have been engaging with is not only of esoteric value to a community of worshippers; it is indicative of questions of the most fundamental import to lives with very different teleologies.

It may be possible, if one is sensitive to the range of human expression, to look for lessons as much in Āṇṭāl as in Gregory of Nyssa, as much in theopoetics as street theatre, as much in classical Tamiḻ as in Spanish, as much in religion as in cinema. But with it comes the responsibility of recognizing the lacunae in one's material. I therefore want to be careful not to overstate the case. To reiterate, this exploration has not got us to looking critically at the gender binary and heteronormativity or at structures of power in language, class/caste, and institutions. Yet it would not be becoming of a student of these Āḻvārs to be too modest about their significance. In their theology, in their poetic power, in the continued if overlooked liturgical significance, they do make us think about how gender may be negotiated between what is given/taken and performed, how boundaries may be acknowledged only to be crossed, and norms symbolically deployed only to reconfigure their meaning. There is still much to be done in thinking through issues of gender through the classical past.

Notes

1 For example, Lloyd (1984); in a very different mode, Zajko and Leonard (2006).
2 I set aside here the complex question of Āṇṭāḷ's identity as more a goddess than an Āḻvār in the community; see Hudson (1993).
3 For an evocative summary of the process, see Shulman (2016: 125–8).
4 The "heroine" in one of the standard persona of the earliest layers of Tamil poetry that falls under the category of "inwardness" (*akam*); Zvelebil (1975: 98 [n. 95]).
5 See the translations in Ramanujan (1985).
6 See Cutler and Ramanujan (1999: 249).
7 I am indebted to Alison Stone for discussion of these issues. Stone (2007) is an admirably clear and helpful orientation to the issues touched upon here; the original ideas laid out in the book belie its modest claim to be an "introduction" to feminist philosophy.
8 Plumwood (1989) is a cool and clear statement of this position.
9 See Moi (1999). Having the notion of an analytic distinction between sex and gender at hand, we need not necessarily follow Moi in saying there should be no "sex/gender" usage at all but only of the "lived body."
10 For an exploration of this process with reference to gender in the *Mahābhārata*, see Ram-Prasad (2018), Chapter 2.
11 Maria Heim and I term this nonmetaphysical, descriptive, analytic, and contextual approach to experience "ecological phenomenology." On its application to *dharma* and emotion, see Heim (2018).
12 For example, Butler (1990 [2007]: 7).

13 Let me acknowledge that the freedom and potential to self-create are constrained by relationships of power, which requires addressing in ways that this chapter cannot do. When talking of gender, I am talking about *the taking on* of a self-declared first-personal voice. There is different task, "of how a female is conceived" in a cultural context, such as Janet Gyatso has touched upon in her study of Buddhist monasticism (Gyatso [2003: 89]), which I cannot undertake here.

14 See Williams (1992: 244).

15 I am indebted to Archana Venkatesan's new translation of Āṇṭāl and mainly follow her rendition of the Tamil in Venkatesan (2010); but the translation by Vidya Dehejia (1990) is also beautiful and well worth reading. Also, I thank Sudha Chakravarthi for conveying to me over the years the beauty and context of Āṇṭāl's words, with the incense-lit, jasmine-fresh dusky afternoon echoing to the *Tiruppāvai*'s enigmatic refrain, *ēl ōr empāvāy*.

16 See Narayanan's (1987: 21) translation.

17 See, for example, Younger (1982).

18 I follow here Venkatesan's sensitive exploration in Venkatesan (2007a).

19 See Venkatesan (2007a), note 11.

20 Here Venkatesan suggests that she is extending an insight about Āṇṭāl from Dennis Hudson (1996): Āṇṭāl tends to offer the mythographic world of Kṛṣṇa in Vṛṇdāvana when talking of and as a *gopī* in the Tiruppāvai, whereas she appears to exist in the densely specific—"material"—world of her locale when in the *Nācciyār Tirumoḻi* she speaks of herself, alone, offering us the contours of a biography.

21 For the following verses of Nammāḻvār with one exception, I use the theologically sensitive rendering in Clooney (2014).

22 For this passage, I use the translation from Narayanan (1987: 43–4).

23 The practice is also discussed by Tirumankai in elaborate echo of earlier Caṇkam literature. See Hardy (1983: 388–402); also Venkatesan (2007b).

24 See Venkatesan (2010) for both a study of the commentary and the bibliography for this long-recognized exegetical feature within the Śrīvaiṣṇava community.

References

Butler, J. ([1990] 2007). *Gender Trouble*. New York: Routledge

Butler, J. (1990a). "Performative Acts and Gender Constitution: An Essay on Phenomenology and Feminist Theory." In Katie Conboy, Nadia Medina, and Sarah Stanbury (eds.), *Writing on the Body: Female Embodiment and Feminist Theory* (pp. 401–18). New York: Columbia University Press.

Clooney, F. (2014). *His Hiding Place Is Darkness: A Hindu-Catholic Theopoetics of Divine Absence*. Stanford, CA: Stanford University Press.

Cutler, N., and A. K. Ramanujan (1999). "From Classicism to Bhakti." In Vinay Dharwadker (ed.), *The Collected Essays of A. K. Ramanujan* (pp. 232–60). New York: Oxford University Press.

Dehejia, V. (1990). *Āṇṭāl and Her Path of Love*. Albany: State University of New York Press.

Gyatso, J. (2003). "One Plus One Makes Three: Buddhist Gender, Monasticism, and the Law of the Non-excluded Middle." *History of Religions* 43(2): 89–115.

Hardy, F. (1983). *Virāha-Bhakti: The Early History of Kṛṣṇa Devotion in South India*. Delhi: Oxford University Press.

Heim, M. (2018). "Emotions." In Donald Davis and Patrick Olivelle (eds.), *The Oxford History of Hinduism: A New History of Dharmasastra* (pp. 419–31). New York: Oxford University Press.

Hollywood, A. (2002). *Sensible Ecstasy: Mysticism, Sexual Difference, and the Demands of History*. Chicago, IL: University of Chicago Press.

Hopkins, S. (2004). "Lovers, Messengers, and Beloved Landscapes: Sandeśakāvya in Comparative Perspective." *International Journal of Hindu Studies* 8(1–3): 29–55.

Hudson, D. (1993). "Āṇṭāl Āḻvār: A Developing Hagiography." *Journal of Vaishnava Studies* 1(2): 27–61.

Hudson, D. (1996). "Andal's Desire." In Stephen J. Rosen (ed.), *Vaiṣṇavī: Women and the Worship of Krishna* (pp. 171–211). New Delhi: Motilal Benarsidass.

Lloyd, G. (1984). *The Man of Reason: "Male" and 'Female" in Western Philosophy*. Minneapolis: University of Minnesota Press

Millett, K. (1979). *Sexual Politics*. London: Virago.

Moi, T. (1999). *What Is a Woman?* Oxford: Oxford University Press.

Narayanan, V. (1987). *The Way and the Goal. Expressions of Devotion in the Early Śrī Vaṣṇava Tradition*. Washington, DC: Institute for Vaishnava Studies Press.

Pechilis, K. (2016). "To Body or Not to Body: Repulsion, Wonder, and the Tamil Saint Kāraikkāl Ammaiyār." In B. A. Hodrege and K. Pechilis (eds.), *Refiguring the Body: Embodiment in South Asian Religions* (pp. 199–228). Albany: State University of New York Press.

Plumwood, V. (1989). "Do We Need a Sex/Gender Distinction?" *Radical Philosophy* 51(2): 2–11.

Ram-Prasad, C. (2018). *Human Being, Bodily Being. Phenomenology from Classical India*. Oxford: Oxford University Press.

Ramanujan, A. K. (1985). *Poems of Love and War from the Eight Anthologies and the Ten Long Poems of Classical Tamiḻ*. New York: Columbia University Press.

Selby, M. (2000). *Grow Long, Blessed Night: Love Poems from Classical India*. New York: Oxford University Press.

Shulman, D. (2016). *Tamil: A Biography*. Cambridge: Harvard University Press.

Stone, A. (2007). *An Introduction to Feminist Philosophy*. Cambridge: Polity Press.

Venkatesan, A. (2007a). "A Woman's Kind of Love: Female Longing in Tamil Alvar Poetry." *Journal of Hindu-Christian Studies* 20: 16–24.

Venkatesan, A. (2007b). "Riding a Horse for Love: A Comparative Look at the Madal Poems of Tirumankaiyalvar and Ceyankontar." In Chelva Kanakanayakam (ed.), *Tropes, Territories and Competing Realities*. Toronto: Toronto South Asian Review.

Venkatesan, A. (2010). *The Secret Garland. Āṇṭāḷ's Tiruppāvai and Nācciyār Tirumoḻi*. New York: Oxford University Press.

Williams, R. (1992). "Macrina's Deathbed Revisted: Gregory of Nyssa on Mind and Passion." In Lionel Wickham and Caroline P. Bammel (eds.), *Christian Faith and Greek Philosophy in Late Antiquity* (pp. 227–46). Leiden: Brill.

Younger, P. (1982). "Singing the Tamiḻ Hymnbook in the Tradition of Rāmānuja: The 'Adyayanōtsava' Festival in Srīraṅkam." *History of Religions* 21(3): 272–93.

Zajko, V., and M. Leonard (eds.) (2006). *Laughing with Medusa: Classical Myth and Feminist Thought*. Oxford: Oxford University Press.

Zvelebil, K. (1975). *Tamil Literature*. Leiden: E.J. Brill.

7

Gender in the Tradition of Sri Ramakrishna

Jeffery D. Long

The Tradition of Sri Ramakrishna: An Overview

The Ramakrishna tradition's understanding of gender is shaped by its approach to transcendence as available equally to women and to men, its orientation toward the Mother Goddess, and the prominent roles played within it by women, particularly in its early history. As we shall see, the Ramakrishna tradition presents a case of an Indic tradition in which, according to its own ideals, femininity is something to be affirmed, while at the same time, institutionally speaking, male domination tends to be the norm. The resources within the tradition for affirming female equality are abundant, but they represent a potential that has yet to be fully realized.

Though it is one of the youngest of Indic traditions, having emerged in the latter half of the nineteenth century, the tradition of Sri Ramakrishna is one of the most influential among the Hindu traditions of the modern period. It is also, although of recent origin, in continuity with many older schools of thought. Its philosophical system draws upon such currents as Advaita Vedānta (with which it is frequently identified), Vaiṣṇava traditions, Tantra, and Buddhism as well as non-Indic traditions, such as Christianity, Islam, and modern science. Indeed, the broad eclecticism or pluralism of this tradition is arguably one of its defining features (Hatcher 1999).

In regard to gender in particular, we shall see that Kālī, the Mother Goddess, has a special role as the preferred deity, or *iṣṭadevatā*, of the tradition's founder. Tantra, too, played a prominent role in the spiritual life of Ramakrishna and informs the tradition's attitudes toward gender issues. Ramakrishna's guru in Tāntric practice, the Bhairavi Brāhmani, was a woman, as was Rani Rasmani, the owner and builder of the Kālī temple at which he served as a priest for most of his life.

The tradition of Sri Ramakrishna, as its name suggests, is rooted in the life and teachings of Sri Ramakrishna (1836–1886), a Bengali Hindu mystic whose life intersected with the wider cultural currents of the Bengal Renaissance. The intersection of Ramakrishna's unique approach to ancient philosophical and Tāntric systems led to the emergence of the tradition that bears his name. Over his lifetime, many male and female householders became his followers. He also initiated a group of young men into monastic life, although the official order, known as the Ramakrishna Order, was established in 1897, eleven years after his passing. After Ramakrishna passed away due to throat cancer in August of 1886, the leadership of his monastic followers fell to one of his closest male disciples: specifically, a young monk named Narendranath Datta (1863–1902), who took up the monastic name of Swami Vivekananda. However, the Ramakrishna movement more broadly, including the Ramakrishna Order, came to follow the informal moral leadership of Ramakrishna's widow, Sarada Devi (1853–1920), also known as the Holy Mother, to whose authority even Swami Vivekananda deferred.

Despite the prominent position of the Holy Mother, the role of gender in the tradition of Sri Ramakrishna is a complex one. Ramakrishna's devotion to the Mother Kālī, on the one hand, his dedication to achieving a state of genderlessness, on the other; Mother Sarada's authoritative role as well as many women's participation in shaping the tradition; and the contemporary monastic order's male-dominated leadership all reveal the complex role that gender has played in the Ramakrishna tradition. After the passing of the Holy Mother, authority in the tradition has been held by the almost entirely male monastic order. Female monastics, nevertheless, have held prominent roles in the tradition. Sister Nivedita (1867–1911), an Irish woman and one of the first Westerners initiated into monastic life by Swami Vivekananda, has held a prominent place in the hearts and minds of adherents of this tradition. And female householders—particularly American devotees, such as Josephine MacLeod—have been among the tradition's most ardent and steadfast supporters. The tradition largely subscribes to the nondualistic philosophy of Advaita Vedanta (although with a prominent place for *bhakti*), which celebrates the Goddess and the Holy Mother herself and encourages its followers to think in a pluralistic and nonexclusive way about the range of philosophies and religions that make up the spiritual heritage of humanity.

Sri Ramakrishna and His Multireligious Practice: One Feminist Perspective

It is not an exaggeration to say that Sri Ramakrishna is one of the most remarkable figures, not only in India but also in all of the history of religion. Barely literate, Ramakrishna was not a philosopher in the sense of having completed any specialized training in the study and elucidation of Sanskrit texts. Rather, he was an inspired seer, consistent with the ancient sages and saints of India. His teachings were based not so much on traditional study in the conventional sense but on his direct experiences, pursued through spiritual practice. The Ramakrishna tradition emphasizes direct experience, in contrast with "book learning," or the type of scholarship traditionally valued in many Indian systems of philosophy. Thus, some scholars see it as forming a break with the ancient scholastic tradition and as distinctively modern (Rambachan 1994). This contrast, however, can be overstated; for it is not that direct experience is undervalued in premodern Indian thought—quite the contrary. Further, many monastics of the Ramakrishna Order are erudite, and some of the best translations of Sanskrit philosophical works into English over the course of the last century have been those by these monks. Experience is also emphasized in premodern Indic traditions, as is evident in the writings of the Upaniṣads and other early texts. But it is certainly the case that, for Sri Ramakrishna himself, direct mystical experience was central and not simply intellectual understanding. For him, truth known only with the mind, through the medium of the intellect, has not yet been fully realized.

One of the unique elements of Sri Ramakrishna's teaching is his combining of Advaita philosophy with devotion to the divine feminine. For Ramakrishna, the *Brahman* of Advaita Vedanta and the Kālī of Tantra are one and the same.

Ramakrishna's Life: Combining Advaita Philosophy and the Worship of the Divine Mother

Ramakrishna was born in February of 1836 to a poor *Brahmin* family in the Bengal village of Kamarpukur. When he was 19 years old, he and his elder brother were hired as priests at a temple dedicated to the Goddess Kālī in Dakshineshwar, on the northern outskirts of Calcutta. Before this time—indeed, going back to his childhood—Ramakrishna was known in his village for his ecstatic trances or *samādhis*. In these altered states of awareness, he would lose consciousness of the outer world and become fully immersed in divine bliss. Both during and after his lifetime, sceptics expressed the view that he might have been suffering from a neurological disorder. He came out of these experiences, though, believing he had become absorbed in God consciousness. He demonstrated a deep knowledge of many of the topics discussed in the Hindu scriptures, even without having studied them. The belief of the tradition that developed around him was that Sri Ramakrishna's knowledge came from his direct experiences of the realities that are described in the scriptures.

One of the most vivid and life-transforming experiences Ramakrishna underwent occurred after he had become a priest of the Goddess Kālī's temple. The Dakshineshwar Kālī temple where he served had been built and was owned by Rani Rasmani, a prominent Calcutta businesswoman. It is noteworthy that a woman—and a lower-caste woman at that—was able to rise to such a level of power in early nineteenth-century Indian society, as Rasmani did. Although both patriarchy and caste are powerful factors in traditional Indian society, and were no less so in nineteenth-century Bengal than at other times and places in Indian history, it would clearly be an error to assume that women and people of low caste have been altogether without agency. It is also worth noting that at the outset of its history, the tradition of Sri Ramakrishna was dependent upon powerful women in many ways. Women played pivotal roles in its formation and its ongoing survival. Ramakrishna and his brother were driven by economic necessity to take up their Dakshineshwar post of priesthood. For his part, Sri Ramakrishna overcame his initial reservations, as a *Brahmin*, about serving in the temple of a low-caste woman, and—in time—Ramakrishna and Rasmani developed a close and respectful relationship. Even when Sri Ramakrishna's path took him in directions that conventional society viewed as eccentric, Rasmani stood by him against those who wanted him to be dismissed from the temple. She came to see Sri Ramakrishna as her guru, as he also grew to appreciate her devotion to the Goddess. Soon, Sri Ramakrishna would come to see caste, and even basic Hindu notions of purity and impurity, as irrelevant on the path of God realization. In this sense, Ramakrishna's sensibility was deeply Tāntric; for Tantra defies the normative conventions of purity and impurity and focuses on the divinity abiding in all forms and all situations.

Apart from the influential female character of Rani Rasmani, another powerful feminine presence in the Ramakrishna tradition is that of the Goddess Herself. Not feeling that he could legitimately serve as a priest of Kālī without experiencing Her presence directly, the young priest Ramakrishna began to pray earnestly and longingly for a vision of the Goddess. He became so desperate for the divine vision that finally, one evening, he threatened to take his own life and reached for a sword that was hanging on the wall of the temple in order to cut his own throat. At that point, the Goddess showed mercy upon him:

> When I jumped up like a madman and seized it [the sword], suddenly the blessed Mother revealed Herself. The buildings with their different parts, the temple, and everything else vanished from my sight, leaving no trace whatsoever, and in their stead, I saw a limitless, infinite, effulgent Ocean of Consciousness. As far as the eye could see, the shining billows were madly rushing at me from all sides with a terrific noise, to swallow me up! I was panting for breath. I was caught in the rush and collapsed, unconscious. What was happening in the outside world I did not know; but within me there was a steady flow of undiluted bliss, altogether new, and I felt the presence of the Divine Mother. (Nikhilananda 1942: 14)

After this powerful vision, Sri Ramakrishna claimed to perceive the Divine Mother's presence everywhere and in all beings. This led to a behavior of ecstasy that many devotees regarded as eccentric. He would feed the food offerings, the *prasād*, left by devotees for the Goddess to a cat, saying he saw the Goddess in the cat no less than in other beings or in the image of the Goddess Kālī to which ritual worship was to be offered. The whole world of Ramakrishna was enlivened with the presence of the Goddess. The divine feminine, for Ramakrishna, pervaded everything.

Ramakrishna continued to have *samādhi* experiences throughout his life. These were often induced by devotional activity, such as the singing of songs on sacred themes. The Dakshineshwar Kālī temple at which he served was on a highly popular pilgrimage route, on the way to the famous Jagannath temple, at Puri. Frequently, holy persons from diverse traditions stopped there and engaged him in discussion of spiritual topics, and he began to develop a reputation for wisdom and insight. One of the ascetics who became fascinated by Sri Ramakrishna was a female Tāntric practitioner known in textual sources as "the Bhairavi Brāhmani." Ramakrishna adopted her as a guru for a period of time. Under the tutelage of the Bhairavi Brāhmani, Ramakrishna followed a variety of Tāntric practices. Each of these disciplines, representing a variety of Tāntric traditions—Śaiva, Śākta, and Vaiṣṇava—led him, eventually, to experience *samādhi*, the highest spiritual state. This state is difficult to attain. Many practitioners observe these disciplines for a lifetime without achieving this result. Observing how easily Sri Ramakrishna attained highly advanced states of consciousness through his various spiritual practices, the Bhairavi Brāhmani believed him to be an *avatāra*, or a divine incarnation, and brought learned teachers to meet Ramakrishna to confirm this belief.

Later, Ramakrishna would follow another guru: the monk, Totapuri. It was from Totapuri that Ramakrishna learned the nondualistic practice of Advaita Vedānta, leading to an experience of the ultimate Reality: *nirguṇa Brahman*, beyond name and form. Totapuri was a *sannyāsin*—a renouncer or monk—of the Daśanāmi order of monks, established by the prominent ninth-century Hindu leader Śaṅkarācārya himself. Totapuri initiated Ramakrishna into *sannyāsa*, or monkhood, thus establishing Ramakrishna, also, in the Daśanāmi lineage. As we have seen, Ramakrishna, in turn, would later initiate a number of his own disciples into monkhood as well. The monks of the Ramakrishna Order are thus also members of the Daśanāmi lineage, through Totapuri.[1] This would have a significant impact on the role of gender, institutionally, in the tradition of Sri Ramakrishna, as the Daśanāmi lineage is a male-dominated monastic tradition.

According to various accounts of his life, Ramakrishna performed *sādhana*, or spiritual practice, following a variety of traditions. His aim was to realize God in as many ways as possible. He thus followed various Hindu traditions—Śākta, Śaiva, and Vaiṣṇava—as well as Christianity and Islam, until he achieved the ultimate realization of the state of *samādhi* through their respective practices. According to the tradition that has developed on the basis of his life and teachings, he achieved God realization through all of them, thus establishing an experiential basis for religious pluralism (Nikhilananda 1942: 60). One of his most famous teachings is *yato mat, tato path*: each system of religion or philosophy is a path to God realization. He taught that all of the world's religions and philosophies contain some kernel of truth and are capable of serving as means to the experience of the divine Reality at the basis of all existence. As he elaborates,

> I have practiced all religions—Hinduism, Islam, Christianity—and I have also followed the paths of the different Hindu sects. I have found that it is the same God toward whom all are directing their steps, though along different paths. He who is called Krishna is also called Shiva, and bears the name of the Primal Energy, Jesus, and Allah as well—the same Rama with a thousand names. (Nikhilananda 1942: 60)

From a feminist perspective, Sri Ramakrishna's pluralism, with the pride of place that it gives to feeling as a valid mode of knowing, in contrast to disembodied or denaturalized discursive reasoning, can be seen as a feminine approach to diversity. The contrast would be with the traditionally masculine approach of noting the logical incompatibilities of the claims of various religions and philosophies and insisting that only one of these systems of thought, at most, can be true. Sri Ramakrishna's approach focuses not simply on the conceptual content of the world's religions, as sets of ideas, but also on their embodied practice. It is through spiritual *practices* that Ramakrishna finds the world's religions true and effective paths, not through comparing their philosophical and theological claims on a conceptual level. As an embodied practice, rather than disembodied and denaturalized logic, Ramakrishna's approach to religious diversity fits a feminist paradigm far more closely than it does a traditional, patriarchal paradigm, focused on logic alone.[2]

This does not mean Ramakrishna's approach to the phenomenon of diversity is illogical or *alogical*. It would be left to his most prominent disciple, Swami Vivekananda, to begin to work out the logical ramifications of Ramakrishna's teaching. Conversely, in this regard many scholars have observed that Swami Vivekananda fits a masculine paradigm more so than his master does. Sri Ramakrishna's approach was bent toward devotionalism, whereas Vivekananda's was toward the intellect—hence his chosen monastic name, *Vivekananda*, which refers to the bliss (*ānanda*) of intellectual discernment (*viveka*).

Of course, it can be problematic to propose that categories such as logic are "masculine" and feeling and embodiment are "feminine"; for women are no less logical than men, and men are no less capable of feeling or embodied practice than women (as Ramakrishna's life demonstrates). But a common feminist critique of patriarchy is its excessive reliance on a certain kind of logic to the exclusion of feeling, which patriarchy relegates to the realm of the feminine (and thus, at least implicitly, diminishes). Feminist critique operates, in part, by revalorizing the categories of feeling and embodiment as a corrective to patriarchy's diminution of these dimensions of the human experience. Therefore, the implication is not that men are more logical or women more emotional, but that the human experience has been artificially bifurcated in this way by patriarchy. Generally, one dimension of experience is overemphasized at the expense of the other. The feminist critique is an attempt to rectify this situation and cultivate a more holistic approach to knowledge.

Interestingly, the patriarchal identification of the *life of the mind* with masculinity and embodied feeling with femininity, and the subsequent modern feminist critique of these gendered identifications, has its analogues in ancient Indian discourse. The Sāṃkhya school of philosophy identifies consciousness with *puruṣa*, the masculine principle, and material nature (including the body, emotions, feelings, and so on) with *prakṛti*, the feminine principle. In the Śākta tradition of Tantra, the relative valuation of these is reversed. This reversal is portrayed iconographically in depictions of Kālī or Śakti (the female power)—who is identified with *prakṛti*—standing on the prone body of Śiva—the cosmic *puruṣa*. The female supersedes the masculine through her power. This is the very icon enshrined at Dakshineshwar, where Sri Ramakrishna practiced his *sādhanas*. This powerful icon symbolizes Ramakrishna's views on gender: the divine feminine, embodied devotion, and his emphasis on a personal realization of nonduality (beyond gender), which cuts through the patriarchal structures of his time and reveals his feminine sensibilities. This becomes even more evident in his relationship with his wife, the Holy Mother Sarada Devi.

Sri Ramakrishna and the Holy Mother Sarada Devi: Divine Love and Religious Authority

The aspect of the life of Ramakrishna that has probably faced the most critical scrutiny is his relationship with his wife, Sarada Devi. The two were married, formally, in May of 1859. At this time, the young Saradamani was only 5 years of age, whereas Sri Ramakrishna was 23. Such arranged marriages between very young girls and older men were common in rural India in the nineteenth century. The rejection of such practices was championed during this period by a variety of Hindu social reformers—particularly in Bengal. Rāja Ram Mohan Roy (1772–1833), the founder of the Brahmo Samaj, the earliest of the Hindu reform organizations of this time, was a staunch critic of various Hindu practices that relegated women to a lower status. However, the intellectual world of the Calcutta-based urban Hindu reformers and their upper-middle-class *bhadralok* (or "gentlemanly") vision of society was far removed from the reality of the rural world in which Ramakrishna and Sarada Devi lived, where village customs of child marriage continued to be practiced.

In fact, Sarada Devi and Ramakrishna's marriage ceremony was more of a betrothal than a marriage. According to the marriage custom of the time, the bride did not leave her family in the village of Jayrambati to go and live with her husband until she was 18. She only briefly visited his family in their nearby village of Kamarpukur. However, during two of these visits, Ramakrishna was not present but was in Dakshineshwar. It seems that they had very little contact before Sarada Devi turned 18.

After she settled in Dakshineshwar, though, Sarada Devi's married life with Ramakrishna proved to be quite unconventional. Ramakrishna did not treat her as his wife but perceived her to be an incarnation of Kālī, the Divine Mother, to whose service he had devoted himself. He therefore literally worshiped Sarada Devi, performing a ritual called the *ṣodaśi pūja*. By one account, this worship took place on the *Amavasya*, or new moon night, of May 25, 1873, though according to another account it took place on the new moon night of June 5, 1872 (Tapasyananda 1986: 329). In the Bengali Śākta tradition of Hinduism (the Hindu tradition that is devoted to Śakti, or Kālī, the wife of Śiva and Divine Mother of the universe), the night of the new moon—when the moon is completely dark—is dedicated to the worship of Kālī. This ritual is significant because Kālī means the "dark goddess," and the worship of her on the dark night of the new moon empowers her devotees. It is said that at the conclusion of the *ṣodaśi puja*—by all accounts a profound and intense experience—Sri Ramakrishna and Sarada Devi lost consciousness in ecstasy and became as one (Gambhirananda 1977: 50):

> Many hours passed in that state. It was past midnight when the Master [Sri Ramakrishna], in a semi-conscious state, offered himself to the deity [Sarada Devi]. He first offered a *bel* leaf (on which was written his name), the rosary [mala, or string of prayer beads], the different articles of clothing and ornaments he had used at the time of his spiritual practices, and also the fruit of his spiritual disciplines; then he offered even himself at the feet of the goddess. (Akshaychaitanya 2009: 50).

This signifies Ramakrishnan's submission to Sarada Devi as the holy divine Mother, not as his wife. Narasingha P. Sil characterizes the *ṣodaśi puja* as "a strange consummation of a strange relationship" (2003: 56).

By all accounts, Sri Ramakrishna and Sarada Devi never had sexual relations (thus making it possible for Totapuri to initiate Ramakrishna into monastic life, despite Ramakrishna's being married). In one biographical account of Ramakrishna, it is said,

> One day while Sarada was massaging the Master's [Ramakrishna's] feet, she asked him, "How do you look upon me?" The Master replied: "The same Mother who is in the temple [the goddess Kālī], the same Mother who gave birth to this body [his biological mother] … that same Mother is now rubbing my feet. Truly, I always see you as a form of the blissful Divine Mother. (Saradananda 2003: 349)

Critical observers may interpret this relationship within the norms of patriarchy. Some may even view his behavior as misogynistic; for the terms of their relationship were defined entirely by Sri Ramakrishna. The first to level this charge was the Brahmo Samaj leader, Pratap Chandra Majumdar, who referred to Ramakrishna's treatment of his wife as "barbarous." On the other hand, the Indologist Max Müller, one of the first biographers of Ramakrishna, "refrained from commenting on Sarada's conjugal life with the caveat that no one had any right to complain against it, because 'she was satisfied with her life'" (Sil 2003: 23–4). Both Majumdar and Müller, though, neglect to look at Sarada Devi's own accounts of her relationship with Ramakrishna.

By Sarada Devi's own accounts, she was not only satisfied but actually delighted in the company of her unusual husband during their years together: "When Sarada spoke of this period later in her life, she would describe it as one of continuous ecstasy; a state of married bliss which was nevertheless absolutely sexless" (Isherwood 1965: 145). The perspective on this topic generally voiced within the Ramakrishna tradition is that, in place of the conventional, sexual relationship of a husband and wife, Sri Ramakrishna and Sarada Devi had a spiritual companionship. Through this relationship Ramakrishna can be seen, in retrospect, to have been preparing his young wife for her future role as *sanghajananī* or mother of the order of monks that carried his message around the world.

Ramakrishna took upon himself the role of his wife's teacher, both in spiritual matters and in worldly affairs (Saradananda 2003: 348; Sil 2003: 82–3). After all, she was much younger than he and was under his guardianship. Of the greatest significance to the subsequent tradition, Sri Ramakrishna "made of [Sarada Devi] a powerful dynamo capable of transmitting spirituality to others" (Saradananda 2003: 719). This refers to one of Sarada Devi's most celebrated contributions to the movement that carried forth the vision of her husband: the "transmission of spirituality" through the medium of *dīkṣa* or initiation into the Ramakrishna tradition through the imparting of a *mantra*. Sarada Devi bestowed this initiation on numerous followers, both male and female. Many of these followers would later go on to become prominent leaders of the Ramakrishna Order during the thirty-four-year period between the death of her husband and her own passing in 1920. It is likely that Sarada Devi had more direct disciples in her lifetime than did Ramakrishna himself. It can be surmised that because of Sarada Devi and Sri Ramakrishna's sacred bond, the tradition was continued through the Holy Mother. This female leadership empowered women in the Ramakrishna Order, especially under the leadership of Swami Vivekananda, the most prominent disciple of Sri Ramakrishna.

The Role of Women in the Career of Swami Vivekananda

Apart from the Holy Mother, Sarada Devi, who was bestowed universal respect by the disciples of Sri Ramakrishna, a number of women played essential roles in the life and the career of Swami Vivekananda. Vivekananda is considered Ramakrishna's most celebrated disciple, largely due to the role he played in making the tradition of Sri Ramakrishna a global phenomenon. This tradition is one of the first Indic traditions (apart from Buddhism) to develop a considerable following outside of India.

Vivekananda, initially a skeptic, gradually became one of Ramakrishna's most ardent disciples. Known among the early disciples of Ramakrishna for his intellectual brilliance and rational bent of mind, as well as his charismatic personality, it was Vivekananda who organized the despondent followers into the Ramakrishna Order after the passing of their master.

Immediately after the passing of Ramakrishna, the young Swami Vivekananda undertook a period of wandering, traversing the length and breadth of the Indian subcontinent as a mendicant. He was dependent on the generosity of householders and gained considerable knowledge about the conditions of the lives of people in various parts of India under British rule. In 1893, at the encouragement of the Mahārāja of the kingdom of Ramnad, in southern India, Vivekananda left India to serve as a delegate at the first Parliament of the World's Religions, which was held in Chicago in September of that year. Vivekananda is famous for, among other things, his first address to the Parliament in Chicago. The young charismatic monk grabbed attention of the American audience when he addressed the crowd, to great acclaim, as "Sisters and Brothers of America." At a time when slavery was still alive, colonialism still a given reality, and the right of women to vote was still a dream, Vivekananda asserted the equality of genders and of races and nations, and he affirmed a vision of Hinduism as all-inclusive and all-accepting. Subsequent to his participation in the Parliament, Vivekananda set forth on a speaking tour of North America. He established the first Vedanta Society in New York in 1894. Upon his return to India, he also established, in 1897, the Ramakrishna Order and the Ramakrishna Mission. He undertook another tour of America and Europe shortly after this and finally returned to India, passing away on the 4th of July, 1902.

Many female devotees were involved during this period of the establishment of the order. The female leadership at this point marks a transition that is different from the Holy Mother's authority as the guru of the tradition. The involvement of these female devotees of Vivekananda, particular his Western devotees, was more directly organizational and financial in nature.

Both by his own accounts and those of contemporaries, much of Vivekananda's work in the last decade of his life was made possible by female devotees—specifically, by Western women. Some of these supporters, such as Sister Nivedita (1867–1911), undertook monastic vows, whereas others gave considerable moral and financial support as householder devotees. Nivedita, born Margaret E. Noble, became a particularly prominent leader in the movement, returning to India with Vivekananda, becoming a close friend of the Holy Mother, and establishing the Sarada Girls' School in Calcutta. Vivekananda's travels in America would likely not have been possible without the support of the women devotees. Vivekananda recognized the support and strength of these women:

> American women! A hundred lives would not be sufficient to pay my deep debt of gratitude to you! I have not words enough to express my gratitude to you … Last year I came to this country in summer, a wandering preacher of a far distant country, without name, fame, wealth, or learning to recommend me—friendless, helpless, almost in a state of destitution—and American women befriended me, gave me shelter and food, took me to their homes and treated me as their own son, their own brother. They stood my friends even when their own priests were trying to persuade them to give up the "dangerous heathen"—even when day after day their best friends told them not to stand by this "unknown foreigner, may be, of dangerous character." But they are better judges of character and soul—for it is the pure mirror that catches the reflection. (Vivekananda 1979: 248)

Vivekananda not only offers his gratitude to the women who supported him but also acknowledges their insightful foresight. Indeed, the support of Western women devotees did not cease after Swami Vivekananda's passing. The building of the Ramakrishna Temple at Belur Math, the monastic headquarters of the Ramakrishna Order—envisioned by Swami Vivekananda but not actually constructed until 1935—was financed by two American women: Helen Stroeber and a Mrs. Wooster of Boston (Gayatriprana, personal communication). These women sealed the lasting mark on the continuation of the tradition in India and the United States. However, among these female devotees, Sister Nivedita holds a particularly high place.

Sister Nivedita and Her Contributions to the Movement

One of Vivekananda's Western disciples who undertook monastic vows was Margaret E. Noble, an Irish woman better known by her monastic name, Sister

Nivedita. Noble pursued her schooling in London, at Halifax College. She found that she had a great love both for learning and teaching and began to pursue a career as a schoolteacher. A deeply religious young woman of the Christian faith, Noble did not find, despite her love for her teaching job, that her life was entirely fulfilled. She had questions that she did not find answered fully, either in the faith of her upbringing or in the scientific secular worldview of the late nineteenth century. Attending one of Swami Vivekananda's lectures in London in 1895, when he was on his way back to India from his first stay in America, Noble believed she had found her purpose in life:

> Suppose he had not come to London that time! Life would have been like a headless dream, for I always knew that I was waiting for something. I always said that a call would come. And it did. But if I had known more of life, I doubt whether, when the time came, I should certainly have recognized it. Fortunately, I knew little and was spared that torture … Always I had this burning voice within, but nothing to utter. How often and often I sat down, pen in hand, to speak, and there was no speech! And now there is no end to it! As surely I am fitted to my world, so surely is my world in need of me, waiting—ready. The arrow has found its place in the bow. But if he had not come! If he had meditated, on the Himalayan peaks! (Parlato)

Noble found her purpose in life when she encountered the young monk, Vivekananda. She and Vivekananda had many shared interests, particularly in regard to the spiritual life. Both shared a fascination with the teaching of the Buddha. And both were also concerned on a very deep level with the sufferings of the poor. Noble joined Vivekananda when he returned to India, where he administered her religious vows in 1898, and she took the name Nivedita, meaning one who has been given or dedicated to God. This was the beginning of her service to the mission of Sri Ramakrishna. That same year, Sister Nivedita established the Ramakrishna Sarada Mission Sister Nivedita Girls' School, which continues to serve girls in India today. After the passing of Swami Vivekananda, Nivedita felt increasingly drawn to the cause of India's independence from colonial rule. Tragically, this required her to distance herself from the Ramakrishna Order and Ramakrishna Mission. Due to theological and practical considerations, this organization has been, from its inception, steadfastly apolitical. Therefore, she committed herself to the service of the tradition and the poor, albeit outside the boundaries of the formal organization.

Nivedita also committed considerable time to writing, authoring a number of major works, including a book on Swami Vivekananda called *The Master as I Saw Him*. She dedicated herself to studying and disseminating knowledge about Hindu traditions in such works as *The Web of Life* and *Religion and*

Dharma as well as coauthoring, along with the famed Sri Lankan art historian and philosopher, Ananda K. Coomaraswamy, a work titled *Myths of the Hindus and Buddhists*.

Even though Nivedita was an influential female follower of the tradition and her leadership was unparalleled in the early twentieth century's patriarchal and colonial context, she emphasized in her theological works that divinity transcends gender. The same Goddess Kālī who manifests to the world as a Divine Mother, she argues, also appears in male forms: including Jesus Christ. Through such interpretation, she connects the tradition with Christianity, demonstrating that its theology is inclusive. In *The Story of Kālī*, written to explain the Goddess to a child, Sister Nivedita writes of Divine Mother's *māyā*, the game of "hide-and-seek" that She plays by appearing in many forms and manifestations:

> There is another game of hide-and-seek that the Great Mother plays. This is more like a fairy story. She hides sometimes in other people. She hides in anything. Any day you might see Her eyes, just looking into mother's, or playing with a kitten, or picking up a bird that had fallen from its nest. Under all these forms you may find God playing at hide-and-seek! When there is something to do for someone—Kali is calling us to play. We love that play. She Herself said once (She was hiding in someone, and He said it for Her), "Inasmuch as ye did it unto one of the least of these, My little ones, ye did it unto Me." Is not that like a fairy story! And what funny places She, the Great Mother, can hide in! Another time She said, "Lift the stone, and thou shalt find Me. Cleave the wood, and there am I!" Did you ever lift a stone or break a piece of wood to see what was inside? Did you ever think *that* was God at the heart of things? How beautifully Kali plays! You might find here *any*where! (Nivedita 2000: 108–9)

Nivedita's portrayal of the Mother Kālī is significant in the following feminist ways: (1) she imagines the Goddess as the Mother who is playful, not authoritarian like the typical male god; (2) the Goddess is omnipresent, equally present in animate and inanimate things; and (3) the Goddess's love is unconditional and is available to all.

Gender in the Tradition of Sri Ramakrishna: A Paradox

After analyzing the theological reverence to the divine feminine and role of some of the early female followers in the tradition, it is important to point out that the approaches to gender found in the tradition of Sri Ramakrishna present something of a paradox; for this institution is laden with male dominance. It is important to note that this paradox is not unique to this tradition. It can be found, to varying degrees and in varying ways, across the spectrum of Indian traditions and, indeed, across the world's religions.

It must, of course, be acknowledged at the outset that all traditions, to some extent, have historically participated in and upheld the dominance of a patriarchal paradigm in the societies in which they have been practiced. In some cases, this upholding of patriarchy is a direct and logical consequence of patriarchal assumptions at the heart of the teachings upon which the tradition is based: traditions in which, for example, God is a father, who is then mediated by an all-male ecclesiastical hierarchy. But in other cases—especially in the Indian traditions—the upholding of patriarchy is in tension with more gender-inclusive visions of the Divine at the theological core of the tradition. Furthermore, in these traditions, both the female and the male identities are seen as manifestations of a deeper, divine reality, and both men and women are generally seen as capable of attaining the heights of spiritual realization.

With regard to Indian traditions, it has been suggested by some scholars that the dominant patriarchy one observes in practice is a more recent overlay upon an ancient ethos with a strong emphasis on the divine feminine.[3] Neela Bhattacharya Saxena refers to this more ancient ethos as the "gynocentric matrix of Indic traditions" and sees it as essential to affirming the view of many of these traditions that the ultimate aim of the spiritual life is to transcend dualities such as gender in order to realize a state of nondual awareness (Saxena 2015: 17). The gynocentric matrix contributes to this realization by unsettling the patriarchal assumptions of conventional society: "Discovery of [this] gynocentric matrix allows [one] to speak forcefully of our spiritual identity, which extends beyond all dualities, including narrow notions of gender" (Saxena 2004: 41). Such nondual spiritual identity was certainly at the core of Ramakrishna's teachings.

One result of a culture of patriarchy being overlaid on a gynocentric deep structure is that it issues in the paradox of metaphysical belief in and profound reverence for the divine feminine principle, while simultaneously affirming patriarchy in practice by adhering to male domination on an institutional level. The tradition of Ramakrishna fits this convention quite well. It is based on the teaching of a figure whose deepest inspiration and primary object of devotion was the Mother Goddess. This Goddess Herself embodies in Her appearance and nature the paradox of simultaneously representing both a fierce guardian and a tenderly loving mother. This teaching is carried forward institutionally by an overwhelmingly male order of ascetic practitioners, many of whose gurus were initiated by a living goddess—the Holy Mother.

This overtly male-dominated tradition raises the question of how a tradition deeply rooted in Goddess worship is upheld and passed on by a male-dominated institution. Is this paradox in some way an outflow of the teaching or the personality of Sri Ramakrishna? Or is it more of an historical accident, an unavoidable reflection of the fact that the larger Indian culture in which this tradition has emerged is itself patriarchal, with its practice therefore inevitably reflecting this broader cultural reality? If one is rooted in this tradition while being simultaneously committed to feminism, the latter reading is more appealing, emphasizing that the essential vision of reality experienced and then expressed by Ramakrishna is gynocentric and ultimately transcendentalist in its orientation toward gender. In such a view, the male dominance of the institution that was developed to advance these teachings is simply a side effect of the times and the society in which this institution emerged. On this perspective, one may hope that as feminist consciousness becomes more widespread, the situation might be gradually rectified with greater female participation at the institutional level. Attractive though this option might be, it nonetheless raises the question of why a basically gynocentric vision of reality has not challenged the dominant patriarchy more forcefully and in a more revolutionary way than it actually has historically. Attending, therefore, to the teachings of Ramakrishna through a feminist lens may still be an illuminating project.

Let us now elaborate on one of Ramakrishna's teachings that might arguably have led the institution to relegate women to subservient roles.

"Woman and Gold": Addressing the Charge of Misogyny in the Teaching of Sri Ramakrishna

One charge that some have leveled against Sri Ramakrishna is that there is a misogynistic streak in his teaching. This charge arises from his many admonitions to his disciples regarding the dangers of "woman and gold." One indeed finds numerous passages in the recorded teachings of Ramakrishna where he gives warnings to his disciples about the temptations of women.

If one is attentive to the original Bengali language that Ramakrishna used, his actual words, *kāminī-kāñcana*, can be literally rendered as "woman and gold." However, a close examination of the context shows that this translation is an unfortunate one and has resulted in an interpretation of Ramakrishna as a misogynist. A much better translation of these terms, to get to the actual gist of Ramakrishna's teaching, is "lust and greed." These vices, not actual women or the substance of gold, are what Sri Ramakrishna finds problematic or obstacles to the spiritual life. Proof of this interpretation can be found in his discourses to female disciples, as Ramakrishna speaks with equal force about the dangers of *puruṣ-kāñcana* or "man and gold." It also must be pointed out that there is a marked difference in emphasis between Ramakrishna's discourses to those of his disciples, male and female, who were intent upon the monastic life, and those to his householder disciples. More of his discourses to monastic disciples have been recorded, which further skews our current perception of Ramakrishna. His instructions to monastics emphasize asceticism (where lust and greed are particularly perilous) but do not represent the totality of his views. Indeed, he approved of and saw it as quite natural for householder devotees to enjoy sexuality and to own possessions. His concern, in this regard, is that householders not become obsessed with material pleasures lest these become impediments to the spiritual life.[4]

The Question of Institutional Male Domination: A Comparison with Buddhism

However, the question arises: if the actual teaching of Sri Ramakrishna is itself free from misogyny, and if God realization and the practices leading to it are available to both men and women, why does this tradition continue to be institutionally male-dominated? Furthermore, this question is pertinent because Ramakrishna had both male and female disciples, and many of the female disciples have played major roles since the tradition's nascent stages. We have discussed the leadership of the Holy Mother and Sister Nivedita as well as the contributions of American women to the movement. One reason seems to be the fact that the Ramakrishna Order, in continuity with Śaṅkarācārya's Daśanāmi Order, is bound by the rules of that Order, some of which do affirm male domination. Most significantly, only male monks may give *dīkṣa*, or spiritual initiation with a *mantra*, to their disciples. But in the Ramakrishna tradition, the Holy Mother initiated thousands, including many monks of the Order. So, how can these two inconsistencies be reconciled?

A comparison of the tradition of Sri Ramakrishna with another Indic tradition with which it shares many similarities may be helpful in regard to the question of institutional male dominance. Buddhism, like the tradition of Sri Ramakrishna, is a tradition institutionally dominated by male ascetics, yet it is also a tradition in which the gynocentric matrix of Indic traditions is evident at the deepest level of its vision of reality. The Buddha's teachings and the practice of the Eightfold Path are available for all, men and women, despite any differences of caste, status, or ethnicity.

The Buddha, when famously asked by his aunt, Mahāprajāpatī (with the help of the monk, Ānanda), whether women were as capable as men of attaining *nirvāṇa*, replied without hesitation that women were no less capable in this regard. Although he was reluctant, at her urging, the Buddha instituted the women's *saṅgha*—the order of Buddhist nuns. He is also, however, said to have predicted that this institution of the women's *saṅgha* would reduce the lifespan of Buddhism over time, saying that this was why he did not open the *saṅgha* to women from the beginning. He also imposed a set of eight additional rules on the women's *saṅgha* that did not apply to the men's *saṅgha*.

From a feminist perspective, this is, of course, a deeply problematic episode in Buddhism. One is left with three possibilities. The first, and probably the most disturbing, of these is that the Buddha's reservations about establishing a women's *saṅgha* reflect the fact that even an enlightened being may have cultural blind spots, including an acceptance of patriarchy. The second possibility is that the Buddha was himself free from such blind spots but was pragmatically conforming to the norms of the patriarchal culture of Buddhism's birthplace. Or, finally, perhaps the reservations of the Buddha were not his at all but were placed in his mouth, so to speak, by later generations of compilers of Buddhist texts who themselves were patriarchal and biased. A prominent Buddhist feminist scholar, Rita Gross, among others, has wrestled with this issue and has reached the conclusion that it is women within religious traditions who finally need to assert their ability to engage in the tradition on an equal level with men, as consistent with the vision of the tradition's founder:

> The equality and common humanity of women and men was not the Buddha's major perception about gender, even after his enlightenment. Differences between women and men and the tensions that arise from their close proximity seem to have been much more evident to him. In short, seeing the negativities of androcentrism through women's eyes simply was not his issue. It took persistent women, fueled by their own experiences of suffering caused by patriarchy, to challenge him to do something unconventional and out of the ordinary regarding gender arrangements. This perhaps could be cited as a shortcoming of the Buddha, a limit to his omniscience, but it is also the unfortunate truth

> that women, not men, are usually the ones who push for non-patriarchal gender arrangements. This is not necessarily due to ill will on men's part, but simply to lack of experience and consciousness. (Gross 1993: 34–5)

Thus, it is women who have to push the boundaries, according to Gross. She goes on to narrate experiences in which male Buddhist leaders, such as the Dalai Lama, have shown openness to greater inclusion of women in the institutional life of the Buddhist *saṅgha* but who had to be made aware by their women devotees of the need for such inclusion. Men do not need to be misogynistic in order to be unaware that patriarchal arrangements are not simply a given part of the natural order of things. This sometimes needs to be pointed out to them. Gross's assessment offers a solution for women to reclaim Ramakrishna's teaching of the equality of male and female on the spiritual path, reverence to the divine feminine, and the leadership of women, as demonstrated by the examples of the Holy Mother and Sister Nivedita.

Conclusion: The Ramakrishna Tradition after Patriarchy

In the tradition of Ramakrishna, one can find abundant resources—theological, spiritual, and institutional—for affirming the equality of both men and women, even if the potential that these resources express has yet to be fully realized. Gender equality lies at the visionary core of this tradition—in the teachings of its founding figures—and at key points throughout its history in which women played pivotal roles. At the same time, male dominance persists in the tradition at the institutional level. Again, this is at least in part due to the wider patriarchal culture in which this tradition emerged and to constraints inherited from the earlier traditions from which it draws. It continues to restrict the right to bestow spiritual initiation only to male monks, with the major exception of the Holy Mother who initiated many of the teachers of those monks who currently make up the Ramakrishna Order. However, the egalitarian potential that is strongly present in the teachings of Ramakrishna, the divinity of the Holy Mother, and the leadership of Sister Nivedita has yet to be fully realized. The unique ideals present in Sri Ramakrishna's teachings and examples can be more fully manifested when women in the tradition have the option to assert themselves and confront the paradoxes that emerge when the profoundly egalitarian teachings of the founder are taken in tandem with women's lived experiences in patriarchal structures.[5]

Notes

1 There is, though, some ambiguity regarding the precise relationship of the Ramakrishna Order to the Daśanāmi Order. See Sinclair-Brull (1997: 23–6).
2 For more on how these ways of thinking are coded "masculine" or "feminine," see Alcoff and Potter (2015).
3 "More recent" here means more recent than the ancient ethos defined by Saxena's gynocentric matrix. Although "more recent" than gynocentrism, patriarchy in India is certainly ancient, being discernible as early as the Vedic literature itself. The question is one of relative chronology.
4 The question of possible misogyny in the teaching of Sri Ramakrishna is explored extensively—and deconstructed—by Swami Tyagananda and Pravrajika Vrajaprana in their jointly authored work titled *Interpreting Ramakrishna: Kālī's Child Revisited* (2010: 239–67).
5 The title of this section is a deliberate homage to Rita Gross's classic book, *Buddhism after Patriarchy.*

References

Akshaychaitanya, B. (2009). *The Compassionate Mother: The Oldest Biography of Sri Sarada Devi.* Translated by Swami Tanmayananda. Mayavati: Advaita Ashrama.

Alcoff, L., and P. Elizabeth (eds.) (2015). *Feminist Epistemology (Thinking Gender).* London: Routledge.

Gross, Rita (1993). *Buddhism after Patriarchy: A Feminist History, Analysis, and Reconstruction.* Albany: State University of New York Press.

Gambhirananda, Swami (1997). *Holy Mother Sri Sarada Devi.* Mylapore: Advaita Ashrama.

Hatcher, B. (1999). *Eclecticism and Modern Hindu Discourse.* Oxford: Oxford University Press.

Isherwood, C. (1965). *Ramakrishna and His Disciples.* Hollywood, CA: Vedanta Press.

Nikhilananda, Swami (trans.) (1942). *The Gospel of Sri Ramakrishna.* New York: Ramakrishna-Vivekananda Center.

Nivedita, Sister (2000). *Kali the Mother.* Mayavati: Advaita Ashrama.

Parlato, F. (ed.) "The Swami and the People He Knew: Sister Nivedita." *Swami Vivekananda.* Accessed July 14, 2017, from http://www.vivekananda.net/PPlHeKnew/SVDisciples/Nivedita.html.

Rambachan, A. (1994). *The Limits of Scripture: Vivekananda's Reinterpretation of the* Vedas. Honolulu: University of Hawaii Press.

Saradananda, Swami (2003). *Sri Ramakrishna and His Divine Play.* Translated by Swami Chetanananda. St. Louis, MO: Vedanta Press.

Saxena-Bhattacharya, N. (2004). *In the Beginning Is Desire: Tracing Kālī's Footprints in Indian Literature*. New Delhi: Indialog.

Saxena-Bhattacharya, N. (2015). *Absent Mother God of the West: A Kālī Lover's Journey into Christianity*. Lanham, MD: Lexington.

Sil, Narasingha P. (2003). *Divine Dowager: The Life and Teachings of Saradamani the Holy Mother*. Selinsgrove, PA: Susquehanna University Press.

Sinclair-Brull, W. (1997). *Female Ascetics: Hierarchy and Purity in an Indian Religious Movement*. London: Routledge.

Tapasyananda, Swami (1986). *Sri Sarada Devi: The Holy Mother*. Mylapore: Advaita Ashrama.

Tyagananda, Swami, and V. Pravrajika (2010). *Interpreting Ramakrishna: Kālī's Child Revisited*. Delhi: Motilal Banarsidass.

Vivekananda, Swami (1979). *Complete Works, Volume 6*. Mayawati: Advaita Ashrama.

Part Three

Androgyny, Gender Hybridity, and Fluidity

8

Divine Androgyny and the Play of Self-Recognition: Revisiting Some Issues in Gender Theory through an Unorthodox Interpretation of Ardhanārīśvara

Geoff Ashton

Introduction

Much of orthodox Indian philosophy centers around the following narrative of human suffering: gain-seeking actions (*karmans*) produce mental impressions or traces, these traces lead to rebirth in suffering, rebirth occurs in terms of past actions (*karmans*), and so on potentially without end. Due to its causal power, *karma* typically gets highlighted as the central problem in this account, with the solution involving knowledge of an unborn self that is wholly detached from action and its results. Taken for granted are gendered associations that get naturalized in terms of the classical Indian dichotomy of liberating self-knowledge and world-binding action. Recognition of one's freedom is conceived in terms of the authentication of a masculinized self over and against a feminized "world" that induces suffering by binding the individual to the causal field of action (*karma*).

The corresponding binaries of action/contemplation, bondage (to the world)/liberation (from the world), and feminine/masculine pervade not only orthodox Indian philosophy but also many of the artistic traditions of India. But Indian artists often evaluated these binaries differently than conservative thinkers and shunned the orthodoxy's disparagement of action, worldly association, and the feminine. This is particularly evident in Indian creation imagery and myths that proceed in terms of male and female principles. Excavations from as early as the Indus Valley period, for example, have unearthed objects that associate anthropomorphic features with the origin of the cosmos and point to ritual worship of both the phallus and the womb.[1] The *Ṛg Veda* and *Upaniṣads* report bi-gendered deities as primordial creators and the aboriginal source(s) out of which unified male-female elements comprise the universe.[2] And a number of *Purāṇic* myths have been inspired by (and were intended to clarify existing iconography concerning) India's foremost androgynous deity, Ardhanārīśvara. Represented at least as early as the first century CE, "The Lord Who is Half-Woman"—derived from *ardha* ("half"), *nārī* ("woman"), and *īśvara* ("lord" or "god")—usually gets portrayed in simple two-armed form; holds a bent posture at the head, torso, and right leg; and is split down the middle showing typically male features on the right half and female on the left.[3] Ardhanārīśvara has appeared in numerous theological contexts, was directly infused with cosmological significance, and displayed explicit narrative associations.

This essay explores a philosophical interpretation of the Ardhanārīśvara motif through the lens of the Pratyabhijñā system. A medieval school of thought from Kashmir, India, Pratyabhijñā reformulates the binaries noted above in order to disclose the nature of the god, Śiva—the deity most often associated with "The Lord Who Is Half-Woman." By situating the iconography and mythology of Ardhanārīśvara within Pratyabhijñā theology, I argue that the Ardhanārīśvara theme suggests neither a mere creation story nor just a means to transcending (and thereby overcoming) identities—contrary to Ellen Goldberg's feminist critique of the image (2002). Rather, it is a guide to enacting a play of self-recognition whereby one realizes the divine in all manifestations, even those that go beyond dualities (i.e., beyond the male-female binary toward alternative genders). From this, I suggest points of dialogue between the Ardhanārīśvara motif and contemporary gender theory. Far from repeating the gender biases of orthodox India, the Ardhanārīśvara image can be read as offering resistance to them in ways that both echo the concerns of contemporary gender theorists and might push existing debates on gender in new directions.

A Feminist Critique of Ardhanārīśvara and Śaivism: Ellen Goldberg's *The Lord Who Is Half-Woman*

Goldberg's recent study, *The Lord Who Is Half-Woman*, makes some valuable insights into Ardhanārīśvara's varied representations; commonalities among these depictions and their respective environments; and their sociocultural, intellectual, historical, and religious contexts. For one, she notes that, while many Indian gods and goddesses have been presented in dual-gender or sex-shifting form, androgynous representations have most often been associated with the god Śiva.[4] She supports this by calling attention to examples from major periods of South Asian civilization. Among them, Indus Valley artifacts that centered around phallus and womb worship present attributes that later became central to representations of Śiva: the Vedic god, Rudra, who likely has pre-Vedic origins and is a clear precursor to Śiva, gets portrayed in the *Śvetāśvatara Upaniṣad* as a bi-gendered creator god; the post-Vedic (e.g., Kushan period) Śiva emerged as the "quintessential" Ardhanārīśvara form; and Purānic stories of Ardhanārīśvara regularly involve Śiva and his female consorts, Pārvatī, Devī, Śakti, and Umā.[5] Second, Goldberg emphasizes the role of orthodox India in developing the Ardhanārīśvara motif in order to embellish its sacred texts. Attending to the sociological context of the ritual worship of Ardhanārīśvara, she identifies what she believes to be an underlying concern to preserve a conservative tradition of theology and philosophy. Sacred scriptural instructions regarding iconographic and textual inscriptions of the image conveyed the normative concerns of the brahmanical elite, argues Goldberg, through "short, factual, and non-optional list[s] of compulsory requirements needed [by religious practitioners] to identify the god" and which in turn were binding for image makers of Ardhanārīśvara.[6] Third, she contends that these same representations of *The Lord Who Is Half-Woman* were intended to promote orthodox Indian social norms. Androgynous representations of Śiva, for example, tended to portray him in his benevolent and peaceful forms (as opposed to his destructive manifestations), oftentimes together with other brahmanical images, as a way of domesticating him in accordance with traditional Indian values (e.g., ritual purification, assuming the role of householder). Goldberg makes clear the implications of this for gender identifications and roles: the image is nothing more than "an orthodox expression" that simply "repeat[s] normative assumptions and traditional idealizations of 'woman' and the 'feminine'" (2002: 143–4).[7]

But as important as Goldberg's study has been for advancing our understanding of the Ardhanārīśvara motif, it bears noting that not only was Ardhanārīśvara commonly depicted as Śiva; conversely, Ardhanārīśvara became one of the most popular iconographic forms for representing Śiva (Yadav 2000: 161).[8] Śaivas (devotees of Śiva) deliberately made use of the Ardhanārīśvara image in order to portray Śiva in their religious practices, and presumably they did so because the main features of this motif (e.g., its bi-gendered nature) had profound theological meaning.[9]

Goldberg might respond to this objection by claiming that, insofar as Ardhanārīśvara is a symbolic representation of Śaiva cosmology and theology, it expresses concerns that are typical of orthodox Indian soteriology, namely, the ultimate experience of nonduality through recognition of the illusoriness of empirical identities and worldly actions. She draws our attention to the visualization and meditation exercises of *haṭha yoga*, an historically long-standing branch of *yoga* associated with Śaivism wherein the adept strives to progressively internalize Śiva in his Ardhanārīśvara form according to appropriate iconographical features and precise ritual instructions. When these activities are brought to their completion, Ardhanārīśvara ceases to be a symbol at all. The aspirant awakens the deity within her own subtle body, dissolving the image within her heart and becoming one with the deity (Eliade 1969: 207–8; Goldberg 2002: 60–2). Goldberg explains how taking Ardhanārīśvara as a soteric goal involves dispensing with Ardhanārīśvara as an external object of worship:

> The desired goal of *haṭha yoga* ascetic and spiritual practice could be conceived of as a recognition or *reintegration* of the two cosmic principles formulated as Śakti and Śiva (or *yoni/liṅga*, sun/moon, *nāda/bindu*, ovum/semen, etc.) within the disciple's own body, similar to the comparative Western notion of *coniunctio oppositorum* ... the attained *yogin/ī* reverses the order of ... emanation [of a world of multiplicity] through a process in which she/he dissolves into undifferentiated or Brahman consciousness, element by element ... [I]gnorance (perceived here as duality and separateness) begins to dissolve, and individual distinction (*asmitā*, I-am-ness) is transcended ... [T]here is no perception of gender, time, space, and so on. There is only the conscious reflection (*darpaṇa*, *buddhi*) of authentic identity. (2002: 67–8)

Through a process that Goldberg terms "subtle androgynization," all opposites (sun/moon, life/death, male/female) are reunited in the practitioner's realization of her true identity as the dual-gendered Śiva. But this experience deepens even further. The effects of and compulsions to action (*karma*) "disappear or dissolve," and all polarities collapse in the realization of absolute nonduality (*advaita*) (2002: 76). Identification through distinction, including "all symptoms or signs of Ardhanārīśvara," completely falls away in this experience of undifferentiated consciousness (i.e., *Brahman* realization) (2002: 82). In keeping with her feminist interpretation of the image, Goldberg emphasizes that in the ultimate recognition of "neutrality" (*śūnyatā*), "there is no gender, no polarity, no form, and no remainder of any kind" (2002: 83).

While Goldberg's assessment of *haṭha yoga* (its links to the Ardhanārīśvara image and Śaivism, the nature of its peculiar soteric goals) is not necessarily inaccurate, it is nonetheless incomplete, and its implications are misleading. For one, her interpretation discounts the fact that the actual employment of these images may have been divorced (at least in part) from the predetermined norms for image making. As noted above, the Ardhanārīśvara image preceded the mythology and textual descriptions that standardized image making of the motif. From this, the image itself may have conveyed philosophical and theological significance that had primacy over the historically later appropriations made by the brahmanical orthodoxy. Second, while it is indeed true that Śaiva communities (which had great power in ensuring the continuity of the Ardhanārīśvara motif) were heavily influenced by the Indian orthodoxy, many of them creatively appropriated the beliefs, ideas, values, and practices of conservative brahmanism in terms of their own theological goals—goals that often clashed with those of the orthodoxy. This is particularly evident through consideration of the Pratyabhijñā school, the idealistic branch of medieval Kashmir Śaivism that developed India's most sophisticated and influential articulation of Śaiva theology and presented its philosophical frameworks as part of a broader axiological critique of the Indian orthodoxy. Not coincidentally, perhaps, Pratyabhijñā discourse receives no consideration in Goldberg's analysis of the interrelation between Śaivism generally and the philosophical, theological, and sociological implications of the Ardhanārīśvara motif. Examination of the parallels between Pratyabhijñā philosophy and Ardhanārīśvara iconography reveals that Goldberg captures only half of the story, as it were, of the meaning of the androgynous Śiva and, along with this, fails to disclose some important dimensions of gender in Indian philosophy and art. In order to fill this gap in our understanding of the Ardhanārīśvara motif, let us investigate the Pratyabhijñā system.

Ardhanārīśvara and the Replication of Orthodox Binaries in Kashmir Śaiva Ontology: The Puzzle of Cosmogony and Transcendence

In both the Śaiva ritual usage of Ardhanārīśvara imagery and the Pratyabhijñā philosophy of Śiva-Śakti, bondage involves a split between gendered principles that occurs in and through the generation of the cosmos. Liberation, meanwhile, is in both contexts equivalent to recognition of one's identity with a fused male-female Śiva body that has reabsorbed the creative process.[10] Given this homologous patterning of the relationship between Śiva and his female consort (Pārvatī or Śakti), examination of the Pratyabhijñā account of the unfolding and cessation of the cosmos can give valuable clues to the metaphysical and spiritual meaning of the Ardhanārīśvara image.[11]

According to this story of the being, becoming, and dissolution of reality, the cosmos is the body of Śiva. In its aboriginal state, this body represents undifferentiated consciousness resting in pure potentiality. But this gets disturbed by the latent presence of the "Mother of the Universe," Śakti, who stirs Śiva from his self-containment and polarizes consciousness into two: a passive, static, masculine subject (Śiva) and an active, ever-changing feminine object (Śakti). These inseparable principles comprise the dual relationship of lived experience, and their vibrant interplay unfurls through thirty-four ensuing stages of rupture, eventually giving way to *māyā* or phenomenal reality as we ordinarily experience it. This is problematic for a couple reasons. First, as Śakti dresses herself in the seductive illusions of *māyā*, Śiva correspondingly forgets his true nature as an original unity with Śakti. Unified subjectivity and being (Śiva) bifurcate into two: a world of multiplicity (Śakti) and an isolated empirical I (Śiva). But Śakti represents not just the *other* to Śiva. Literally meaning "power" in Sanskrit, "Śakti" represents Śiva's power (or powers) that manifest as if operating of their own accord—that is, as if they are happening *to* the I instead of deriving *from* the I.

Prakāśa and *vimarśa* mark the two poles of this unfolding body of consciousness. *Prakāśa* represents Śiva as the self-revealing light of transcendental consciousness that illuminates all things. *Vimarśa*, meanwhile, enacts the *śaktis* or powers that emanate a real world of diverse beings. Traditional commentators often use the mango seed-mango tree analogy in order to explicate this. Just as the characteristics of a mango tree lie dormant in a mango seed, so too does *vimarśa* (the active phase) rest latently within the phase of passive alertness (*prakāśa*), wherein the seeds of the manifest universe are preserved. Conversely, as a mango tree begets mangos, which themselves bear mango seeds, each phase of procreation, or *vimarśa*, generates further seeds of potentiality that germinate during the period of rest in order to later bring about the next phase of action-production (*vimarśa*). But this leads to a curious problem: just as vibrant *vimarśa* divides a self-contained one-without-an-other into a multitude (e.g., one mango seed eventually produces numerous *other* mango seeds), it creates diversity in the phenomenal world and causes the previously unified Śiva body to thereby forget its true nature as self-revealing pure consciousness.

In making sense of this curious situation, Pratyabhijñā thinkers drew upon many of the core themes, ideas, and conceptual binaries of the orthodox philosophical systems. Advaita (or "Nondual") Vedānta is perhaps the most conservative of these, and it had a tremendous influence upon the Pratyabhijñā school. It recognizes that our active participation in a feminine-gendered world (*māyā*) binds us more and more to illusory empirical identities, including our own self-identifications. To counter this, Advaita Vedāntins advocate knowing the true self to be undefiled by action (*karma*) and ignorance, and they ground the authentic I in a single ultimate reality or cosmic consciousness (*Brahman*) that stands juxtaposed against *māyā*. The Pratyabhijñā system similarly operates with these three associated dichotomies: action/knowledge, bondage/liberation, and feminine/masculine. Moreover, it advocates a reversal of consciousness' unfolding into a field of action and diversity, employing philosophy in order to redirect consciousness toward the transcendence of its mundane condition.

My analysis thus far corroborates Goldberg's findings in her own study of the interrelation between Śaivism and the Ardhanārīśvara icon. Particularly similar to *haṭha yogic* practitioners who transcend their individuality through a *coniunctio oppositorum* of gendered principles (i.e., male and female, Śiva and Śakti) and dissolve worldly identities in a cosmic, undifferentiated consciousness, Pratyabhijñā philosophers believed that created reality is comprised of a fractured multitude that gets reconciled through a contemplative knowing that recuperates the primordial unity of an androgynous Śiva consciousness. This unity, Pratyabhijñā philosophers argued, entails the overcoming of gender identities. This would seem to suggest that the meaning of the Ardhanārīśvara image in its Śaiva contexts replicates the normative assumptions of the Indian orthodoxy, including the conceptual binaries noted above. But consider the following paradox: in the Pratyabhijñā orientation, consciousness spins out its creation from powers that originally belong to Śiva. The driving force behind the unfurling of consciousness is the desire or volition of Śiva himself. However, Śiva qua the individual subject experiences phenomenal reality as a field of ignorance and suffering that happens to him as if against his will. In other words, Śiva undergoes a loss of wholeness and power due to the enactment of his own creative intentionality.[12] This raises a puzzle: why would a ubiquitous, omniscient, all-powerful being (i.e., Śiva) voluntarily bifurcate into two and endure a diminishing of his self-knowledge and power? The following section responds to this question by demonstrating how the Ardhanārīśvara motif actually contests the norms and doctrines of the brahmanical orthodoxy with which Goldberg associates the image.

Ardhanārīśvara and the Absorption of Orthodox Binaries into the Myth of Śiva-Śakti: From the Mirror of the Self to Performing Recognitive Self-Awareness as the Actor-Dancer

In anticipation of the Pratyabhijñā reply to this paradox and its implications for reinterpreting the Ardhanārīśvara motif, consider two common features from among the various representations of Ardhanārīśvara. First, the Pārvatī (or Śakti) half of the deity is sometimes portrayed holding a mirror in one of her hands.[13] Second, Ardhanārīśvara is often portrayed as a performing dancer, with one of the names associated with this deity including "Ardhanārīnaṭeśvara" or "The Lord of Dance Who Is Half-Woman."[14]

To examine the possible meaning of Pārvatī's mirror, let us further explore how the core concepts of Pratyabhijñā philosophy (namely, *prakāśa* and *vimarśa*) are much more than cosmological. *Prakāśa*, for example, refers not just to the aboriginal Śiva as a body of unified consciousness and being wherefrom a world of duality unfolds. Instead, it signifies a phase wherein consciousness begins to withdraw upon itself by reuniting the manifold differentiations. One by one, the diversity of phenomena and their underlying principles or stages of manifestation become reabsorbed into pure being; all phenomena reveal that they are mere reflections of the light of consciousness that illuminates them.[15] Accordingly, *prakāśa* denotes not just a phase of potentiality but also one of return: division and multiplicity get reassimilated into the universal, undivided, and transcendent consciousness that is Paramaśiva (or "The Ultimate Śiva"). This points to that most characteristic feature of Śiva's creative intentionality: the growth of recognitive awareness. Whereas during the *vimarśa* phase of Śiva's self-bifurcation empirical objects get revealed *as objectified others*, during the *prakāśa* phase these same objects manifest in order to give birth to self-awareness through the other. Depictions of the female half of Ardhanārīśvara holding a mirror can be viewed correspondingly. Pārvatī's mirror gets angled not in order to see herself but so that Śiva (the "I") can perceive his own reflection together with his other, Pārvatī. Unifying male and female elements in a single frame conveys not just the generation of new life. Going beyond creation myth, it indicates hidden meanings that are made explicit in the Pratyabhijñā doctrine of *prakāśa*. The female half of Ardhanārīśvara becomes the means by which Śiva recognizes himself; Pārvatī (or Śakti) *is* the mirror of self-recognition.[16]

The underlying meaning of *vimarśa* further highlights how Śiva's androgyny is a mechanism for the devotee's recognizing herself in and through the other.

Recall that the *vimarśa* phase sets in motion consciousness's *othering* of itself and that this corresponds to the emergence of Śiva's other, Śakti. But this is only half the story in this narrative account of reality's unfolding and reabsorption.[17] After reflecting a distinct other, during the *prakāśa* phase *vimarśa* enacts a hermeneutic retrieval: consciousness bends back upon itself and gives way to reflective self-awareness or the recognition that the empirical object is meant for the subject's own self-recognition in the other. Rather than occurring separately, *prakāśa* and *vimarśa* are here involved in the same synthetic function by which the seeming otherness of a world of multiplicity gets recovered in the discernment of unifying oneness. Importantly, identity and differentiation do not get elided in a cosmic, nondual ocean of bliss, as it does with Advaita Vedānta's conception of *Brahman*. Rather, the alterity of others gets preserved in the midst of their being seen as endowed with the same essential consciousness as oneself.

This reexamination of Pratyabhijñā terminology provides valuable clues to the question of why an omnipotent Śiva would voluntarily *other* himself. As just explained, the field of myriad others is not devoid of consciousness. Rather than concealing consciousness, it reveals it. Furthermore, distinction is not a function of *māyā* (illusion); it does not stand counterposed to consciousness, as Advaita Vedānta argues. To the contrary, consciousness enjoys its own proliferation through distinction and time because its unfolding is a mode of consciousness itself (i.e., the *vimarśa* aspect). This has deep soteriological implications: Śiva undergoes this bifurcation in order to make space for an ongoing play of separation and return. The Pratyabhijñā philosopher, Abhinavagupta, explains,

> The Supreme Lord, who has the nature of awareness, makes His own Self into an object of cognition, even though it is not an object of cognition, because the Cognizer is unitary ... As He recognitively apprehends [*parāmṛśati*] His Self, so, because everything is contained within Him, He appears as blue, etc.[18]

The world and our place in it (as alienated subjects) is born of Śiva's desire for an inner blissful vibration that moves from union to bifurcation to self-recognition in the other. In brief, Śiva undergoes his own self-fragmentation because without an other, he could not play.

As explained in the previous section, this recovery of primordial union with the other—as symbolized in the female half of Ardhanārīśvara holding the mirror—entails retrieval of the powers (*śaktis*) that had been lost during the *othering* phase of consciousness. This has significant implications for how Pratyabhijñā thinkers theorized that most essential concern of India's religio-philosophical traditions: *karma* or action. *Karma* is often associated with the *vimarśa* phase of consciousness, wherein gain-seeking actions create division between the individual subject and the object as yet to be obtained (but not still as *other*). But according to the Pratyabhijñā school, only those actions born of ignorance about one's true identity are damaging in this way.[19] The more pressing theological problem is the will of the imagination. The limitation of the individual agent results from the self-forgetfulness of one's perfection as Śiva, and this can be recuperated through a shift in imagining oneself in relation to the field of otherness and action (*vimarśa*). However, this shift requires the obtainment of various powers (*śaktis*) to creatively reenact the play of Śiva-Śakti. Through the practice of contemplating ideas such as "I am Śiva"—an act of imagining that can be performed in the here and now independently of past deeds (*karmans*)—the adept experiences "the actual state of affairs of objects as the emanation of monistic Consciousness" (Lawrence 1999: 63). This does not involve a wholesale elimination of thought patterns and conceptual constructions (per the Advaita Vedānta cognitive model). Rather, it entails the obtainment of power over them through the realization that they are to be determined not by the object but by the subject in whom the object has been absorbed.

This has significant implications for both the object and the empirical subject. Instead of appearing as resting in itself, the absorbed object presents itself as desiring relatedness and recognition in the intentional awareness of a conscious subject. The individual ego likewise decenters or purifies itself of its limitedness with a view to recentering itself in the relational middle between cognized object and (limited) cognizing subject. Arindam Chakrabarti explains, "Repose becomes freedom in every sense when the heart witnesses its own great power of creating and effacing differences and relishes the egoless 'middle' of that process of tasting any sensation or experience without getting fettered to either the taster or the tasted" (2005: 35). Due to this retrieved power (*śakti*), one now perceives the object as simply pretending to be distinct in its otherness. Recognizing the object as an emanation of consciousness, the subject enters into the interiority of the other. This reveals to the individual agent an additional capacity: namely, the ability to experiment with invariant structural features that manifest within objects. Through participation in the rich visualization exercises of Kashmir Śaivism, for example, one's consciousness awakens to a ceaseless desire to propagate meaning by disclosing every nook and cranny of the object. One's attitude toward the object transforms from literal mindedness to polymorphic mindedness. With the object no longer a mere *other*, all tiredness vanishes in "exploring the unending contentment of self-discovery" (Chakrabarti 2005: 33). Immersion in a world of multiplicity is now found to be both liberating and rapturous as the adept seizes upon her power as a relation maker, revealing objects in their unhiddenness out of a desire for wonder and as an expression of her power to reenact the narrative play of Śiva-Śakti.

Contextualizing the representation of Śiva within the Pratyabhijñā concern for recovering the powers of self-recognition anticipates my analysis of the second feature of Ardhanārīśvara imagery noted at the start of this section: Ardhanārīśvara as Ardhanārīnaṭeśvara or "The Lord of Dance Who Is Half-Woman." This particular depiction of the androgynous god expresses a point of resistance toward the Indian orthodoxy—something adhered to not just by Pratyabhijñā thinkers but by Kashmir Śaivas generally. The Pratyabhijñā philosopher, Vasugupta, nicely articulates this opposition when he writes, "The self [*ātmā*] is the actor. The stage is the inner self. The spectators are the senses ... A compact mass of delusion, the soul is subject to *karma*" (3.9–3.11, 3.36 [Dyczkowski 1987: 113–16, 153]). Conservative schools of Indian thought (Advaita Vedānta foremost among them) hold that active involvement (*karma*) in a feminized field of diversity (e.g., *māyā*) is an obstacle to spiritual liberation. Vasugupta's assertion similarly recognizes the perils of *karma*. However, his emphasis upon the liberated self as a dance performer secures worldly involvement by reformulating bondage in terms of a lack of power over the will of the imagination. "Delusion" (or ignorance) reproduces worlds and propels one into relation with others by "acting out" one's compulsions. By contrast, the liberated agent is a kind of theatrical actor-dancer who imaginatively explores alternative identities in and through powers of cognition ("I am Rama," "I am Hamlet") and action (the actor's performing the role of Rama, Hamlet, etc.). Moreover, this mode of performativity enacts a deep identification with the other (i.e., one's audience) in order to spawn new worlds and relations in terms of a kind of transpersonal consciousness.

I argue that this reflects typically Śaiva associations of freedom with power—and not just powers of contemplation but of actively constructing reality. Meanwhile, when construing the meaning of Ardhanārīśvara as Ardhanārīnaṭeśvara through a Pratyabhijñā lens, the image signifies the totality that lies not just behind *but among* all possible dualities—for example, subject/object, action/knowledge, bondage/liberation, feminine/masculine. The associations of Ardhanārīśvara with fertility and abundant growth can be understood accordingly. The androgynous Śiva dancer represents not just the reproductive power of nature (to generate new material creations) but also the power of I-consciousness to unify the cosmos by performing its own growth in recognitive awareness.

This interpretation challenges Goldberg's findings concerning the philosophical and theological associations of the Ardhanārīśvara image. Realizing one's identification with Śiva in his androgynous form entails not just the transcendence of dualities and recognizing the emptiness of identifications, it involves recovering the powers (*śaktis*) through which one radically affirms and creatively interacts with all objects as expressions of the play intentionality of consciousness. Out of a desire for constantly separating off from and rediscovering his identity with the other, the Śaiva devotee engages in an endless drama of hide and seek. Having mastered the powers of cosmic creation, the adept encounters phenomenal reality as a theater for manifesting his agential freedom. The other, meanwhile, is not a mere projection of the adept's wish fulfillments. Rather, the other gets experienced as the objectification of Śiva consciousness. One's awareness now enters into the interiority of the other and imaginatively performs the act of *being* that other, ultimately with the purpose of focusing one's attention to the relational middle between self and other. By interpreting one's own lived reality as a theater play contained within the field of consciousness and freedom, one encounters the world as the stage whereupon the self adopts all roles. Accordingly, the Śaiva practitioner does not seek an overcoming of his active involvement in the world, his relations with others, or his self-identifications. Rather, he fills the world with ecstasy and wonder as an expression of his own divine, creative will.

Conclusion: Toward a Dialogue between Kashmir Śaivism, Ardhanārīśvara, and Contemporary Gender Theory

By way of a rather long conclusion, I offer some thoughts on how gender theory and Pratyabhijñā philosophy might be able to converse with one another through the image of Ardhanārīśvara.

Gender Categories as Instruments of Ontological Analysis

In keeping with contemporary gender theory, Pratyabhijñā thinkers hold gender identity and gendered representations to be central categories of analysis. Consider that Kashmir Śaivism represents an axiological challenge to the Indian orthodoxy, with the Pratyabhijñā system refuting and/or reformulating many basic terms within brahmanical discourse. Though thinkers such as Utpaladeva and Abhinavagupta never developed gender as a philosophical theme to the same extent that they did other issues (e.g., *karma*, *prakāśa*, etc.), they reject the essentialism of orthodox Indian thought and reevaluate the correlative dichotomizations of action/contemplation, bondage/liberation, and feminine/masculine. Importantly, they dispute the orthodox assumption that liberation corresponds to masculinity. Contrary to many gender theorists, however, Pratyabhijñā philosophers took "feminine" and "masculine" to be categories of ontological analysis. Irreducible to a sociological phenomenon, gender is thoroughly written into the fabric of things.[20] One might argue that these are nothing more than metaphors for modes of mental activity that project the illusion of difference. But there is little to suggest that Kashmir Śaivas did not hold these categories to be metaphysical principles. Further, the gendered difference between self and other is not illusory; it is simply incomplete insofar as the recognition of such difference is not seen to rest in the repose of Śiva consciousness.

Gender as Relational

Gender studies tends to focus upon constructions of gender through relations between and across genders.[21] The Pratyabhijñā system echoes this by situating the feminine and masculine genders in relation to each other and acknowledging the deep interconnectedness of the two—a stance that is in deliberate contrast with the orthodoxy, which often emphasizes either the ultimate illusoriness of cross-gender relations (Advaita Vedānta) or the radical disjunction of masculine and feminine (consider the Sāṃkhya school). The soteriological ideal of Kashmir Śaivism as symbolized in Ardhanārīśvara exhibits the primacy of gender relations. Liberating self-realization excludes neither the feminine gender (contrary to orthodox Indian soteriologies) nor gender as such; difference between the genders does not get negated, nor does the ideal of androgyny in Kashmir Śaivism promote sameness between genders. Central to Kashmir Śaiva liberation, gender identification includes all genders and their cross-relations as essential to the self's natural state. Further, Kashmir Śaivism does not approach gender as a freestanding category but as one that intersects with other relations of power, such as sexuality, class, ethnicity, and religion. The tantric-yogic rituals of medieval Kashmir Śaivism, for example, contribute to a larger social, cultural, and political critique of the structures of subordination and power on display in orthodox brahmanism.[22] Kashmir Śaivas were largely intent upon antagonizing the power dynamics of the Indian orthodoxy, including those that essentialized gender identities and gendered representations. This critique was often waged by reversing orthodox thinking about these issues, such as by denaturalizing gender identities, gendered representations, and gender relations, in order to bring them into the domain of interrogation.

Power of the Feminine and Power-in-Common

In some respects, we can understand the Pratyabhijñā system as an inquiry into the life of power. Not only does this examination affirm feminine power, power itself gets feminized. Śakti is both the consort of Śiva and power itself. Derived from the root verb, √*śak*, or "to be capable of," the term *śakti* both refers to the goddess, Śakti, and connotes "power" as the ability to move consciousness in particular directions. This runs counter to the paternalistic and oftentimes misogynistic tendencies exhibited within orthodox Indian culture and early Western theorizing about gender. Pratyabhijñā thinkers organized femininity and masculinity according to different structures than, for example, Freud (for whom women were disfigured and had to accept their lack of a penis) or Lacan (who situates femininity and masculinity according to different unconscious arrangements than Freud but still reduces the feminine to a supplementary role in the "phallic" organization). Quite the contrary, one might read Kashmir Śaiva myth and its ontology as suggesting that men must learn to accept their lack of a vagina and the subordination of masculinity to feminine power.

Having said that, in Kashmir Śaiva myth and metaphysics, Śakti can be viewed as secondary to Śiva insofar as she is to be (re)acquired and controlled by her male lover. Of principal concern in Śaivism is the story of Śiva, while Śakti plays only a supporting role as Śiva's consort—a consort who gets lost or misplaced and later repossessed by Śiva.[23] This reveals a curious feature of the Śaiva conceptualization of power: at one moment power is Śakti herself (the goddess who reigns over Śiva), while at another moment the *śaktis* belong to Śiva (even when they are estranged from him, he is the agent of their being lost and recovered). Puzzling questions result from this: is Ardhanārīśvara a combination of two genders, or is he the extension of one essentially male deity with bisexual features; is power Śakti's alone, or do Śakti (and her various *śaktis*) belong to Śiva; is power Śakti's to own and voluntarily give to Śiva, or are Śakti and her *śaktis* subordinate to the will of Śiva? Various Śakta cults have responded to the subordination of the feminine in Indian culture by venerating the goddess as the supreme being, emphasizing creation as emerging from the female body (it is Śakti's body, not Śiva's, that divides into male and female halves) and depicting the right (i.e., dominant) side of the androgynous image's body as female and the left as male, which is contrary to the practice of depicting the right, superior side of the dual-gendered body as male.[24]

Another response to these questions is to claim that the iconography and mythology of Ardhanārīśvara leave open the question, "To whom do the *śaktis* belong?" Indeed, power is gendered, but its gender is ambiguous and constantly shifting in the relational between-ness of Śiva and Śakti at play. Seen in this light, power is perhaps better conceived as shared, irreducible to either gendered pole, and having a normative dimension: power is to be exercised not with a view to "power-over-and-against" but "power-in-common." Neither gender has absolute power over its other. Rather, the two are mutually complementary. Seen in this light, the Ardhanārīśvara image does not convey the hostility of a power polemic between sexes (as in Freud's theory and some contemporary feminist writings) or a more subtle subordination of one gender to the other (via a supplementary role, as in Lacan's thinking). Rather, we observe a creative tension wherein true power emerges through bringing feminine and masculine energies into right relationship.

Enacting Gender through Dramatic-Dance Performance

Gender is performed, contemporary theorists tell us, rather than essential to one's nature. This critique of traditional thinking about gender in Western literature is reflected in Pratyabhijñā discourse, which counters not only the ortho-*doxy* of India but its ortho-*praxy* as well. Consider its various soteriological practices (some of which have been discussed briefly above). Whether they be performances of ritual, visualization, and mantra exercises, or logical syllogisms, these exercises enable the Śaiva adept to realize her true identity as Śiva by reenacting the mythico-ritual play of Śiva-Śakti. Through these enactments, the play of Śiva-Śakti becomes realized as a model for the movements of the practitioner's own consciousness in its varied spheres of activity. Upon recognizing that the true self is the actor (*naṭa*) in this cosmic drama, action and cognition are no longer juxtaposed but are recognized as different modes for expressing one's identity with the narrative unfolding and return of consciousness. Moreover, by enacting one's true identity à la the model of the dance performer, the very performance of the dance-like movements of Śiva-Śakti gets realized as the end itself. Free from the compulsive desires and habits of action of the *karmic* actor, and yet fully engaged in the world (its conventions, limitations of time, space, etc.), performing the androgynous gender of Śiva as the dancer-actor represents both the means and the goal of liberation. The adept simultaneously affirms self-identity qua worldly categories, specifically gendered identities, and enters into relation with others while retaining a measure of detachment from her identities and her relations. Instead of operating from narcissistic attachment, the Śaiva adept establishes psychical distance with respect to her personal life stories in order to *perform* herself and her relation to the other rather than merely *acting out* herself as juxtaposed against the other.[25]

Exploring Multiple Gendered Identities through Renarrativization

Kashmir Śaiva metaphysics is best understood narratologically, that is, in terms of a narrative interplay of Śiva and Śakti that leads to the realization of the self as the dance performer who brings into being a world of dualities and then reabsorbs them (without eliding or reducing them to a single gender) through the growth of recognitive self-awareness. Gender studies, of course, is well-known for its challenging grand narratives. But the story of Śiva-Śakti is better understood as a meta-narrative that, in almost postmodern-like style, liberates its adherents from the fixity of social conventions, empirical identities, and so on. That which enables the adept to successfully challenge the naturalization of categories is *śakti* (power), whose recovery gets represented in the figure, Ardhanārīśvara. Power is liberating in both Kashmir Śaivism and gender theory because it disturbs, among other things, the hegemony of gender constructs and oversimplified male-female difference. However, for Kashmir Śaivas this occurs in order to make room for imaginative exploration of plural femininities and masculinities. Keeping in view the central problematic of Kashmir Śaivism—namely, forgetting one's true identity with the unending play of consciousness—the solution entails discovering (and rediscovering) different expressions of self-identity (including gendered identities) through the renarrativization of one's own life. This postulation is not incompatible with an observation held by most gender theorists: the development of gender identity is an ongoing process based upon sociocultural circumstances and so on. However, in contrast with those theorists who advocate a kind of gender neutrality, Kashmir Śaivism advocates celebrating the diversity of gender identities as expressions of the play of Śiva-Śakti. Indeed, we should resist naturalizing the self according to fixed identities, but this need not lead to cancelling empirical identities. The goal of the Pratyabhijñā system is not the realization of disembodiment, gender neutrality, or escape from the "prison of gender" but unending investigation of the self through its countless manifestations—including its variegated masculinities and femininities as well as those gender minorities that oppose gender binarism, such as "queer."[26] In this respect, the ideal of Ardhanārīśvara can be understood as radically inclusive: its challenge to the dichotomization of genders exceeds even masculine-feminine binaries in order to recognize all possible manifestations as expressions of one's desire for self-exploration.

Notes

1 *Liṅga*-shaped objects (likely part of a cult of phallus worship) and artifacts devoted to "female fertility deities" have been unearthed from Indus Valley civilization sites. These findings may anticipate historically later imagery of Śiva with prominent upward phallus (*ūrdhvaliṅga*). Phallus and earth goddess worship appear to have been especially prevalent in the non-Aryan tribes of this period. For more on this topic, see Goldberg (2002: 146).

2 *Puruṣa* and *prakṛti* are examples of generative principles that pertain to male and female genders, respectively, and are found in this early literature. One of the more well-known creation myths from the *Ṛg Veda* is the *Hiranyagarbha Sūkta* ("Hymn of the Golden Womb").

3 Ardhanārīśvara art originated and evolved significantly during the Kushan era (30–375 CE), while its "golden age" is the Gupta period (320–550 CE). For more on this, see Goldberg (2002: 13) and Rao (1916: 330–2).

4 Tamil poets frequently expressed devotion to Viṣṇu, for example, as a kind of Ardhanārīśvara figure.

5 Among the *Purāṇas* that depict Ardhanārīśvara as a fused Śiva-Pārvatī, the *Śiva Purāṇa* relates how the creator god, Brahmā, in search of help in generating male and female beings (after the male Prajāpati deities were unable to procreate by themselves), summons Ardhanārīśvara, who then unites the *liṅga* and *yoni* (as symbolized in the deities, Śiva and Pārvatī), respectively. See Kramrisch (1981: 200–3, 207–8). Other *Purāṇas* (including the *Liṅga*, *Vāyu*, *Viṣṇu*, *Skaṇḍa*, *Kūrma*, and *Markaṇḍeya Purāṇas*) tell of a Rudra-Śiva deity appearing as Ardhanārīśvara and emerging from various parts of Brahmā's body in order to quicken the pace of creation. See Kramrisch (1981: 200–8).

6 Goldberg (2002: 17) concurs with Dagens (1989: 153). She elaborates on Dagens' claim: "Indian temple architecture and, to a lesser extent, Indian art, have for the most part extrapolated their formulaic descriptions from preexisting monuments" (Dagens 1989: 151). In other words, Dagens argues that image precedes text, and this is clearly the status with images of Ardhanārīśvara (2002: 17). These prescriptions for image production were likely pan-Indian.

7 In support of her argument, Goldberg draws upon Pollock's work on how the *śāstric* tradition typifies the "desire to codify" and "textualize" the iconographic

tradition by extending its reach to all domains of human activity, teaching people "what they should and should not do." See Pollock (1989: 15, 18–19); c.f., Goldberg (2002: 19–20).

8 This can be observed in temples and shrines devoted to Śiva throughout India and Southeast Asia.

9 Interestingly, Śiva's consort, Pārvatī, does not appear during the earliest phase of Śaiva iconography (the post-Vedic era), though his Ardhanārīśvara form does. This suggests that the Ardhanārīśvara image was an independent interpretation of Śiva, not a combination of the two deities (Śiva and Pārvatī [or Śakti]). For this and other reasons, it is likely that the Ardhanārīśvara representation originally derived its female iconography from Indus Valley civilization conceptions of the Mother Goddess, which is entirely lacking in the brahmanical collection of deities from this early period of Śaiva art. See Goldberg (2002).

10 Realizing ultimate identification with Śiva is not the goal of all Śaiva traditions, many of which worship Śiva merely as an object of devotion (and hence preserve the separation between devotee [the empirical subject] and object of devotion [Śiva]). In the Pratyabhijñā system, however, liberation entails collapsing this gap between devotee and Śiva.

11 I borrow this notion of a "narrative ontology" from David Lawrence (1999).

12 In this respect, Śaivas adhere to an ontology that is agent-centered or what Lawrence terms an "agential narrative ontology." See Lawrence (1999).

13 This gets depicted in a number of Ardhanārīśvara representations, including a mid-first-century Kushan era stela in the Mathura Museum, a sculpture at the Paraśurāmeśvara Temple in Bhubaneswar, and a sculpture at Darasuram. See Dehejia (1997: 115).

14 Ardhanārīśvara is known by other names, such as Ardhanāranārī ("The Half Man-Woman"), Ardhanārīśa ("The Lord Who Is Half-Woman"), and Ardhanārīnaṭeśvara ("The Lord of Dance Who Is Half-Woman"), among others. Correspondingly, one of the most popular portrayals of Śiva is as the dancing god, Nāṭarāja.

15 Mark Dyczowski explains how the recovery of primal unity occurs in terms of Śiva's *prakāśa* aspect: "Typically, the Pratyabhijñā establishes that all things participate in the one reality by arguing that nothing 'shines' (i.e., appears, manifests or exists in its apparent form) if it is not illuminated by the light of consciousness [*prakāśa*]. If phenomena were to be anything but 'light,' they could not 'shine,' that is, exist" (1987: 26). Literally meaning "light" in the context of Kashmir Śaivism, *prakāśa* means the light of transcendental consciousness that illuminates all phenomena and can never be separated from or restricted to the seer (*prakāśaka*) or the seen (*prakāśya*). Pratyabhijñā literature regularly draws upon analogies with the properties of light in order to explain the nature of manifestation as necessarily sharing in Śiva consciousness. It represents the power of self-revelation by which

supreme consciousness (Śiva) shines and all things eventually become manifest as identical with it. In short, *prakāśa* designates the unity of Śiva and Śakti, whereby *prakāśa* is *sva-prakāśa* or self-aware luminosity. In this state, Śiva is always aware of himself as the supreme lord through a kind of immediate, *a priori* intuition.

16 Not coincidentally, the very name of the Pratyabhijñā school means "recognition."

17 Commonly translated as "emanation," "reflexivity," and "diversity," in the context of Pratyabhijñā doctrine, *vimarśa* also means "reflective awareness" or "self-awareness" (see Dyczkowski [1987: 59, 73]).

18 See Abhinavagupta and Bhāskara (1987: 1.5.15, 1:267–68). C.f., Lawrence (1999: 121).

19 *Karma* is only one of three illusory taints or *malas*, with *karma mala* understood as only an incomplete realization of one's omnipotent identity with Śiva-Śakti. The *Karma Mala* originates in the lack of awareness that the only real agent is Śiva (not the empirical ego) and results in the reduction of the universal power of action to a finite power. For more on this, see Chatterji (1986).

20 Goldberg rightly concludes that, according to Śaivas, the universe is essentially androgynous. See Goldberg (2002: 135).

21 According to Brod, the field of men's studies (by contrast) tends to examine masculinities by focusing upon relations between men and excluding from consideration the role of women in men's lives and formulations of masculinity. See Brod (1994).

22 For more on this topic, see the work of Alexis Sanderson, in particular, 1985.

23 One possible way (among others) of avoiding the sexist implications of this account is by noting that the audience of much of medieval Kashmir Śaiva philosophy likely was male and hence was designed to appeal to the perspective of males by presenting a male protagonist, Śiva.

24 Goldberg offers a critique of the Ardhanārīśvara image. For one, she argues that the very name suggests a gender hierarchy through its subordination of the female (*nārī* or "woman") to the male (*īśvara* or "lord," "master," "god") (2002: 1). She also provides a translation of the *Ardhanārīśvara Stotra* and subjects its imagery to a thorough analysis in order to uncover its gender markers. She asserts that rather than uncritically accepting "the illusion of equality in androdgynous images" (be they "Western" or "Eastern"), what is required is a critique of their "subtle" gender constructions (2002: 103–11). Elsewhere, she draws our attention to *Purāṇic* myths that maintain a codependency and complementarity between Śiva and Śakti but reverse the primary relationship between the two deities—with Śiva taking on the supplementary role as consort to Śakti, who is ultimately superior. This can be seen in various *purāṇic* portrayals of the Great Goddess (Mahādevī, e.g., in the *Devī Bhāgavata Purāṇa*) as the "creator, preserver, and destroyer of the universe, as well as the eternal source of compassion necessary to take those beings suffering in

saṃsāra to liberation" (2002: 145). Śakta cults, meanwhile, were known to challenge the power dynamics of the orthodox brahmanical tradition and to identify the Devī (e.g., Śakti, Pārvatī, Kālī), not Śiva, as the source of all manifestation. This is evident in rare depictions of the Ardhanārīśvara image (e.g., the Ardhanārī sculpture at Vedopusīśvara Temple, Thanjavur District, Tiruvedikudi, Madras, ninth century) wherein the dominant right side shows female features and the subordinate left side displays characteristically male attributes. See Goldberg (2002: 145–9).

25 For more on how liberation can be realized in Indian philosophy through a kind of theatrical performativity, see Ashton (2013).

26 The "prison of gender" refers to Carolyn Heilbrun's "Toward a Recognition of Androgyny," where she argues that the ideal of androgyny can serve as an emancipatory paradigm by helping women to transcend gender distinctions and realize psychological and sociological equality between men and women (1973: x, 115). While in some sense the realization of one's true nature as nondual Śiva consciousness overcomes phenomenal identities (and hence, all distinction), this movement still gives way to a return to worldly involvement. Identifications of all kinds then—gender identifications included—are not to be overcome, per se, but embraced and celebrated. In this respect, gender is not a "prison" but a gateway to self-realization. My comments here echo some of Phil Hine's insights regarding the meaning of the Ardhanārīśvara image. He comments that the quasi-Jungian way of reading the image in terms of a symbolic union of opposites "can lead to other possibilities being overlooked" (2013). Indeed, the practitioner is to realize that her own true nature is in some sense androgynous. However, the *coniunctio oppositorum* comparative model (emphasized in Goldberg's study) may in fact conceal a key feature of the image: namely, that it intends to move us beyond binary thinking itself (2013).

References

Abhinavagupta (1938–43). *Īśvarapratyabhijñāvivṛtivimarśinī*, vols. 1–3. Edited by M. K. Shastri. Bombay: Kashmir Sanskrit Texts Series 60, 62, 65.

Abhinavagupta and Bhāskara (1987). *Īśvarapratyabhijñāvimarśinī of Abhinavagupta, Doctrine of Divine Recognition*, vols. 1–2 are Sanskrit text with *Bhāskarī*. Edited by K. A. Subramania Iyer and K. C. Pandey. Reprint, Delhi: Motilal Banarsidass.

Abhinavagupta and Bhāskara (1987). *Īśvarapratyabhijñāvimarśinī of Abhinavagupta, Doctrine of Divine Recognition*, vol. 3. Translated by K. C. Pandey. Reprint, Delhi: Motilal Banarsidass.

Ashton, G. (2013). "The Soteriology of Role-Play in the *Bhagavad Gītā*." *Asian Philosophy: An International Journal of the Philosophical Traditions of the East* 23: 1–23.

Brod, H. (1994). "Some Thoughts on Some Histories of Some Masculinities: Jews and Other Others." In D. S. David and R. Brannon (eds.), *Theorizing Masculinities* (pp. 82–96). Thousand Oaks, CA: Sage.

Chakrabarti, A. (2005). "The Heart of Repose, the Repose of the Heart: A Phenomenological Analysis of the Concept of *Viśrānti*." In Sadananda Das and Ernst Furlinger (eds.), *Sāmarasya: Studies in Indian Arts, Philosophy and Interreligious Dialogue*, 27–36. New Delhi: D. K. Printworld.

Chatterji, J. C. (1986). *Kashmir Shaivism*, Albany, NY: SUNY Press.

Dagens, B. (1989). "Iconography in *Śaivāgamas*: Description or Prescription?" In Anna Libera Dahmen-Dallapiccola (ed.), *Shastric Traditions in Indian Arts, vol. 1* (pp. 151–53). Stuttgart: Steiner Verlag Wiesbaden.

Dehejia, H. (1997). *Pārvatīdarpaṇa: An Exposition of Kāśmir Śaivism through the Images of Śiva and Pārvatī*. Delhi: Motilal Banarsidass.

Dyczkowski, M. (1987). *The Doctrine of Vibration: An Analysis of the Doctrines and Practices of Kashmir Shaivism*. Albany, NY: SUNY Press.

Eliade, M. (1969). *Yoga Immortality and Freedom*. Princeton, NJ: Bollingen Foundation.

Goldberg, E. (2002). *The Lord Who Is Half-Woman: Ardhanārīśvara in Indian and Feminist Perspective*. Albany, NY: SUNY Press.

Heilbrun, C. (1973), *Toward a Recognition of Androgyny*. New York: Knopf.

Hine, P. (2013, July 29). "On Queering Deity: Ardhanārīśvara and Other Conundrums of Gender." *Enfolding*. Accessed September 13, 2017, from http://enfolding.org/on-queering-deity-ardhanarishvara-and-other-conundrums-of-gender/.

Kramrisch, S. (1981). *The Presence of Śiva*. Princeton, NJ: Princeton University Press.

Lawrence, D. (1999). *Rediscovering God with Transcendental Argument: A Contemporary Interpretation of Monistic Kashmiri Śaiva Philosophy*. Albany, NY: SUNY Press.

Pollock, Sheldon (1989). "The Idea of Śāstra in Traditional India." In Anna Libera Dahmen-Dallapiccola (ed.), *Shastric Traditions in Indian Arts*, vol. 1 (pp. 27–36). Stuttgart: Steiner Verlag Wiesbaden.

Rao, T. (1916). *Elements of Hindu Iconography, Vol. 2: Part I*. Chennai: Law Printing House.

Sanderson, A. (1985). "Purity and Power among the Brāhmans of Kashmir." In M. Carrithers, S. Collins, and S. Lukes (eds.), *The Category of the Person: Anthropology, Philosophy, History* (pp. 190–216). Cambridge: Cambridge University Press.

Vasugupta (1992). *The Aphorisms of Śiva: The Śiva Sūtra with Bhāskara's Commentary, the Vārttika*. Translated by Mark S. G. Dyczkowski. Albany, NY: SUNY Press.

Yadav, N. (2000). *Ardhanārīśvara in Art and Literature*. New Delhi: D. K. Printworld.

9

Gender in Pāli Buddhist Traditions

Carol S. Anderson

Examining gender in Pāli Buddhist literature (the early texts of Theravāda Buddhism) requires a certain familiarity with the body of Buddhist literature written in the Pāli language. Steven Collins has articulated the concept of the "Pāli imaginaire," which refers to the "ensemble of what is imagined" by those who recited, compiled, and recorded the texts within the world of Pāli Buddhism (Collins 1998: 83). This key concept sets the stage for the present exploration of gender in Pāli literature. I draw upon the material found in the Pāli Buddhist canon, which was likely composed over a span of several centuries, beginning in the first century or two BCE continuing into the first few centuries of the Common Era.

As with all Indian religious texts from this period, the works in this canon were first composed orally and then gradually committed to writing, initially on palm leaf manuscripts. In order to ensure the stability of the oral recitations, there were groups of monks charged with memorizing and reciting the various sections of the canon (called *bhaṇaka*s or reciters), although the system was complex. For example, the story of the Buddha's passing describes how his followers gathered together the morning after he passed into *parinirvāṇa*. Ostensibly, there were groups of monks charged with reciting different portions of the canon, but since the canon was not fully systematized, the assignment of sections may have been rather unorganized (Norman 2006: 47–8).[1] Furthermore, as was the case with religious literature from South Asia in this early period, the body of the Pāli canon and its commentaries were composed entirely by men and were passed down by male monks. At the same time, a number of collected teachings and stories were written from women's points of view and even in women's first-person voices. These works provide a wealth of material for those examining gender and gendered asymmetries in the Pāli *imaginaire*. Even so,

Collins' caution is worth citing: "I doubt that the lived world of any individual, let alone any group, has ever coincided precisely, with no remainder, with the *imaginaire* of (some or all) Pali texts" (1998: 76). This simply means that the world described by the Pāli texts is larger and more expansive than any single person who may have lived at the time; we need to realize that our sources are not straightforward narratives that can be interpreted in a historical fashion. When it comes to gender, scholars have suggested that the Pāli sources reflect an essentialist binary system in which biologically sexed bodies are mapped directly onto culturally gendered living beings; this chapter will demonstrate that this model is not as accurate as has been suggested (Sweet and Zwilling 1993: 604).

The Pāli Canon and Its Various Threads

The sources at our disposal are written texts that we can reliably trace to three to four centuries after the Buddha's passing into the state of *parinirvāṇa* (final passing). This is the Pāli Buddhist canon of the Theravāda tradition, and it became the most well-known collection of teachings for Indian Buddhism until its decline in the subcontinent during the tenth century CE. Other collections of the canon have been recorded in Sanskrit and in Chinese, but this chapter examines only those teachings that have been recorded in Pāli, a dialect of Sanskrit.

The Pāli canon, known as *Tipiṭaka*, is made up of three *piṭaka*s, a term that is usually translated as "basket." We get a clearer sense of the word *piṭaka*, however, if we translate it as "thread," specifically as a thread of the teachings that eventually became identified as the Buddhist canon (Collins 1990: 89–126). The three *piṭaka*s are the *Sutta-piṭaka*, *Vinaya-piṭaka*, and the *Abhidhamma-piṭaka*. The first contains four different collections of sayings, stories, and narrative teachings of the Buddha. The four different collections in the *Sutta-piṭaka* are organized according to length and number. The first two of these four, the *Dīgha-nikāya* and the *Majjhima-nikāya*, are the "Collection of Long Sayings of the Buddha" and the "Middle Length Sayings of the Buddha," respectively. The third, the *Saṃyutta-nikāya*, is based on connected sayings or "Groups of Verses on Related Topics." The final collection, the *Aṅguttara-nikāya*, is organized according to number: teachings that are singular are grouped together as "ones," "twos," and so on, up to twelve. Taken together, the collections of the *Sutta-piṭaka* provided reciters with a way to ensure some continuity in the teachings since the different teachings of the Buddha were organized in different ways (long sayings, medium-length sayings, sayings by connected topics, and by number). The second "thread," or *piṭaka*, is the *Vinaya-piṭaka*, which contains the rules necessary for regulating the monastic orders of both monks and nuns. The *vinaya* rules were formulated on a case-by-case basis as they became needed to ensure order within the evolving monastic community. The rules have generally been understood throughout history as necessary for both spiritual development as well as defining the social and ethical norms for the monastic community. Spiritually, they prohibited nuns and monks from engaging in behaviors considered to be at odds with progress along the path (Wijayaratna 1990: 94–5). Finally, the teachings in the final "thread," the *Abhidhamma-piṭaka*, are examinations of the "higher *dhamma*" or the more philosophical and analytical categories of the Buddha's teachings. All of these three "threads" of the Pāli canon are interrelated and show us different dimensions of the Pāli *imaginaire*, particularly regarding gender.

The Buddhist Cosmos and the Various Kinds of Gendered Beings

The Buddhist cosmos is filled with a wide variety of living beings. Humans occupy the most propitious realm, which is earth. On earth, there is a balance between those things that hurt us (pain) and the things that make us feel good (pleasure), with the effect being that we are not overwhelmed by either. According to the Buddha, life involves "pain" and "suffering," but it is possible for all humans to end the cycle of rebirth and death by eliminating the cause of our attachments. This simplified version of the path is based on the Buddha's first sermon on *dhamma*, "The Sermon on the Turning of the *Dhamma* Wheel" (*Dhammacakkappavattāna-sutta*). This talk is one of the best-known talks given by the Buddha to his five companions, who were on the search for enlightenment with him just prior to his solitary enlightenment under the Bodhi tree. When he decided to turn the wheel of *dharma* loose in the world, he did so by preaching on the four noble truths: there is pain in the world, there is a cause for pain, there is an end to the cause of pain, and there is a path to the ending of pain.

There is more to imagine though. While humans (as gendered beings) are located at the center of all Buddhist teachings, they are only one class of living beings among others. The gods in the heavens above are overwhelmed with pleasure and, therefore, are not likely to realize that they, too, should seek to escape the rounds of *saṃsara*. Conversely, the beings that reside in various hells, such as animals and hungry ghosts, are too overwhelmed by pain to realize that they may also seek an escape from the cycle of rebirth and death. The cosmology drawn from the *Sutta-piṭaka* commonly identifies five classes of living beings: gods, humans, animals, ghosts, and hell dwellers. However, the *Vinaya-piṭaka* talks most often about three classifications of living beings: humans, nonhumans, and animals. The *Vinaya-piṭaka* talks explicitly about the ways in which these three kinds of living beings are gendered whereas the *Sutta-piṭaka* does not. Bodies—human and animal as well as living and dead—are regulated in the *vinaya* for the purpose of regulating the *saṅgha*, and questions of sex and gender are systematically addressed in *vinaya* teachings.

Four different kinds of gendered beings are described in the section of the *Vinaya-piṭaka*, which speaks of the first *parājika* or rule that prohibits sexual intercourse for all monks and nuns. The explanation provided goes into excruciating detail about just how monks and nuns should not violate the rule against sexual intercourse. The purpose of the rules of discipline is to enable the spiritual life for monks and nuns; prohibiting intercourse for monks and nuns is one of the central ways in which the boundaries of monastic life are delineated from lay Buddhists. Hence, it makes sense that the texts would want to explicate the permutations of the rule against sexual intercourse. In the discussion of the specific ways in which monks should not have intercourse, because they are forbidden from all sexual intercourse as monks, the passages explain that sexual intercourse is forbidden with three kinds of *itthi*s (female human, nonhuman, and animals), three kinds of *ubhatobyañjanaka*s or intersex (human, nonhuman, and animal), three kinds of *paṇḍaka*s (human, nonhuman, and animal), and three kinds of *puruṣa*s (male human, nonhuman, and animal) (Horner 1938: 48–9; Oldenberg 1882: 28–39). Lest there be any confusion about what distinguishes these different kinds of beings, the text explains that there are three "ways" (i.e., openings in the physical body) in which a monk can break this rule with females (mouth, anus, and vagina) and *ubhatobyañjanakas*, and two ways with *paṇḍakas* and males (mouth and anus). Thus, the texts' detailed explication of how monks should not break the rules against sexual intercourse is also explicit in defining relationships between physically sexed bodies and gendered bodies.

"Male" and "Female"

More precisely, the Pāli Vinaya (text of monastic rules) maps four kinds of gendered beings onto two types of biologically sexed bodies: those with two openings and those with three. "Male" and "female" are not difficult to understand, as male humans and female humans are simply men and women, biological humans who are born biologically male and female with a penis for men and a vagina for women. While this sounds rather reductive, it is precisely how the *Vinaya-piṭaka* defines male beings and female beings. Elsewhere in the Pāli canon, in the *Abhidhamma-piṭaka* and the *Sutta-piṭaka*, male and female are described in terms of the "faculties" and in terms of behavior and appearance.

According to classic Buddhist teachings, the faculties (*indriyas*) are constitutive elements of living beings that are established at the moment of conception. The *Abhidhamma-piṭaka* includes the faculties of masculinity and femininity among a longer list of twenty-two *indriyas* (Rhys Davids and Tin 1920: 122, 411–17). For all beings born in a womb, including humans, the twenty-two faculties (*indriyas*) present from conception include those of the bodily sensation, mind, masculinity or femininity, vitality, happiness or indifference, faith, energy, mindfulness, concentration, and wisdom (Rhys Davids and Tin 1920: 411–17). All faculties (*indriyas*), and thus the faculties of masculinity and femininity, are basic aspects or capacities of living beings, which are present from the time of conception and which may have their roots in the karmic past of an individual.

However, we need to be careful when we translate the terms *itthindriya* and *purisa-indriya* into English. The terms are usually translated as "feminine faculties" and "masculine faculties," or "male" and "female" faculties, largely because of the differences in biological sex and the subsequent cultural constructions of gender, usually denoted with the adjectives of "feminine" or "masculine." When it comes to the traditions based on the Pāli canon, however, we cannot argue that the faculties are the product of biology or culture; no such distinction is made. Masculine and feminine faculties are explained and defined in the *Abhidhamma-piṭaka* in terms of the physical appearance of men and women. Both feminine (*itthi-*) and masculine (*purisa-*) faculties are defined as the physical appearance (*itthākappo*), deportment (*itthikuttaṃ*), marks (*itthinimittaṃ*), and features (*itthiliṅgaṃ*) peculiar to women—women's being or nature (*itthibhāvo*) and the condition of being a woman (*itthattaṃ*) (Müeller 1885: 143, 151f, 163f; Rhys Davids and Tin 1920: 122–3). So, too, a masculine faculty means the physical appearance unique to a man or the state or condition of masculinity or being male (*purisatta* or *purisabhāva*). The *Aṅguttara-nikāya* in the *Sutta-piṭaka* shares this framework when it defines both male and female faculties as forms of attachment. These explanations of what it means to be "feminine" and "masculine" are all based on behavior and appearance, which are ultimately rooted in one's faculty of masculinity or femininity with which one is born:

> A woman, *bhikkhus*, is aware of the female faculty (*itthindriyaṃ*) in herself: feminine deportment (*itthikuttaṃ*), feminine appearance (*itthākappaṃ*), feminine manner (*itthividhaṃ*), feminine impulses (*itthicchandaṃ*), feminine voice (*itthissaraṃ*), [and] feminine adornment (*itthālaṅkāraṃ*). (Karunadasa 1967: 55; Morris, Hardy, and Rhys Davids 1955: 57–8, 194)

This passage is repeated *verbatim* for men and the male faculty, using *purisa-* instead of *itthi-* as a prefix in the compounds. This accord is precisely what we expect to find in a gendered system based on biological differences between male and female: there is a correlation between a conception of female-ness or male-ness that encompasses one's physical appearance, behavior, and attire. According to these passages in the Pāli tradition, to be possessed of the female or male faculty is to possess a set of qualities rooted in one's biological sex. José Cabezón compares these sex faculties across different South Asian religious traditions in *Sexuality in Classical South Asian Buddhism* (Cabezón 2017: 359 ff.).

Male and female are not equal in any sense of the term anywhere in the *Pāli imaginaire* or the world of the Buddhist teachings recorded in Pāli. Stories found in the *Sutta-piṭaka* describe the subordinate status of women in some detail, whether there are tales of unjust marriages, the burdens laid on women workers, or the self-evident misogyny found at various points. Alan Sponberg has outlined four different attitudes toward women in early Buddhism (not just Pāli teachings): soteriological inclusiveness, institutional androcentrism, ascetic misogyny, and soteriological androgyny (Sponberg 1992). The androcentrism of Buddhism has been long debated in any number of articles and books.[2] I suggest that Sponberg's four models should probably be *reduced to two* when considering the Pāli canon and commentaries: those of cultural androcentrism and soteriological equity. Briefly, the cultural traditions of androcentrism that valued and placed males in positions of power shaped the institutions of Buddhism (institutional androcentrism) as well as the negative attitudes toward women (ascetic misogyny), and in a similar fashion, both of Sponberg's types of soteriology can readily be conflated into a single category.

There are many stories about the second-class status of women; the Buddha's foster mother and aunt, Mahāprajāpati, is perhaps the best example of this. When she approached the Buddha to seek permission to create the order of nuns, he at first denied her request. And when he reluctantly agreed, the Buddha declared that—because of this decision—the period of time during which his teachings would be influential in the world would be reduced by half. The *Abhidhamma* contains the clear statement that women are born as women due to bad *karma* (such as incurred through adultery, etc.), and this analysis is also repeated in the *Vinaya-piṭaka* (Analāyo 2014). Furthermore, we need to recognize that both those models (nuns and monks) are heterosexist, insofar the Pāli canon and commentaries are quite clear that only "properly" gendered and sexed male and female human bodies may be ordained.

Ubhatobyañjanakas

In the normatively two-gendered and heterosexual world of the Pāli *imaginaire*, only normatively sexed female and male humans may be ordained as Buddhist monks or nuns. However, there are other classes of gendered beings discussed in some detail, including mentions of beings who are "both natured"; that is, they are both male and female (*ubhatobyañjanaka*s) and *paṇḍaka*s (discussed in the following section). English translations for these terms are difficult. While it seems logical to translate *ubhatobyañjanaka* as "hermaphrodite," that term has been called into question in recent scholarship because it reflects the preoccupations of the nineteenth- and twentieth-century scholars of human sexuality (Dreger 1998). There is ideally a move to use the term "intersex" instead of hermaphrodite. Although it would be better to leave the term untranslated, I have not done that throughout this chapter for ease of reading.

The *Atthasālinī*, a fifth-century commentary on the *Abhidhamma* texts of the Pāli canon, explains that differences in faculties give rise to the physical differences between men and women. It takes an interesting turn when the argument is applied to *ubhatobyañjanaka*s or intersex beings. The problem for the *Atthasālinī* is the fact that an *ubhatobyañjanaka* cannot always (*sadā*) have two sets of "marks" or genitals. According to the author of the *Atthasālinī*, intersex beings are either sexually *active*, which means that s/he is the one who "penetrates women with the genitals of a man," or *passive*, which means "having aroused another, s/he has the genitals of a woman." There are, the commentary explains, two kinds of *ubhatobyañjanaka*s: female and male. The passage then turns to the relationship between the faculties and the physical differences between the sexes by explaining how the genitals "work" in *ubhatobyañjanaka*s:

> Does an intersex possess one faculty or two? One, and that is a female faculty to a female intersex and a male faculty to a male intersex. This being true, the second mark of an intersex should not exist. The female faculty is said to be the

> reason for the marks (*vyañjana*). In such [male intersex] the female faculty is not the reason of the mark, because it [i.e., the (female) mark] does not exist. When a female intersex has a lustful thought for a woman, then the masculine mark is manifested, and the feminine mark is hidden and concealed; and *vice versa.* And if in these [people] the faculty was the cause of the second mark, then both marks would always persist. But in reality there is no such persistence. Hence it is to be understood that in a hermaphrodite the faculty is not the reason for the marks. (Müeller 1897: 322; Rhys Davids 1920: 421)

The logic here is fairly straightforward, albeit complex. An intersex being (*ubhatobyañjanaka*) should, according to all that we have examined up until this point, have two faculties—one female and one male. However, the author of the commentary cannot conceive of a being that *always* has two faculties—despite his understanding that intersex individuals have the genitals (marks) of both sexes.[3] The commentary rules out the possibility that female faculty (*itthīndriyaṃ*) is responsible for the marks in a male intersex, on the basis that a male intersex does not have female genitalia. But the commentary still needs to account for the class of *ubhatobyañjanaka* (intersex), and thus it explains that "lustful thoughts" (*rāgacittaṃ*) are the catalyst for the different genitalia to emerge—depending, of course, on the sex of the person to whom the lustful thoughts are directed (Müeller 1897: 322; Takakusu and Makoto 1924: 1024).

In other words, according to the commentaries, *ubhatobyañjanaka* cannot always have two faculties and the genitals of both sexes. The explanation, then, is that lust is the motivating factor that enables different genitalia to emerge in an intersex being, according to a heterosexist model. For example, male intersex who are attracted to women manifest male genitalia and the opposite for female intersex. The commentaries conclude this explanation by saying that if the faculties (*indriyāni*) *were* the cause for the genitals (or "marks"), then there would always be two sets of genitals. But there are not two sets of genitals in this definition of intersex; therefore, in intersex beings, the faculties are not the cause for the existence of the genitals. Instead, desire is the cause: "Lustful thought, friend of (past) kamma, is the reason" (Müeller 1897: 322). Furthermore, manifesting and hiding the genitals are not the commentary's last word on intersex beings. The ability to manifest and hide one's genitalia extends to pregnancy:

> Because there is only one faculty in an intersex being, therefore the female intersex herself becomes pregnant and causes another to become pregnant; the male intersex causes another to become pregnant but himself does not become so. (Müeller 1897: 322; Takakusu and Makoto 1924: 1024)

In other words, a male *ubhatobyañjanaka* (intersex) cannot become pregnant but a female can. In the *Samantapāsādikā*, Buddhaghosa adds a slightly different explanation for the intersex that he attributes to one of his authorities: "Kurundī has said if there are male sexual characteristics at conception, female sexual characteristics emerge as a natural process; if there are female sexual characteristics at conception, male sexual characteristics emerge as a natural process" (Takakusu and Makoto 1924: 1024).[4] Buddhaghosa closes this passage in the *Samantapāsādikā* with the declaration that intersex should not be considered for any kind of ordination into Buddhistic monasticism—and neither are *paṇḍaka*s eligible for ordination. Only normatively heterosexual sexed men and women may be ordained.

Paṇḍakas

Just as intersexed beings were not permitted to be ordained as monks or nuns, so too were *paṇḍaka*s. Using the same logic for *paṇḍaka*s as we did for *ubhatobyañjanaka*s, we should also leave the word *paṇḍaka* untranslated because we have no clear etymology for the word (Analāyo 2014: 439).[5] An early etymology proposed by Leonard Zwilling parsed the term *paṇḍaka* into *apa* (without) + *aṇḍa* (testicles) + *ka* (suffix) (1992: 204). Janet Gyatso correctly rejected this etymology on the grounds that there are no other examples of *apa-* becoming *pa-* in the Pāli language (Gyatso 2003: 94). Leonard Zwilling construed the term broadly, suggesting that it means roughly what we might mean when we say that a man "has no balls." Based on an explanation of the term as *napuṃsaka* (not male or masculine, neuter), Bernard Faure understands the term to refer to passive homosexuals, although he recognizes the deficiency of that translation (1998: 73). L. P. N. Perera offers a different etymology, suggesting that the root *paṇḍ-* may have been borrowed from non-Aryan sources, suggesting the root *peṇ*, which has given rise to *pēḍi* in Telugu and *peṇṭakan* in Tamil, both of which Perera says have been translated as "eunuch" or "hermaphrodite" (1993: 114, 138).[6] Current scholarship in Buddhist Studies suggests that the term *paṇḍaka* remain untranslated.

Paṇḍaka individuals are biologically male insofar as they have two "openings," an anus and a mouth. Buddhaghosa, the fifth-century commentator on the Pāli canon provides a list of five kinds of *paṇḍaka*s in his commentary on the *Vinaya-piṭaka*. This list of five types of *paṇḍaka*s is found throughout Indian Buddhist Vinaya literature and is distinct from the lists found in non-Buddhist literature. Terms used in non-Buddhist sources include *klība*, *ṣaṇḍha(ka)*, and *napuṃsaka*. In contrast, Pāli sources use *paṇḍaka* almost exclusively while Buddhist Sanskrit sources use *ṣaṇḍha(ka)* and *paṇḍaka*.[7] This concept is not unique to Buddhist texts; Hindu and Jain texts also discuss this term. However, the Buddhist typology for *paṇḍaka*s is different from those laid out in the Indian medical texts and also different from those found in Jain texts.[8] Kenneth Zysk has suggested that classical Indian medical texts and redactors constructed the system of *āyurvedic* medicine on the foundations of Buddhist medicine, and thus the reconfiguration of *āyurvedic* medicine means that it is not surprising to find a different list in the Buddhist texts than in the Hindu texts (1991).[9]

This set of five *paṇḍakas* is consistent throughout the Pāli postcanonical commentaries and sub-commentaries (*ṭīkā*).[10] These *paṇḍakas* define the gender categories as follows: (1) one who is not male (*napuṃsakapaṇḍaka*); Buddhaghosa explains that this state is congenital and defines it as having "no nature" (*abhāvako*), which is probably a parallel construction to women's nature (*itthibhāva*) and men's nature (*purisabhāva*), which he uses throughout his commentaries; (2) one who, out of jealousy, watches others engage in sexual intercourse (*usūyapaṇḍaka*/*īrṣyāpaṇḍaka*); Zwilling translates this as a voyeur, as does Gyatso; (3) one who is a *paṇḍaka* during the "dark" days of the month (full moon until the new moon), due to bad *karma* (*akusalavipākā nubhāvena*), and whose passions are calm during the bright days of the month (*pakkhapaṇḍaka*/*pakṣapaṇḍaka*); (4) one who takes the penis of another into the mouth and is sprinkled with impurity (*āsittapaṇḍaka*/*āsekapaṇḍaka*); and (5) one whose seeds have been removed by means of some (medical) remedy (*opakkamikapaṇḍaka*). This leaves open the possibility that some *paṇḍaka*s were eunuchs, although other Buddhist sources vary on this definition. Buddhaghosa further describes *paṇḍaka*s: "They are filled with defiling passions (*kilesā*), their lust is not calm, and they lack masculinity (*napuṃsakā*). Overcome by the force of their lust, they desire friendship with anyone" (Takakusu and Makoto 1924: 991–2).[11] In Buddhist Sanskrit sources, *paṇḍaka*s were considered unfit for monastic life, as were *ubhatobyañjanaka*s.

There is one term that indicates that *paṇḍaka*s were not necessarily always male. At several points in the Pāli *vinaya* and postcanonical commentaries, we find the unusual term, *itthipaṇḍakā* (or *itthipaṇḍikā*), which actually means "female *paṇḍaka*." Buddhaghosa explains that an *itthipaṇḍakā* is someone without genitals (*animitta*), thus reinforcing his assumption that all *paṇḍaka*s were biologically sexed males regardless of their other characteristics (Takakusu and Makoto 1924: 548–9). However, the term *itthipaṇḍakā* appears in a list of biologically nonnormative women in the Pāli canon, so despite Buddhaghosa's definition of *itthipaṇḍakā* as someone without genitals, the Pāli sources consider the possibility of a female *paṇḍaka* (Anderson 2016).

Furthermore, four different kinds of gendered beings are found in the Pāli canon and commentaries: female, male, *ubhatobyañjanaka*s, and *paṇḍaka*s. These four genders may be human, nonhuman, or animal. Even though the texts catalog four genders, the root of that system is still female and male faculties and female and male sexual genitalia—in other words, a dimorphic system based on the sexual characteristics manifested at conception. *Ubhatobyañjanaka*s drew Buddhaghosa to develop a series of somewhat circular explanations when it came to the relationship between male and female faculties and the manifestation of male and female genitalia (to the point of pregnancy). *Paṇḍaka*s never raised questions about the faculties because they were all regarded as male—with the exception of the "female *paṇḍaka*s." The explanation for the relationship between female and male faculties, one's performance of gender, and genitalia and the state of being female (or male) is quite clear, as discussed above: feminine (*itthi-*) and masculine (*purisa-*) faculties are defined in terms of the physical appearance (*-akappo*), deportment (*-kuttaṃ*), marks (*-nimittaṃ*), and features/genitals (*-liṅgaṃ*) peculiar to each gender, women or men. Put differently, the male and female faculties are evident according to one's physical appearance, what we would explain as one's performance of gender, and the state or nature of being a woman or a man. So far, one's biological sex appears to be the means by which the faculties are discovered, and an individual's biological sex is closely connected to the performance of one's gender and is not distinct from one's nature of being male or female—even if that state of being male or female changes in *ubhatobyañjanaka*s due to one's sexual attractions.

Faculties, Biology, and Gender

Thus far we have seen that the Pāli canon and commentaries draw a close correlation between biologically sexed bodies (with two openings or three), male and female faculties, and the behavioral aspects of what we would call gender today: how women and men comport themselves, dress, adorn themselves, what occupations they hold, and so on. According to the argument that has been analyzed up to this point, there is a strong biological basis to the differences between men and women because the faculties come into being at the moment of conception, even before birth. In other words, up to this point, biology seems to determine the faculties and thus the characteristics of gendered behavior in men, women, intersex, and *paṇḍakas*. However, biology is not the ultimate determinate of one's gender in the Pāli Buddhist *imaginaire*—the faculties (*indriyas*) are.

The male and female faculties are, instead, the mechanisms that shape what we understand today to be both biological sex and gender. These explanations are found throughout the commentaries, and the *Atthasālinī* (fifth century CE) commentary explains that female faculty (*itthindriya*) is *not* the same thing as the physical differences between the sexes that we call "feminine" and "masculine." The key term in the following commentarial passage is *liṅgaṃ*, which may be translated as anything from "features," "characteristics," "gender" (in grammar or as we use it today), "genitals," "sexual organs," and so on. The following quote from the *Atthasālinī* commentary parses the *Abhidhamma* canonical statement, "by whatever cause a woman has female features/characteristics/genitals (*itthiliṅgaṃ*) and so on" and explains,

> [In that sentence] "feature" (*liṅgaṃ*) means shape. That is, the shape of a woman's hands, feet, neck, breast, and so on is not like a man's. A woman's lower body is wide, the upper body is narrow. The hands and feet are small, the mouth is small … The female breasts are noticeable. The face is without beard or moustache. The dressing of the hair, the wearing of the clothes are also unlike those of a man. "Occupation" (*kuttaṃ*) means action. As children, women play with tiny shallow baskets, pestles and mortars, different dolls, and weave string with clay-fiber. "Deportment" (*ākappo*) is a way of going, or one's gait. There is a lack of assertiveness (*avisadaṃ*) in women's walking, standing, lying down, sitting, eating, and swallowing. Indeed, when a man of that description is seen (*purisam pi hi avisadaṃ disvā*), people say, "He walks and stands like a woman." (Müeller 1897: 321)[12]

The above passage is followed by an equally detailed description of male features (*purisaliṅgaṃ*), which includes the same distinctions as for women: men's bodies are broader at the top, narrower at the hips; they have facial hair, and in childhood they play with chariots and plows and make sand piles and dig ponds (Müeller 1897: 321). Here, the author explains that "female features" (*itthiliṅgaṃ*) refer to the features or markers of women. The *Atthasālinī* has a clear description of the features that distinguish men and women—voice, posture, and so on—and the text also explains that the cause of these features lie in the faculties (Müeller 1897: 321–2). This passage makes it clear that there is a correlation between female and male "features" or "sexual characteristics" (*liṅgaṃ*) and what boys and girls like to do—but it also emphasizes that the control of such features lies in the faculties not in one's biological sex.

The *Atthasālinī* defines the terms "the state of being a woman" (*itthattaṃ*) and "female being" (*itthibhāvo*) by explaining that both of these terms have one meaning: "female nature" (*itthisabhāvo*), "which is born of *kamma* and produced at the instant of conception" (Müeller 1897: 321; Rhys Davids and Tin 1920: 419). Likewise, the same holds for men; the male being (*purisabhāvo*) is born of *kamma* and produced at the moment of conception. Here, the text comments on the passage in the *Dhammasaṅgaṇī* (one of the original *Abhidhamma* texts of the Pāli canon), which has claimed that male and female faculties are *the same as* the "state or condition of male or female." The commentary clarifies the *Dhammasaṅgaṇī* when it states the following: "But female features and so on (*itthiliṅgādi*) are *not* the female faculty (*itthindriyaṃ*)—female features are produced in due course as a result of the female faculty," just like a tree grows from a seed (Müller 1897: 321). By extension, the same is true of male features and the male faculty.

We have, then, two different explanations for the relationship between the female and male faculties: (a) the physical appearance of being a man or a woman, women's and men's "nature" or "being" (*bhāvo*), and (b) the state or condition of being a man or a woman (*itthatta* and *purisatta*). The Pāli texts, *Dhammasaṅgaṇī*, *Vibhaṅga*, and the *Aṅguttara-nikāya* say that they are all the same.[13] The *Atthasālinī*, on the other hand, concludes that the faculties are the *cause* of men's and women's features (*liṅgaṃ*), not that they are the same as men's as women's features. This clearly follows from the idea that women's being (*itthibhāvo*) and men's being (*purisabhāvo*), and women's nature (*itthisabhāvo*), are present from the time of conception. The *Atthasālinī* also claims that "female features" and "male features," while produced in the same way (as a result of the faculties), are not equal: "Of the two, men's features are superior (*uttamaṃ*), women's features are inferior (*hīnaṃ*)" (Müeller 1897: 322). Remember that *liṅgaṃ* may be translated as genitals as well as features and at many points should be translated as the physical genitals. In short, male and female faculties give rise to one's physical markers of sexual difference. Realizing that the male and female faculties are the cause for male and female *liṅgaṃ* makes a bit more sense of Buddhaghosa's explanation of how *ubhatobyañjanaka*s manifest female and male faculties and *liṅgaṃ*. The category of "both natures" (intersex) is a problem for a biologically based gender binary, insofar as there is no conceptual way to conceive of a female *ubhatobyañjanaka* who can give birth. If, however, we realize that the faculties are the basis of gender in the Pāli world, it allows for the mutability of both biological sex and gender.

In summary, we need to recognize that that the key categories accounting for the differences between "male and female" are *seed-like faculties* and not gross biological markers of sexual difference—even though "male or female being" is established at the moment of conception. According to the texts, these defining aspects of being male and female in society cannot be simplistically reduced to a biologically essentialist framework, precisely because the faculties are inscribed on humans at the point of conception. The role of the male and female faculties is the key. Even though male and female faculties come into being at the moment of conception—and as a result of *karma*—"female and male" faculties determine an individual's biological sex, not the reverse.[14]

The Issue of Change of Sex or Gender

The Pāli texts not only provide an insight into sex and gender but also into the issues of the stability of sex and gender. There are two passages in the *Vinaya-piṭaka* of the Pāli Buddhist canon that describe cases involving a change of sex or gender. These sentences are cited throughout the canon and commentaries as the root text for change of sex. In keeping with the logic of how the rules may be broken, the Buddha's response focuses on what kind of offense change of sex entails for monks and for nuns:

> Now at that time the sexual features of a woman appeared on a certain monk. They told the Blessed One about this matter. [He said,] "Monks, I prescribe the same teacher, the same ordination, the same rainy seasons together with the nuns. I prescribe reinstatement among the nuns for those offenses that nuns share in common with monks. According to those offenses of monks that are not shared in common with nuns, there is no offense."
>
> (Oldenberg 1882)[15]

There is much to be understood from this passage. The word I have translated as "features" is *liṅga*, a word that carries a wealth of different interpretations and connotations, as has been mentioned earlier. It can refer to the actual sexual genitalia of males and females (for humans as well as nonhumans), the linguistic markers of gender in language, or even to what we would today call gender—the cultural meanings assigned to the biological organs of males and females. Other common translations of *liṅgaṃ* include "sign," "characteristic," "feature," "sex," or "organ." When paired with "male" (*purisa*) or "female" (*itthi*), the compound should properly be construed as "the features/organs of a male/man" and "the features/organ of a female/woman." Any of these terms would work equally well in the translation of the passage above, but there is one key element of these passages that should lead to the translation of *liṅgaṃ* as "sex" or "genitals." The reason for this is that the Buddha is quite clear that a change of *liṅgaṃ* requires the monk or nun in question to change their primary residence from a monastery to a nunnery or vice versa. This means that these cases are not just talking about changing one's appearance, and as we have seen above, one's gendered performance and genitals are conditioned by the male and female faculties, which are, in turn, conditioned by one's *karma*. The commentaries are quite clear: good *karma* leads to a sex change from female to male, and weak or bad *karma* leads to a change in sex from male to female.

These cases are introduced in the *Vinaya-piṭaka* as a straightforward observation made by his followers, brought to the Buddha for his consideration and his response. This passage appears in the discussion of the first rule for monks and for nuns, the rule against sexual intercourse—the first of four rules for monks and the first of eight rules for nuns that result in the expulsion of a monk or a nun from the order. The audience is the Buddha's followers, and the passage has no details about who the monks or nuns who experienced this change of sex were, unlike other passages found in the description of this first rule. We have, then, an unnamed monk and an unnamed nun whose characteristics or features that denote sexual difference—their genitalia—have changed. The Buddha's response is equally telling; the passage does not note any unusual response to this fact of sex change. Given this focus on how the rules are broken, the Buddha's response to the stories about the monk and nun in whom the sexual features of the opposite sex appeared is not particularly remarkable. The Buddha's response is solely in terms of how this sex change affects the monk's or nun's teacher, seniority, and relationship to the new order of nuns and monks to which the transformed monk and nun, respectively, should now belong. The Buddha explains that the monk and the nun can have the same teacher, *upajjhāya*, the same ordination, and the same number of rainy seasons (the same number of years spent as a monk or a nun). There are traditionally two kinds of teachers named in the Pāli canon, the *upajjhāya*, who may be considered to be the more senior of the two, and the *ācariya*, who is subordinate category. Similarly, a male monk who has female genitalia is still ordained and the female nun who now has male genitalia is still ordained, but as a monk. Nothing changes for the monk (now a nun) or the nun (now a monk) except their biological sex and the fact that they now have to belong to the order of nuns or the order of monks. The fact of sexual transformation is regarded in this passage as a rather ordinary thing, to be dealt with solely in terms of one's seniority in the order of monks or nuns.[16]

Conclusion

The Pāli *imaginaire*—worlds shaped by the ideas, teachings, and practices of Pāli Buddhism—recognizes four different genders: females, males, *ubhatobyañjanakas*, and *paṇḍakas*. These four exist among humans, nonhumans (gods as well as beings in the hells), and animals. The relationship between biologically sexed bodies and the performance of gender is no less complicated in the early periods of Pāli Buddhism than it is in Christian traditions and those of other religious traditions; the notion that humanity has only recently come to recognize that biological sex and gender have a complex relationship with each other is an erroneous assumption. For Pāli Buddhism, we can identify two different explanations for the relationship between the faculties (*indriyāni*) that are present in womb-born beings from the moment of conception, biological sex, and gender. The first explanation says that the faculties are displayed and manifested in one's biological sex and gender, as evidenced in such ways as one's deportment, occupation, fashion, and so on. The second explanation, however, argues that the male and female faculties are ultimately the cause of one's biological sex and also the basis for the gender that one performs. The intricacy of these analyses demonstrates that Pāli Buddhism is more complex than an essentialist, sexually dimorphic system. Sex change is possible; the faculties are the mechanisms by which one's *karma* determines one's conception and birth and thus one's biologically sexed body and one's gender.

Notes

1 For more, see also Norman (2006), chapters 3, 4, 5.

2 There are a handful of excellent, and recent, bibliographies on women in Buddhism for those not familiar with the literature. See Janet Gyatso (2003: 89–115), Wilson (2003), Analāyo (2014: 109–53), and Collett (2014). Finally, see Cabezón (2017).

3 ubhatobyañjanako 'ti itthīnimittuppādanakammato, Samantapasadika, 1024.

4 Compare this to Bapat (1957: 15–17).

5 See Analāyo (2015).

6 Perera cites *A Dravidian Etymological Dictionary* for this suggestion. Perera's work, while published in 1993, was completed in 1973, and, thus, his use of terms such as "eunuch" and "hermaphrodite" should be recognized as now dated.

7 Compare this to Gyatso (2003: 94–5, n. 11)

8 Compare this to Sweet and Zwilling (1993).

9 Sweet and Zwilling (1993: 898). Compare to Gyatso (2003: 109).

10 Discussed in Kassapa's *Vimattivinodanī-ṭīkā* from the twelfth century and the *Vinayālaṅkāra-ṭīkā*, composed by Taung Phila Sayadaw (1578–1651). See Bode (1909: 53–4).

11 The passage in Pāli is "paṇḍakā 'ti ussannakilesā avūpasantapariḷāhā napuṃsakā. pariḷāhavegābhibhūtā yena kenaci saddhiṃ mittabhāvaṃ patthenti." In his discussion of this passage, Zwilling seems to have conflated two different passages. In this passage, there is no mention of *thulakumarikā* (coarse young girls) (Zwilling 1992: 205). However, *Vinaya-piṭaka* 1.70 lists the five places that monks should not visit for alms. Those five areas or resorts that are "off limits" to monks are prostitutes (*vesiyāgocaro*), widows (*vidhavāgocaro*), grown girls (*thullakumārikagocaro*; see Horner's note on this), paṇḍakas (*paṇḍakagocaro*), and nuns (*bhikkhunīgocaro*) (Horner 1938: n. 4.87).

12 This translation is from Müeller (1897) but also adapted with help from C. A. F. Rhys Davids and Pe Maung Tin's translation in the *The Expositor: Atthasālinī, Buddhaghosa's Commentary on the Dhammasaṅgaṇi, the First Book of the Abhidhamma-piṭaka* ([1920] 1958: 419). The Maung Tin and Rhys Davids translation of the *Atthasālinī* in *The Expositor* is generally accurate, though I have modified it slightly to make it more readable in English.

13 Karunadasa points out that there is another anomaly with regard to the faculties of femininity and masculinity: in the *Paṭṭhāna* of the *Abhidhamma-piṭaka*, he writes, "With the sole exception of *itthindriya* and *purisindriya*, all the *indriyas* are postulated as *indriya-paccaya*, 'condition by way of faculty'" (1967: 55). This observation has implications for how the male and female faculties are understood in the commentaries, which must be the subject for a different study.

14 Janet Gyatso has made this point with reference to the category of *paṇḍakas*, using Nāgārjuna's deconstruction of essentialist and dualistic points of view. See Gyatso (2003: 103).

15 My translation. In the original it reads: tena kho pana samayena aññatarassa bhikkhuno itthiliṅgaṃ pātubhūtaṃ hoti and tena kho pana samayena aññatarissā bhikkhuniyā purisaliṅgaṃ pātubhūtaṃ hoti (*Vinaya-piṭaka*, vol. 3, 35, in Oldenberg 1964)

16 Compare this to Gyatso (2003: 110–11) and Gyatso (2015).

References

Analāyo, B. (2014). "Karma and Female Birth." *Journal of Buddhist Ethics* 21: 109–53. Accessed November 11, 2017, from http://blogs.dickinson.edu/buddhistethics/files/2014/01/Anaalayo-KarmaFemale-final.pdf.

Analāyo, B. (2015). "The *Cullavagga* on *Bhikkhunī* Ordination." *Journal of Buddhist Ethics* 22: 439.

Anderson, C. (2016). "Regulating Women's Bodies in Indian Buddhist Canonical Literature." In Karen Pechilis and Barbara Holdredge (eds.), *Re-Figuring the Body: Embodiment in South Asian Religions*, Conference on the Study of Religions of India Series. Albany, NY: SUNY Press.

Bapat, P. (1957). "Bisexualism in Buddhist Literature." *Palaeologia* 6(1): 15–17.

Bode, M. (1909). *The Pali Literature of Burma*. London: Royal Asiatic Society.

Cabezón, José I. (2017). *Sexuality in Classical South Asian Buddhism*. Somerville, MA: Wisdom.

Collett, A. (ed.). (2014). *Women in Early Indian Buddhism: Comparative Textual Studies*. Oxford: Oxford University Press.

Collins, S. (1990). "On the Very Idea of the Pāli Canon," *Journal of the Pali Text Society* XV (1990): 89–126.

Collins, S. (1998). *Nirvāṇa and Other Buddhist Felicities: Utopias of the Pāli Imaginaire*. Cambridge: Cambridge University Press.

Dreger, A. (1998). *Hermaphrodites and the Medical Invention of Sex*. Cambridge: Harvard University Press.

Faure, B. (1998). *The Red Thread: Buddhist Approaches to Sexuality*, Princeton, NJ: Princeton University Press.

Gyatso, J. (2003). "One Plus One Makes Three: Buddhist Gender, Monasticism, and the Law of the Non-Excluded Middle." *History of Religions* 43(2): 89–115.

Gyatso, J. (2015). *Being Human in a Buddhist World: An Intellectual History of Medicine in Early Modern Tibet*. New York: Columbia University Press.

Horner, I. B. (trans.) (1938). *The Book of the Discipline (Vinayapiṭaka)*. London: Pali Text Society. Reprint edition 2000.

Karunadasa, Y. (1967). *Buddhist Analysis of Matter*. Colombo: Department of Cultural Affairs.

Morris, R., E. Hardy, and C. A. F. Rhys Davids (eds.) (1955). *Aṅguttara-nikāya*. London: Pali Text Society.

Müeller, E. (ed.) (1885), *Dhammasaṅgaṇi*. London: Pali Text Society. Reprint edition 1978.

Müeller, E. (ed.) (1897). *Atthasālinī: Buddhaghosa's Commentary on the Dhammasaṅgaṇi*. London: Pali Text Society. Reprint edition 1979.

Norman, K. R. (2006). *A Philological Approach to Buddhism*, 2nd edn. Lancaster: Pali Text Society.

Oldenberg, H. (ed.) (1882). *Vinaya-piṭakaṃ*. London: Pali Text Society. Reprint edition 1964.

Perera, L. P. N. (1993). *Sexuality in Ancient India: A Study Based on the Pali Vinayapitaka*, Kelaniya: Postgraduate Institute of Pali and Buddhist Studies.

Rhys Davids, C. A. F., and P. M. Tin (trans.) (1920). *The Expositor: Atthasālinī, Buddhaghosa's Commentary on the Dhammasaṅgaṇi, the First Book of the Abhidhamma-piṭaka*. London: Pali Text Society. Reprint edition 1958.

Sponberg, A. (1992). "Attitudes toward Women and the Feminine in Early Buddhism." In José I. Cabezón (ed.), *Buddhism, Gender, and Sex* (pp. 3–36). Albany, NY: SUNY Press.

Sweet, M., and L. Zwilling. (1993). "The First Medicalization: The Taxonomy and Etiology of Queerness in Classical Indian Medicine." *Journal of the History of Sexuality* 3(4): 590–607.

Takakusu, J., and N. Makoto (eds.) (1924). *Samantapāsādikā: Buddhaghosa's Commentary on the Vinaya-piṭaka*. Lancaster: Pali Text Society. Reprint edition 2006.

Wijayaratna, M. (1990). *Buddhist Monastic Life: According to the Texts of the Theravada Tradition*. New York: Cambridge University Press.

Zwilling, L. (1992). "Homosexuality as Seen in Indian Buddhist Texts." In José I. Cabezón (ed.), *Buddhism, Sexuality, and Gender* (pp. 203–14). Albany, NY: SUNY Press.

Zysk, K. (1991). *Asceticism and Healing in Ancient India: Medicine in the Buddhist Monastery*. Dehli: Motilal Banarsidass.

10

Narrative of Ambā in the *Mahābhārata*: Female Body, Gender, and the Namesake of the Divine Feminine

Veena R. Howard

The Kāśi princess Ambā blazes through life as a female avenger. The *Ambā-Upākhyāna* (the subtale of Ambā) of the *Mahābhārata* begins with the Kuru patriarch Bhīṣma violently abducting Ambā, with the intent of giving her as a bride to his half brother Vicitravīrya. This abduction tragically prevents Ambā from marrying her love Śālva (whom she chose in secret), thus depriving her of her *strī-dharma* (prescribed duties for wife and mother). Entirely dedicated to Ambā's story, the *Ambā-Upākhyāna* details her pursuit of vengeance as she resolves to seek justice against the powerful Bhīṣma.[1] Ambā's story extends over the course of two lifetimes and recounts her fierce resolve to kill Bhīṣma, her undertaking of extreme austerities to accomplish this goal, and finally, her intentional sex change to secure Bhīṣma's death.[2]

Central to the story is Ambā's defiance of the normative gender conventions that circumscribe the female body. Throughout this narrative, Ambā asserts her agency and expresses her formidable will to revenge her wrongdoer, all of which are unusual for a woman characterized as "the beautiful Kāśi princess." However, most scholarship of the *Mahābhārata* has used gender essentialist and psychoanalytical approaches,[3] generally focusing on the issues of patriarchal oppression, purity, the female body, sexuality, transsexuality, marriage, and violence against women. Through such analyses, Ambā emerges as a tragic figure who has been deprived of marriage and motherhood. Through a close literal analysis of the narrative, with insight from feminist scholars including Gayatri Spivak and Luce Irigaray, as well as a consideration of the motif of the Divine Feminine, this chapter concentrates on underexamined aspects of Ambā's story. The themes of this chapter include the insistent depiction of Ambā's agency (which feminist scholars often overlook, not recognizing Ambā's autonomy), an exposé of oppressive patriarchal structures, and the failings of eminent men in the story (considered as *dharma* guardians) who fail in their duty to protect women.[4]

The following four sections address the ways in which Ambā's female identity and gender ambiguity directly challenge gender normative structures and women's social roles prescribed in the *Mahābhārata* and Hindu law books. The first section gives an overview of the narrative structure and the narrator of the *Ambā-Upākhyāna*, providing a foundation for the analysis of the narrative. For a complete view of Ambā's character and actions, we must evaluate the narrator of Ambā's story, Bhīṣma, who is also the cause of Ambā's plight. The second section focuses on Ambā's defiance of patriarchal norms through her speeches. Ambā's acumen and fierce willpower is revealed through her confrontation with both Bhīṣma and Śālva, her monologue in which she curses men, and her conversations (*saṃvāda*) with the male ascetics in which she sorts out her dilemma. The third section explores Ambā's demonstration of willpower through her austerities, her fierce individuality in the female body, and her decision to change her sex to take revenge. Finally, the essay evaluates the resonances between Ambā and the Goddess of her namesake, Ambā also being the name of the Goddess Durgā who defies evildoers through her prowess. The closing section argues that Ambā emerges as a powerful female protagonist who wages war against patriarchal structures and undermines Bhīṣma, the symbol of a powerful patriarchy. The chapter as a whole draws attention to how narrative portrays a female character who defies gender and sexual norms, unlike many other narratives in the *Mahābhārata* that depict women with traits of obedience, bound within normative patriarchal structures.

The Narrative and the Narrator: Issues in the Female Right to Speak and Ambā's Agency

To appreciate the value of Ambā's tale, it is important to understand the purpose of *upākhyānas*—or subtales—in the *Mahābhārata*. Alf Hiltebeitel catalogues sixty-seven *Upākhyānas* as "*dharmayāṇī*" or "concerned with *dharma*", connoting duty/virtue/obligation/law (Hiltebeitel 2011: 223). According to Hiltebeitel, the *Upākhyānas* are often "vehicles of unofficial law" (2011: 224). Of the sixty-seven, only five subtales are named after a central female character: "Śākuntalā" and "Tapatī" (Book 1), "Sāvitrī" and "Sukanyā" (Book 3), and "Ambā" (Book 5). All five women display immense willpower and agency, and all challenge normative marriage laws. The first four women are married, and they prevail in their challenges by adhering to the *strī-dharma* of *pativrata* (absolute devotion to husband). These stories of marriage all conclude "happily ever after."

Ambā's tale stands in contrast to these stories, with their pleasant endings and moral victories: Ambā's marriage never actually occurs; she wins no miraculous, happy outcome. In fact, the intended guardian of moral order in the story, Bhīṣma, so profoundly transgresses the conventions of marriage that Ambā is left utterly bereft of any champion and must rectify the situation herself. She challenges laws that limit women's autonomy. Other subtales are morality tales that are meant to reinforce the belief that a wife's primary duty is devotion to her husband, while Ambā's tale—by getting rid of the conventional "happy marriage" ending—challenges this belief as well as laws limiting female choice. Is the lesson of this tale to empower women in the face of difficult situations and oppressive systems? By naming the female protagonist Ambā (a name of Goddess Durgā), the tale evokes defiant female agency and *śakti* (the feminine power).

The narrative begins when Bhīṣma abducts the three sisters—Ambā, Ambikā, and Ambālika—at their *svayaṃvara*, the ceremony in which they choose their bridegroom.[5] Bhīṣma does not abduct the sisters for himself—as he already has committed himself to a life of celibacy—but for his younger brother, Vicitravīrya. Ambā discloses to her captor Bhīṣma that she and King Śālva had chosen each other in secret, unbeknownst to her father. Considering that she had already selected another man, Bhīṣma releases her and sends her back to Śālva. Ambā happily returns to her lover Śālva, only to suffer Śālva's rejection—despite her heartfelt pleas. He bases his rejection of her upon the law of *rākṣasa* marriage (marriage by abduction), which determines the woman to be forcibly married to the man who abducted her. Dejected and humiliated, Ambā returns to Bhīṣma, demanding that he himself marry her, but he also rejects her based on his lifelong vow of celibacy. Deciding not to return to her parents' home, Ambā takes a course seldom available to single young women in Indian texts, wandering off alone, eventually arriving at a hermitage of ascetics in the forest.

The second part of the narrative, comprised of the ascetics' consolation of and conversations with Ambā, focuses on her plight and despair at the hermitage and her unequivocal determination to revenge herself on Bhīṣma. The ascetics voice their concern for her situation and offer solutions to her predicament. The ascetics conclude that Bhīṣma is the cause of her misfortune. In this section, Bhīṣma's guru, powerful sage Rāma Jāmadagnya, decides to fight Bhīṣma for having deprived Ambā of her *strī-dharma*. However, Bhīṣma is unyielding and his pride unwavering in the face of this confrontation, and eventually, Rāma accepts defeat in the battle. Despite such a setback, Ambā remains undeterred; she resolves to "bring Bhīṣma down in battle" (5.187.8) herself as she disappears into the deep woods.

In the final section of Ambā's story, Bhīṣma recounts her resoluteness: she resorts to fierce austerities to gain the spiritual power necessary to kill him. Her austerities include "going without food" and "standing in the water" (5.187.20). Significantly, she undertakes these austerities not for attaining spiritual realization but rather to destroy the supposed guardian of patriarchal laws who deceptively quotes the laws of marriage. Ambā is so resolute in practicing her austerities that she moves Lord Śiva, who appears in front of her to grant a boon, granting her request that she will attain manhood and get her revenge in her next life. Bhīṣma also tells the details of how Ambā is reborn as Śikhaṇḍinī—King Drupada's daughter—and is later transformed into a man—Śikhaṇḍin, who eventually faces Bhīṣma in battle.[6]

As the narrator, Bhīṣma concludes by saying that the daughter of Drupada received her desire to be transformed into a man, and that he will not break his vow (of not lifting arms against women) and kill Śikhaṇḍin in the battle because of Śikhaṇḍin's femaleness.[7] Even though Śikhaṇḍin has a male body, Bhīṣma sees him as Ambā—although her sex has been changed. It is Ambā's femaleness that causes Bhīṣma—the great patriarch— to give up in the battle and eventually meet his death.

Narrator Bhīṣma: The Issue of Male Sexual Control and Control of Women's Sexuality

For literary analysis, it is important to note that the Kuru patriarch Bhīṣma, erudite in the nuances of *dharma* laws, serves as the narrator of many *Upākhyānas* in the *Mahābhārata*, but, among those, the tale of Ambā is the only one with a female protagonist. Ironically, Bhīṣma, who has been spying on Ambā throughout her wanderings and next birth, narrates her story and divulges his own fear of the young maiden. Unlike many other tales, scholars see *Ambā-Upākhyāna* to not impart any apparent *dharma* lesson but only as explaining Bhīṣma's impending demise at the hands of Śikhaṇḍin whom he recognizes as Ambā from a previous birth.[8] However, my reading of the text demonstrates this tale's didactic import: it exposes oppressive systems of patriarchy through the lens of a woman's journey to confront the symbol of patriarchy—Bhīṣma—who commodifies women throughout his life, treating them simply as tools for progeny.

The *Mahābhārata* largely portrays Bhīṣma as a man symbolizing royal power, wisdom, self-restraint, and sacrifice. He stands in almost every regard as a pillar of moral rectitude, an upholder of the laws of *dharma*, duty. He receives the name Bhīṣma—literally, "terrible"—because of his vow of lifelong celibacy taken in his youth—a vow simultaneously entailing voluntary renunciation of personal pleasures and political right to the throne. As a young prince, Bhīṣma takes the vow to abdicate the right to his father's throne to assure Satyavatī (a fisherwoman with whom his father was in love) that her sons will be his rightful heirs. In return for this sacrifice of denying himself conjugal pleasures and fatherhood, the gods bestow upon Bhīṣma the boon of *icchā mṛtyu*—death at his own will—making him invincible to any warrior, no matter how great. Bhīṣma gives up the right to the throne of the Kuru clan but simultaneously pledges to become the guardian of the throne of the Kauravas. To ensure the succession of that clan, he organizes the marriages of his male relatives to secure the Kaurava patrilineage.[9] As a renunciate who rejects any relations with women, Bhīṣma never has to deal with women as wives or daughters. But with regard to women, his actions with consistent with the norms of patriarchal society in which "a man's honour depended on his legitimately 'owning' his woman's sextuality."[10] He views women impersonally, largely as instruments to sustain the Kuru and Kaurava clan and essential to the higher goals of the state's security. This chauvinistic outlook most clearly shows itself in the Ambā story, in which his abduction of three sisters for his half brother ultimately leads to his own demise.

Bhīṣma's life story reveals that he tends to reduce women to objects of exchange between males and values them only as givers of progeny, even in his vow of celibacy. Celibacy is an utmost expression of male agency over the male body. In the epic, Bhīṣma shows his aversion for all women other than his mother. Bhīṣma clandestinely arranges the marriage of princess Gāndhārī with Dhṛtarāṣṭra, without informing her of her future husband's blindness. He remains silent while Prince Duryodhana shamelessly disrobes Draupadī before the entire court until she is rescued by the divine intervention of Kṛṣṇa. He is so obsessed with saving the Kuru line that he does not hesitate to use any means to protect the throne, including his violent abduction of the sisters Ambālikā, Ambikā, and Ambā. As Irawati Karve notes, "The Mahabharata does not reveal that there was any attitude of chivalry towards women. But no man had shown the utter callousness that Bhishma had" (1974: 16). In Bhīṣma's own telling, his devastation of Ambā's chances for marriage and his lawlessness toward her lead directly to his destruction—a seemingly indomitable man—by a mere woman.

Bhīṣma's Surrender: Unveiling the Cause of His Own Demise

Bhīṣma is the last person in the world one would imagine telling Ambā's tale. In it, he himself unveils the cause of his own death, his Achilles' heel, as it were. Before the great war of the *Mahābhārata*, Duryodhana beseeches Bhīṣma to take command of the Kaurava army, exclaiming, "when we are guided by you as the celestials are by Śakra, we shall surely become invincible" (5.153.15). Bhīṣma accepts command of the army, but forewarns, "Arjuna, Vāsudeva and other kings there I shall beat back as soon as I see them, Bhārata, but I shall not, strong-armed king, kill Śikhaṇḍin of Pāñcāla … I shall not fight him" (5.169.15–20). Bhīṣma addresses Śikhaṇḍin as "strong armed," but he fears him not because of his physical prowess. Bhīṣma recognizes him as the female Ambā from a previous incarnation rather than as the son of King Drupada.

The reader might be surprised to hear Bhīṣma's own account of his mishaps and his willing compliance to Ambā's wish to kill him. However, the following reasons warrant that he only unveils the truth of his unlawfulness, even though he never overtly admits his masculine aggressions. First, even though Bhīṣma transgresses the marriage law while abducting Ambā and her sisters, he overall symbolizes truth and righteousness. Bhīṣma's willing acceptance of the consequences of the abuse of the marriage laws demonstrates the consequential nature of the laws of *dharma*, which cannot be transgressed with impunity. Second, Bhīṣma alone witnesses Ambā's journey spanning over two lifetimes. He follows Ambā's musings and her actions through the reports of the spies that he had sent to follow her. Such stealthy pursuing of the young maiden Ambā signals his anxiety about her. Although Bhīṣma calls her blameless, he never admits his violation of Ambā's sanctity. Further, as an exemplar of *dharma* in almost every other instance, Bhīṣma must inevitably recognize that he had even distorted the *rākṣasa* marriage laws in his fixation on advancing the Kuru clan. Third, Bhīṣma tells Ambā's story before the war commences, foretelling the overthrow of the forces of *adharma* under Duryodhana. Bhīṣma accepts in advance his defeat by Śikhaṇḍin as the just consequence of his own deed of *adharma* toward Ambā. His death will leave the Kaurava army unprotected. Finally, that Bhīṣma serves as the narrator of a female character's life substantiates Ambā's stature as an agent of *dharma* herself. It is Bhīṣma's one act of *adharma* toward Ambā that brings down the entire Kaurava army.

Thus, it is only fitting that epic authors choose Bhīṣma to be the narrator of Ambā's tale, the only woman's tale (*upākhyāna*) that he chronicles and tells in a great detail. He does not detest Ambā's wrath nor does he cast her as a helpless female. The following sections focus on Bhīṣma's recounting of how Ambā confronts patriarchal norms, reveals the flaws of *kṣatriya* prowess, defies Brahmanical structures meant to suppress women, and otherwise asserts her autonomy.

Ambā's Speeches and the Question of the Right to Speak

In her essay, "Can the Subaltern Speak?," Spivak draws attention to Brahmanical laws that circumscribe women's agency and voice. Spivak's approach is helpful when analyzing Ambā's defiance in speaking for herself—first with Bhīṣma and Śālva and then with the ascetics. According to Spivak, "There is no space from which the sexed subaltern subject can speak" (1994: 103). Nevertheless, Ambā's sudden release from the normative role of a wife in the structure of *dharma* laws when she is rejected both by Śālva and Bhīṣma opens up a "space" for her from which she can speak. Her words and actions tell us that Ambā *can*, and *does*, speak. She most clearly articulates her thoughts as a woman only when she is single. She claims her autonomy when she is not under the control of Śālva, who betrays her emotionally and psychologically, or Bhīṣma, who uses martial power to control her, or her father, who seeks to control her legally. In contrast to the patriarchal forces that silence her voice, the male ascetics at the hermitage, who have stepped out of the ordinary world of gender and caste discriminations, provide a space for her to speak, through which she reclaims her female autonomy.

When Ambā speaks, she makes the most invulnerable man—the man of "terrible" vow, Bhīṣma—tremble. The recursive power of the feminine nature in Hinduism resonates through Ambā's voice, as represented in her soliloquy and dialogues with Bhīṣma, Śālva, and the sages. She expresses her agency as a woman in a way that warrants closer scrutiny. Speech serves as a form of action that deconstructs the structures of power. The *Chāṇdogya Upaniṣad* celebrates the power of speech or *vāk* (a feminine gendered noun): "Had speech (*vāk*) not been there, no one would be able to make known the distinction between just and unjust, true and false … It is speech which makes all these known" (VII.2.1).[11] Ambā's speeches echo the wisdom expressed through the *Upaniṣad's mahāvākyas* (great sayings) in her discernment of the just from the unjust. In his book, *Strī: Feminine Power in the Mahābhārata*, Kevin McGrath differentiates between the use of speech acts made by men and women heroes in the epic, stating that women

> are *knowers* of dharma—that which is valued as appropriate—and in speech proclaim what *karma* is right at certain moments in the narrative. They are the vocal interpreters of what is worthwhile. (2011: 13)

Ambā provides a vocal analysis of how she is wronged by the chauvinistic interpretation of the marriage laws. We will see how Bhīṣma in fact breaks the *rākṣasa* marriage laws while proclaiming to be following them, laws that should in fact have protected her wishes in marriage, and how her beloved, Śālva, heartlessly abandons her, deferring to the patriarchal letter of the law fearing his own dishonor. The following section focuses on how her discursive arguments expose the injustices of patriarchal laws invoked by both Bhīṣma and Śālva.

Ambā's Defiance of Draconian Marriage Laws

Ambā uses her intelligence to defend her decision to choose her own bridegroom and to contest Bhīṣma's unjust abduction of herself and her sisters. She defies the normative tradition by choosing a bridegroom (*vara*) for herself in secret, which some consider to be the root of her dilemma. Uma Chakravarti (2009: 49) observes that Ambā's narrative "works to discipline female choice."[12] Chakravarti views the hardships of Ambā's life as punishment for her choice. Alternatively, I argue that the narrative presents a unique illustration of female defiance and of a woman's reclamation of control after she loses her choice. She eventually confronts the great warrior Bhīṣma in battle, a move that challenges the draconian marriage law of *rākṣasa* (marriage by abduction).

Bhīṣma publicly proclaims *rākṣasa* marriage as "the highest" form of marriage when he abducts Ambā and her sisters (as narrated by Vaiśaṃpāyana in Book 1).[13] The *Laws of Manu* recognize marriage by force among various forms of marriages but as one of the lowest forms. Bhīṣma's proclamation shows his own interpretation of the law. Rather than bowing to his mandate like her sisters, Ambā fearlessly approaches Bhīṣma protesting that she has already chosen Śālva as her lord. According to the *Dharma Śāstras*, she cannot have two lords at the same time.[14] She knows not only the laws of marriage but also right conduct for a woman. She addresses Bhīṣma as someone "wise in law and learned in all scriptures (*dharmajñaḥ sarvaśāstraviśāradaḥ*)" to invoke his sensibilities and pleads,

> Pray listen and act toward me in a lawful fashion [*dharmayam*]. In my heart I had chosen [*vrata*] the king of Śālva as my bridegroom, and he too has chosen me secretly ... How can you, who have learned the scriptures, force me to dwell

in this house, when I am in love with someone else ... Take pity on me, strong-armed upholder of the Law [*dharma*], for you, so we have heard, are known on earth for being true to your vows. (5.171.5)

Ambā's words are calculated. She addresses Bhīṣma as a *cognoscenti* of *dharma* and beseeches him to listen because the law (*dharma*) of marriage is in question. Furthermore, she appeals to Bhīṣma's sense of righteousness to help him see beyond his obsessive allegiance to the Kuru throne, for which he snatches the three princesses from their *svayaṃvara*. Throughout the *Mahābhārata*, Bhīṣma demonstrates unwavering dedication for continuing the Kuru clan, and most of his mishaps are the result of this commitment.[15] When Bhīṣma crashes the wedding party to kidnap the princesses, he sets a dangerous precedent when he says that "the students of the Law hold that the bride is the best who is carried off by force" (1.96.13). Bhīṣma valorizes the *rākṣasa* (demonic) form of marriage, which is mentioned only as the seventh option of the eight forms of marriages.[16] Marriage by force is considered to be demonic because it uses violence and is traumatic to the bride and her family. Thus, it is not the superior form of marriage.

Bhīṣma's abduction of Ambā for his half brother indicates an even more aberrant interpretation of the draconian marriage laws. Ambā is pointing out the danger of blind adherences to the laws. In his essay, "Moral Doubts, Moral Dilemmas and Situational Ethics," P. K. Sen says, "The *Mahābhārata* is full of instances wherein actions performed on the basis of blind adherence to scriptures or social practices either resulted or could have resulted in disastrous consequences" (2014: 194). Sen cites Bhīṣma's abduction of the three maidens and Ambā's ensuing trouble as one such example. Ambā's words draw attention to the objectification of the female body and casting of her identity as solely a child-bearing object, both of which have been confronted by modern feminists. In her Stanford Encyclopedia essay on Luce Irigaray, Sarah Donovan summarizes Irigaray's perceptive analysis of how women have "historically been associated with the role of 'mother'" and how they have "not been considered as full subjects."[17] For Bhīṣma, Ambā's body has only one purpose: the advancement of the Kuru clan. Ambā's not acquiescing to the patriarch of the Kuru clan calls into question the treatment of women as commodified objects. Ambā begins and rests her case by appealing to Bhīṣma's wisdom and his promise to uphold *dharma*—*dharma*, meaning law, virtue, and justice.[18]

Alternatively, Ambā is scolding Bhīṣma for not even properly adhering to the letter and intent of the lowly *rākṣasa* form of marriage, in that the groom did not abduct her himself, so Bhīṣma's very laying of his hands upon the women technically puts Ambā and her sisters into marriage with him, not his half-brother. Ambā demonstrates not only courage when she speaks out against the patriarch but also knowledge of marriage laws. She is aware of the legal quandary that he has left her in as well as the *dharma* problem that Bhīṣma has created for himself by abducting her in a rash attempt to fulfill his duty (*dharma*) to preserve the Kuru lineage. However, Bhīṣma fails to acknowledge that he has destroyed Ambā's future and marred his own destiny. Without deliberating on this question, he sends her back to Prince Śālva, intending to correct the error that he has inadvertently made but lacking the foresight of the looming trouble he has created for Ambā.

Who Does Ambā Belong to? Ambā's Exposé of the Violence of Patriarchy

In her essay, "Women on the Market" (1985: 186), Irigaray analyzes the position of women in male-dominated societies and draws attention to a system involving the "commodification" of women. She points out that the virgin woman is esteemed as the "pure exchange value," but she does not provide any examples of real or *mythical* women to prove her point. The Classical Hindu Dharma (Law) books clearly state how only the virgin woman is fit for carrying the patrilineal line. Ambā's story presents a unique example in which a woman both exposes the absurdity of these laws and curses them for reducing women to objects. Ambā's conversation with Śālva reveals the unjust nature of marriage laws as interpreted by both Bhīṣma and Śālva.

Because of Bhīṣma's actions, Ambā finds herself involved with *gandharva* and *rākṣasa* marriages: one by love (Śālva), the other by abduction (Bhīṣma). Arti Dhand discusses the laws of marriage, saying,

> By whatever means a partner may have been acquired, however, women are expected to have only one sexual partner in their lifetimes. This would appear to be the case even in unions in which a woman was abducted or assaulted—as in the case of Ambā. (2008: 105)

The fact that Ambā is forcefully dragged from the marriage hall and had already chosen another man in her heart raises the question: "To whom does she belong?" That Bhīṣma is oblivious of her situation shows how the patriarch is unconcerned about the plight he causes her by his action. Thus, it is only apposite that the *Mahābhārata* does not let this act go unpunished but appoints Ambā as the cause of the death of this invincible man. As we mentioned earlier, Bhīṣma himself narrates the tale, essentially accepting the cause of his own death.

When released by Bhīṣma, Ambā happily approaches her beloved Śālva with the expectation that they will be reconciled. He turns a cold shoulder to her and replies,

> I do not want you as my wife: you have been another man's before, fair woman. Go back to the Bhārata my dear. I do not desire you after Bhīṣma's forcible abduction of you … How can a king like me, who has learned his lessons and preaches the Law, allow into his house a woman who has been another man's? Go where you please, dear, don't let the time go by. (5.172.5)

Śālva invokes the same *rākṣasa* marriage law that Bhīṣma invoked at the wedding and in one stroke annuls their mutual love. In Śālva's eyes Ambā is now tainted and not worthy of him—another patriarchal entrapment that further degrades Ambā. He chooses not to confront the dilemma and demonstrates cruelty toward the one he supposedly loved once so dearly.

Significantly, in most instances in the *Mahābhārata*, the bride is a willing party in the *rākṣasa* form of marriage and is abducted by the groom himself, not by another man on someone else's behalf. Ambā is anything but a willing party; furthermore, she is abducted by Bhīṣma on his half-brother's behalf. Śālva takes the *rākṣasa* marriage law literally and insists that Ambā now belongs to Bhīṣma. Ambā is caught in the middle of two patriarchal laws—*gandharva* (marriage by love) and *rākṣasa* (marriage by force). She uses poignant words to her beloved Śālva:

> He abducted me by force … Love me who love[s] you, an innocent girl, King Śālva, for the abandonment of loving people is not praised in the Laws … I swear by my head that I have never dreamed of anyone at all but you, King Śālva, tiger among men! It is not as another man's previous woman that I have come to you. I speak the truth, Śālva. (5.172.10–15)

Ambā seeks to prove her purity and reminds him of their mutual love.[19] Ambā knows that Śālva's rejection is a doomsday scenario for her because she will be bereft of the *dharma* of both a wife and mother. She has been stolen by Bhīṣma and is now considered his property.

Irigaray draws from the anthropological insights on the commodification of women by saying, "The society we know, our own culture, is based upon the exchange of women" (1985: 170). In Śālva's estimation, Ambā has been stolen by Bhīṣma and thus he forfeits his right to her, saying, "Go, now go! I fear Bhīṣma, fair-hipped woman, and you are Bhīṣma's chattel" (5.172.20). He even considers her to now be Bhīṣma's spoiled goods. Wendy Doniger muses, "Amba epitomizes the no-win situation of a woman tossed like a shuttlecock between two men, each of whom ricochets between inflicting sexual excess or sexual rejection upon her" (1999: 283). But Ambā refuses to be tossed about by powerful men and exposes the violence of the patriarchy. In her story, Ambā and the reader witness the failing of Bhīṣma, who is widely known as the upholder of *dharma*. Furthermore, she realizes the fickleness of her lover Śālva, who claims to know *dharma* but rejects his beloved (Ambā) as a "snake casts off its worn-out skin" (5.172.20).

Bhīṣma and Śālva both reject Ambā—despite her pleas—insofar as they both see themselves as having abdicated the right to her body. Śālva believes that she belongs to Bhīṣma—who dragged her body off—and Bhīṣma believes that she belongs to Śālva—to whom she has previously offered to commit her body in love. She is "othered" as nonessential by both men, to use Simone de Beauvoir's term. In *The Second Sex* de Beauvoir writes,

> For him she is sex, so she is it in the absolute. She is determined and differentiated in relation to man, while he is not in relation to her; she is inessential in front of the essential. He is the Subject, he is the Absolute—she is the Other. (2011: 26)

Both Bhīṣma and Śālva reject her as inessential. Yet, these rejections open a space for Ambā to show her feminine force. Ambā is rejected, but she simultaneously has been released from the constraints of patriarchal laws. Now she is an autonomous woman and expresses her subjectivity through her monologue and her dialogues with the sages, which reveal Ambā's fierce nature in contrast to the pleading and pitiable woman in the courts of the two men. Ambā on her own emerges as a force to be reckoned with.

Ambā's Monologue and Her Emergence as an Autonomous Woman

Ambā's soliloquy in the forest, narrated by Bhīṣma, offers a fierce feminist critique of patriarchy. Her rage signals a proto-feminist rise to power against the patriarchal forces that have controlled her life. She is a woman left to fend for herself without patriarchal protection. According to *Mānava Dharma Śāstra*, a woman should always be guarded by her father, husband, or son. Furthermore, Ambā has been defiled by Bhīṣma, whose abduction has been viewed as the equivalent of rape, "socially, if not physically" (Doniger 2014: 353).[20] Dejected,

Ambā proclaims, "May the strict [*santaḥ*] be my shelter" (5.172.20). Significantly, Ambā chooses to seek refuge in the *santaḥ*—the strict men of wisdom and truth. She is not rejecting law per se; she is objecting to its unjust law and unfair application.

By not returning home to her father, she rejects the world ruled by patriarchal laws—laws that have been critiqued by modern feminists seeking autonomy and equal respect. What is unique about Ambā is that she does not just deliberate on the atrocities done to her but actively seeks to challenge them. She returns neither to Bhīṣma's Hastināpur nor to her father's home (as many would expect) but leaves the city and goes to the hermitage of holy ascetics—notably, a cultural oasis where marriage is not relevant. Her soliloquy reveals her rage toward the patriarchal system as well as the reality of the laws that relegate women to a lower status. Ambā's character as a fierce feminine force emerges. She is in such a rage that she views the custom of *svayaṃvara*—a contest at which a woman supposedly chooses her own husband—as another patriarchal ploy and an occasion to display *kṣatriya* prowess. Ambā's articulation of such grievances—narrated by Bhīṣma himself—brings razor-sharp focus to the indignity of patriarchal social customs imposed upon women, including forced marriage and men's right to the woman's body. Bhīṣma, who has been following her through his secret agents, recounts Ambā's monologue:

> A curse on Bhīṣma, a curse on my dull-witted mindless father, who dangled me like a harlot for the bride price of some derring-do. A curse on myself, a curse on King Śālva, a curse on the Placer [*Daiva*; hand of Fate/god]. Thanks to the folly of all of them I have come to this sorry impasse. Man always gets what his fate has in store. However, Bhīṣma Śāṃtanava was the beginning of my misfortune. (5.173.5)

Ambā ends with a resolve unprecedented in the *Mahābhārata*: "I see now that I have to revenge myself on Bhīṣma, by austerities [*tapasā*] or battle [*yuddha vāpi*], for I consider him the cause of my misery" (5.173.8). Here, we find an outraged woman, in stark contrast to the commonly obedient, subservient, and meek women. Draupadī, after her molestation in the court of elderly patriarchs, including Bhīṣma, is also outraged, but she remains within the boundaries of the propriety expected of a woman in patriarchy. Ambā's statement seems as if it belongs to a modern feminist heroine's biography, resolving that she must instead set things right for herself. She furiously asserts her agency as a free woman and ventures to enter into the male-dominated spaces of *tapas* (asceticism) and *yuddha* (war).

Ambā's Rage and Her Rational Deliberation in the Hermitage

In recent years, feminist thinkers have become "increasingly attuned to the liberatory aspects of anger," writes Jennifer McWeeny. She draws on feminist analyses that cast anger not as "irrational" but "lucid and appropriate," saying, "Our angers empower us, because within them we *know* our own agency and self-worth … we *know* [emphasis in the original] we have been wronged … we *know* the patterns and functions of the oppressive structures that work on us" (2010: 123). Ambā's fury exposes the oppressive patriarchy, and through it she discovers her agency. We see her anger throughout her speeches and conversations: it is intentional and focused on the fact that she has been wronged by Bhīṣma. The ascetics, with whom she takes refuge and who are embodiments of tranquility (*nivṛtti*), side with Ambā's rage. The ascetics' sympathy toward Ambā's plight stands in contraposition to the laws that circumscribe women's conduct. That Ambā, a single woman, spends the night "surrounded by ascetics" (presumably all male) and narrates her story in detail [*savistaram*] is a testament of the liberal spirit of sages (5.173.10).

It is noteworthy that they address Ambā as "the good woman" not as rebellious. One of the sages asks helplessly, "What can ascetics do in these circumstances, good woman, lordly and great-spirited hermitage dwellers deep into austerities?" (5.173.10). Ambā does not ask for protection but rather for permission to "wander forth" (*pravrājitum*) and practice "severe asceticism" (*tapastapasyāmi duścaram*). "I want you to instruct me in asceticism," she beseeches. Indeed, Ambā's request is nontraditional—there exist few examples, if any, of a single unmarried woman living in a hermitage of male ascetics. Bhīṣma narrates how the ascetics worry about the girl and debate among themselves the right course of action.

The sages deliberate on various options and give her advice that is within the accepted laws:

> The husband is her recourse when things go smoothly, the father when things are rough. Wandering forth is quite difficult, especially for a delicate woman like you, a princess by nature dainty, radiant woman. (5.174.5-10)

The sages put things into perspective: Ambā's affluent upbringing and her ascetic resolve are incompatible. Nonetheless, she wishes to practice austerities. Even though the general convention in the stories of the *Mahābhārata* is that people often submit to the advice of ascetics, Ambā defies traditional norms and refuses to return to her father's home in humiliation. Ambā, once removed from male domination, is free to make her own decisions, despite the first counsel of the ascetics. The ascetics' concern for Ambā's situation, and their deliberations, have not received adequate attention from scholars.

In the theatrical and popular portrayals, Ambā is shown as erratic and mad with anger. However, despite her furious mental state, Ambā never acts recklessly. The narrative depicts the ascetics in the forest showing concern, tenderness, and affection for Ambā, anguished by her predicament. All are intent on securing justice for Ambā. Ambā's recounting of her story is repeated to three ascetics: (1) Hotravāhana, (2) Akṛtavraṇa, and (3) the sage Rāma Jāmadagnya. Both Hotravāhana and Akṛtavraṇa consider seeking the help of Rāma Jāmadagnya—the great ascetic and the guru of Bhīṣma—to put Bhīṣma in place. Even though Ambā blames Bhīṣma, her response to the ascetics is deliberate and reasoned:

> Bhīṣma acted in ignorance when he abducted me, reverend lord, for he did not know that my heart was set on Śālva. That you should take into consideration, sir, and pass judgment justly and dispose accordingly. Take appropriate measures in the case of either the Kuru tiger Bhīṣma, or King Śālva, or both, brahmin. I have told you the source of my grief precisely as it is, pray take measures about it as reason [*vidhāna*] dictates, reverend lord. (5.176.5)

Ambā demonstrates her rational approach—not weakness of heart. Since both men were at fault, she rationally refuses to solely blame Bhīṣma. However, Akṛtavraṇa determines it is Bhīṣma who is the primary aggressor, saying,

> What you say concerning the Law is correct, fair woman. Now listen to what I have to say, my dear … Since you have in fact been won and abducted, dear glowing maiden with the pretty waist, King Śālva has reason to doubt you. So Bhīṣma is the one, a self-styled hero flushed with the glow of victory, hence it is proper that you avenge yourself on him. (5.176.10)

This conversation reveals the sage conversing with Ambā on equal terms and concurring with her argument. Ambā's cogent ideas are acknowledged when they are not drowned out by the interests of men tethered to patriarchal dharmas.

Furthermore, Sage Rāma Jāmadagnya (who is Bhīṣma's own guru) shows empathy for Ambā's sorrow; his poignant submission to Ambā's decision to fight Bhīṣma illustrates the eminent ascetic's wish to fight for justice. Outraged by Ambā's predicament, Rāma Jāmadagnya himself offers to take up arms to secure justice for the maiden: "Daughter of Kāśi, say the word and Bhīṣma, however deserving of honor, will touch your feet with his head at my orders!" (5.177.5)[21] This statement is shocking: Bhīṣma is the Kuru patriarch, and his gesture of touching Ambā's feet mirrors the ritual of touching the feet of a goddess—a man touches the feet only of his mother or the Divine Mother. It is almost unimaginable that Bhīṣma the "terrible" would touch the feet of a young woman whom he so lightly dispensed with. I will return to this theme later in the paper.

Rāma Jāmadagnya declares, "I shall take the girl and go myself wherever Bhīṣma is. If battle-famed Bhīṣma does not [do] as I tell him, I shall kill the swaggerer" (5.177.20). The fact that Rāma Jāmadagnya is enraged enough to fight his own disciple attests to Ambā's anger being justified. However, Bhīṣma rejects his guru Rāma Jāmadagnya's command to bow to Ambā, which leads to an apocalyptic battle between the sage and the great warrior. The battle ends in the sage's withdrawal (5.187.1). Bhīṣma recounts that even in the face of her defender's defeat, Ambā is undeterred: "I shall on no condition whatever go back to Bhīṣma again. Rather I shall go there when I myself can bring Bhīṣma down in battle" (5.187.5). She decides to accomplish the task herself.

Scholars who have overlooked Ambā's conversations above have missed her agency and determination. They have also failed to notice the sages' willingness to subvert the normative laws of *strī-dharma* and to consider Ambā on the side of right (*dharma*), taking her grievances seriously enough to go to aid her in revenging Bhīṣma. The ascetics never accuse Ambā of irrational behavior; on the contrary, they allow her to express her rage and seek to ensure that injustice and misogyny toward a woman do not go unpunished.

Ambā's Austerities: Generating the Heat to Consume the Source of Injustice

Ambā stokes the power of rage through austerities—the heat of her *tapas*. Both her *tapas* and free wandering show her to be an example of rebellion against male-dominated conventions (as elaborated by feminist scholars such as Irigaray, de Beauvoir, and Spivak) that circumscribe a woman's agency and control her body and decisions. Her fierce feminism reveals itself as she masters her own body through *tapas* (austerities), in her transgression of all quotidian *dharma* restrictions on women, and in her ultimate decision to change her gender. Other examples exist in the *Mahābhārata* of women "undertaking *mahāvratas*, or extreme ascetic practices directed toward finite goals," writes Dhand (2008: 84). She names Draupadī, Śruvavatī, and Umā, who all undergo rigorous *tapas* to gain the husband of their desire. In this vein she notes, "Ambā displays dogged determination in her austerities, undertaken to accomplish the death of Bhīṣma" (2008: 84). Ambā undertakes *tapas* for the goal of vengeance, not for marital bliss.

The sages of the forest support her desire to perform *tapas*, even though it has as its goal the negative end of wreaking revenge on Bhīṣma. They mentor Ambā in methods to formally renounce the world (*pravraja*). The fact that the ascetics mentor her in *tapas* to kill Bhiṣmā is unparalleled in the Indian sacred literature. *Tapas*—literally "heat"—is generally taken up for spiritual attainments. The heat generated by the fire of austerities yields supernatural powers. Even gods fear the power of *tapas*. Through *tapas,* Ambā emerges as an unstoppable force. Bhīṣma portrays her as the maiden with "her eyes rolling in anger, and she set her mind on austerities, brooding on my death" (5.187.10). She engages in her austerities—not to achieve ultimate spiritual or marital bliss—but to bring down the icon of patriarchal structures. Her determination shakes even the heart of Bhīṣma, who was not shaken by any mighty forces, including those of his Guru who subdued generations of *kṣatriyas*. Anticipating his death, Bhīṣma is deeply troubled by Ambā's decision to undertake austerities:

> From the very day that the maiden departed for the forest set on austerities, I became troubled, wretched, and well-nigh lost my wits. For no baron can defeat me in battle with his prowess ... except one who knows the *brahman* and whose vows have been honed by austerity. (5.187.15)

What is so unique about Ambā's austerities that they trouble Bhīṣma? Perhaps he is disturbed by Ambā's austerities because she is a woman and a woman who is neither married nor unmarried.[22] The Patriarch no doubt feels threatened by the fact that Ambā's motivation for *tapas* is not to find a good husband but to gain the power to slay him. Bhīṣma must feel uneasy of the power of a woman because he has taken a vow never to fight a woman. His vow of celibacy earned him power and fame but has made him fearful of women. He described women as morally "frail and infirm" but also likened them to "blazing fire" (Dhand 2008: 134–5). This spiritual fire (*tapas*) coupled with Ambā's fury is doubly dangerous.

Ambā's *Tapas* and Self-Immolation: Self-Control and Agency

According to Walter Kaelber, "Among the connotations of the Sanskrit root *tap* are 'to consume or destroy by heat' and 'to injure [with heat].'" He notes that "connotations of injury and consuming destruction are, in fact, the most prevalent meanings of the root *tap* and *tap*-derivatives in the Ṛg Veda." He provides examples in which "deities are invoked to injure and destroy enemies by means of *tapas*" (Kaelber 1979: 192–3). Clearly, Ambā's *tapas* is meant to bring about Bhīṣma's death. To attain it, Ambā exercises complete control over her body and decisions. Her intrepid wanderings and fierce austerities are unparalleled in the *Mahābhārata*'s universe—even as a universe inhabited by many powerful women. Bhīṣma narrates the details of Ambā's wanderings to far pilgrimage places, her ascetic practices, Śiva's boon foretelling Bhīṣma's death, and Ambā's next life as Drupada's daughter who—by way of a sex change—becomes the male Śikhaṇḍin who ultimately confronts Bhīṣma in battle. Bhīṣma's spies report all these details of Ambā's actions. This section of the narrative shows how Ambā, as a woman, takes control over her destiny and her gendered body, manipulating it as she wishes for the singular purpose of revenge.

Ambā's time in the forest, during which she is unguarded by her father or any other man, portrays both her freedom and fearlessness. Any women—even in the present world—might covet Ambā's adventures: wandering off to the hermitages of "great ascetics of holy habits," journeying to the sacred fords of different regions, bathing in holy waters, and performing sacred rites. The text provides a catalog of pilgrimage sites:

> There, bathing her body at sacred fords day and night, the daughter of the Kāśi roamed about, ranging at will—at the hermitages of Nanda … the hermitage of Cyavana, the Site of Brahmā, and Prayāga, the sacrificial terrain of the gods … At all those fords the maiden bathed her limbs … and performed severe austerities. (5.187.25-28)

The long list of names of the hermitages and sacred fords suggests that Ambā travelled extensively, as a woman unencumbered by *strī-dharma*. Examples of a single woman roaming freely are rare in the Indian sacred narratives—but nowhere does the text judge her autonomy harshly. Furthermore, the ritual bathing of her body is symbolic of her efforts to purify what has been defiled by the violent abduction of Bhīṣma.

The details of Ambā's austerities (*tapa*s) indicate her strong will power and independence. Ambā resorts to

> superhuman self-mortification. Going without food, emaciated, coarsened, with matted hair, caked with dirt, she lived for six months on air, a stock-still ascetic … she wore through another year standing in the water, without food, glowering. Another year she spent in subsisting on one withered leaf, ferocious in her wrath, while standing on tiptoe. For fourteen years she set heaven and

> earth aglow, and though dissuaded by her relatives, she was to not to be stopped. (5.187.20)

She controls her own body—her body is not for any man. When asked, "Good woman, why do you inflict pain on yourself?" Ambā responds unequivocally,

> Bhīṣma was not defeated by Rāma, so who else would try to vanquish that lord of the earth with ready arrows? I myself shall undertake the most gruesome self-mortifications for the destruction of Bhīṣma. I roam the earth ... so that I may kill the king. May this be the fruit of my vow in another body. (5.187.30)

Ambā knows that there is no man who is equal to Bhīṣma in military prowess, and that she will have to take another birth because her female body prevents her from going to battle with the mighty warrior. Although her feminine gender (she is identified as a female) is constant, Ambā's biological sex is transformed and used as an instrument for her revenge.

Ambā, the Woman of "Terrible" Vow: The Norm-Defying Female

In the *Mahābhārata*, an ideal woman is celebrated because of her religious nature and devotional vow to her husband (*pativrata*). A devoted wife is held in high regard for her single-minded devotion to her husband and often gods shower boons on her. Ambā is not a *pativrata* woman. She is a *single* woman, and it is her unwavering vow to kill that terrifies Bhīṣma. In her resolve, Ambā defies the misogynist attitude often found in Indian religious and philosophical texts that cast women in a fickle, impulsive light. Even though aged, Ambā continues her austerities and, over the course of time, the fire of her vengeance grows proportionate with the fire of her *tapas*. Even in the face of dissuasion by the ascetics and others, she remains undeterred:

> I am consecrated to his death, not to a higher world, ascetics! I have resolved that only by killing Bhīṣma I shall find peace. I shall not desist, brahmins, until I have slain Gangā's son in battle, him because of whom I have found this everlasting life of misery, deprived of the world of husband, neither a woman nor a man! That resolve is lodged in my heart, and for that I have undertaken this vow ... I want to pay Bhīṣma back, I am not to be diverted. (5.188.1)

In vowing to slay Bhīṣma, Ambā describes herself as "neither a woman nor man." This is not because she has been "unsexed" or lost her femaleness but because she has been deprived of the *strī-dharma* of being a wife and mother—considered in her context to be the source of meaning in a woman's life. She is not a man, either, because the patriarchal norms prevent her from participating in battle.

Ambā's intense *tapas* becomes threatening. Bhīṣma, his mother Gaṅgā, ascetics, and gods all grow wary of the power of Ambā's *tapas*. Her terrible vow shakes the heart of celestials, as Bhīṣma's vow of celibacy did. She is not a "shuttlecock" as Doniger termed it but has taken power in her hand. Even Lord Śiva, "the God who wields the Trident, the Consort of Umā, appeared in his own form to the maiden in the midst of the great seers" (5.188.10). Śiva offers Ambā a boon and she chooses Bhīṣma's defeat. "Thou shall smite him," Śiva tells her. Notably, Ambā does not accept the boon with delight—she questions Śiva's promise. She is well aware that her woman's body prevents her from participating in the battle:

> 'How can it be that I, a woman, will triumph in battle, for since I am a woman, my heart is meek [*śāntaḥ*] to its core, Consort of Umā. Yet, Lord of Ghosts [bhuteṣu, creatures], thou hast promised Bhīṣma's defeat, therefore act so that his defeat comes true … that I may encounter Bhīṣma Śāṃtanava and slay him in battle! (5.188.10)

Śiva assures her, "My voice speaks no lies, good woman—it shall come true. Thou shall attain manhood and slay Bhīṣma in battle. And thou shalt remember everything when thou hast gone to a new body" (5.188.15). Immediately after receiving this boon guaranteeing Bhīṣma's demise, Ambā gathers firewood and makes a high pyre, and proclaiming, "For Bhīṣma's death!" she enters into it. This episode offers salient insights into Ambā's character and her wish to kill her nemesis that scholars have overlooked:

1. Ambā acknowledges her womanhood and refers to her heart as "meek," which may seem to contradict her many earlier conversations and actions that demonstrate her courage and fierce will. Notably, it is the Sanskrit term *śānta* (peaceful) that has been translated as "meek" and "still." Ambā presents herself not as a *śāntaḥ strī* (a peaceful woman) but a woman whose mind (*manaḥ*) is at peace (*śāntaḥ*). Perhaps austerities have purified Ambā's body and brought peace to her heart, without diminishing her indomitable intent to bring about Bhīṣma's death for his unpardonable violation of her. Ambā's victimization, the intense austerities, the ascetics' verdict against Bhīṣma, and Guru Rāma's unmet demand for Bhīṣma's rectifying his misdeed—all of these reasons justify why Bhīṣma must be punished (5.179.5).[23]
2. Ambā's austerities had created ample heat to bring Bhīṣma down, but she wants to be certain that Śiva's boon seals Bhīṣma's death. She needs the

body of a man, which can only be achieved by the grace of God. Ambā's self-immolation may appear evocative of the custom of *satī*—widows ascending on the pyre with their deceased husbands—but it is in fact contrary to that practice. Not having a husband, Ambā is not bound to the *dharma* of a devoted wife. Unlike widowed women who sacrifice their bodies on the funeral pyre (*satī*) for no personal advantage, Ambā's self-immolation is intentional: it is for the sake of her personal goal to kill Bhīṣma. In her analysis of the custom of *satī*, Spivak notes that Hindu laws permit self-sacrifice, not self-killing (1994: 95).

Ambā's self-immolation is self-*sacrifice*, not suicide. Traditionally, a widowed woman is the helpless victim of the patriarchal customs that sanctify practice of *satī*. Contrary to this, Ambā's self-immolation is symbolic of her agency in both life and death. Her collecting of the wood is evocative of lighting the fire of *yajña*, to which she offers her body like a last oblation, invoking the death of Bhīṣma. Ambā's body has already been purified by *tapas* (fire of austerities) and by bathing in the sacred fords. Her self-immolation can be considered as an extension of *tapas*, in which she offers her body.

Furthermore, Ambā as an ascetic woman has withdrawn any ties from her relatives who would traditionally perform her funeral rites. Per Hindu understanding, cremation not only purifies the body but also serves to more quickly release the soul from the body (*Ṛg Veda*: 10:16).[24] Wishing to be reborn as speedily as possible to slay Bhīṣma per Śiva's promise, and having no one to cremate her dead body, Ambā makes the choice of self-immolation when approaching the time of her death.

3. Finally, in this episode Bhīṣma characterizes her as "blameless" (*anindita*) and "fair-complexioned" (*varavarṇiṇī*) before she enters in the fire. By calling Ambā "blameless," Bhīṣma accepts the blame for her self-sacrifice. Or rather, by witnessing Ambā's plight and by closely scrutinizing the trials and trepidations of a woman's life, Bhīṣma—one with the terrible vow of celibacy—is able to better realize his participation in the iniquities of draconian marriage laws.

Ambā's Next Birth: Shifting Sex, Gendered Female Body

Many scholars have noted the gender-bending motifs in the *Mahābhārata* through which gender roles are subverted. Many see Ambā's sex change as simply a ploy to overcome the limitations of being a woman. In doing so, scholars often miss the story's details showing that the other characters always view Ambā as a woman, even when in a male body.

Despite Śiva's boon, Ambā is born as King Drupada's daughter in her next life, not as his son. Scholars give ample attention to this section of the tale for the following reasons: (1) the patriarchal mores continue in Ambā's next life because she is born in a female body (despite the boon from Lord Śiva); (2) the sexual themes of transvestism, transsexuality, and sexual ambivalence; and (3) Ambā (Śikhaṇḍin in her next life) does not actually kill Bhīṣma—it is *Arjuna* who kills Bhīṣma. Andrea Custodi sums up Ambā's plight, saying, "Even though Ambā pursues a life of austerities, receives a guarantee from a god, and finally immolates herself in the fire to be reborn a man—*and* her future father Drupada performs rites for a son—Ambā is actually reborn as a female." (2007: 216). Hence, Ambā's journey has often been interpreted as a failure. Nevertheless, we must focus on some important issues that have been overlooked.

The story of Ambā's next birth begins with King Drupada's austerities and Lord Śiva's promise to this sonless king: "You will have a man child who is a woman ... it shall never be otherwise" (5.189.5). "The man child who is a woman" references the reborn Ambā, who despite her sex change to become the male Śikhaṇḍin remains a woman. The story chronicles the ensuing complexities arising out of the birth of Ambā as Drupada's daughter Śikhaṇḍinī. Her parents conceal her female sex, hoping for a miraculous sex change, trusting Śiva's boon.[25] Śikhaṇḍinī, concealed as a male, is married to a woman, but after marriage she is humiliated when the truth of her sex is revealed. Śikhaṇḍinī transforms into the male Shikhaṇḍin after borrowing the male sexual organ from a *yakṣa*. Indeed, from the viewpoint of patriarchal norms and a psychoanalytical lens, it seems unfortunate that Ambā is reborn as woman rather than a man. However, her birth in a female body is ominous for Bhīṣma.

Ambā's rebirth as a female is essential to her fulfilling her vow to kill Bhīṣma. Ambā is recognized as "female" even after she transitions into a male body (Śikhaṇḍin). If Śiva's boon is inalterable (as boons often are) and if only men can go to battle, then Ambā's transition to a male body is the only way she can fulfill what has already been destined. Robert Goldman and Doniger read Ambā's birth as a woman and her sexual transformation from a psychoanalytical perspective, interpreting it as yet another injustice to Ambā. But a close reading of the text shows that the logic of the entire story of Śikhaṇḍinī's sexual transformation demands that she be born female so that Bhīṣma recognizes Śikhaṇḍin as a female. Born as a woman, Ambā avenges herself on behalf of all women.

Scholars such as Madhusraba Dasgupta misconstrue Ambā's life as a failure: "Ambā's resistance disrupted the social norm and brought her nothing but trouble and unhappiness . . . For all her single-minded efforts, Ambā did not, after all have, the satisfaction of exacting vengeance on her own" (2000: 51–2). On the contrary, the text shows that Ambā in fact succeeds in causing the death of the great patriarch Bhīṣma. All the characters of the *Mahābhārata* unanimously consider Ambā the cause of Bhīṣmā's death. During the war, Śikhaṇḍin does not need to attack Bhīṣmā because the great warrior has already accepted his own defeat. Ambā effectually causes Bhīṣmā's death by virtue of her austerities and fierce vow.

Ambā's intense austerities and her feminine power (*śakti*) evocate comparison to Goddess Pārvatī's *tapas*. Being a single woman, her mission to destroy her nemesis, Bhīṣma, invincible even to the gods, and her name Ambā (name of the Goddess Durgā)—all invite an examination of theological resonances in the *Ambā-Upākhyāna* with the Goddess mythology.

Resonance of Goddess Themes and Concluding Insights

Thomas B. Coburn observes the *Mahābhārata*'s assimilation of philosophical and Purāṇic themes in its overall design and draw attention to the presence of the Goddess Durgā in the *Mahābhārata* war (1991: 20). Significantly, the character who kills Bhīṣma bears the name Ambā, the Divine Mother. Hindu philosophical texts name the feminine power or principle variously as *Prakṛti*, *Māyā*, and *Śakti*, the feminine divine power; and devotional and Purāṇic mythology identify the Divine Feminine principle by the several forms of the Goddess (1991: 20–2). Ambā, with the popular name of Goddess Durgā, emerges as "a warrior goddess." According to David Kinsley's analysis,

> In many respects Durgā violates the model of the Hindu woman. She is not submissive, she is not subordinated to a male deity, she does not fulfill household duties, and she excels at what is traditionally a male function, fighting in battle. (1988: 97)

In the Purāṇic texts and even in a modern context, gods and heroes summon Mother Durgā to ensure victory. In the twentieth century, many freedom fighters invoked the imagery of the goddess during India's Independence Movement. Before the commencement of the *Mahābhārata* war, Kṛṣṇa asks Arjuna to seek Durgā's grace to defy his enemies.[26]

Even though the traditional conventions of battle prohibit women from participating in battle, I focus on the resemblance of Ambā's acts with those of Mother Durgā, who symbolizes the feminist value of defying patriarchal structure. No one's consort, Durgā depends on no male figure. She singly embodies raw power and does not hesitate to decapitate demons.[27] In my reading of the *Mahābhārata*, the placement of Ambā's story between the only two hymns devoted to Durgā provides a clue to Ambā's resemblance to this feminist Goddess. Ambā's rage, intense austerities, her autonomy, and single-minded focus to kill Bhīṣma evoke Goddess Durgā, who defeats demons impossible even for gods.[28]

The only two *Durgā Stotras* (hymns) in the *Mahābhārata* surround Ambā's story as bookends on either side of her tale in the *Udyoga Parva* (Book 5). The first Durgā hymn appears in the *Virāṭa Parva* (Book 4) in which Yudhiṣṭhira praises Goddess Durgā before entering the city of Virāṭa (4.6.1-35). In this text, the Goddess promises the king, "You will achieve victory in battle soon" (4.6.27). The second *stotra* appears in the *Bhīṣma Parva* (6.23.4-21), before the beginning of the great war of Kurukṣetra in which Ambā—now as Śikhaṇḍin— participates on the Pāṇḍava side. On the first day of the battle, Lord Kṛṣṇa (right before the *Bhagavad Gītā* begins) asks the great warrior Arjuna to invoke Goddess Durgā for help. Arjuna descends from his chariot and chants the hymn to Durgā. Pleased, Durgā appears to Arjuna and blesses him, proclaiming, "You shall relinquish your enemies within a very short time. You are Nara, unassailable hero, and you have Nārāyaṇa by your side" (6.23.18).

Durgā has promised Arjuna swift victory, yet the gruesome war between Kaurava and Pāṇḍava goes on for days. The Kaurava army protected by Bhīṣma unleashes great havoc on the Pāṇḍavas. Even after battling for nine consecutive days, no warrior stands a chance in defeating Bhīṣma. He suggests a solution that will eventually orchestrate his own death and the Pāṇḍavas' victory. Having received Bhīṣma's advice Yudhiṣṭhira becomes emboldened shouting, "Placing Śikhaṇḍin in our van we will assuredly conquer Bhīṣma in battle" (6.116.20). Bhīṣma, who has followed Ambā's journey throughout her new birth, recognizes the male Śikhaṇḍin as Ambā.[29]Arjuna places Śikhaṇḍin in front as a shield and showers arrows on Bhīṣma, which cause him to fall. Surrendering himself to Ambā in the form of Śikhaṇḍin, Bhīṣma willingly accepts his destiny and does not fight back. Custodi quotes Doniger emphasizing that "for Bhīṣma it is imperative that 'Śikhaṇḍin is in essence a woman, despite her outer male form' " (Custodi 2007: 217). Ambā's femaleness and resolve cause Bhīṣma's death.

Scholars such as Goldman and Doniger discuss Arjuna placing Śikhaṇḍin before him as a shield from a psychoanalytic perspective and dismiss Ambā's agency in Bhīṣma's demise. Doniger says, "Śikhaṇḍin does not kill Bhīṣma outright but merely functions as a human bulwark for Arjuna (or in Robert P. Goldman's nice phrasing, Bhīṣma is slain by 'Arjuna hiding, as it were, behind the skirts of his 'mother' Ambā in his sexually ambiguous form of Śikhaṇḍin')" (Custodi 2007: 217). Notwithstanding sexual ambiguity of Śikhaṇḍin, it is Ambā, embodying the energy of Divine Mother, who protects Arjuna from the arrows of the invincible man and causes the downfall of Bhīṣma. He himself recognizes Ambā as the sole individual who can bring about his death: (1) because she has been reborn female in line with the conditions of Bhīṣma's vow not to fight against a woman and (2) because in her physical form of the male Śikhaṇḍin, Ambā can now enter the battlefield. The *Mahābhārata* recounts, "Bhīṣma laughingly said, 'Whether thou chooses to strike me or not, I will never fight with thee. Thou are that Śikhaṇḍin still which the Creator first made thee [a woman]'" (6.109.43–45).[30] Bhīṣma's laughter is significant: ironically, many great warriors were unable to defeat the Kuru patriarch, but a woman whom he despised and rejected became the cause of this celibate warrior's death. Śikhaṇḍin's placement at the front of Arjuna's chariot is a strategic move only, sealing Bhīṣma's fateful death, set in motion long ago by Ambā's resolve. The mere sight of Śikhaṇḍin in front of him on the battlefield causes Bhīṣma to set down his weapons and accept his defeat. McGarth (2009) rightly places Ambā in the list of women heroes in the *Mahābhārata* saying: "In a temporal and morphological sense, Ambā is thoroughly feminine, and the term which Bhīṣma repeatedly employs to indicate this intensity is *strī*: for *strī* is inviolable and irrefragible [sic]" (113).

Ambā—as Śikhaṇḍin—initiates the beginning of the end of this chapter of the war by standing with Nara and Nārāyaṇa against her victimizer, the Kuru chief Bhīṣma.[31] Durgā has already promised to protect the sons of Pāṇḍu. When Ambā brings down Bhīṣma in battle, she prevents the slaughter of untold numbers of the Pāṇḍava warriors. Hence, the image of Śikhaṇḍin riding on the chariot with Nara (Arjuna) and Nārāyaṇa (Lord Kṛṣṇa) and standing between the two represents the protective power of the Divine Goddess in action. Bhīṣma's demise signals the beginning of the victory of the Pāṇḍavas as promised by Goddess Durgā. Vishwa Adluri aptly notes that *Ambā Upākhyāna* allows us to see the superlative symbol of patriarchy— Bhīṣma —is not only raised by a female goddess but also brought down by a warrior who is born female (Adluri 2016: 309). Earlier in the tale, when Ambā enters into the fire, Bhīṣma characterizes her as *varavarṇinī* (fair complexioned one), the same epithet Arjuna uses for Goddess Durgā in his invocation to the Goddess on the battlefield. The themes of intense passion in confronting evil, the ascetic prowess of the single woman Ambā, and her fierce autonomy, all indicate Ambā's association with Durgā.

Conclusion

An in-depth reading of the *Ambā-Upākhyāna* reveals that Ambā's narrative does not merely explain of Bhīṣma's death by Śikhaṇḍin, as many scholars suggest. Further, Ambā's story represents not the spiteful vengefulness of a spurned woman. It is neither another account of the victimization of a woman entrapped by patriarchal customs nor a tale of scintillating gender themes. Instead, it intensely focuses light on the *Mahābhārata*'s theme of *dharma*—restoring justice to those who are on the side of right. Through her deliberate consultations with the ascetics, autonomous decisions, and resolute actions, Ambā confronts archaic marriage laws, women's oppression, and issues pertaining to the female body and women's agency. I see the text as confronting the oppression of patriarchal *dharma* laws—an oppression that must be confronted by an equally powerful feminine force. *Brahmacarya* (celibacy) was the source of Bhīṣma's power, but Ambā's austerities proved equal in potency—evidenced by Bhīṣma's surrendering himself without shooting even one arrow. By the force of her resolve and austerities, Ambā transforms herself from the Kāśi princess into the personified power of Durgā, a force to be reckoned with, challenging the tyrannical oppression of patriarchy.

Ambā, who defies normative restrictions on women, exercises complete agency over her mind and body and retains her feminine gender in the eyes of Bhīṣma, even after her sexual transformation. In Hindu myths the Mother Goddess fights as a woman, but Ambā in her male-dominated world has to take on a male body. Ambā becomes the cause of Bhīṣma's death as a woman when she made the vow, performed fierce austerities, acquired the boon, and entered the fire with the wish to kill her nemesis. A close literary and feminist reading offers new insights into how Ambā employs her female body—the body that was violated, rejected, and humiliated—to challenge patriarchal structures. She was born yet again as a woman—as Drupada's daughter—and her sexual transformation became an instrument by which to confront Bhīṣma, who already had accepted his death by her hands. By the force of her resolve and austerities, Ambā transforms herself from the Kāśi princess into the personified power of Durgā, a force that destroys injustice and evil.

Notes

1 In this chapter, the textual references from the *Ādi Parvan* (Book 1) and the *Udyoga Parvan* (Book 5), which contains *Ambopākhyāna*, are from J. B. Van Buitenen's (1980) translation in Volume 1 and 3. The other references from *Virātaparvan* (Book 4) and *Bhīṣmaparvan* (Book 6) are from M. N. Dutt's and K. M. Ganguli's translations (2008, 2001). In some instances, I provide my own translation for clarity.

2 Ambā's tale is narrated by Bhīṣma himself before the Kurukṣetra war. This war is central to the *Mahābhārata*. It was fought between the two sets of cousins of the Kuru clan but involved the participations of regional kingdom siding with one or the other side. Bhīṣma had been spying on Ambā for two lifetimes. The story of Ambā is recounted in three places in the epic. It is first mentioned in the *Mahābhārata* 1.96; then, there is a brief reference at 5.49.31–34; finally, a brief outline of the story appears at 5.169.16–21, followed by a more extensive narration beginning the next chapter (5.170–193). Kevin McGrath (2009) notes that the account of the "the life of Ambā is not given in a micro-narrative within the epic, but is a sub-plot that runs in and out of the main course of the epic …" (109).

3 Scholarship on the *Ambopākhyāna* primarily focuses on the following themes:
   1. Patriarchal Hindu laws, women's powerlessness, and the *Mahābhārata*'s overarching theme of disciplining female choice: For example, see Dasgupta (2000: 21–32) and Chakravarti (2009).
   2. Transsexuality focusing on Ambā's sexual transformation in her next life from female to male in order to get revenge (e.g., Wendy Doniger)
   3. Psychoanalytical themes or, more precisely, theories around the oedipal undertones (Fitzgerald; Goldman). See Doniger (2002: 57–72).4. Psychoanalytical themes of oedipal complex and gender bending (e.g., Fitzgerald, James, "Bhīṣma beyond Freud: Bhīṣma in the Mahābhārata" (2007: 189–207). Custodi summarizes feminist and psychoanalytic themes saying, "Several feminist and psychoanalytic themes emerge in the Ambā story, one of which Doniger calls 'lethal transsexuality'—frustrated by love, denied fulfillment in marriage" (2007: 208–29).5. Theological resonances of the goddess theology in the narrative (e.g., Vish Adluri's "The Divine Androgyne: Crossing Gender and Breaking Hegemonies in the Ambā-Upākhyāna of the *Mahābhārata*" (2016) and Coburn [1991]).

4 Meenashi Reddy Madhavan's *Girls of the Mahabharata: The One Who Had Two Lives* is a modern retelling of Ambā's journey that extends over two lifetimes. It validates the continuing interest in this life story of the strong-willed woman character of the *Mahābhārata.*

5 *Svayaṃvara* is an ancient Indian custom of the *kṣatriya* caste of choosing a husband. A marriageable woman chooses a suitor from a list of suitors in a public ceremony. The examples are found in the *Mahābhārata* and the *Rāmāyaṇa.*

6 In "Change of Sex as a Hindu Story Motif," Norman Brown (1921) elaborates on five common ways a sex change is brought about in the classical Indian literature, including "exchanging sex with a *yakṣa*," which is pertinent to the story of Ambā (Śikhaṇḍinī's sex change to the male Śikhaṇḍin falls in this category).

7 This section of narrative is the longest, spanning about fifteen sections (5.173–88). It focuses on Ambā's plight and despair and her unequivocal determination that "I have to revenge myself on Bhīṣma" (5.173.10).

8 Chakravarthi Ram-Prasad analyzes the episode of the invincible Bhīṣma's surrender to Śikhaṇḍin because the latter was a woman in his early life and Bhīṣma's "extraordinary withdrawal from the sexual life and his deliberate courting of death through a particular aetiology of gender" (2018: 58–98).

9 See Allen (2007: 176–88).

10 See Trikha (2006: 110-111).

11 See Chakrabarti (2014: 244–83).

12 Both Wendy Doniger and Uma Chakravarti make this point. See Doniger, *On Hinduism*, 351; Chakravarti, *Of Meta-Narratives and "Master" Paradigms*, 49.

13 The *Laws of Manu* describe eight forms of marriages: "The rite of Brahman (*Brahmā*), that of the gods (*Daiva*), that of the Ṛṣis (*ārṣa*), that of Prajāpati (*Prājāpatya*), that of the Āsuras (*Āsura*), that of the Gandharvas (*Gandharva*), that of the Rākṣasas (*Rākṣasa*), and that of the Pisaca" (*Mānava Dharma Śāstra*: III: 21). Manu calls the first four types of marriages the highest and last four types of marriages "blamable."

14 Draupadī's marriage to five husbands was an exception to this rule.

15 Irawati Karve (1974: 18) deliberates, "We cannot say Bhishma committed all this cruelty deliberately. It seems he was indifferent to it. Did this indifference arise out of his obsession with one goal—the perpetuation of the Kuru line?"

16 Bhīṣma is cognizant of all forms of marriages sanctioned in law books, but he arrogantly declares the marriage by abduction as "the best" (1.96.10).

17 https://www.iep.utm.edu/irigaray/. Accessed July 20, 2018.

18 If Ambā and Śālva both have chosen one another in love, they have performed what is known as *gandharva* marriage (voluntary union of a maiden and her lover) as Śākuntalā does in Book I. In that tale, King Duṣyanta coaxes Śākuntalā by saying, "*Gandharva* and *rākṣasa* marriage are lawful for the baronage, have no fear for

that" (1. 67.10). According to this law, Ambā may be considered already bound by the commitment of love. *Dharma Śāstras* (Hindu law books), including the *Manu Smṛti*, dictate prescriptive laws for guardianship of women in the protection of male.

19 Ambā's plea reminds us of Śākuntalā when she was discarded by Duṣyanta, but Śākuntalā has a child and thus has earned a place as a woman.

20 According to Doniger, "She is socially, if not physically, raped by Bhīṣmā (for his abduction of her made her second-hand goods from the standpoint of the man she loved)."

21 *rāma uvāca kāśikanye punar brūhi bhīṣmas te caraṇāv ubhau śirasā vandanārho 'pi grahīṣyati girā mama.*

22 Irigaray, for instance, draws attention to the three roles available in a patriarchal value system: mother, virgin, and prostitute (1985: 184). In India's patriarchal traditions, the roles are limited to wife, mother, and *sannyāsinī* (renunciate, *tapasvinī*).

23 The Guru characterizes Bhīṣma as "a fool," "a lover of war," and a "sick man."

24 "Release him again, O Agni, to the fathers. The one offered to you now proceeds to his destiny. Putting on new life, let him approach the surviving, let him reunite with a [new] body, All-Knowing One!" (10.16.5).

25 Drupada was offered a boon by Lord Śiva that he will obtain a son, but a girl was born. The parents concealed the girl's sex hoping for a miracle because of the promise of the god.

26 "There are also two hymns in the *Mahābhārata* that are directed to a goddess named *Durgā* ... Although these hymns have been excised from the critical edition of the epic, they would appear to be older than the *Devī-Māhātmya*" (Coburn 1991: 20–1).The references to Goddess are found in the *Mahābhārata* translations by M. N. Dutt and K. M. Ganguli.

27 Coburn (2002) suggests not a "precise correspondence" but an "underlying continuity" between the Mbh Ambā and the *ambā* of the *Devī Māhātmya* (202).

28 In his excellent analysis, Vishwa Adluri focuses on the theological architecture of the *Mahābhārata* and draws connections of its heroes/heroines with various deities. Ambā's "relation to Indian notions of divinity, especially ambiguous power of the goddess" (2016: 277–9).

29 "*Nāhaṁ hanyāṁ śikhaṇḍinam śrūyate strī hy asau pūrvaṁ tasmād varjyo raṇe mama*" (6.16.100).

30 The translation is from Ganguli, Volume II, 109: 274–5.

31 According to Coburn, "In setting the context for our translation of this hymn, which appears as an insertion near or at the end of MbH 4.5, little need to be said about its relationship with to the constituted text at this juncture. The opening line establishes a thread of its continuity with that text" (2002: 267).

References

Adluri, V. (2016). "The Divine Androgyne: Crossing Gender and Breaking Hegemonies in the Ambā-Upākhyāna of the *Mahābhārata*." In Vishwa Adluri and Joydeep Bagchee (eds.), *Argument and Design: The Unity of the Mahābhārata* (pp. 275–319). London: Brill.

Allen, N. (2007). "Bhīṣma as Match-Maker." In Simon Brodbeck and Brian Black (eds.), *Gender and Narrative in the Mahābhārata* (pp. 176–88). New York: Routledge.

Brodbeck, S., and S. Black (eds.). (2007). *Gender and Narrative in the Mahābhārata*. New York: Routledge.

Brown, N. (1921). "Change of Sex as a Hindu Story Motif." *Journal of the American Oriental Society* 47: 3–24.

Chakrabarti, A. (2014). "Just Words: An Ethics of Conversation in the Mahābhārata." In Arindam Chakrabarti and Sibaji Bandopadhyay (eds.), *Mahābhharata Now: Narration, Aesthetics, Ethics*. New York: Routledge.

Chakravarthi, R. P. (2018). *Human Being, Bodily Being: Phenomenology from Classical India* (pp. 58–98). New York: Oxford University Press.

Chakravarti, U. (2009) *Of Meta-Narratives and "Master" Paradigms: Sexuality and the Reification of Women in Early India*. New Delhi: Center for Women's Development Studies.

Coburn, T. B. (1991). *Encountering the Goddess: A Translation of the Devī-Māhātmya and a Study of Its Interpretation*. New York: SUNY Press.

Coburn, T. B. (2002; 1984). *Devi Māhātmya: The Crystallization of the Goddess Tradition*. India: Motilal Banarsidass.

Custodi, Andrea. (2007). "'Show You Are a Man!': Transsexuality and Gender Bending in the Characters of Arjuna/Bṛhannaḍa and Ambā/Śikhaṇḍin(ī)." In Simon Brodbeck and Brian Black (eds.), *Gender and Narrative in the Mahābhārata* (pp. 208–29). New York: Routledge.

Dasgupta, M. (2000). "Usable Women. The Tales of Ambā and Mādhavī." In Mandakranta Bose (ed.), *Faces of the Feminine in Ancient, Medieval, and Modern India* (pp. 48–55). New York: Oxford University Press.

De Beauvoir, S. (2011). *The Second Sex*. New York: Vintage.

Dhand, A. (2008). *Woman as Fire, Woman as Sage: Sexual Ideology in the Mahābhārata*. New York: SUNY Press.

Doniger, W. (1999). *Splitting the Difference: Gender and Myth in Ancient Greece and India*. Chicago, IL: University of Chicago Press.

Doniger, W. (2002). "Transformations of Subjectivity and Memory in the Mahābhārata and the Rāmāyaṇa." In D. Shulman and Guy S. Stroumsa (eds.), *Self and Self-Transformation in the History of Religions* (pp. 57–72). Oxford: Oxford University Press.

Doniger, W. (2014). *On Hinduism*. New York: Oxford University Press.

Donovan, Sarah K. "Luce Irigaray." *The Internet Encyclopedia of Philosophy*. Accessed from https://www.iep.utm.edu/irigaray/.

Dutt, M. N. (2008), *Mahābhārata: Sanskrit Text with English Translaiton* (9 Volumes). Delhi: Parimal Publications.

Ganguli, K. M. (trans.). (2004). *The Mahābhārata*, vol. II. Delhi: Munshiram Monoharlal.

Hiltebeitel, A. (2011). *Reading the Fifth Veda: Studies on the Mahābhārata—Essays by Alf Hiltebeitel*. Edited by Vishwa Adluri and Joydeep Bagchee . Netherlands: Brill.

Irigaray, L. (1985). *This Sex Which Is Not One*. New York: Cornell University Press.

Kaelber, W. (1979). "Tapas and Purification in Early Hinduism." *Numen* 26(2): 192–214.

Karve, I. (1974). *Yuganta: The End of an Epoch*. Delhi: Orient Blackswan.

Kinsley, D. (1988). *Hindu Goddesses: Visions of the Divine Feminine in the Hindu Religious Tradition*. California: University of California Press.

McGrath, K. (2011). *Strī: Feminine Power in the Mahābhārata*. New Delhi, India: Orient Blackswan.

McWeeny, J. (2010). "Liberating Anger, Embodying Knowledge: A Comparative Study of María Lugones and Zen Master Hakuin." In J. McWeeny and A. Butnor (eds.), *Asian and Feminist Philosophies in Dialogue: Liberating Traditions* (pp. 123–46). New York: Columbia University Press.

Madhavan, M. R. (2018). *Girls of the Mahabharata: The One Who Had Two Lives*. India: HarperCollins.

Sen, P. K. (2014). "Moral Doubts, Moral Dilemmas, and Situation Ethics." In A. Chakrabarti and S. Bandopadhyay (eds.), *Mahābhārata Now: Narration, Aesthetics, Ethics* (pp. 153–202). New York: Routledge.

Spivak, Gayatri C. (1994). "Can the Subaltern Speak?" In P. Williams and L. Chrisman (eds.), *Colonial Discourse and Post-Colonial Theory: A Reader*. New York: Columbia University Press.

Trikha, P. (2006). *Textuality and Intertexuality in the Mahābhārata: Myth, Meaning, and Metamorphosis*. New Delhi: Sarup.

van Buitenen, J. A. B. (1973 & 1980). *The Mahābhārata: Volume 1 (Book 1—the Book of Beginning)* and Volume 3 (*Book 4—the Book of the Virāta; Book 5—the Book of the Effort*). Chicago, IL: University of Chicago Press.

Part Four

Gender and the Feminine Divine

11

God the Mother and Her Sacred Text: A Hindu Vision of Divine Immanence

Rita D. Sherma

The absence of the Feminine Divine in Christian traditions has received reflection by feminist theologians and ministers who have sought resources for the evocation of a feminine aspect of the Christian conception of the Divine.[1] In contradistinction, from the second millennia BCE, India's philosophical and religious traditions have included the feminine principle in diverse ways, as the chapters in this volume explore. Hindu philosophical and theological schools, in particular, have foregrounded the immanental divine presence in terms of creative, cosmogonic power (*śakti*) envisioned as feminine. While there are elements of the feminine principle in Buddhist thought and practice—female *bodhisattva*s, *yogini*s, *ḍākinī*s, and other enlightened beings populate the Mahāyāna and Vajrayāna Buddhist canons—their ontologies and functions are distinct from that of the Hindu Mahādevī and cannot be conflated.

The feminine principle is ubiquitous in Hindu thought and practice—whether (1) as the dynamic power of a masculine-gendered supreme deity or more radically, (2) as the absolute, ultimate divinity itself. Specifically, Hindu texts offer the only extant, widely accepted, *systematic theological vision* of God the Mother as the Supreme Divinity in a global religion. She is transcendent and immanent, the efficient and material cause of creation, the ground of sustenance, and the final destination of all existence. Much of the scholarship on Hinduism's Divine Feminine has focused not on Her theology per se, but on the liturgical, ritual, festive, pilgrimage, and other elements of practice associated with Her. Some examine the impact of the strong presence of the Feminine Divine on the lives and liberties of actual women.

However, such efforts at understanding a phenomenon that is unique to a specific tradition's thought system are most often undertaken without consideration of the underlying structure of philosophical theology associated with the Divine Feminine. This oversight is understandable. Hindu philosophical theology—for example, Advaita Vedānta or Viśiṣṭādvaita—emerges from extensive theological commentaries (*bhāṣya*) on scripture, is highly systematized, and is associated with a particular denominational lineage (*sampradāya*). In contradistinction, *mystical or praxis-oriented theology* is often arrayed in the language of mythopoeia allowing for the narrative structure of the theological text to be transformed into popular recitation and ritual, feasts and festivals, ceremony and liturgy, as well as esoteric theology and praxis, often accessible only to the initiated. The philosophical elements that infuse such theology are often subtle and, therefore, often disregarded. The theology of God the Mother, Śakti, falls into this latter category.

Philosophical Influences in the Theology of the Mahādevī

She is known to Hindu texts as Śakti (divine power), Devī (the Divine Feminine), Mahādevī (Great Goddess), and Īśvarī (God, in terms of a feminine pronoun), among many other titles. She is understood, worshipped, and experienced as God the Mother—creator, sustainer, and dissolver. She is both the efficient and material cause of creation, sustenance, and dissolution, as both the process and the product. The earliest text to present a cohesive and clear theological vision of the Mahādevī is the *Devī Māhātmyam* (DM, *c* sixth century CE), canonical for Śākta-s (who view Śakti as the supreme divinity).[2] In explorations of the rich variance of practices afforded by Her mystical theology as presented by the text, the philosophical and theological content can recede into the background—hidden, but in plain sight.

Nevertheless, though often overlooked, foundational philosophical categories do play an important part in the vision and definition of the theology of the Mahādevī and is evident in the conception of divine nature presented by the DM. The modern conventional disjunctive bipolarity of philosophy and theology has not been the traditional norm for Hindu thought in which the two categories often interpenetrate and inform each other. Philosophical principles such as *prakṛti* (matter/primal components of the physical world); the *guṇa*-s (the three foundational characteristics/tendencies of matter); *mūlapradhāna*[3] (the root material cause of creation); *māyā* (the cosmological power of veiling the Ultimate Reality); and conceptual paradigms such as *satkāryavāda* (postulating the presence of the cause *within* the effect) and *pariṇāmavāda* (positing transformation of the cause *into* the effect) are deeply imbued in the structure of the Śākta theology advanced by this seminal text.

Among the numerous commentaries on the DM, the two most influential were written more than a millennia after the composition of the text by the late-seventeenth- to mid-eighteenth-century Śākta theologian Bhāskararāya and his older contemporary Nāgoji Bhaṭṭa.[4] Both commentaries explicitly align with the ontology of Advaita Vedānta that views reality as singular and indivisible, and liberation and bliss lying in the experiential realization of this truth: that only *Brahman* exists. Both cite Śaṅkarācārya extensively but whereas Bhāskararāya views *Brahman*/Śakti as transforming into physical reality (*pariṇāmavāda*), Nāgoji Bhaṭṭa perceives the multiplicity of the material universe as appearance only (*vivartavāda*). The DM's clarity about Her ultimate nature as primordial *prakṛti* strongly counters such an exegesis, stating "you, the Mahādevī, who has become everything, granting heaven and ultimate liberation"(DM 11.6), and glorifying Her as "the eternal one, who becomes the capacity of creation, sustenance, and dissolution, abiding in the characteristics of primordial matter, indeed consisting of those characteristics" (DM 11.10). The supreme statement is offered by the DM's verse 4.6, which describes Her as the cause of all that is possessed of the three *guṇa*-s; as this world of multiplicity; and the primordial, unmanifested *prakṛti*. The text supports the *pariṇāmavāda* of Bhāskararāya whose work shows awareness of the deep grounding of Śākta theology, in all its forms, in the immersive, consciousness-infused, agentic materiality of the Feminine Divine.

Feminine Deity in the Hindu World

Feminine deity, in the Hindu tradition, is ubiquitous for a number of reasons. Across diverse Hindu theologies, the Feminine Divine is associated with divine power (*śakti*), the force of active creation (*kriyā-śakti*)[5], the material cause of creation (*prakṛti-śakti*), various natural forms and phenomena (such as rivers, forests, the dawn, water, and the earth itself), as well as certain inherent capacities that exist in the cosmic manifold (and within humans who are part of the cosmos) such as, for example, the divine potency of abundance (Lakṣmī).[6] Yet, however wide-ranging the conceptions of the feminine principle are in Hindu thought and practice across the historical record, the specific understanding of the Divine Feminine as the Supreme Reality, is first glimpsed in a hymn from the *Ṛg Veda* (1900–1700 BCE)—the earliest texts of the Hindu canon—known as the

Devī Sūktam ("Hymn of Praise to the Divine Feminine," RV 10.125). The hymn envisions the Feminine Divine as Ultimate Source, Creative Force, Pervasive Universal Power, and as Supreme Divinity. The *Ṛg Veda* contains 1,028 hymns and 10,600 verses, systematized into ten books. The *Devī Sūktam*, believed to be authored by a renowned woman sage (*ṛṣikā*) known as Vāgāmbhṛṇī, appears to have been composed in a state of ecstatic, unitary mystical experience of the Self as pervasive, unlimited, and nonlocal. Verses from the hymn bear testimony to her experience (*Ṛg Veda* 10.125, *Devī Sūktam*):

> I am the Queen, the gatherer of treasures, established in/as Ultimate Reality, the Primary Object of Worship.
>
> The Luminous Divine Powers (*devāḥ*) have dispersed me in many places, having many abodes, causing me to be All-Pervasive.
>
> (Verse 3)

> Even eating, seeing, breathing, or hearing the spoken word is accomplished through me alone. Even the non-perceivers amongst you dwell near me. Hear me, for I reveal the truth.
>
> (Verse 4)

> While creating all beings, I merely breathe forth like the wind. So expansive is my power, possessing a greatness beyond heaven and earth.
>
> (Verse 8).[7]

The *Devī Sūktam* is a testament to the early Vedic authority granted to women's enlightened awareness and an initial harbinger of the vision of the Divine Feminine as immanent, experienceable, creative power and presence. Nearly four millennia later, the *Devī Sūktam* is still recited as part of the DM, the sacred text of God the Mother and, here, the subject of our exploration. Its integration into the DM is a testimony to the ongoing stream of the vision of the Divine Feminine as the pervasive supreme reality in the Hindu experience of the phenomenal world.

Śiva, Śakti, and the Nature of the Masculine and Feminine Principles

In Hindu philosophy and theology, the feminine principle functions as the active and creative pole of the ontological binary that is posited across schools of thought. In addition, "God" (in Hindu theism), or "the Divine," (in Hindu nondualism) is dyadic—an integrated divinity that includes and integrates both the Divine Masculine and Divine Feminine. As such, the two major visions of God (distinct but related) in Hindu theology—that of Viṣṇu and Śiva—are incomplete without their feminine and dynamic counterparts. The feminine counterparts, respectively Lakṣmī and Pārvatī (who is strongly identified with Śakti/Mahādevī), are presented in mythic theological narratives as the divine feminine aspect/consort/partner. Yet, the theological understanding interprets the divine masculine and feminine as *coterminous*, *co-necessary*, and *coeval*. They form two modes of a divine dyad. We have briefly examined the position of Śakti/Mahādevī vis-à-vis the masculine Supreme Deity with whom She is associated. We will examine, in the DM, the vision of Mahādevī in Śākta texts in which She does not just *infuse* the nature of the Absolute but where She *is* also the Absolute.[8]

Hindu philosophical theology is most often structured in terms of a divine biunity. The binaries of reality are cast as the masculine and feminine principles. Such biune pairs—particularly when associated with Śiva and Śakti—represent complementary binaries that include, but are not limited to, the following:

- Transcendence–Immanence
- Consciousness–Matter/Energy
- Stasis–Dynamism
- Infinitude–Finitude
- Eternality–Temporality
- Divine Potential–Phenomenal Actualization
- Being–Becoming

The *Divine Feminine principle* (Śakti/ Mahādevī) is associated/identified with (1) immanence and creativity, (2) matter–energy, (3) dynamism, (4) genesis and emergence of forms and phenomena, (5) the body–mind, (6) transitions and transformations, (7) the power inherent in the cosmos, and (8) both the Formless Absolute *and* the Divine Mother. The *divine masculine principle*, in theologies associated with Śiva, is identified as (1) Transcendence over Time, (2) Pure Consciousness, (3) Divine Quiescence/Stillness, (4) Infinite Potentiality, (5) Ground of Being/Reality, (6) the Ultimate Subject/Self who Experiences all things through Sentient Beings, (7) the Wielder of Cosmic Power, and (8) both the Formless Absolute *and* the Divine Lord/Creator.

Śiva in the form of "Rudra" is one of many *devatā*-s in the *Ṛg Veda Saṃhitā*, but is envisioned as the Supreme Lord in the *Śvetāśvatara Upaniṣad* (400–200 BC), presenting the earliest textual roots of theistic devotion to Rudra-Śiva. He is identified as the creator of the cosmos and liberator of souls. The era from 200 BCE to 100 CE also marks the beginning of the Śaiva tradition focused on the worship of Śiva as the Supreme Divine. Śiva is associated with Pārvatī, the gentle aspect of Śakti/Mahādevī. By the period of the composition of the *Purāṇa*-s (from *c* 400 BCE to 400 CE), she is identified clearly as the feminine aspect of the divine dyad of Śiva-Śakti. In the DM, Pārvatī is explicitly associated with the Mahādevī in all Her forms, thereby theologically linking the Devī of the DM to Śiva in the minds of worshippers.

The *Devī Māhātmyam*

The (i) vision of the Absolute as feminine, presented in the *Devī Sūktam* of the *Ṛg Veda*; (ii) the principle of *Brahman* (Ultimate Reality) central to the Upaniṣad-s; and (iii) the concepts (*prakṛiti*, the *guṇa*-s, *śakti*s, and *māyā*, amongst others)—that characterize the feminine principle of the philosophical systems—transform into the Feminine Divine in the DM. It is appropriate to begin any exploration of the nature and function of Śakti in Śākta texts with the DM, a seminal text for the theology, liturgy, and ritual life of Śākta-s. The DM can be translated as the "Inherent Greatness of the Devi" and the glorification of the Devī as the "Great Supreme Self." In this text, framed clearly for the first time, is the vision of the Mahādevī that now colors the various strands of the Śākta tradition. This vision is what N. N. Bhattacharya has famously called "independent Śaktism" as opposed to the "dependent Śaktism" of Śaiva and Vaiṣṇava theological systems (1996: 96).

The DM of the *Mārkaṇḍeya Purāṇa* comprises chapters 81–93 of the *Purāṇa*, one of the early Sanskrit *Purāṇa*-s (a category of Sacred Text that interweaves theology with mythic and legendary narratives), and is attributed to the sage Mārkaṇḍeya. The thirteen chapters of the DM are divided into three major episodes. Among the important forms of the Divine Feminine introduced by the DM into Hindu Theology is Kālī.[9]

The text is known by several other names, the most renowned of which are: *Durgā Saptaśatī* (700 Verses to Durgā: the sacred name by which She is referenced in the text); *Caṇḍī* (one of the names of Durgā); and *Caṇḍī Pāṭha* ("*pāṭha*" means liturgical recitation). The fact that the text is known as a "recitation," points to its primary function. Although the text forms the basis of Śākta *theology*, it is most commonly viewed as a 700-verse *mantra* to be chanted, rather than a theological text to be commented on. *Mantra* itself has a history of nearly four millennia in the Hindu tradition and is the basis of Hindu "sonic theology," (Beck 2009) whereby specific sound vibrations are associated with certain states of awareness: the *mantra* is meant to be orally and aurally experienced as transformative to one's consciousness.

Composed *c* 400–600 CE, the DM is highly significant as the foundation, testament, summation, and the theological heart of the Śākta tradition, and has been translated into most Indian languages. As noted, there are several commentaries on the text, and numerous ritual manuals associated with it. The commentaries and ritual manuals differ according to region. This variegation has led to a democratization of the text and its popularity and availability to the rural poor, those outside the scholastic theological circles, and to women across social, linguistic, and educational demarcations.

The elaboration of the theology of the Mahādevī that first occurs in the DM melds together various philosophical constructs (noted earlier)—and the encompassing vision of Ultimate Reality (*Brahman*)—to create a portrait of God the Mother who births, includes, and transcends all forms. The text portrays Her as the causal agent of creation and implicitly identifies Her with the ground of being—thereby endowing Her with transcendence. As Śakti, She is the creative, nurturing, and reabsorptive power underlying the manifest cosmos (DM 11.10). She is the matrix of the universe and, as *prakṛti*, its material substratum. Hence, She is fully immanent in the world as its cause and essence. Indeed, according to the DM, the Mahādevī does not employ a specific power or force to create the world. Ultimately, She *is* the world and all its diverse forms are aspects of Her Being. Yet, Her creation does not delimit Her and She maintains the power of transcendence.

Thomas Coburn has noted that while this "comprehensive statement" of Her identity is not the earliest example of devotion to the Feminine Divine, it is undoubtedly the first in which this devotion is anchored to the heritage of the important category of texts known as the *Purāṇas* (a category that, I would suggest, can be generally termed "narrative theology"), and to the two great epics of Hindu sacred literature. This anchoring occurs through the incorporation of the theological functions and narratives from the mythos and logos associated with other divinities so that the Mahādevī is able to include and sublimate other conceptions of Deity.

The DM is most widely known as the *Durgā Saptaśatī*. Indeed, although the Mahādevī is addressed by many titles and epithets in the text, Durgā has become the name consistently associated with the Mahādevī in a pan-Hindu context. The text itself has a life of its own and is widely used in both India and abroad in numerous worship scenarios including the popular *jāgrata*, which are all-night vigils devoted to the liturgical chanting of the text. This form of praxis is common in the Hindu diaspora where it can be performed in private homes among friends and family. The text is also variously applied in temple contexts in centers dedicated to different aspects of the Mahādevī. There are numerous liturgical manuals associated with the text.

For our purposes, however, it is the theological elements embedded in the narrative that are of greatest interest. The vision of the Divine expressed in the DM is encyclopedic in a theological sense. It attempts to appropriate to Her all the capacities, functions, and powers of both the masculine and feminine principles that have been attributed, in other texts, to the Supreme Divinity—variously conceived. Theological elements are not explicitly delineated in the text but are woven, instead, through the strands of the mythic narrative in which the theology of the Mahādevī is framed. The account begins with a king who has lost his kingdom, and a merchant who has been cheated out of his wealth and property by his own kin. Both men are at the hermitage of a sage. They turn to the sage for counsel in dealing with the pain and suffering associated with their losses. The sage tells them about the grace of the Mahādevī and discloses to them Her theology, elaborated in different episodes in which She acts to restore justice and eradicate the preeminence of evil by offering a potent vision of Śākta theodicy. The narrated episodes are punctuated with hymns of praise that glorify Her majesty and benevolent care for creation and reveal, through their verses, the hidden theology of the Mahādevī.

One episode requires Viṣṇu to eradicate two malevolent beings (*asuras*) but He is under the influence of a deep sleep induced by the Devī Herself in Her form as Mahāmāyā. Brahmā, contemplating the manifestation of the next cycle of the universe at Viṣṇu's behest, is prevented from his creative work by the two *asuras*. Brahmā sings a hymn to the Mahādevī that presents Her theology through the glorification of Her names, and invokes Her presence for the release of Viṣṇu from His cosmic slumber. She does so and Viṣṇu is able to awaken and dispatch the *asuras* (DM: 1.66–70). This mythic narrative is a reformulation of an earlier narrative centered on Viṣṇu but, here, Viṣṇu is under the active control of the Mahādevī. Through this narrative, two primary masculine divinities, Viṣṇu and Brahmā, are conceptualized as divine agents dependent on the Mahādevī. She is presented as the power that allows the cosmic order to be restored and as having primary agency.

Another episode presents Śākta theodicy and Her care for the world that carries a very specific vison of the nature of evil. The Mahādevī, in the form known as Caṇḍī, represents the irresistible force of divine justice when released against malevolence. The world is under attack by Mahiṣāsura, a potent and wildly destructive *asura* who, in a number of popular accounts, is morphogenic—just as malevolence always changes form according to circumstances. The *devatās*, diverse divine beings, are unable to counter Mahiṣāsura, and endow the Devī with their potencies and capacities. She is henceforth envisioned as the wielder of all divine powers. Astride a lion (representing majesty), She destroys the *asura* who has taken the form of a buffalo. Through this act, she not only dissolves the power of the *asura* but liberates his spirit as well. Chaos dissolves and order emerges.

In the *Mahābhārata*, before the cataclysmic battle, Kṛṣṇa asks Arjuna to recite the *Durgā Stotram* for conquering his enemies.[10] Arjuna praises the Goddess and Durgā appears and bestows upon him the boon of victory. Thomas Coburn notes,

> The conclusion seems inevitable: The conception of deity as periodically incarnate for the sake of redeeming the world has been employed in the service of both Kṛṣṇa and the Goddess [Mahādevī] .... That this affinity is not merely casual is suggested by the fact that virtually all the other early hymns to the Goddess [Mahādevī] as found in the *Mahābhārata* . . . contain this same emphasis on salvific activity in the teeth of adversity....
>
> The synthesis that is accomplished in the *Devī-Māhātmya* [*sic*] is therefore extraordinarily and uniquely broad. It reaches deep into the Sanskritic heritage, identifying the [Mahādevī] with central motifs, names, and concepts in the Vedic traditions. (1991: 27)

Coburn also comments on the many tales that are enfolded into the text. Śākta theodicy is further explored by the episode involving the *asura* named Raktabīja. The segment presents the Mahādevī as manifesting different forms of Herself from within. A unity is established between Śakti in her aspects as the gentle Pārvatī, the dark Kālikā, and the motherly but fierce Ambikā. Entreated by the celestial *devatās*, who have encountered the ascendance of pernicious forces, the Mahādevī once again enters the arena of duality and counters evil. In the cosmic battle that ensues, the ferocious Kālī arises in a burst of light from the Mahādevī's forehead as a manifestation of the fierce love of the Divine Mother for creation. Each drop of blood shed by the *asura*, Raktabīja, morphs into a brand new *asura* as it touches the earth. Kālī laps up every drop of the blood spilled by Raktabīja the moment it falls, thereby inhibiting the emergence of new clones of this specific form of malevolence. In the concluding battle, Devī absorbs Kālī back into her being. From each of the masculine divine powers present, their *śakti*s (feminine powers, counterparts, capacities) emerge and join the cosmic battle for justice, and thereby return the world to luminous peace and harmony. Eventually, the Mahādevī absorbs all the *śakti*s into Herself (DM: 9.3–10.28). At the conclusion of the episodes, *devatā*s and the celestial hosts praise her protective powers: "You have become the sole support of the world, for you abide in the form of the earth. By you who exist in the form of water, all this universe is filled up, O one of inviolable valor" (DM 11.3–4).[11] After accepting the devotional praise of the grateful, the Mahādevī proclaims that whenever any form of profound danger threatens the flourishing of creation, divine care and restoration will occur, proclaiming that She will come to the rescue "Once again, when there has been no rain, no water, on the earth for a hundred years" (DM 11.42–45). This divine care and interest is highly significant. As Howard points out, in the introduction of this volume, feminist scholars continue to call for the envisioning of divine models that are not transcendent or aloof, but engaged in the care of the universe.

These passages have been, and continue to be, read on many levels. For example, Śākta practitioner and teacher, Devadatta Kali offers a commonly held interpretation of these episodes of war between the Devi and the *asura*s allegorically. He states that the *asura*s

> represent the all too human impulses arising from the pursuit of power, possessions, and pleasure, and from illusions of self-importance. Like the battlefield of the *Bhagavad Gītā*, the *Devī Māhātmyam*'s battlegrounds represents the field of human consciousness on which the drama of individual lives plays out in joy and sorrow, in wisdom and folly. (Kali 2003: xvii)

There are other overlapping points including an alignment with the *avatāra* doctrine clearly elucidated in the *Bhagavad Gītā* (4: 4–9). Similarly, a doctrine of divine care and benevolence is asserted by the DM (11.37–51). In the *Pradhānika Rahasya*—one of the ancillary ritual texts (*aṅga*s) associated with the DM—king Suratha states that "I have been told about the *avatāra*s of Caṇḍīka (a principal name of the Devī)" and inquires as to the primal form that gives rise to the *avatāra*s of the Devī who exist, not in historical time, but in timeless presence. In Her response to the *devatā*s, in the eleventh chapter of the text, the Mahādevī promises to return whenever and wherever She is needed—whether it is for the reestablishment of justice, or for provision of protection from the effects of natural disasters (DM 11.42) such as extreme drought. Although eternal, She takes forms in the world repeatedly in order to offer protection and providence

(DM 12.33) and yet, as the Devī discloses, She will also manifest without actual physical birth (DM 11.42).

The DM diverges from other conceptions of Deity, including that of the *Bhagavad Gītā* in terms of the unique *organicity* of the ontology of God the Mother as presented in the text, and further intensified in the later Śākta *bhakti* tradition. That is, the ontological relationship between the Mahādevī and physical reality is far more intimate and integral than that of other renditions of the Deity because, in a very *material* way, She is convergent with Her creation at its emergence (DM 1.57). Her best-known epithets are divine power (*Śakti*) and primal matter (*Prakṛti*) unfolding itself. Yet, She remains free of the flaws of materiality—as the primal *Prakṛti*, as the unmanifest creative power and potential of physical reality (DM 4.6).

The Nature of Supreme Divinity

The Goddess, in the DM, is the creator of the universe (1.43), the very process of temporality and change within it (11.8), all-pervasive and eternal (1.47) cause of the cosmic creation (1.56), maintenance (1.53, 5.66), and dissolution (1.57). She is, at once, the gnosis that liberates (1.44, 1.58) and the illusory nature of experiential knowledge (1.58). While She is the divine redemptress for those seeking liberation, She is also the source of fulfillment for those seeking worldly satisfaction (12.38). She is identified with the primary modes of the feminine principle such as *māyā* (5.12), and *prakṛti* (1.59, 4.6)—with its three innate characteristics (*guṇa*-s) of luminous purity, dynamic activity, and dissolutive or entropic states—that weave through and condition all of matter. But at the same time, She is the self-existent, timeless divinity (11.10). She is characterized as both tremendous and awe-inspiring in Her power (1.61) and the epitome of gentleness (l.62). Within all life, She resides as the consciousness (5.13), intelligence (5.14), power (5.18), activity, perception (5.27), and compassion (5.29). She is the intrinsic and enveloping divine immanence (5.33–34) in the material universe, comprising all forms and phenomena which are Her transformations (11.6). She is the divine source of genesis, nurturance, and dissolution: “O you, the eternal, who become the power of creation, sustenance and destruction, Abiding in the qualities of primordial matter, actually consisting of these qualities” (11:10). Ultimate Reality, as presented by the text, is none other than the Devī of the DM.

Descriptions of the nature of the Mahādevī are woven through the text in the form of songs of praise and invocation. These descriptions, names, and epithets are not elaborated upon but, nonetheless, given the use of these terms of reference in the *Purāṇic* theology and other theological literature, the implications are clear. The descriptions of the glory of God the Mother contain a great deal of implicit theology, elucidated by some of the theological commentaries on the text. From these hymns of embedded theology worshippers have surmised much about the nature of the Divine that is put forward by the DM. Of the many hymns of evocation that offer the theology of the Mahādevī as poetic renditions, one that is particularly pertinent to our discussion is the *Tantroktaṃ Devī Sūktam*. Below are examples of verses from the hymn that allows for an appreciation of the use of epithets to signify the nature of the Divine. They demonstrate how philosophical principles of *śakti*, *prakṛti*, and Self-existent Reality (*sat*) are theologized in the DM.

Selections from: Tantroktaṃ Devī Sūktam[12]
Devī Māhātmyam

Hymn to Aparājitā ("In Praise of the One Who is Undefeated")

Namo Devyai Mahādevyai
Śivāyai satataṁ namaḥ
Namaḥ Prakṛtyai Bhadrāyai
niyatāḥ praṇatāḥ smatām (5.7)

Glory to the Goddess, to the great Goddess, to the energy of the auspicious one.
Praise to Prakṛti, to She who is pure beneficence.
Salutations to Her

Raudrāyai namo Nityāyai
Gauryai Dhātryai namo namaḥ
Jyothsnāyai cendurūpiṇyai
Sukhāyai satataṁ namaḥ (5.8)

Glory to the tremendous one, to the eternal, to Gaurī Devī, to the embodiment of the luminous. Salutations to the One who manifests as the form of moonlight,
Salutations to the One who is endless joy.

Kalyānyai praṇatāṁ vṛddhyai
Siddhyai kurmo namo namaḥ
Nairṛtīyai bhūbṛtām Lakṣmyai
Śarvāṇyai te namo namaḥ. (5.9)

Glory to the benevolent One, to the power of growth, success, to Nairṛtī,
And to the abundance that supports the earth,
To the consort of Śiva, salutations to you.

Yā devi sarva-bhūteṣu
cetane-tyabhidhīyate
Namas-tasyai, namas-tasyai
namas-tasyai namo namaḥ. (5.13)

Glory to the Devī immanent in all, who abides as
Consciousness in all beings
Salutations to Her, again and again

Yā devi sarva-bhūteṣu
buddhi-rūpeṇa saṃsthitā
Namas-tasyai, namas-tasyai,
namas-tasyai namo namaḥ. (5.14)

Glory to the Devī immanent in all, who abides in the form of
Wisdom
Salutations to Her, again and again

Yā devi sarva-bhūteṣu
śakti-rūpeṇa saṃsthitā
Namas-tasyai, namas-tasyai
namas-tasyai namo namaḥ. (5.18)

Glory to the Devī immanent in all, who abides in the form of
Divine Energy
Salutations to Her, again and again

Yā devi sarva-bhūteṣu
śānti-rupeṇa saṃsthitā
Namas-tasyai, namas-tasyai
namas-tasyai namo namaḥ. (5.23)

Glory to the Devī immanent in all, who abides in the form of
Tranquility
Salutations to Her, again and again

Yā devi sarva-bhūteṣu
śraddhā-rūpeṇa saṃsthitā
Namas-tasyai, namas-tasyai
namas-tasyai namo namaḥ. (5.24)

Glory to the Devī immanent in all, who abides in the form of
Faith
Salutations to Her, again and again

> *Yā devi sarva-bhūteṣu*
> *matṛ-rūpeṇa saṃsthitā*
> *Namas-tasyai, namas-tasyai*
> *namas-tasyai namo namaḥ.* (5.31)
>
> Glory to the Devī immanent in all, who abides in the form of
> Mother (maternality)
> Salutations to Her, again and again

Both Her transcendent qualities and Her engaged conventionally "maternal" attributes of compassion, love, and care are equally highlighted through the full *sūktam*. The theology of the Divine Feminine in Her full glory is revealed through these verses.

Conclusion

The Divine as the Mother, in the DM is all in all and, yet, cares deeply for the welfare of sentient beings, a model of divinity that reflects deep immanence and caring presence. For those who seek enlightened liberation, She is the liberator. For those seeking satisfaction in life, She is the source of blessings. The DM identifies Her with materiality and transformation but, at the same time, proclaims that She is the self-existent, eternal, unconditioned Absolute. She is characterized as fierce and powerful and, simultaneously, the personification of nurturance evinced by Her care for creation.

The tales narrated by the sage to the dispossessed king and the duped merchant are often viewed as metaphors for both psychological and physical life experience.[13] The *asuras*, the forces of malevolence that are confronted by the Devī, are emblematic of the worst of human tendencies: they seek to overpower the divine order in their delusion and craving for power, pleasure, and possessions. *They are the inner unawareness of human beings in regard to the teleological thrust of the cosmos towards emergence, order, symbiosis.*

The DM's battlefields represent the field of human effort and endeavor and can be analogized to the battlefield of the *Bhagavad Gītā*. The Devī, envisioned as one Supreme Divinity that contains all other divinities, challenges the inner demons of the human mind: that of the delusional ego forgetting that nothing belongs to oneself but everything belongs to the Supreme Self. The mystical theology of the Devī is revealed by the DM as it describes the adoration offered to the Devī, envisioned as the Divine who unlocks the possibility of transcending one's lower nature.

Intriguingly, in chapter 1, Brahmā—the *deva* always shown with four faces for the four directions—proclaims that the Devī has created everything *including himself*. God the Mother, the Primordial Power (Ādi-Śakti), is presented as the source of all other divine potencies and forces, embodying the combined energy of the luminous cosmic powers (*deva*s). She possesses both material and causal agency.

Through this abrogation of powers, capacities, and agency—that are normatively the purview of the masculine and feminine principles, respectively, in Hindu philosophical theology—the text integrates the ontological binaries, which I have discussed earlier, and protects against any potential disjunction between transcendence and immanence. And yet, as the Devī surpasses all oppositional binaries and pluralities including gender(s), She remains victoriously, viscerally, and experientially feminine.

Notes

Note: This essay draws on my earlier research, published in various journals. I acknowledge, in particular, the publication of my lecture titled "The 24th Reading of the Sacred Texts Lecture, 2016" by *Berkeley Journal of Religion and Theology*, vol. 2, no. 1. Berkeley: Graduate Theological Union, 2016.

1 See, for example: Cynthia Bourgeault and Rami Shapiro, *The Divine Feminine in Biblical Wisdom: Selections Annotated and Explained* (Nashville, TN: SkyLight Paths, 2011); and June Boyce-Tillman, *Unconventional Wisdom: Gender, Theology and Spirituality* (New York, Routledge, 2014).

2 Raj Balkaran in his chapter in this volume (Chapter 12) analyzes the frame story of the *Devī Māhātmyam* while focusing on the myth of Saṃjñā.

3 The *Śatapatha Brāhmaṇa* (7.15.27) presents *pradhāna* as the foundational *material* cause of creation; Sāṃkhya philosophy uses the term to imply the root cause or material source.

4 *Bhāskararāya Makhin* (1690–1785) is widely considered an authority on issues pertaining to the worship of the Divine Mother.

5 In the Pratyabhijñā philosophy of Kashmir Śaivism, *Śakti* is understood to have three primary modes of manifestation which are *Icchā Śakti* (the divine volitional power/energy), *Jñāna Śakti* (the power/energy of knowing which manifests first in the divine consciousness before concrete manifestation can occur), and *Kriyā Śakti* (the power/energy of action).

6 For an extensive overview of various goddesses in the Hindu tradition, see David Kinsely, *Hindu Goddesses: Visions of the Divine Feminine in the Hindu Religious Tradition* (New Delhi: Motilal Banarsidass Publishers, 1988).

7 This is a modification of Griffith's translation (pp. 571–2).

8 For example, *Kulārṇava Tantra* elevates *Śakti* to the status of the Supreme.

9 See Thomas Colburn on the historical setting of the DM. He notes that the Devī Māhātmya "cannot be considered a 'typical' *Purāṇic* text . . . it has a high degree of integrity." Furthermore, he draws attention to the text's "fixed, reified quality" (1991: 8, 9).

10 The *Durgā Stotram* is found right before the *Bhagavad Gītā* in some manuscripts of the *Mahābhārata*. See Coburn 1991: 26–7.

11 Translation is from Coburn (1991).

12 Translation by Rita D. Sherma.

13 Such interpretations have also been articulated in the Buddhist philosophy.

References

Beck, G. (2009). *Sonic Theology: Hinduism and Sacred Sound*. Columbia, SC: University of South Carolina Press.

Bhattacharyya, N. N. (1996). *The History of the Śākta Religion*, 2nd edn. New Delhi: Munshiram Manoharlal Publishers.

Bourgeault C., and Shapiro, R. (2011). *The Divine Feminine in Biblical Wisdom: Selections Annotated and Explained*. Nashville, TN: SkyLight Paths.

Boyce-Tillman, J. (2014). *Unconventional Wisdom: Gender, Theology and Spirituality*. New York: Routledge.

Coburn, T. (1991). *Encountering the Goddess: A Translation of the Devī-Māhātmyam and a Study of Its Interpretation*. Albany: SUNY Press.

Griffith, R. T. H. (1963). *Hymns of the Rigveda*. Varanasi: Chowkhamba Sanskrit Series Office.

Kali, D. (2003). *In Praise of the Goddess: The Devīmāhātmyam and Its Meaning*. Lake Worth, FL: Nicolas-Hays.

Kinsley, D. (1988). *Hindu Goddesses: Visions of the Divine Feminine in the Hindu Religious Tradition*. Los Angeles: University of California Press.

12

The Story of Saṃjñā, Mother of Manu: Shadow and Light in the *Mārkaṇḍeya Purāṇa*

Raj Balkaran

The Sanskrit narrative text *Devī Māhātmya*, "The Greatness of The Goddess" (henceforth DM), extols the triumphs of an all-powerful Goddess, Durgā, over universe-imperiling demons. The exploits of this formidable figure constitute the first known Sanskrit articulation of a Great Goddess within the Indian subcontinent, indeed the first occasion where the ultimate divine principle is accorded femininity. Believed to have emerged somewhere along the Narmada River *c* fifth century CE (Kinsley, 1982: 153), the DM is preserved in thousands of manuscripts across India, in remarkably stable fashion. It is recited as liturgy to Durgā in temples, during individual daily spiritual practice, and at temples and homes during the autumnal *Navarātri* (nine nights) Hindu festival. While the DM equates supreme reality with the feminine Hindu concepts of *māyā*, *śakti*, and *prakṛti*, it posits no systematic theory; instead, it masterfully interweaves these philosophical strands—as only narrative can—into the visage of a Feminine Divine whose power surpasses that of the Vedic pantheon, and even that of the cosmic *trimūrti* comprised of the great gods Brahmā, Viṣṇu, and Śiva. Hindu narrative literature is enormously didactic in nature, functioning to preserve philosophical principles and religious ideology across the centuries. Therefore, the overwhelming scholarly emphasis on philosophical texts over narrative literature has proven problematic. Recent scholars have argued in favor of locating religious authority within narrative text,[1] hence the enterprise at hand culling "philosophy" from "mythology." But how exactly *should* we go about reading narrative texts?

Western scholarship on the *Purāṇas* has been riddled with misgivings about the trustworthiness of these texts as we have them. The first wave of colonial scholarship on the *Purāṇas* condemned them as disorganized, debased, "corrupted" texts, coopting them for philological agendas. The second wave of Romantic Era scholars too mined these tales in search for historical and mythic data. The first approach was based on the assumption that the "real" text no longer exists (and probably never did), and the second resorted to dissecting the text that we have in hand. What about more modern scholarship on the *Purāṇas*? Inaugurated by the twin auspices of literary criticism and structuralism, the third, modern wave of scholarship has nevertheless been somewhat preoccupied with mining the *Purāṇas* for mythological motifs. The most significant figure in this enterprise is Wendy Doniger, who has spent nearly half a century plucking mythic moments from across vast spans of time and boundaries of genre and region to bring them into conversation within the rubric of structuralist discourse. However, in this essay, I take a different hermeneutic approach, carefully analyzing the text itself, taking cue from its own narrative content in order to ascertain its deeper philosophical meaning, and broader cultural significance.

The story of Saṃjñā that we find in the *Mārkaṇḍeya Purāṇa* (MkP) is as significant as it is mesmerizing, especially in light of its role as the backstory for the *Devī Māhāmtya* (DM), immediately following it in the MkP. It indeed "stands at the threshold of another tradition, the beginning of the incorporation of the worship of the Goddess into Sanskrit texts" (Doniger 1999: 55). Doniger, the most prolific voice in interpreting this myth, further remarks that "since the *Mārkaṇḍeya Purāṇa* tells the tale of Saṃjñā not once but twice and regards her as the mother of the Manu who rules in our age, the whole *Devī Māhāmtya* is, in a sense, a footnote to the story of the shadow of Saranyu" (Doniger 1999: 55).[2] However, the fact that the Saṃjñā myth is told twice is not necessarily indicative of its double importance (as compared to the DM), but rather, of its framing function of the DM: it is told immediately before and after the DM, serving to thematically contextualize the exploits of the Goddess. From the perspective of the DM—which glorifies the great goddess whose might surpasses even the creator's, and whose grace is responsible for installing the next Manu—it is the story of Saṃjñā which ornaments, and echoes, the Goddess's grandeur. But why would this be? What is it about the story of Saṃjñā that warrants its use as a foyer into the grandeur of the Great Goddess? How does the story of Saṃjñā—entailing an exchange between Sūrya, the Sun, and his wives Saṃjñā and Chāyā—orient us in broaching the Goddess of the DM?

Implicit in asking *what* the story of Saṃjñā tells us are the pre-suppositions (1) *that* it tells us anything at all and (2) that we may intelligently go about deciphering that meaning. Harkening to Umberto Eco's notion that texts are essentially machines designed for interpretation, positing a "model reader" by virtue of their very contents, this chapter bases its conclusions on a close synchronic reading of the world within the text, countering two centuries of Indological scholarship. Only in safeguarding the text from historicism, philological and structuralist reductions, may we begin to hear what it is trying to say. This approach demonstrates the agency of the text to serve as its own hermeneutic guide, prioritizing material through cues comprising its inherent structure. It therefore contributes not only to *what* we see in the text but also *how* we go about seeing it. In doing so, I moreover demonstrate that the story of Saṃjñā is purposefully wedded to the visage of the feminine we see in the DM because it is no mere tale of an ill-treated goddess who abandons her children and whose actions are the source of the evil of death. Rather, Saṃjñā's tale bespeaks monumental feminine resourcefulness, faith, and tenacity of spirit.

Structuralist Sleight of Hand

Frame narratives function as guides to interpretation. A frame of course cannot function as a strict, dogmatic fail-safe against dynamic, ongoing mythic exegesis, or else the fluidity of the *Purāṇic* genre freezes into cultural obsoletion. They are more like irrigational guides, designed to channel the narrative flow into fertile grounds for embellishment and interpretation. While much might be gained by plucking a given myth out of its narrative context so as to compare it to myths of similar content, affording purvey of the structural functions of elements of the myth, too much is lost in the process. Furthermore, this approach implicitly holds subsequent articulations accountable to earlier versions (consciously or unconsciously), operating under the premise that earlier articulations are "more authentic" in some way or another. Of course, both diachronic and synchronic methodologies constitute viable means of gaining insight into the "meaning" of a given narrative. However, I contend that if one is interested in grappling with a specific articulation of a narrative, one needs to commence with fully unpacking it within the narrative content proper to its articulation before (rather than instead of) proceeding to compare it to others of its kind. An individual mythic articulation need not be held accountable to its previous or subsequent incarnations. Yet, when we compare mythic articulations from different historical horizons (which, to be sure, is a useful and important exercise), the process itself often constitutes a "sleight of hand" of sorts, causing us to perceive contortions and occlusions that are very much functions of our methodological lens and not necessarily proper to their articulations themselves.

Wendy Doniger addresses the story of Saṃjñā at seven junctures throughout her work, in publications spanning 40 years (1976, 1980: 174–85; 1996, 1999: chapter One; 2000: chapters One and Nine; 2004: 60–2, 65–70; O'Flaherty 1973: 276, 292). She does so largely through the lens of earlier Vedic articulations of the myth and thus against the grain of the mythology of the Sun found in the MkP. In her 1976 publication, *The Origins of Evil in Hindu Mythology*, Wendy Doniger writes that "an important Vedic myth of two mothers is the story of Saṃjñā, the wife of the sun" (1980: 349). It is important for our purposes to unpack her methodological approach. While she uses a modified structuralist technique in her first publication (O'Flaherty, 1973), Doniger writes that "the problem of evil does not easily lend itself to a structuralist approach, perhaps because so many of its jagged facets prove stubbornly irreducible . . . I have therefore used any tool that would do the job – a bit of philology, a measure of theology, lashings of comparative religion, a soupcon of anthropology, even a dash of psychoanalysis" (Doniger 1976: 9). Despite this announcement, it appears that structuralism pervades the methodological milieu of this work nevertheless. Articulations of the Saṃjñā story (and its Vedic correlates pertaining to the goddess Saraṇyū, whom Doniger equates with Saṃjñā) appear at several junctures of Indian lore, ranging from Vedas to the *Upaniṣads* to, of course, the *Purāṇas*.[3] One might question the ability of any given author to translate and render thirteen mythic junctures ranging across two millennia of cultural and textual history in one fell swoop—but, graced by the powers of structuralist analysis, Doniger does just that. She presents "the" myth as follows:

> Saṃjñā gave birth to twins, Yama and Yamī, and then left her husband, creating as a substitute in her place an identical goddess called Chāyā ("dark shadow"). Her husband discovered the deception only when Chāyā mistreated her stepson, Yama; Yama tried to kick Chāyā and was cursed by her to lose his leg, a curse which his father later modified so that Yama fell to the underworld, the first mortal to die and king of all subsequent dead people. Vivasvat pursued Saṃjñā, who had taken the form of a mare, and in the form of a stallion (whose seed she drank) he begat the twin Aśvins upon her. (Doniger 1976: 349)

She then proceeds to offer analysis of her translation under the section heading "The Good and Evil Mother" as follows:

> The oppositional pairs of the good and bad mother, the bright image (saṃjñā) and dark shadow, are linked with the motif of the fertile solar stallion pursuing

> the erotic, destructive mare. The sun himself is said to have been rejected and pushed from the breast by his mother, Aditi, or to have been threatened by her asceticism while still in her womb, becoming mortal because of this [fn. 143 reads RV10.72.8–9] . . . Chāyā's hatred of her stepson results in a curse that makes Yama into the king of the dead. Thus the wicked, false mother is the source of the greatest of all evils, the kingdom of the dead. (Doniger 1976: 349)

In the first section of her analysis above, Doniger draws upon a binary pair of opposites—the good and the bad mother—in order to explain how Saṃjñā and Chāyā relate to each other and their purpose in the myth as a whole: the ill-treatment of Yama. She furthermore links this binary with a second pair of opposites, namely the fertile solar stallion and the erotic destructive mare. These theoretical tropes curtail the individual articulations of this tale in ways that can be (as is the case in the MkP's telling) contrary to *what we actually see in the text*. It is, for example, mystifying how one could perceive, based upon the MkP account, an "erotic, destructive mare" when we are explicitly told that Saṃjñā in her equine form performed austerities and fasted "like a chaste wife," (106.12), and that her efforts were geared towards pacification of her destructive husband. It is in fact Saṃjñā's steadfast celibate austerity that spiritually empowers her to reckon with her husband's overbearing *tejas*. Doniger nevertheless asserts elsewhere that sexual insatiability "is the telltale characteristic of the mare in Hindu mythology" (Doniger 1999: 48), and that this insatiability serves as an essential clue to Saṃjñā's "flight from marriage and motherhood" (Doniger 1999: 48). If Saṃjñā cared not for motherhood, it is doubtful that she would bother to craft a double and especially doubtful that she would instruct it to care for her children in her absence. Likewise, if she cared not for marriage, it is doubtful she would undertake austerities to ameliorate her husband's form. She flees from the Sun's excessive sharpness; once this is quelled, she gladly returns to both marriage and motherhood.

Reading the myths of the MkP through the lens of their "older, original" correlates is misguided, for, understandably in doing so, one might quite sensibly argue that "the fact the Saraṇyū myth is a hierogamy between a mortal and an immortal accounts for both Saraṇyū's desertion of her husband and her 'trimming' of him: either the sun is impotent and abandoned by the goddess or he is too powerful and is therefore castrated, a no-win situation if ever there was one" (Doniger 1980: 183). Similarly, as Robert Goldman points out, "the sun, of course, is the mortal par excellence in the Veda" (Goldman 1969: 278), and furthermore that he is "a progenitor of mortals." In the *Ṛg Veda,* itself, he is said to be the father both of Manu (VIII. 52.1) and Yama (X. 14.1)" (Goldman 1969: 279). However, the Sun is certainly not a mortal in the MkP. Therefore, while the myth of Saraṇyū and her husband in the *Ṛg Veda* may very well be one wherein "the male is a mortal while the female is immortal" (Goldman 1969: 275), this simply cannot be said to be true of the myth of Saṃjñā and her husband in the MkP. Not only is the Sun said to be immortal, he is described as the prime being among immortals, lauded variously as "the supreme light that was at the beginning" (103.7), "the eternal one" (104.19), "without birth" (107.4), "self-existent" (107.5), "lord without beginning" (109.72). Therefore, the mythology of Saṃjñā and Sūrya in the MkP is not a hierogamy between a mortal and an immortal, so this cannot possibly account for Saṃjñā's flight, nor the pairing down of Sūrya. Nor does it appear sensible to attribute Saṃjñā's flight in the MkP to either a distaste for motherhood or an insatiable sexual appetite. Saṃjñā in equine form is portrayed as neither destructive nor erotic; on the contrary, she maintains ascetic chastity in order to quell the destructive tendencies of an overbearing husband.

Let us now turn to the second section of the above analysis, regarding Chāyā's alleged hatred for her stepson, causing her to curse Yama and become "the source of the greatest of all evils, the kingdom of the dead" (Doniger 1976: 349). Neither account in the MkP correlates Chāyā's curse (that Yama's foot should fall off) with his status as the lord of the departed: the first account tells us that "because he is righteous of eye, impartial to friend and foe, therefore the dispeller of darkness appointed him over the southern region" (78.29) (Pargiter 1904: 506), while the second account tells us that the Sun "appointed him to the southern region; his adorable father gave to him the duty of protecting the world, O brahman, and the lordship over the pitṛis" (106.18–19) (Pargiter 1904: 575–6). Furthermore, as we have seen above, it is Sūrya's curse (based on Saṃjñā restraining her eyes) that causes Yama, "the restrainer" to be born to her. Yama and his role are inseparable; he was accorded this status before birth. More crucial to engaging this myth is the fact that while the myth of a primordial mother figure causing humanity's fall from blissful immortality to tragic mortality might prevail in the Abrahamic mythic imagination, it, alas, is deeply incommensurate with the myth at hand, both with respect to its specific articulation and to the cultural imagination authoring it. Doniger's distortion results from uprooting the myth from its narrative and cultural contexts, which she does in the interest of embellishing the discourse of a "bifurcated Hindu feminine," a trope abounding throughout her work. While Doniger does indeed mention the MkP among the various literary spaces with which the Sūrya–Saṃjñā–Chāyā episode is furnished,[4] she neglects to register the import of the myth's narrative context therein. We ought not to read the myth as if Chāyā were some "other" mate chosen by Sūrya and forced to contend with her husband's children of a previous marriage (as the term "stepmother" might connote). Chāyā was created by Saṃjñā through an act of self-cloning, one reminiscent of the yogic attainment (*siddhi*) of bilocation wherein the yogī is able to project a duplicate of his form, known as a shadow self (*chāyā mūrti*). We must note that shadow here does not connote nefariousness as it might in English, but merely reflection. Furthermore, this reflected self of Saṃjñā was explicitly instructed to treat the children well. The text does not indicate hatred nor ill-treatment toward any of the children. Rather, it indicates favoritism shown toward the younger children, which as anyone familiar with the dynamics of childrearing in a South Asian context can readily attest, would likely have been the case, even where all of the children were of the same parents. If this sort of favoritism were unconventional, it would have in itself aroused suspicion. Chāyā is not suspected as being other than Saṃjñā through her favoritism toward the younger children, but through her very human reaction to Yama's egregious insult, a reaction which only a mother might, under ideal circumstances, have been able to suppress.

In the MkP account, Chāyā is not demonized as "the wicked stepmother"—far from it. She succeeds in mothering children who are Sūrya's legitimate offspring, who have crucial cosmic roles, no less so than Sūrya's children by Saṃjñā.[5] Despite Doniger chalking up Yama's inauspicious post as the result of Chāyā's curse, Mārkaṇḍeya informs us that envious of Chāyā's favoritism of the three younger siblings, Yama threatened to kick her due to "both anger and childishness." As inappropriate a thing this is to do in Western culture, it would be absolutely inexcusable in an Indian context not only because of one's duty to respect elders and to revere one's parents as gods on earth, but especially because it is an expression of utter disregard to touch someone with one's foot, not to mention kicking them. So stigmatized is this that injunctions persist about even displaying the soles of one's feet toward a teacher or person of respect. One would not think to kick even inanimate objects that deserve respect, such as books. Chāyā curses Yama for his atrocious "unfilial conduct" (Pargiter 1904: 566). It is clear in the text that Yama is well aware that the transgression is his, not Chāyā's; he runs to his father to beg pardon and intersession of the curse, confessing that he "lifted my foot against her, but did not let it fall on her body; whether *it was* through childishness or through foolishness, do thou, Sir, deign to pardon it" (MkP 106.24. See Pargiter 1904: 568). He asks forgiveness because he has done wrong. Sūrya, in like manner, begins his response thus: "Without doubt, my son, this curse must take effect here, since anger entered into thee" (MkP 106.25. See Pargiter 1904: 568). Even the overbearing Sūrya can recognize that the fault here lies with Yama's conduct. If Chāyā is faulted in this myth, it is only for falling short of exhibiting saintly compassion in the face of atrocious disrespect on behalf on the part of a haughty youth.

The "wicked step-mother" motif—that is, the notion that "behind this complex myth we may discern a few repeated, familiar themes [such as the dual nature of Saṃjñā expressed as] the loving mother and the wicked step-mother" (Doniger 1980: 177)—is problematic, to say the least. The theme of the wicked stepmother may indeed be a "familiar" one, but only to those familiar with western fairy tales, and not necessarily their Indian mythic counterparts. In seeking to chart the "origins of evil" in Hindu mythology, one is confronted with two interconnected obstacles with respect to the conception of evil therein: first, the cosmos itself, much less any aspect of it, is fundamentally beginning-less, a notion which undercuts discourse of origins; second, one cannot treat as a separate entity that which is conceived as an aspect of a greater whole. The lines between good and evil are incredibly (and intentionally) blurred in *Purāṇic* discourse where gods may behave nefariously (typically for a greater good) and demons may exhibit extraordinary piety, particular in devotional milieus, for the sake of acquiring power. For example, the gods (*sura*s) and the demons (more literally, the anti-gods, *asura*s) not only share an ancestry but, as we are reminded of in the myth of the churning of the ocean, are kindred polarities which must collaborate to generate the creative tension engendering all of the universe's riches and even immortality itself. That these forces appear to oppose each other is so only from a limited perspective. From a grander perspective, these forces are like two separate hands pressed together in *añjali mudrā*, stemming from the same ground of being, producing a unified gesture.

In maintaining the evil stepmother motif, one silences what the MkP has to say; Doniger therefore writes,

> this transition from good mother to evil mother is highly significant in the Indian context; Indeed, some *Purāṇic* texts tried to restore a modicum of maternal spirit to Saraṇyū by stating that she turned away from the stallion because she feared that he might be some man other than her husband (MkP: 103–5). This gloss . . . is untrue to the original spirit of the myth. (Doniger 1980: 185)

From what perspective should we gauge what is authentic? Doniger bases the "original spirit" of "the" myth upon her understanding of its earliest known incarnations and thus eclipses the authority of the composers of the MkP themselves, along with the communities that preserve, invoke, and depend upon its current articulation in their religious lives. She not only reads the myth of Saṃjñā in the MkP at large through the lens of its earlier Vedic correlates, but she goes so far as to outright dismiss as inauthentic the elements that do not conform to that lens. To my mind, this outcome comprises the central hazard to uprooting *Purāṇic* tales from their narrative soil, intended to support, not thwart, their religious transmission; a compromise of their religious authority.

Sixteen years after her publication of the *Origins of Evil in Hindu Mythology*, Doniger produces a 1996 article dedicated to Saṃjñā/Saraṇyū (Doniger, 1996) wherein she perpetuates the practice of plucking from myth cycle across vast spans of time and reading later articulations as distortions of earlier ones. She draws her data from *Ṛg Veda* 10.17.1–2 (Doniger 1996: 171)[6] the *Harivaṃśa*,[7] the MkP, along with an episode from the classic series Indian comics, *Amar Chitra Katha* (Doniger 1996: 172).[8] Rather than chart the functions of the single character of Saṃjñā across three millennia of cultural history, it is perhaps more commensurate to the *Purāṇic* textual transformations to study in detail how that character relates to the whole within a single articulation of the myth cycle in a given *Purāṇa*. It is, for example, crucial to note that the *Purāṇic* authors never refer to the figure in question as Saraṇyū, but only as Saṃjñā, which suggests a distancing, if not radical reconfiguring, from the figure we find in Vedic lore to the one that graces the *Purāṇas*. As a result of this conscious transformation, tension arises while reading *Purāṇic* iterations and all the while harkening to Vedic articulations in order to understand "the myth" in itself. Hence Doniger, upon completing her discussion of Saraṇyū in the Vedic literature, refers to the articulation of this found in the *Harivaṃśa* and the *Purāṇas* as "later variants" (Doniger 1996: 158) wherein the goddess is not named Saraṇyū, but Saṃjñā (Doniger 1996: 158). This attitude of course echoes the trenchant bias toward the *Purāṇas* as corruptions of older texts. Keeping in line with her "variant from Vedic version" discussion, Doniger further notes that "Saṃjñā's surrogate is no longer said to be of the same kind or type but is rather her chāyā, her mirror image or shadow, creature who is not exactly like her but is her opposite in terms either of inversion (the mirror image) or of color (the shadow)" (Doniger 1996: 158). This note regarding color keeps in line with her interest in question of race (Doniger 1996: 154), yet is problematized by the fact that Saṃjñā addresses Saṃjñā as "fair one" (MkP 106.7) in her instructions prior to fleeing.[9] Regardless, these notable developments entailing the transition of Saraṇyū and Sāvarṇa to Saṃjñā and Chāyā, respectively, ought not be viewed as deviations from the original Vedic myth, but as important *Purāṇic* articulations in their own right, whose religious vision is equally authentic to its contemporaries as the Vedic myths were to theirs.

In the section of her article discussing the MkP, Doniger translates the opening of the first account of the Saṃjñā myth as follows:

> Samjna was the daughter of Tvastr and the wife of Martanda, the Sun. He produced in her Manu, called Manu Vaivasvata, since he was Vivasvant's son. But when the sun looked at her, Samjna used to shut her eyes, and so the sun got angry and spoke sharply to Samjna: "Since you always restrain (samyamam) your eyes when you see me, therefore you will bring forth a twin (yama) who will restrain (samyamanam) creatures." Then the goddess became agitated by terror, and her gaze flickered; and when he saw that her gaze darted about, he said to her again, "Since now your gaze darts about when you see me, therefore you will bring forth a daughter who will be a river that darts about." And so because of her husband's curse Yama and Yamuna were born in her. (MkP 74.1–7) (Doniger 1996: 164)

Doniger then proceeds to offer the following analysis: "where Manu is named after his father, and is blessed, Yama is named after his mother, and is cursed; for he is named not after her name but after her evil deeds" (Doniger 1996: 164). First, let us be reminded that, it is not Yama who is named after his mother. Rather, it is the second Manu, Sāvarṇi, who is named after Chāyā, known also as Sāvarṇā (i.e., She of the Likeness). Second and more important, the fact that this exchange is designed to paint the Sun (and not Saṃjñā) in less than favorable light is corroborated throughout the solar myths to be found in the MkP. They unanimously warn us of the danger and disruption which ensues when the Sun is excessive in his intensity. This is unsurprising to a people born of a climate wherein when the Sun is too intense, drought ensues, hence his epithet, "Robber of the Waters." The aforementioned portion of the myth, accounting for Yama's birth, tells us that death (Yama) is fathered by the wrath of the Sun. Recall this entire episode is framed by the mythology of the Sun who is unbearable even to the creator himself and constitutes a threat to cosmic order. That this episode (between Brahmā and Sūrya) occurs before the Sūrya–Saṃjñā episode is, of course, significant: the earlier serves to frame the later.

There can be little doubt that the MkP is sympathetic to the plight of Saṃjñā: for who is able to gaze at the Sun full on, in its full fury, without squinting? The text portrays an overbearing husband rather than a nefarious wife. The Sun curses Saṃjñā in this moment but the text clearly sides with Saṃjñā; hence she flees and is never once admonished for doing so, neither by her husband, her sons, her father, nor the narrator of the text. Recall that Sūrya himself realizes the folly of his ways and *volunteers* to be pared down toward the conclusion of this telling. In the Sun's rash cruelty, he curses his own unborn children, but let us not forget that Yama's curse is ultimately reconfigured as a cosmic benediction insofar as Yama became the righteous-eyed judge because of it. Doniger misguidedly argues that "as anthropogonies, these stories are saying that the primeval children, our ancestors, were abandoned by their mother" (1996: 170). Even to entertain that this angle of inquiry as central to the contours of this myth (which, as Doniger herself admits, is probably not the case—a wise move considering Indian deities are rarely rendered as exemplars for human conduct), can we sensibly arrive at this conclusion when we are told that our primordial mother (1) was unable to remain due to our father's excessive sharpness, (2) that she made arrangements for our care during her necessary respite, cloning herself and commanding her clone to treat us well, (3) that she engaged in religious practices in order to restore balance to our family, and (4) that she was successful in neutralizing our father's overbearing wrath and restoring balance, such that she ended up returning to us and so didn't ultimately abandon us at all? It is perhaps precisely due to the resilient faces of the Feminine Divine pervading the MkP, such as that of Saṃjñā, that the DM is happily at home therein.

Doniger's own words point to the incommensurability between her hermeneutic approach and the myth we find in the MkP. She states at the outset of her Saṃjñā study that she is primarily interested in "questions of gender and race" (Doniger 1996: 154), but must admit that nothing is said of the Sun's "ugliness or dark color" in the MkP's accounts of his mythology, which leave only questions of gender. With respect to such questions, she appears intent on painting the picture of humanity's fall from grace due to the evils of a primordial stepmother (a motif familiar to anyone acquainted with Abrahamic religion), that she fails to address the obvious feminist gems of this myth cycle: first that wives and mothers are thought to hold tremendous power over the domestic sphere and thus exert great influence over their families through their religious activities; and second, rather than the typical motif of the daughter being made to succumb to the pressures of the mother-in-law, we have a shocking and refreshing reversal: a son-in-law (the Sun himself no less) who submits to the hammering down of his father-in-law for the safety and comfort of his wife, family, and society as a whole. When Doninger does turn her attention to the fact that the versions of this myth cycle occurring in the MkP (along with the one occurring in the *Harivaṃśa*) "give new prominence to an old, silent character: the father-in-law, Tvastr" (Doniger 1996: 165), she does so in order to argue that "the aggression of the bride's father against her husband" (Doniger

1996: 166) (a statement that itself cannot be said to apply to the MkP's tellings) "lends weight, retrospectively, to the possibly incestuous connection that some Indologists have seen between Tvastr and Saranyu in the Vedic corpus" (Doniger 1996: 166).

Strangely, she opts to read the father-in-law's willingness to pare down the Sun's splendor (at the Sun's behest) for the sake of the welfare of his daughter as grounds for reading into the *Purāṇic* telling conjecture into a possible incestuous relationship held by some Indologists in reference to myths composed two millennia earlier, rather than register that the myth serves as a salient reminder to overbearing husbands that daughters are always welcomed (albeit temporarily) to their fathers' homes post-marriage. Not only does Doniger appear disinterested in this dimension of the myth, she also claims that Saṃjñā took the form of a mare "when her father threw her out of his house" (Doniger 1996: 163). Similarly, in *Hindu Myths*, wherein she translates this same passage from the MkP, she writes that Saṃjña's father "admonished her again and again to go to her husband" (Doniger 2004: 66). She fails to mention that the MkP tells us that Saṃjñā remained in her father's house "unreproached" (*aninditā*, 77.16), or that her father, "after praising her and prefacing his speech with love and much respect," (*stutvā ca tanayāṃ premabahumānapuraḥ saram*, 77.17) advises her to leave since it is improper for a married woman to remain among her kinsmen (i.e., away from her husband) for a long time, and that she was welcome to return in the future. The text goes out of its way to indicate that Saṃjñā was welcome in her father's home and that her father lovingly sends her back for the sake of her honor, all the while unaware that she was imperiled by her husband's overbearing nature. It is the Sun, and not Saṃjñā, who mends his ways in the MkP. In portraying this mother of the Manus, the MkP certainly does not paint a portrait of an absentee mother nor wicked stepmother nor ultimately disenfranchised wife. Rather, it portrays a resilient feminine figure who succeeds in softening overbearing masculinity when she is imperiled by the dangers of its sharpness.

Seminal Splendor and the Transmission of *Tejas*

Despite the richness of the term *tejas* (fiery energy, vital power, spirit), and its obvious connotations to majesty, Wendy Doniger, in her reading of this myth, favors one of its more figurative meanings: semen.[10] She therefore translates the encounter as follows:

> Then Vivasvant's body was beautiful, and had no excessive fiery energy. He went to his wife, the mare, in the form of a stallion. But when she saw him approaching she feared it might be another male, and so she turned to face him, determined to protect her hindquarters. Their noses joined as they touched, and the seed of the Sun flowed from his two nostrils into the mare and came out of her mouth, and in that way the equine twin gods called the Asvins were born. (Doniger 1996: 165)

She notes that "impregnation by drinking semen is a world-wide theme, and it is particularly well developed in India. In the Vedic story of Saṃjñā, the mare becomes pregnant by smelling or absorbing through her nostrils the seed of her husband" (O'Flaherty 1973: 276). Therefore, she reads the sun's excessive splendor (*tejas*) as his overbearing sexuality, from which Saṃjñā must flee. She reasons that it is significant that the word for "energy" (*tejas*) is also a word for semen since Saṃjñā "in her anthropomorphic form avoids the Sun's energy, while in her mare form she avoids the stallion's semen" (Doniger 1996: 163). However, this comparison is lopsided: Saṃjñā does not merely avoid the Sun's energy, she flees from it out of desperation. With respect to the "strange" male, she does not flee but merely averts penetration and engages him face to face. Furthermore, Saṃjñā here does not fear Sūrya's semen but the semen of "another male." She fled from the overbearing majesty of the Sun, not his procreative proclivity, hence the begetting of three children with him prior to fleeing. This fear results not merely as a threat to her womanhood (or marehood rather) but as a threat to the celibate austerities in which she was engaged, along with a threat to her marital fidelity. In other words, she was not afraid because it was Sūrya (from whose sexuality she needed to flee) but precisely *because it wasn't Sūrya* (or so she thought), on account of her commitment to whom, sexual engagement with another ought to be avoided at all costs. These sources of anxiety may not be simplified as tantamount to fearing male sexuality at large, and particularly not her husband's.

The text could not possibly be referring to the stallion's literal semen flowing into Saṃjñā since it was emitted through his nose, not his genitals. She also received it through her nose, and receiving liquid through one's nose, as we know, is an unpleasant and dangerous experience. Saṃjñā birthed the Aśvins through her mouth, and not her genitals. It is noteworthy that the verb "to drink" (*pā*) appears nowhere in this passage, despite Doniger's claim that the worldwide theme of impregnation through drinking semen has been particularly well developed in India (O'Flaherty 1973: 276). Even if seminal *fluid* was involved, Saṃjñā doesn't drink it since it would have then passed from her nose to her mouth; drinking involves swallowing. The supernormal dimension of this encounter strongly suggests that we are to literally take it that the Sun conceived the celestial twins with his literal *tejas*, his spiritual power. If the authors meant to signify physical semen, they could have easily used the term *retas*, which would very conveniently serve the prosodic demands of both meter and stress, and much better connote seminal fluid than does *tejas*. That the Aśvins were conceived with such miraculous power befits their own miraculous healing ability. We are told that the Sun and Saṃjñā in equine form "joined their noses" (Pargiter 1904: 460)[11], an act that is bereft of physical penetration. We are soon thereafter told that Revanta was born at the end of the flow (*retaso 'ante*), presumably of the Sun's transmission. *Retas*, as noted above, also connotes the flow of semen. Thus, in *Hindu Myths*, Doniger translates this as "and when the seed ceased to flow [*retaso' ante*, 'at the end of the seed'] Revanta was born" (Doniger 2004: 69). However, there is only one mention of *retas*, which cannot be translated twice as both "seed" and "flow." Therefore, it may be translated as "as the end of the seed" or "at the end of the flow." It is less forced to translate *retas* as 'flow' [i.e., of *tejas*] in this context given the absence of reproductive organs or penetration involved in the encounter. Also the phrase *retaso' ante* is a play on the name Revanta, which cleverly evokes "*revato 'ante*", that is, at the end of the constellation *Revati* where one finds the constellation Aśvini, the same asterism over which the Aśvin twins preside. Interestingly, there is an account of a previous Manu (the fifth one) Raivata whose backstory is heavily interspersed with the constellation Revati. Perhaps it is not without design that we hear the tale of a Manu whose backstory invokes Revatī before hearing a tale of a Manu whose backstory invokes Aśvini, at the end of Revati (revato'ante).

Given the supernormal, non-penetrative, voluntary encounter between Sūrya and Saṃjñā, Doniger's claim that Saṃjñā was "raped by the Sun stallion and brought home again . . . [since] in the end she must submit to her husband's sexual demands, just like a human woman" (Doniger 1999: 49) is most mystifying to my mind. This reading presents the myth out of the context of its various narrative frames. Narrative frames bear tremendous thematic import, devised to ideologically orient one's reading of myth. Doniger's reading presumes that Saṃjñā attains equine form to enjoy sexual freedom. But if Saṃjñā had the gumption to devise and implement an escape plan so that she didn't have to contend with the energetic threat of her husband while in anthropomorphic form, could we really think she would hesitate to gallop away from the sexual threat of a strange male while in equine form? How can this stallion be portrayed as a threat when she turns and unflinchingly encounters him face to face? Post-encounter, the MkP unambiguously informs us that Saṃjñā is *pleased* at the sight of her husband's pared-down form and describes her as the Sun's "loving wife." The passage reads, "then the Sun displayed his own peerless form, and she gazing upon his true form felt a keen joy; and the Sun, the robber of the waters, brought home this his loving wife Saṃjñā restored to her own shape."[12] One is unable to locate within this passage indications of sexual coercion of any kind, nor evidence supporting the presumption that Saṃjñā is dragged home.

That Saṃjñā opts not to flee indicates no sign of struggle, and that she voluntarily joins noses with the equine-Sun is consistent with what the text tells us: she is afraid of union with another male, intent on guarding her chastity She attains the form of a mare to practice *chaste* austerities, rather than indulge her sexual appetite. And if the text indeed intended to portray a Saṃjñā who wished to sow her wild oats, it is doubtful that the idyllic land of the Northern Kurus[13] would be the place to do so, since it is a location where folks are born in pairs and each partner has the same lifespan so that blissful monogamy may ensue. Had they intended to invoke the theme of sexual freedom, the others of this episode would have much better served their cause by (1) refraining from having Saṃjñā guard her rear and (2) choosing any of the several other regions described in the MkP than one explicitly associated with contented monogamy. The resilient and resourceful Saṃjñā of the MkP was neither raped, nor "dragged" anywhere; she left home because of her husband's overbearing *tejas*, and while we may debate about what that *tejas* might be said to represent, there is no question that the Sun had his *tejas* checked by his father-in-law. Since the cause of her discontent and flight were eliminated, what reason do we have to assume her discontent continued? She conceives the Aśvins and joyfully returns home. While Saṃjñā suffers to conceive death (Yama) when the Sun's *tejas* is overbearing, she readily receives his pared-down energy to conceive health through the healer twins. In his fierce form, the Sun fathers death. In his contained, pleasant form, he births divine medicine in the idyllic Northern Kurus. And this latter achievement is directly attributed to the equine austerities of an empowered Saṃjñā.

In addition to discourse on *tejas* and the birth of the Aśvins, there are a number of notable themes running through the MkP's account of the mythology of Sūrya. In particular, this myth cycle is redolent with the overarching theme of mirror images: not only does Chāyā mirror Saṃjñā but we are, as well, presented with the production of two sets of children, the second of which set mirrors the first. Manu Vaivasvata, Yama, and Yamī are mirrored by their younger stepfamily Manu Sāvarṇi, Śanaiścara, and Tapatī (the current Manu, the planet Saturn, and the Narmadā river, respectively). Thus we hear the tale of two Manus, two gods of human suffering, and two dark rivers. Interestingly, there is a tertiary dimension to the duality of this mythology: (1) each stepfamily consists of a threesome, not just a pair; (2) the Sun and Saṃjñā, while in equine form, beget a third set of triple offspring comprised of the Aśvin twins and Revanta. We seem to be presented with an intriguing triplet motif comprised of "a pair and a third entity": the daughters are the third appendage to the pairs of sons, Revanta is the third entity to be born in tandem with the Aśvins, and the entire equine family itself is a tertiary emanation of Sūrya's two anthropomorphic families.[14] Perhaps this tertiary dynamic is fitting considering it is spawned by the threefold intertwining of Sūrya, Saṃjñā, and Chāyā. An object cannot be reflected in the absence of light. Arguably, the most trenchant expression of mirroring featured in this myth consists of the interplay between shadow and light. This interplay (like the set of offspring noted above) is not merely a binary one (as might be expected in this case) but, intriguingly, is tertiary. The main actors are Sūrya as emblematic of the primal, self-effulgent progenitor of the universe, along with his primary consort Saṃjñā, and his secondary consort (born of the interplay of Sūrya and Saṃjñā), that is, Chāyā. Saṃjñā casts behind her own shadow, unable to bear the Sun. For a shadow to exist before a source of light, there must be a third entity: an object to cast its shadow.

Shadow and Light in the MkP

In my view, the brilliance of this myth is to be found in its treatment of the interplay between shadow and light: given that it is ultimately Sūrya's brilliance (*tejas*) that causes Saṃjñā to cast behind her shadow in her stead, who is to blame for Saṃjñā's flight? When Sūrya ventures to his father-in-law's[15] home in search of Saṃjñā (clarity), he requests that his father-in-law Viśvakarman pare down his form so that it is once again bearable (MkP 106.36–38. See Pargiter 1904: 569). One sees clearly neither in the dark nor when the light is too bright. Doniger reads this as an encounter where Viśvakarman "finally mutilates [Saṃjñā's] husband in order to make him acceptable to her" (Doniger 1996: 166). Mutilation connotes forceful disfigurement resulting in unsightliness and suffering and can hardly be said to properly refer to a voluntary act of beautification and pacification, undertaken by a "mutilator" all the while full of songful praise of his object of mutilation. It is the Sun's overbearing aspect that results in Saṃjñā's flight,[16] an aspect so overpowering that at the dawn of time, the creator himself must pare down that aspect for creation to successfully occur. Rather than fault Saṃjñā, the MkP expresses a *necessity* for Sūrya to be pared down, a task accomplished at the hands of the divine tinkerer, who is conveniently cast as Saṃjñā's father. The Sun never chastises Saṃjñā for fleeing, but rather is so much in agreement with the dangers of his overbearing nature that he *voluntarily* acquiesces to being pared down.

The Sun does not disown his children born of shadow (Chāyā); rather, he promotes them in rank to statuses parallel to those of his children born of Saṃjñā. Sūrya fathers three children with each of these wives and these stepfamilies are parallels of one another: Saṃjñā mothers Vaivasvata (the current Manu), Yama (the god of the dead, as the shadow of that Manu), and Yamunā (a river known for turning black, also named Kālindī) (Mani 1975: 894) while Chāyā mothers three children: Sāvarṇi (the next Manu), Śanaiścara (Saturn, the lord of karmic retribution), and Tapatī, who eventually receives a blessing from Sūrya whereby she becomes the Narmadā river, flowing west from the Vindhya mountains (Mani 1975: 798).

Chāyā's daughter, Tapatī, has an ever far more significant role to play in the unfolding of *itihāsa*. The MkP sums this up in the following line: "The third of them, the daughter named Tapatī, had a son, Kuru, king of men, by king Samvaraṇa."[17] In the *Mahābhārata*, Arjuna asks the Gandharva in the forest why the Gandharva not only addresses him with the matronymic Kaunteya, son of Kuntī, but also as Tāpatya, son of Tapatī.[18] The Gandharva then dedicates a subtale[19] to explaining that radiant Tapatī was wedded by King Saṃvaraṇa (himself a devotee of the Sun), upon whom was begotten Kuru, that great ancestor of the entire lineage. Tapatī is not only the mother of Arjuna, she is the mother of the entire line of kings populating both Pāṇḍava and Kaurava camps.[20] The Sun is so inextricable from the symbolism of kingship that even the lunar line of kings showcased in the *Mahābhārata* attributes their lineage to the seed of the Sun. The legitimacy of both of the Sun's stepfamilies (along with the legitimacy of the solar race mothered by one branch of that family tree through Tapatī, daughter of Chāyā) bespeaks of the legitimacy of both of the *śaktis* (powers, consorts) of the Sun to whom both shadow and light must ultimately be attributed for him to retain primordial supremacy within the solar myths as the cause of all creation. Therefore, rather than being a story of a wicked stepmother or absentee birthmother, a raped wife, or a mutilated son-in-law, the Sūrya–Saṃjñā–Chāyā exchange, couched in a section of the MkP dedicated to the splendor of the Sun, perhaps more directly comments on the symbiosis of light and dark.[21]

Doniger concludes her study by confessing that questions of sociology are not the dominant questions entertained by this myth. She states that this myth cycle, rather,

> raises theological questions about the origin of the human race and of human death, about appearance and reality, about the relationship between male and female divine powers, and about the nature of the relationship between humans and the divine . . . But that is yet another story, best left for another time. (Doniger 1996: 170–1)

Despite the tantalizing hope of having these seminal aspects of this myth cycle addressed, yet another eighteen years elapsed before this article on Saṃjñā reappears in Doniger's 2014 collection *On Hinduism*, relatively unaltered from its 1996 state. It is no wonder that she writes at the very outset of her discussion that despite having addressed it "variously in various books," the mythology of Saraṇyū/Saṃjñā "still accuses [her] of not even having begun to plumb its depths" (Doniger 2014a: 607 See fn. 1). Yet, she tells the same story in this article as she did in her 1996 article and one is left wondering about this profound story "best left for another time" (Doniger 2014b: 287) as again quoted at the conclusion of the 2013 edition. This present study, at long last, begins to tell the tale of this captivating myth cycle that Doniger has broached only in passing for forty years; for it is these very issues pertaining to "the relationship between male and female divine powers, and about the nature of the relationship between humans and the divine" (Doniger 1996: 171) which the DM addresses and furthermore, why its composers opted to dovetail its narration alongside the mythology of the Sun found in the MkP. Both mythologies bespeak powerful feminine divinities whose efforts restore order in the face of peril, and both bespeak the danger that results when fiery figures, though required to preserve our world, exceed safe bounds.

Reading the story of Saṃjñā as merely a tale of an ill-treated goddess who abandons her children and whose actions are the source of the evil of death is fundamentally incommensurate with the vision of the Feminine Divine that the authors of the DM present and by virtue of this, incommensurate with their understanding of Saṃjñā with who's mythology they yolk the grandeur of the Goddess to the fabric of the MkP. Saṃjñā's tale is the one that demonstrates feminine resourcefulness, faith, and tenacity of spirit that ultimately restores cosmic balance. Saṃjñā, through her austerity, causes the destructive aspect of the Sun to keep at bay and thus ensures the preservation not only of self and family, but also of the cosmos as a whole. It is primarily her efforts, and only secondarily her husband's (once he realizes the motivation for her penance), which restores cosmic balance. Doniger writes that "on the metaphysical level the myth of Saṃjñā seems to be saying that we, the descendants of Manu, are the children of the image—the children of *māyā*, not the children of the real thing" (Doniger 1996: 170) and that "these myths embody the Vedantic view that we are born into illusion, live in illusion, and can only know illusion" (Doniger 1996: 170). But in my estimation, this myth, in the context of the MkP (especially given its vital association to the DM), goes well beyond the values of Vedantic binary, succeeding in subverting them by positing a supremacy on the part of that illusion insofar as it is inextricable from anything conceived to be superior to it. We are told at the very beginning of the DM, for example, that King Suratha is made the lord of an age by the might of Mahāmāyā. To be the children of Mahāmāyā is to be children of the divine mother and arguably, to be children of the future: while the current Manu, the child of Saṃjñā, is patrilineally named Vaivasvata (after Vivasvat, the Sun), the Manu Sāvarṇi, primordial overlord of the *next* epoch, is named after his mother, Sāvarṇa,[22] She of the Likeness. Her Likeness, through Sāvarṇi, our primordial forefather to come, shall populate an entire age. Bolstered by its *Purāṇic* context, the DM affirms that the diversity of this phenomenal world, along with the myriad of life forms finding homes herein, is as supreme as that dynamic feminine mystery which engenders, supports, and governs it, compelled through compassion toward colossal acts of cosmic preservation.[23]

Appendix 1: Synopsis of Saṃjñā Story

The mythic juncture in question comprises the opening frame of discourse on the seventh Manu whereby the first telling of MkP informs us straight away (at the outset of Canto 77) that the Sun and his wife Saṃjñā[24] (77.1–2) beget a famous and learned Manu, namely the current Manu Vaivasvata, that is, "He of Vivasvat," which is an epithet of the Sun. The text next tells us that Saṃjñā would shut her eyes when met with the Sun's gaze (77.3) and the Sun, angered, curses her to bring forth Yama, the imprisoner (*samyamanam yamam*), given that her eyes remained imprisoned (*netrasaṃyamam)* at the sight of him (77.4). Saṃjñā "unnerved by fear, became wild-eyed" (Pargiter 1904: 455), and the Sun again curses her (77.5) through means of a second wordplay to bring forth the tumultuous river Vilolā (Yamunā) due to her tumultuous glances (77.6). Thus Manu Vaivasvata's siblings Yama and Yamunā are born (77.7).

Saṃjñā, having suffered the sharpness (*tejas*) of the Sun for some time (77.8) and unable to bear it further, decides to take refuge with her father (77.8–10). In order to do so, she "fashioned her body, that the Sun loved, in shadow-form, and addressed her shadow-self: 'Remain thou here in the Sun's house even as I; and behave thou becomingly to the children even as to the Sun.'" (77.11–12). Chāyā-Saṃjñā (Saṃjñā's "shadow-self" or "reflected-self," used herein interchangeably with Chāyā for the sake of simplicity) agrees to remain in Saṃjñā's stead, holding up the ruse as ordered, even to the point of being seized by her hair or drawing curses upon herself (77.13–14). The goddess Saṃjñā, "receiving this assurance, then went to her father's abode" (77.15). We are told that the great Tvaṣṭṛ[25] ("cleansed from stain by means of austerities" 77.15) honored her with much respect (77.16) and that she "remained in her father's house some time, unreproached" (*tasthau pitṛgṛhe sā tu kañcitkālam aninditā*, 77.16). Then after having dwelt there for a short time, her father, "after praising her and prefacing his speech with love and much respect," (*stutvā ca tanayāṃ premabahumānapuraḥ saram*, 77.17) advises her thus:

> Now while I have been seeing thee my child, the days though very many may be reckoned as equal to half a moment; nevertheless righteousness suffers loss. Dwelling a long time among kinsmen brings no good repute to women; kinsmen hold a woman's proper residence is in her husband's house. Such art thou, and thou art mated to a husband, the Sun, the lord of the three worlds; deign not my daughter to dwell a long time in thy father's house. Being such, go thou to thy husband's home. I am pleased; thou hast been honoured by me. Thou must come again to see me, my beautiful one. (77.18–21[26])

Agreeing to his counsel, she salutes her father respectfully and secretly departs for the Northern Kurus, unbeknownst to him, still fearing the sharp splendor of the Sun. She practices austerities and changes herself into the form of a mare (77.22–23).[27]

Meanwhile the Sun, unaware of the ruse, begets a second family with Chāyā, one reflecting the first family by consisting also of two sons and a daughter, Manu, Śanaiścara, and Tapatī. Yama exhibits petty envy when the younger children are favored (77.24–25) and goes so far as to raise his foot in anger against his own mother (i.e., Chāyā, whom he believes at this point to be his own mother). Astonished at his appalling behavior, Chāyā curses Yama that his foot would fall to earth that very day. She cleverly gives her reason for her curse that he insulted his father's wife (*pituḥ patnīm*) as opposed to his mother (77.26–29). Yama, terrified of the curse, runs to his father, Sūrya (77.30), and complains as follows:

> O father, this great marvel was never seen by any one, that a mother casting love away imprecates a curse on her son. She is not mother to me in the same way as Manu calls her his mother; no mother would abandon her good qualities even towards sons devoid of good qualities (77.31–32).[28]

We are told that upon hearing these words from his son, the "illustrious dispeller of darkness" (*bhagavāṃs timirāpahaḥ*) summons Chāyā and apparently seeing through the ruse, asks, "Where has she gone?" (77.33). Though Chāyā answers that she is his wife, Saṃjñā, and the mother of his children (77.34), the Sun repeatedly questions her and, eventually, enraged by her silence on the matter, threatens to curse her (7.35). Although she promised to hold to the false story, even to the point of bringing curses upon herself, the Sun's glare succeeds in breaking through Chāyā's pretense. She confesses the truth, at which point Sūrya goes to pay a visit to his father-in-law, Tvaṣṭṛ, in order to reclaim Saṃjñā (77.36). Once there, he is received with honor and "with sublime faith" (77.37). Tvaṣṭṛ, upon being asked after his daughter, responds, "She came indeed here to my house, saying she had been verily sent by thee" (77.38).

Upon hearing this, the great Maker of Day (*divākaraḥ*) concentrates his mind in yogic meditation and inwardly sees his wife in the form of a mare, practicing austerities in the Northern Kurus (*samādhistho vaḍavārūpadhāriṇīm / tapaścarantīṃ dadṛśe uttareṣu kuruṣvatha*, 77.39). Through his yogic attainment, he is furthermore able to perceive the purpose of her penance, namely that her husband should acquire a gentle form, beautiful to behold (77.40). Upon becoming aware of this, the Sun immediately asks of his father-in-law that his sharp splendor be pared down (77.41), to which Viśvakarman of course reverently complies (77.42). Thus ends the first canto of the first telling.

The following Canto (78) commences with the praise of the gods and divine seers (*devarṣayaḥ*) who had assembled for the cosmic event, that is, the paring down of the Sun. Interestingly, this event appears to be construed as an auspicious one. While, for example, the waning of the moon is considered inauspicious, this appears to be a different scenario wherein excess energy is reabsorbed by the universe to grant the Sun a more balanced, benign form. Immediately following the fourteen-verse praise,[29] the Sun begins to shed his splendor (78.15), which not only comprises the earth, sky, and heaven (*svarga*) from the aspects of him which comprised the *Ṛg*, *Yajur*, and *Sāma Veda*, respectively (78.16), but the "fifteen shreds of his splendour which were pared off by Tvaṣṭṛ" (78.17) were used to craft Śiva's trident (78.17), Viṣṇu's discus, "the Vasus, the very terrible weapon of Śankara," Agni's spear, Kubera's *palki* (78.18), "and all the fierce weapons of the others who are the gods' foes, and of the Yakṣas and Vidyādharas" (78.19). The Sun at this point, therefore, "bears only a sixteenth part . . . of his splendour [which] was pared off by Viśva-karmaṇ into fifteen [other] parts" (78.20). Having successfully shed himself of his extraneous sharpness (which was harnessed to craft the weapons of gods and demons alike), the Sun assumes the form of a stallion and journeys to the Northern Kurus where he encounters Saṃjñā in her equine guise (78.21). Upon seeing the stallion approach, Saṃjñā was "afraid of [an encounter by] a strange male," and so she "went towards him face to face, intent on guarding her rear" (78.22). As their noses met, two sons were born in Saṃjña's mouth, namely Nāsatya and Dasra (78.23), better known as the Aśvin twins. At the end of the Sun's emission, Revanta was born (78.24). The Sun then reveals his "own peerless form, and she gazing upon his true form felt a keen joy" (78.25). Then the Sun "brought home this his loving wife Sañjñā restored to her own shape" (78.26).

The myth then recounts the posts appointed to the children of the Sun as follows (78.27–34):

> Her eldest son then became Vaivasvata Manu; and her second son Yama became the righteous-eyed judge because of the curse . . . And Yamunā became the river which flows from the recesses of Mount Kalinda. The Aśvins were made the gods' physicians by their high-souled father. And Revanta also was appointed king of the Guhyakas. Hear also from me the places assigned to the Shadow-Sañjñā's sons. The eldest son of the Shadow-Sañjñā was equal to Manu the eldest-born; hence this son of the Sun obtained the title Sāvarṇika. He also shall be a Manu when Bali shall become Indra. He was appointed by his father as the planet Saturn among the planets. The third of them, the daughter named Tapatī.

Let us now turn to the second occurrence of this myth, situated a little later in the MkP at the beginning of the section on genealogies. While the telling therein is part of a sequence of myths glorifying the sun termed herein the Sūrya Māhātmya (to be discussed in greater detail below), the segment recapitulating the exploits of Sūrya, Saṃjñā, and Chāyā-Saṃjñā (i.e., the mythic locus giving rise to Sāvarṇi, who as we know, is none other than a future incarnation of King Suratha, by the grace of the Goddess) are self-contained in Cantos 106 through

108. I will present a more abridged version of this telling, emphasizing only the elements that depart from the first telling.

This telling makes no mention of the Sun's curses to Saṃjñā but merely informs us that "He, *Vivasvat,* lord of the *heavenly* cattle, begot three children of her, two most illustrious sons and a daughter Yamuna . . . Manu Vaivasvata was the eldest...then were born Yama and Yami as twins" (106.4–5). The account tells us that the sun's exceeding splendor

> scorched the three worlds and the moveable and immoveable things therein very grievously [and that] Sañjña saw Vivasvat's globe-like form and, being impatient of his great splendour, gazed at her own shadow *C'haya* and spoke: 'Fare thee well! I will go to my father's very own abode. Yet thou must stay here without change at my command, O fair one; and thou must show honour to these two boys for me and to *this* daughter who is of noble rank; and thou must not declare this at all to the god. (106.5–8)

In like manner as the first telling, Chāyā promises to maintain the charade even amid the seizing of her hair and the incurring of curses, promising to never divulge Saṃjñā's design (106.9).

Saṃjñā again retreats to her father's abode, who repeatedly advises her to return to her husband. Then Saṃjñā turns herself into a mare and departs for the Northern Kurus (106.11). In this version, she apparently already possesses the power to assume equine form and does not need austerities to do so. However, as with the first telling, once she arrives there, "like a chaste wife, she practiced austerities, fasting" (106.12). And again, the Sun proceeds with Chāyā as with Saṃjñā and "the adorable Sun begat of her, *he* thinking *it was* of Saṃjñā, two sons in addition and a daughter. The firstborn of the two sons was equal to the eldest *son* Manu, hence he was *called* Sāvarṇi, O best of dvijas. And the other, who was the second *son,* became the planet Saturn. And the daughter who was Tapatī" (106.13–15). And again Chāyā favors the younger threesome, and while Manu nobly accepts the favoritism, Yama does not, and "by reason of both anger and childishness and indeed by the force of predestination, threatened C'haya-Sañjña with his foot . . . and thereupon *the Shadow-Sañjña,*[30] full of resentment, cursed Yama severely" (106.18–19). The same sequence of events ensues: Chāyā curses Yama and Yama complains to Sūrya. However even in his own complaint, Yama confesses his own culpability in the matter. Sūrya again promises to alter the curse, whereupon he confronts Chāyā, and this time it is through his yogic vision that he is able to perceive the truth that the form before him was not Saṃjñā (106.33–34). Again the Shadow weakens by the glare of the Sun and on the brink of being cursed, Chāyā relays what had transpired, which again sets the Sun in motion toward the residence of his father-in-law Viśvakarman. Viśvakarman is again quite reverent to the Sun and succeeds in pacifying the Sun's wrath with the following words:

> Permeated with surpassing glory is this thy form which is so hardly endurable; hence Saṃjñā, unable to endure it, practices austerities in the forest in sooth. Thou shalt now see her, Sir, thy own wife, beautiful in her behaviour, practicing most arduous austerities in the forest on account of thy *too glorious* form. I remember Brahma's word: if it please thee, my lord, I *will* restrain thy beloved form, O lord of heaven. (106.36–38)

In this version, it is Viśvakarman's suggestion that the Sun be pared down, though he readily agrees. When he is being pared down, there is great chaos amid the heavens and the earth (106.39–47), and the gods again praise the Sun (106.48–65). Then Viśvakarman offers his own praise (107.1–10) while paring down the Sun's glory to one-sixteenth of its original status, forging with the remaining fifteen-sixteenths "Vishṇu's discus, and Siva's trident, Kubera's *palki*, the rod of the lord of the dead, and the spear of the gods' general [along with] brilliant weapons of the other gods with the Sun's splendour for the quelling of their foes" (108.3–5). We are told at the end that "He whose splendour had been thus pared down shone with no excessive splendour.

Figure 12.1 The Mārkaṇḍeya Purāṇa Solar Family Tree

Sūrya (the Sun)
    + his wife Saṃjñā
        begets → Vaivasvata, 7th (current) Manu
        → Yama, god of the dead
        → Yamī / Yamunā River

Sūrya
    + his wife Chāyā
        begets → Sāvarṇi, the 8th (next) Manu
        → Śanaiścara, the planet of karmic retribution
        → Tapatī / Narmadā River

equine-Sūrya
    + equine-Saṃjñā (while in equine form)
        begets → Nāsatya (first of the Aśvin twins, divine physician)
        → Daśra (second of the Aśvin twins, divine physician)
        → Revanta

Mārtaṇḍa retained a body resplendent in every limb" (108.6). The remainder of the canto details the same sequence of events and the same allotment of posts as in the first telling.

Notes

1 Cheever Mackenzie Brown, "Purāṇa as Scripture: From Sound to Image of the Holy Word in the Hindu Tradition," *History of Religions* 26, no. 1 (August 1, 1986): 68–86; Arti Dhand, "The Dharma of Ethics, the Ethics of Dharma: Quizzing the Ideals of Hinduism," *Journal of Religious Ethics* 30, no. 3 (October 1, 2002): 347–72; Thomas B. Coburn, "The Study of the Purāṇas and the Study of Religion," *Religious Studies* 16, no. 3 (September 1, 1980): 341–52; McComas Taylor, "What Enables Canonical Literature to Function as 'True'? The Case of the Hindu Purāṇas," *International Journal of Hindu Studies* 12, no. 3 (December 1, 2008): 309–28.

2 Wendy Doniger has written profusely on Hindu mythology throughout her career. Hers has certainly been the most acclaimed scholarly pen of the last half-century to have drawn from the ink of *Purāṇic* lore. Western scholars of *Purāṇa* are deeply indebted to her work and as a discipline, the extent of her influence on approaches to Hindu myth is only beginning to become clear. While Doniger has written voluminously on Indian mythology, this discussion confines itself to her work on the mythology of the Sun and his wife, Saṃjñā, as appearing in the MkP. Unless otherwise specified, translations from the MkP are F. E. Pargiter's, see: Pargiter, 1904. You can find a synopsis of the Saṃjñā story in Appendix 1 at the end of this article.

3 Doniger, 1976, p. 349. See fn. 142, whereby Doniger lists the following textual sources for this myth: *Ṛg Veda* 10.17.1–2: Nirukta 12.10: Śatapatha Brāhmaṇa 1.1.4.14; Taittirīya Brāhmaṇa 1.1.4.4; 1.1.9.10; 3.2.5.9; Taittirīya Saṃhitā. 2.6.7.1; 6.5.6.1; 6.6.6.1; Mārkaṇḍeya Purāṇa 103–105; Mahābhārata 1.66; Brahmāṇḍa Purāṇa 3.59–60; Matsya Purāṇa 11; Padma Purāṇa 5.8; Vāyu Purāṇa 2.3; Viṣṇu Purāṇa 3.2; Gopatha Brāhmaṇa 1.1.3.

4 Doniger, 1976, p. 349. See fn. 142, whereby Doniger cites, among other sources, *Mārkaṇḍeya Purāṇa* 103–5.

5 For example, in his study of the MkP, Desai discusses the statuses accorded to all of Sūrya's offspring, without feeling the need to distinguish whether Saṃjñā was in his original form, her Chāyā form, or her mare form, at the time of their conception: "He then allotted different offices to his children. Thus Vaivasvata became the lord of the seventh manvantara, Yama the lord of manes, Yamunā the river flowing from the recesses of mount Kalinda, two Aśvins the physicians of gods, Revanta the lord of Guhyakas, Sāvarṇi the lord of the eight manvantara, Śanaiścara the planet and Tapatī the river." Desai 1968: 164.

6 See fn 2, which references "Rig Veda, with the commentary of Sayana, 6 vols. (Benares: Chowkhamba Sanskrit Series no. 99, 1966), 10.17.1–2.

7 *Harivaṃśa*, critical edition; Poona: Bhandarkar Oriental Research Institute, 1969.

8 See fn 31, which references "Sūrya," retold by Mayah Balse, Amar Chitra Katha no. 58, ed. Anant Pai (Bombay: India Book Trust, n.d.), as "retold from the Mārkaṇḍeya Purāṇa" (Doniger 1996: 166 The comic cover is labelled "Sūrya," depicting Sūrya and Saraṇyū (Hindi edition), Amar Chitra Katha comic book no. 58,. Bombay: India Book House, n.d.)

9 MkP 106.7–8 reads: "Fare thee well! I will go to my father's very own abode. Yet thou must stay here without change at my command, O fair one; and thou must show honour to these two boys for me and to this daughter who is of noble rank; and thou must not declare this at all to the god." See: Pargiter 1904: 566–7.

10 Corroboration of the primary meaning of the word *tejas* can be taken from its antithesis: *atejas*. The Monier Williams entry for the antonym at hand specifies the following meanings: "n. absence of brightness or vigour"; "dimness, shade, shadow"; "feebleness, dulness, insignificance"; "not bright, dim, not vigorous." While the listlessness associated with these meanings can surely be symbolically applied to render a sense of (sexual) impotence, seminal fluid is far from the primary connotation of the term *tejas*. Furthermore, the verbal root *tij* (which, as mentioned, means to "be or become sharp," does not carry with it the connotation of "to inseminate.")

11 The Sanskrit reads: tato *'śvarūpadhṛgbhānuruttarānagamat kurūn / tadṛśe tatra saṃjñāñca vaḍavārūpadhāriṇīm // 78.21 // sā ca dṛṣṭvā tamāyāntaṃ parapuṃso viśaṅkayā / jagāma saṃmukhaṃ tasya pṛṣṭharakṣaṇatatparā // 78.22 // tataśca nāsikāyogaṃ tayostatra sametayoḥ / nāsatyadastrau tanayāvaśvīvaktravinirgatau // 78.23 // retaso 'nte ca revantaḥ khaḍgī carmo tanutradhṛk / aśvārūḍhaḥ samudbhūto bāṇatūṇasamanvitaḥ // 78.24 //)*

12 MkP 78.25–26: *tataḥ svarūpamatulaṃ darśayāmāsa bhānumān | tasyaiṣā ca samālokya svarūpaṃ mudamādade* || 78.25 ||

> *svarūpadhāriṇīñcaimāmāninḁya nijāśrayam | saṃjñāṃ bhāryāṃ prītimatīṃ bhāskaro vāritaskaraḥ* || 78.26 ||

13 Mārkaṇḍeya describes the Northern Kurus thus: "Next I will tell thee of the Northern Kurus; hearken to me now. There the trees yield sweet fruit, they bear blossoms and fruit in constant succession; and they produce garments and ornaments inside their fruits; verily they bestow all one's desire; they yield fruit according to all one's desire. The ground abounds with precious stones; the air is fragrant and always delightful. Mankind are born there, when they quit the world of the gods. They are born in pairs; the pairs abide an equal time, and are as fond of each other as c'akravakas. Their stay there is fourteen and a half thousands of years

indeed. And C'andra-kanta is the chief of the mountains, and Surya-kanta is the next; they are the two mountain ranges in that continent. And in the midst thereof the great river Bhadra-soma flows through the earth with a volume of sacred and pure water. And there are other rivers by thousands in that northern continent; and some flow with milk and others flow with ghee. And there are lakes of curdled milk there, and others lie among the various hills. And fruits of various kinds, which taste rather like amṛta, are produced by hundreds and thousands in the woods in those continents." MkP 59.18–26. See Pargiter 1904: 389.

14 See Figure 12.1, "The MkP Solar Family Tree."

15 Saṃjñā is the daughter of Viśvakarmā, the divine architect, who functions in many myths as a tinkerer type, much akin to Hephaestus of Greek mythology, the god of the forge whose handyman prowess was utilized in cracking open the skull of Zeus at the time of Athena's birthing. As you will see, this function is integral to the myth since Viśvakarmā alone among the gods would possess the skill and the tools to hammer away at the overbearing might of the Sun.

16 And the Mārkaṇḍeya *Purāṇa* in no way faults her for fleeing. Recall that Sūrya's luster was unbearable to Brahmā (and indeed imperiled the universe), and also originally unbearable to Aditi, the mother of the demons and the gods, in whose womb he agreed to take birth.

17 See Pargiter (1904: 461). Pargiter's footnote reads, "She married the Paurava king Saṃvaraṇa and was the twelfth ancestress of the Pāṇḍavas." However, if he means she was twelve generations removed from them, I am unsure of how he arrived at this number since the Pāṇḍavas were her sixth-generation descendants.

18 While this matronymic Kaunteya of course is self-evident to him (and the reader) given that his mother's name is Kuntī, both he and the reader wonder how he can be said to be the son of Tapatī. His query reads (MBh I.11.60.1–2): tāpatya iti yad vākyam uktavān asi mām iha | tad ahaṁ jñātum icchāmi tāpatyārthaviniścayam || tapatī nāma kā caiṣā tāpatyā yatkṛte vayam | kaunteyā hi vayaṁ sādho tattvam icchāmi veditum ||

19 The tributary is named "Tapatī," to be found at MBh I.160–163 (see Buitenen 1973: 324–9).

20 Also of use for the purposes is this discussion is that fact that Saṃvaraṇa, upon wedding Tapatī "frolicked on the mountain like an Immortal" (so 'pi rājā girau tasmin vijahārāmaropamaḥ, I.163.13 (Buitenen 1973: 329)), making love with her for twelve years. The implication here is that Tapatī, daughter of an immortal (the Sun), is already immortal, and it is the mortal Saṃvaraṇa who has the chance to experience the life of an immortal due to her company.

21 It also partakes in a clever mythological encoding of the astronomical timing of the Nine Nights Goddess festival, see (Balkaran 2018).

22 Sāvarṇa literally denotes one having the same color or appearance, similar to, or equal to.

23 The theme of preservation is invoked at the very outset of the MkP, and perhaps accounts for why the DM was included within its *Purāṇic* fold. See Balkaran (2017).

24 Saṃjñā is the daughter of Tvaṣṭṛ, also known as Viśvakarman, the divine architect-tinkerer figure who roughly correlates to Hephaestus of the Grecian mythological heavens.

25 Saṃjñā's father; see fn 6.

26 *tvāntu me paśyato vatse dināni subahūnyapi / muhūrtārdhasamāni syuḥ kintu dharmo vilupyate // 77.18 // bāndhaveṣu ciraṃ vāso nārīṇāṃ na yaśaskaraḥ / manoratho bāndhavānāṃ nāryā bhartṛgṛhe sthitiḥ // 77.19 // sā tvaṃ trailokyanāthena bhartrā sūryeṇa saṅgatā / pitṛgehe ciraṃ kālaṃ vastuṃ nārhasi putrike // 77.20 // sā tvaṃ bhartṛgṛhaṃ gaccha tuṣṭo 'haṃ pūjitāsi me / punarāgamanaṃ kāryaṃ darśanāya śubhe mama // 77.21*

27 *ityuktā sā tadā pitrā tathetyuktvā ca sā mune / saṃpūjayitvā pitaraṃ jagāmāthottarān kurūn // 77.22 //*

> *sūryatāpamanicchantī tejasastasya bibhyatī / tapaścacāra tatrāpi vaḍavārūpadhāriṇī // 77.23 //*

28 *tātaitanmahadāścaryaṃ na dṛṣṭamiti kenacit / mātā vātsalyamutsṛjya śāpaṃ putre prayacchati // 77.31 //*

> *yathā manurmamācaṣṭe neyaṃ matā tathā mama / viguṇeṣvapi putreṣu na mātā viguṇā bhavet // 77.32 //*

29 Included in Appendix 1.

30 This must be *C'haya-Sañjña;* but both editions read *Sañjṇa.*

References

Balkaran, R. (2017). "The Essence of Avatāra: Probing Preservation in the Mārkaṇḍeya Purāṇa." *Journal of Vaishnava Studies*, 26(1): 25–36.

Balkaran, R. (2018). "The Splendor of the Sun: Brightening the Bridge between Mārkaṇḍeya Purāṇa and Devī Māhātmya in Light of Navarātri Ritual Timing." In C. Simmons, Sen, Moumita, and Rodrigues, Hillary (eds.), *Nine Nights of the Goddess: The Navarātri Festival in South Asia*. New York: SUNY Press.

Buitenen, Johannes Adrianus Bernardus van (1973). *Mahābhārata: Volume 1: Book 1: The Book of the Beginning*. Vol. I. Chicago, IL: University of Chicago Press.

Desai, Nileshvari Y. (1968). *Ancient Indian Society, Religion, and Mythology as Depicted in the Mārkaṇḍeya-Purāna; A Critical Study*. Baroda: Faculty of Arts, M.S. University of Baroda.

Doniger, Wendy (1976). *The Origins of Evil in Hindu Mythology*. Berkeley: University of California Press.

Doniger, Wendy (1980). *Women, Androgynes, and Other Mythical Beasts*. Chicago, IL: University of Chicago Press.

Doniger, Wendy (1996). "Saraṇyū/Saṃjñā: The Sun and The Shadow." In John Stratton Hawley and Donna Marie Wulff (eds.), *Devī: Goddesses of India* (pp. 154–72). Berkeley: University of California Press.

Doniger, Wendy (1999). *Splitting the Difference: Gender and Myth in Ancient Greece and India*. Chicago, IL: University of Chicago Press.

Doniger, Wendy (2000). *The Bedtrick: Tales of Sex and Masquerade*. Chicago, IL: University of Chicago Press.

Doniger, Wendy, ed. (2004). *Hindu Myths: A Sourcebook Translated from the Sanskrit*. London: Penguin.

Doniger, Wendy (2014a). *On Hinduism*. New York: Oxford University Press.

Doniger, Wendy (2014b). "Saranyu/Samjna: The Sun and The Shadow." In *On Hinduism* (pp. 269–87). New York: Oxford University Press.

Eco, Umberto (1994). *Six Walks in the Fictional Woods*. Cambridge, MA: Harvard University Press.

Goldman, Robert P. (1969). "Mortal Man and Immortal Woman: An Interpretation of Three Akhyana Hymns of the Rg Veda." *Journal of the Oriental Institute of Baroda* 18(4): 274–303.

Mani, Vettam (1975). *Puranic Encyclopaedia: A Comprehensive Dictionary with Special Reference to the Epic and Puranic Literature*. Delhi: Motilal Banarsidass.

O'Flaherty, Wendy Doniger (1973). *Asceticism and Eroticism in the Mythology of the Śiva*. London: Oxford University Press.

Kinsley, David (1984). "Consort of None, Śakti of All: The Vision of the Devī-Māhātmya." In Stratton Hawley and Thomas B. Coburn (eds.), *The Divine Consort: Radha and the Goddesses of India*. Delhi: Motilal Banarsidass.

Pargiter, F. Eden (1904). *Mārkaṇḍeya Purāṇa*. Calcutta: Asiatic Society of Bengal.

Smith, Jonathan Z. (1978). "The Wobbling Pivot." In *Map Is Not Territory: Studies in the History of Religions*. Leiden: Brill.

Part Five

Gender Transcendence

13

Male–Female Dialogues on Gender, Sexuality, and Dharma in the Hindu Epics

Ruth Vanita

Introduction

This essay examines the paradoxes that arise in the course of two dialogues between male and female sages in the *Mahābhārata*. These dialogues underscore the tension between the Hindu philosophical view of gender as ultimately unreal and Hinduism's acknowledgment of bodily materiality. The dialogues address these ontological questions and also the ethical issues to which they give rise.

These philosophical dialogues occur in the epic narrative of the *Mahābhārata*. Some might therefore dismiss them as literary rather than philosophical dialogues. As Andrew Nicholson points out, Western scholars have perpetuated a bias against narrative texts like the epics and *Purāṇas*, considering them mythological and therefore lacking in philosophical rigor. However, as he demonstrates, premodern Hindu philosophers readily quoted from these texts to support their arguments (2010: 74–5, 148).[1] Texts that today are not classified as philosophical—such as the *Mahābhārata*—encompass accounts of the doctrines of various schools of Indian philosophy, including Sāṃkhya and Yoga. Thus, to construct a divide between narrative and philosophical texts would be anachronistic. I here focus on discourses that are clearly philosophical.

I examine two dialogues in the *Mahābhārata*. In one, the interlocutors are female ascetic Sulabhā and philosopher-king Janaka.[2] This dialogue centers on the ontology and epistemology of gender, focusing on three questions: What is a man? What is a woman? How should gender be perceived? It also addresses ethical questions related to gender, such as: Should men and women act differently? Can a woman be independent?[3] The other dialogue occurs between a female sage Diśā and a male sage Aṣṭāvakra. This dialogue has thus far received scarcely any attention. This dialogue explicitly questions the philosophical concept of non-difference with regard to existential reality.[4] The doctrine of non-difference, which is central to the *Bhagavad Gītā*, is based on the presupposition that living beings are not essentially different from one another. This is because they are all manifestations of the unchanging Self, while apparent differences of body, species, gender, abilities, and community identity are ever-changing and transient. This dialogue explicitly brings bodily pleasure and sexual desire into the picture, thus complicating the notion of non-difference. Furthermore, both the dialogues I examine directly address the *Mānavadharmaśāstra*'s notorious dictum, repeated also in the *Mahābhārata*, that a woman must always be under a father's, husband's, or son's protection, and must never be independent.[5] From different perspectives, both dialogues demonstrate the invalidity of this dictum.

While Hindu philosophical compendia, such as the *Upaniṣads*, are "often framed as a dialogue between teacher and student,"[6] the two dialogues I examine are not between teacher and student (Black and Patton, 2015: 1). Both participants in these dialogues are equals, although the woman interlocutor does end up instructing the man. In different ways, both bring *pravṛtti-dharma* (the social *dharma* that is different for each embodied self) into dialogue with *nivṛtti-dharma* (the universal *dharma* of every being, which is to achieve liberation from the cycle of rebirth).[7]

In addition, I briefly consider two more dialogic narratives from the two epics the *Rāmāyaṇa* and the *Mahābhārata*. All these dialogues provide access to philosophical notions of gender. Through a comparative analysis of these four texts, I explore the complex and widely varied ways in which they frame and interrogate gender difference, likeness, and equality in relation to *dharma*, variously defined.

The Ontology of Wholeness or Non-duality of Gender?

Early Hindu philosophical texts indicate that the Ultimate Being or universal Self (*Ātman*) is one but becomes many (*Chāndogya Upaniṣad*, VI. 2.3).[8] Even those philosophers who incline toward what may be termed a type of dualism, such as adherents of Sāṃkhya, Dvaita, Dvaitādvaita, and Bhedābheda Vedānta, would not be likely to argue that a particular self in a female body is made up of the feminine principle (*prakṛti*) alone. Rather, every individual being is made up of both *Puruṣa*/*Ātman*/*Brahman* (Self/Spirit), which is conventionally gendered male, and also of *Prakṛti/Māyā* (Nature/Matter in Motion), the principle that is conventionally gendered female.

Composed relatively later, the *Śvetāśvatara Upaniṣad* defines the non-gendered nature of *Ātman* (Self): "It is not female nor is it male nor is it neuter/ It is joined with whatever body it takes" (Tyagisananda, 1949: 5.10).[9] In the same *Upaniṣad*, the Supreme Self is addressed as dual-gendered, both feminine and masculine: "You are woman, you are man, you are boy and you are girl" (Tyagisananda, 1949: 4.3). The three verses that follow gesture toward the relationship between individual self and universal Self—first, by deploying the metaphor of sexual union to envision the attachment of the eternal Self to eternal Nature, and, second, by repeating the *Ṛg Veda's* metaphor of two inseparable birds seated on the same branch. In this famous metaphor, one bird eats the fruit of the tree (and can thus be interpreted as the acting individual self) while the other watches (and can thus be interpreted as the universal Self that witnesses action but does not participate in it).

In various Hindu interpretations of this relationship between the two selves, it is scarcely ever disputed that bodily sex and gender, like other physical and social attributes, such as species, are transitory appurtenances not intrinsic to the Self. Hence the *Bhagavad Gītā's* declarations that the body is like clothing put on at birth and discarded at death, and that a wise person sees the same universal Self in a learned *brāhman*, a cow, an elephant, a dog, and a dog-eater. The fourteenth-century *Aṣṭāvakra Gītā* explicitly adds gender to this list:

> *sukhe duḥkhe nare nāryāṃ sampatsu ca vipatsu ca /*
> *viśeṣo naiva dhīrasya sarvatra samadarśinaḥ //*
> [The wise one, who sees the same everywhere,
> finds no difference
> between happiness and misery,
> man and woman, fortune and misfortune.] (Mukerjee, XVII: 15)[10]

How does this formulation of gender as nonessential work in a world of sexed bodies and gendered persons? A popular 1981 Hindi film, *Āhistā Āhistā* (Gradually), directly addresses this philosophical question. In the film, a learned *brāhman* named Dayanand debates with his conventional wife, Kaveri, the propriety of accepting a neighboring courtesan's daughter Chandra into their family. Dayanand, a connoisseur of music, includes Chandra in family worship. This results in friendship between her and Dayanand's son Kunal. When they eventually grow up and want to marry, Kaveri objects. Dayanand tells her, "All this business about caste and community, family and household, is like clothing. One comes into the world without clothes and one leaves these clothes behind when one leaves the world." Kaveri does not challenge the truth of this premise, but she nevertheless silences her husband with her retort: "As long as one is alive one has to wear clothes."[11]

Kaveri's argument addresses the reality of the living body, which is gendered and circumscribed by various bodily qualities. Furthermore, in most Hindu narratives, relatively unreal appurtenances of the body persist through successive lifetimes; this is suggestive with regard to the tenacious reality of the phenomenal world. For example, in the *Mahābhārata*'s *Anuśāsana Parva*, Bhīṣma tells Yudhiṣṭhira that over many births and a period of hundreds of thousands of years, beings change their species from animal to human, and as humans all are first born as a *śūdra*—(lower *varṇa*)—it takes many more hundreds of thousands of lifetimes to transition from being a *śūdra* to a *brāhman* (13.28.2). He does not, however, indicate how gender changes from one lifetime to another.

As I have argued elsewhere, evidence from epic *Purāṇic* and Buddhist narratives suggests that changing *varṇa*, class, and even species over a series of births is easier than changing gender (Vanita: 2005).[12] In fact, it may be easier to change gender by miraculous means within a lifetime than to change it from one birth to the next. An example of the difficulty of changing gender is seen in the story of Ambā, who prays to be reborn as a man so that she may take revenge on Bhīṣma, but she is then reborn as a woman named Śikhaṇḍinī. As Śikhaṇḍinī, she manages to exchange her sex with a *yakṣa* (forest-spirit). This miraculous sex-change occurs within one lifetime. Further, it may be easier for a man to be reborn as a woman than for a woman to be reborn as a man. There are a few stories in the *Purāṇas* of men being reborn as women. This often occurs in the context of Vaiṣṇava devotion where men wish to become milkmaids in order to participate in love-sport with Kṛṣṇa.

Despite this, the story of King Purañjana explicitly illustrates the point that the Self is not gendered. Due to excessive attachment to his wife and children, he is reborn as a woman named Vaidarbhī. When her husband dies, Vaidarbhī is about to burn herself with his corpse. A sage appears and reminds her that the true Self is neither male nor female. The sage tells Vaidarbhī that she should not regard herself as man or woman: "You are neither" (Śrīmad Bhāgavatam: IV.28.61). It is the female, Vaidarbhī—not the male, Purañjana—who achieves the realization that gender is ultimately unreal, and this realization comes as she is about to burn herself alive. Perhaps the text suggests that it is more important for women to realize the relative unreality of gender, as they suffer more of the negative social consequences of gender as a category. Likewise, it is the female ascetic Sulabhā who clearly understands the unimportance of gender, and the supposedly liberated Janaka has to learn this from her.

Ever-Changing Bodies

In the *Śānti Parvan* of the *Mahābhārata*, Bhīṣma recounts the Sulabhā–Janaka debate in response to a question from Yudhiṣṭhira regarding the path to liberation (12.308–310). Yudhiṣṭhira's question is not explicitly about gender—he asks whether liberation from the cycle of rebirth can be attained while leading a domestic life, or whether renunciation is necessary for liberation. Implicitly, the question may pertain more to women than to men because larger numbers of men than women renounce domesticity and become ascetics. Bhīṣma's answer is significant because it also addresses the question of whether women can match men in asceticism and whether asceticism conflicts with the specific *dharma* of women, which, elsewhere in the epic, is repeatedly described as requiring them to be under men's protection and to marry and serve their husbands. Bhīṣma tells the story of a debate between Sulabhā—a female ascetic who has renounced the world—and Janaka—a male sage who has not yet renounced the world. Janaka considers himself liberated, even though he continues to live as a king and a householder.[13]

Janaka questions the genuineness of Sulabhā's renunciation because she is a young and beautiful woman (this is a form she has assumed, but he takes it at face value). He doubts that it is possible for her to subdue her senses. This doubt is a conventional one—Yudhiṣṭhira and Bhīṣma in the course of their dialogue several times remark that women are incapable of restraining their senses, not finding it necessary to justify this view with evidence.

Janaka begins his denunciation of Sulabhā by asking who she is, to whom she belongs, and where she has come from (12.308.20), and ends it by asking about her nature, her *varṇa*, and her intentions (12.308.75). His question of "whom she belongs to" is based on the dictum, often repeated in the *Mahābhārata* (including elsewhere in the Bhīṣma–Yudhiṣṭhira dialogue), that a woman cannot be independent but must always reside under the control of a father, husband, or son.

Bhīṣma comments that although Janaka spoke to her in an unpleasing, illogical, and imbalanced manner, Sulabhā replied in a speech more beautiful than her physical beauty. After an initial explication of the nature of rational speech, Sulabhā answers Janaka's questions: who she is, to whom she belongs, and where she has come from. She does this by building on certain basic philosophical premises, which she assumes that both she and Janaka accept.

The first ontological premise is that all bodies are constituted of the same elements and are in constant flux, since minute particles of the body are born and die every moment. The beauty of Sulabhā's language on which Bhīṣma remarks can be seen in two successive verses where she deploys two widely different tropes to express the nature of physical and mental change. It is very important to remember that in Indian thought the mind is part of the body and is distinct from Spirit/Self/Consciousness. She compares the constantly changing but imperceptible phases in a body's existence to the movements of a lamp's flame (12.308.122).[14] Then she compares the change in all beings to a galloping horse (12.308.123).[15]

These images perfectly convey the paradoxical nature of bodily change—it occurs imperceptibly yet it is rapid. One is unaware of it as it occurs and therefore one assumes the stability of the bodily self, but looking back one realizes how swiftly that self has changed. All bodies and minds change in this way—there is no difference between male and female bodies and minds in this regard. This constant change is perhaps the most important aspect of existence.

The conclusion that Sulabhā draws from this premise is that bodies cannot be possessed by anyone because of their constantly changing nature: "Who then has come from where or where not, whose is it or whose is it not, where is it and where is it not?" (12.308.123–4).[16] These are real, not rhetorical, questions, and they point simultaneously in two directions. No particular body (and this would include all human, animal, plant, and mineral bodies) belongs to anyone, but at the same time every body belongs to everyone ("whose is it not?").

What this means is that one does not possess even one's own body. It follows, then—importantly for our purposes—that no one can possess the body of another. Therefore, the requirement for a woman to be under the control of a father, a husband, or a son is based on an ontological impossibility. From the ontological perspective, only change controls the body (including the mind).

From the bodily self, Sulabhā moves on to the *Ātman* or Self/Spirit/Consciousness that is manifested in all individual selves. *Prakṛti* is the cause of all bodies and *Puruṣa* is the cause of all selves. It follows that there is no difference between the nonmaterial selves of existing beings:

> Just as you see your self in your self
> In the same way, why do you not see your self in others' selves?

> If you perceive sameness between your self and others
> Then for what purpose did you ask me who I am and whose I am?
> "This is mine, this is not mine"—O king of Mithila, if you are free from such duality,
> What is the point of saying, who are you, whose are you, where are you from? (12.308.126–7)[17]

Right perception shows that a woman as *Ātman* cannot belong to father, husband, or son because all individual selves are really manifestations of the same one Self.

Sulabhā's discourse also demonstrates the ultimate unreality of *varṇa* and *jāti*, or what much later came to be called "caste." Janaka, having assumed from her ascetic appearance that she is a *brāhman*, objects to her entering into yogic union with himself, a *kṣatriya*. Such a union would necessarily be, according to him, an inter-*varṇa* union. Sulabhā informs him that she too is a *kṣatriya* but, more importantly, she states that *varṇas* and *āśramas* (phases or modes of life) are not really different from one another and also do not attach to the Self, and therefore there is no question of their intermingling or not intermingling (12.308.177)[18]. She states that just as one may hold a pot with milk in it where a fly may sit on the milk, yet in one's hand the milk, the pot, and the fly all remain distinct, so also *varṇa* and *āśrama* may exist with a person but yet remain distinct from the self of that person.

Cross-Gender Yogic Union

Janaka is arguing in the context of a normative law, which stipulates that a woman should always be under a man's protection. This law prevents a married woman from entering into extramarital unions and also prohibits an unmarried woman from engaging in any union, marital or otherwise, which is not sanctioned by her father. The fear of interaction between unrelated men and women is one of the main reasons for the restriction of women's freedom. By introducing the concept of cross-gender yogic union, the text questions the assumption that all unions between unrelated men and women must necessarily be sexual.

Yogic union is distinct from marital union in being nonphysical, temporary, and imperceptible by others. Bhīṣma tells two stories in which yogic union involves one person tying up another with yogic bonds by penetrating the other with their gaze and then entering into their body without touching them. The first story is one in which a woman (Sulabhā) imposes this union on a man (Janaka). In the other story, a man (Vipula), employing his yogic powers, enters into the body of a beautiful woman (Ruci). The uninitiated may mistake yogic union for sexual union, particularly because it is described in words that could apply to sexual relations (*praveśa*, to enter; *saṃyoga*, union). But in these two stories, even the wise become anxious about the propriety of such unions.

Sulabhā uses her yogic powers to enter into Janaka's body and remain there for a while. She restrains the rays of light from his eyes with the rays from her own, enters him, and binds him with yogic bonds (12.308.16–17).[19] If gender is ultimately unreal, then this nonphysical union between two persons should not incur opprobrium. But although it is not a physical union, it nevertheless creates anxieties about impropriety, which suggests how difficult it is for even an enlightened being to ignore gender difference.

Sulabhā's yogic union with Janaka angers him and he objects to it as an inappropriate physical union that she has undertaken without his permission. She proves that his analysis is incorrect because, she says, it is not a physical union. She undertook this union to examine him because she had doubts about his having achieved the highest goal of liberation. She points out that she has not touched him with any part of her body (12.308.169)[20] and that she is staying in him without touching him just as a drop of water stays on a lotus leaf without making it wet (12.308.173).[21]

Exactly these images and terms are used to describe the yogic union that the sage Vipula undertakes to protect his teacher Devaśarman's wife—Ruci—from seduction by Indra. While Sulabhā's yogic union demonstrates equality and the irrelevance of gender, Vipula's yogic union reaffirms gender difference. This is a good example of how the epic depicts a range of approaches to gender among philosophers and sages. In this narrative, Devaśarman, who is an ascetic, considers it is his duty to guard his wife from other males, and thinks that she is not capable of doing this herself. He therefore appoints his student Vipula to guard her.

Since Indra is known to take all kinds of forms, including the form of wind, to approach women, Vipula cannot think of any way to restrain Ruci except by entering her body with his yogic powers so that he can control her. Deploying the same image as Sulabhā does, he decides that it would not be wrong for him to do this, because he will remain in her body without touching her just as a drop of water lies on a lotus leaf without making it wet (13.40.52).[22] Vipula achieves this union by uniting (*saṃyojya*) the rays of light from his eyes with the rays from hers and entering (*viveśa*) Ruci's body as the wind enters space. Unlike

Janaka, who is aware of Sulabhā's entering him, Ruci is unaware of Vipula's union with her. When Indra appears and tries to seduce her, she wants to rise and welcome him, but she is unable to move. It is Vipula who speaks through her, asking Indra why he has come.[23] After releasing her, Vipula also speaks to Indra in his own person.

Bhīṣma says that Vipula thus becomes the only man who has ever succeeded in protecting a woman. However, Vipula is not entirely comfortable with the mode of protection he adopts and is therefore hesitant to disclose his act to his teacher. Later, he hears predictions that he will inhabit various hells after this lifetime for not telling his teacher the truth. When he finally decides to tell his teacher Devaśarman the truth, he discovers that Devaśarman already knows about it and so does Ruci by then. Presumably, her husband has told her. Devaśarman disapproves, not of the yogic union but of its having been concealed from him. He forgives Vipula and frees him from the consequences of the concealment.

Even Sulabhā, who in every other respect seems free from conventions, reproaches Janaka for having spoken publicly about the yogic union between a woman and a man. The nuances of what kind of male–female union may be spoken of in whose presence seem very delicate. Vipula should have told Devaśarman about his yogic union with the latter's wife, but Janaka should not have spoken in public about Sulabhā's yogic union with him. Although not a sexual union, yogic union between an unrelated man and woman seems uncomfortably close to the body and therefore creates anxiety and doubt about the propriety or impropriety of speaking about it. If yogic non-bodily union creates such anxieties, marriage, which is generally a bodily union, raises even more questions pertaining to the differences between body and Self, between two individual selves, and between men and women.

Marriage, Gender, and *Dharma*

In the *Anuśāsana Parva* of the *Mahābhārata* (13.1.1–9), Yudhiṣṭhira asks Bhīṣma a series of questions about marriage, explicitly and implicitly raising several issues, including those of difference and likeness between men and women. Why, Yudhiṣṭhira asks, is marriage defined as a companionship in *dharma*, and why is it said that jointly practicing *dharma* in marriage leads to heaven? Yudhiṣṭhira raises a number of objections to this definition of marriage. First, he points out, couples rarely die together. If the one who dies first goes to heaven, what becomes of the other who can no longer practice *dharma* in union? This is a meaningful ontological question. Marriage is a social and sexual arrangement within a lifetime, while the Self moves from one life to another. Each being has its own *karma* and attachments and moves to the next life at a different time. How is marriage to be viewed in the context of numerous lifetimes? This question would arise even if the genders were socially equal.

Yudhiṣṭhira's second objection addresses gender difference. He states that human beings behave in widely diverse ways and have to incur the consequences of their actions. Reminding Bhīṣma of his own words that described human beings having varied natural tendencies and women in particular as disordered in their behavior, Yudhiṣṭhira asks, how can marriage be a union for the shared practice of *dharma*? While acknowledging that all human beings perform some disordered acts that have bad consequences for them, Yudhiṣṭhira insists that women are *anṛtāḥ*, that is, they do not adhere to *ṛta* (the Vedic term for the cosmic order on which *dharma* is based). One interpretation of his formulation might indicate that the female gender is innately at odds with cosmic order. Another reading might suggest that women have to work harder to overcome the innate disorderliness of their sex in order to attain either heaven or liberation or a better rebirth. Either way, Yudhiṣṭhira suggests that women are inherently more disordered than men are.

Yudhiṣṭhira's question raises the issue not so much of gender equality as of gender likeness and difference. He says that in the hand-taking ritual in the wedding ceremony (*pāṇigrahaṇa*), the spouses are instructed to perform *dharma* together (*sahadharma*). It is for this reason, one may note, that a wife is termed *sahadharmiṇī*, a partner in *dharma*. But a partnership suggests that there is at least likeness of some sort between the partners if not complete equality. Only two beings who are like one another can be conceived of as sharing *dharma*. Yudhiṣṭhira's questions are somewhat similar to those that Aristotle addresses in the *Nicomachean Ethics*. Aristotle claims that true friendship can exist only between those who bear a likeness to one another, and that the best friendship is therefore one that subsists between two virtuous men. Marriage is a form of friendship in which the wife is an inferior partner who must be educated by her husband (Aristotle, 1925: 203).

Yudhiṣṭhira goes on to say that the injunction to share *dharma* in marriage could have three different meanings, and he asks Bhīṣma which meaning is correct. First, the word *dharma* in its original etymology can apply to inherent nature or the law of one's being, which necessitates a range of functions, many of which are neither meritorious nor unmeritorious (to cite a common example, it is the *dharma* of iron to sink and of wood to float). He asks whether the word *dharma* is used in the context of marriage in this grammatical sense rather than in a moral sense. Second, it may refer simply to sexual pleasure, that is, to the fact that sex within marriage is both a duty and a pleasure in accordance with *dharma*. Third, it may pertain to the *dharma* of producing children within marriage.

His implication is that companionship in *dharma* for a woman and a man may pertain either to sex or to reproduction but cannot pertain to other acts. This is not only because each self has its own *karma* and *dharma*, but also because women are innately more disordered than men and are thus unsuitable companions in *dharma*. Yudhiṣṭhira even states that his opinion is contrary (*viruddha iti me matiḥ*, 13.19.3)[24] to that of the ancient sages who decreed that marriage is for the sharing of all *dharma*. It is important to note that Yudhiṣṭhira mentions only producing children but not raising them. Raising children, as we shall see later, requires sharing a number of different activities and ideas.

Bhīṣma does not directly answer the question. His response, instead, is to tell the nuanced and ambiguous story of an encounter between the male sage Aṣṭāvakra and the female sage Diśā in the context of marriage. Bhīṣma draws no explicit conclusions from this story. The reader is left to decipher the answers to Yudhiṣṭhira's questions.

Scholars have largely ignored the philosophical implications of this story and dialogue, perhaps because its magical dimensions and its focus on sexual relations seem to relegate it to the realm of so-called "mythology." As I demonstrate though, the dialogue addresses philosophical issues pertaining to the nature of men and of women, desire, the body, and marriage. Bhīṣma's story maps out a landscape of desire, first, male heterosexual desire, second, female heterosexual desire, and third, undifferentiated desire that is bodily but that presumably anyone of any gender can experience.

Marriage and Likeness

Bhīṣma begins the story by saying that Sage Aṣṭāvakra loses his heart to sage Vādanya's daughter Suprabhā the moment she looks at him. As a precondition for their marriage, Vādanya sends Aṣṭāvakra to meet the female sage Diśā who lives in the Himalayan region. Vādanya says that Diśā is beautiful like Lakṣmī herself.

Performing many rituals along the way, Aṣṭāvakra meets various deities, including Kuvera, god of wealth. Kuvera entertains him with a dance of *apsarās* (celestial nymphs), nineteen of whom the texts names. So charmed is Aṣṭāvakra by their music and dance that he spends a year there without realizing it, and Kuvera has to gently remind him of his mission. He then proceeds through a delightful landscape to Diśā's wonderfully decorated dwelling where seven beautiful girls greet him and each one of them steals his heart as he looks at her (*mano'harat*, 13.20.41).[25] The phrase used here is the same as that pertaining to his falling in love with Suprabhā (*mano jahāra*, 13.19.13).

With great difficulty, he controls himself and goes in to meet Diśā, who appears as an old and decrepit lady. He then commands all the girls to leave, saying that only the one who is wise (*suprajñātā*) and calm (*supraśāntā*) should stay (13.20.46). This injunction, which puts the girls on a plane lower than himself and Diśā, can be read as motivated by the need to protect himself from being distracted by them. That night, Diśā makes sexual advances to him, but she finds that when she touches him, he is lifeless like wood. She then tries to verbally persuade him to have sex with her, arguing that the union will be a reward for his austerities, that she will please him in every way and bestow all her wealth on him, and that women desire sexual union above all else and will even destroy the family to obtain it.[26]

Aṣṭāvakra responds that he never approaches other men's wives, and furthermore that he is not interested in pleasure of any kind, intending to marry only in order to have children since sons are needed to attain heaven. Not only is this statement untrue (because Aṣṭāvakra was attracted both to Suprabhā and to the seven maidens, and he also enjoyed the pleasures of music and dance), but it addresses Yudhiṣṭhira's question as well. Aṣṭāvakra seems to indicate that marriage is meant not for sexual pleasure but for children; this is a common ascetic claim. When Diśā presses him, he indirectly admits that she is not to his taste and that desire springs from liking or inclination (*ruciram*). Diśā then asks him to stay a while and see whether he develops a liking for her, which he agrees to do.

The text then reveals the reality behind Aṣṭāvakra's high-minded claims; it tells us that he is tortured by worry (*cintāṃ … saṃtapta*, 13.20.71)[27] throughout the next day. He keeps looking at Diśā but is unable to feel any desire because he is displeased by her looks (*nāramat*) and, in a powerful phrase, his vision is defeated (i.e., repelled) by her form (*dṛṣṭī rūpaparājitā*, 13.20.72).[28]

One may note here that in Hindu thought, repulsion is a form of attachment. Therefore, Aṣṭāvakra's strong aversion to ugliness, like his earlier positive reaction to beauty, shows that he is not free from attachment. His rejection of Diśā is based on her ugliness, not on his freedom from desire. That evening,

Diśā sets about pleasuring Aṣṭāvakra in various ways. This is reminiscent of the *Kāmasūtra*, where sexual pleasure is just one of many pleasures that fall under the rubric of *kāma*.

Aṣṭāvakra, who had claimed to be indifferent to all pleasures, finds his senses engaged by Diśā as she gives him an oil massage, and then seats him on a splendid seat, and bathes him with pleasure-giving hands. So pleasant is the bath that the whole night passes without his noticing. Similarly, the next day passes unnoticed while he eats delicious food that she cooks for him. The unnoticed passage of time indicates the intensity of these pleasures, just as was the case in his earlier experience at Kuvera's palace. The list of pleasures that Aṣṭāvakra enjoys overlaps a good deal with the list of pleasures that Bhīṣma, in his preface to the Vipula–Ruci story, says that women enjoy (along with sexual pleasure). Bhīṣma says that because women have powerful senses and are incapable of restraint, they are disposed to enjoy "beds, seats, ornaments, food and drink"[29] (*Anuśāsana Parva*, 13:40.12).[30] When Aṣṭāvakra enjoys these same pleasures, we see that he is not immune to pleasure as he had claimed to be. We also see that women and men respond to the same sensual stimulants.

Woman as Independent Agent

When Diśā again comes to his bed that night, Aṣṭāvakra changes his reasons for rejecting her. He no longer claims to be immune to pleasure, but instead repeats that he cannot have intercourse with the wife of another. This displays a step forward in self-knowledge, as he appears to have realized that he is not, in fact, indifferent to pleasure as he had earlier claimed to be. Diśā now replies, "I am self-governed" (*svatantrāsmi*, 13.21.11)[31], indicating that she is not married. Aṣṭāvakra responds that according to scripture a woman can never be self-governed or independent but instead must be dependent on a man; in various phases of life this man may be a father, a husband, or a son. Thus, the text returns to the famous dictum that Janaka had alluded to in his speech to Sulabhā, and which she refuted by demonstrating the unreality of gender.

Diśā counters the dictum in a different manner. She says that Aṣṭāvakra incurs *adharma* by refusing her request for sexual intercourse (*maithunam*) (13.21.13).[32] This appears to be a reference to texts such as the *Chāṇḍogya Upaniṣad* (13.2), which instruct a man never to refuse a woman who comes to him requesting sexual relations. This is an impasse of sorts. If the dictum about woman's dependence is always valid, then a woman who requests sexual relations must always do so at the behest of a father, husband, or son. However, the *Chāṇḍogya Upaniṣad*, which is a Vedic text, places no such modifications on its statement that a man should always yield to a woman's sexual desire.

Diśā now moves from proposing sexual relations to proposing marriage. She says that if Aṣṭāvakra considers it wrong to have sex with one who is not his wife, she is willing to marry him. Using the same term for the hand-taking ceremony that Yudhiṣṭhira had referred to in his opening question, she says, "take my hand" (*pāṇiṃ gṛhṇīṣva me*, 13.21.16)[33] and again adds that she can make this proposal because she governs herself. It is noteworthy that Diśā initially proposes sexual union with Aṣṭāvakra and proposes marriage only as a concession to him because he is reluctant to unite with her.

Aṣṭāvakra insists again that a woman cannot be independent and asks her how she has come to be so. Diśā's answer rebuts the idea that a woman must always be under a man's protection. She states that she has been celibate since girlhood and is still a virgin. If celibacy is an option for a woman (and the epics mentioning many celibate women demonstrates that it is), then the dictum that a woman must always remain under the control of father, husband, or son collapses on a third score. A father would normally die before his daughter dies, and a celibate woman would normally not have a husband or a son, so she would have to govern herself.

Aṣṭāvakra now suddenly changes his stance and replies, "As you are to me, so am I to you." This indicates that a balance has been achieved between the two of them: *Yathā mama tathā tubhyaṃ yathā tava tathā mama* (13.21.21).[34] He here acknowledges, as she had predicted, that after spending time with her he has developed a liking for her, and now feels desire for her as she does for him.

The succeeding verses ambiguously reveal this change, when he appears to speak to himself, wondering how the old lady has suddenly been transformed into a beautiful girl, and what sage Vādanya would wish him to do. He appears to be in a quandary, but he decides to maintain his restraint. The text is somewhat cryptic here, and it is unclear whether we are to understand it to mean that Diśā[35] has changed her form, or that Aṣṭāvakra now apprehends her as beautiful. Perhaps this ambiguity is deliberate, suggesting that beauty may be in the eye of the beholder.

Vādanya told Aṣṭāvakra at the outset that Diśā is as beautiful as Lakṣmī. Had she used her yogic powers to transform herself into an old woman in order to prove a point to Aṣṭāvakra? Or has she now used her powers to appear young to him? Or has Aṣṭāvakra's way of seeing changed? No definitive explanation is provided. Perhaps the reader's questions regarding the reality or otherwise of her beauty and ugliness are themselves flawed. As Sulabhā pointed out, bodies are always changing. Age and youth, ugliness and beauty are passing appearances. A body that at one time appears young later appears old, but a body that appears old and ugly may also in a certain light or to a certain person appear young and beautiful.

Aṣṭāvakra questions Diśā about her changing form, but unlike Sulabhā, she does not explain it. Ignoring his question, she instead gives unclear and somewhat self-contradictory explanations of why she tried to seduce him. On the one hand, she says she was testing and teaching him as was desired by her friend Vādanya. On the other hand, she says she approached him because she desired him and that this proves even old women experience desire.

The one unambiguous statement she does make is that sexual desire cannot be overcome in the three worlds. Thus, she modifies her earlier claim that women are sex-crazed, now suggesting that no being, regardless of gender or other status, can overcome desire. She tells him to marry the girl he has chosen and predicts that he will have a son. He then returns and takes Suprabhā's hand with great joy.

In answer to Yudhiṣṭhira's initial question about shared *dharma* in marriage, then, Bhīṣma's story represents at least three types of marriage (as outlined in the *Dharma* literature). The first type of marriage is for reproduction alone. This is the kind of marriage Aṣṭāvakra refers to when he tells Diśā that he has overcome desire and wishes to marry only in order to have a child. In such a marriage, the shared *dharma* would be that of parenthood, although one may wonder whether it is possible for a man to reproduce without experiencing at least some modicum of sexual desire.

The second type of marriage is for sexual pleasure. This is the kind Diśā refers to when she proposes marriage in order to fulfil her desire, but it is important to note that she also states that she is devoted to Aṣṭāvakra. In this context, her appearing old and decrepit is important. As an old woman, she presumably cannot reproduce but she still feels desire and emotion. She states unambiguously that even old people experience desire. This suggests that people who cannot reproduce may also marry to satisfy desire.

The third type of marriage is the kind that Aṣṭāvakra undertakes with Suprabhā. It is said to fill him with delight, which suggests that it fulfills desire. It also produces a child. The question, though, is whether it enables the spouses to jointly fulfill *dharma* beyond sex and reproduction. The story does not definitively resolve Yudhiṣṭhira's doubts. Rather, it produces a dialectic of its own, in which evidence of both difference and likeness appears, allowing different readers to draw different conclusions.

Alike or Different?

On the one hand, the story seems to demonstrate that men and women are not as different as Yudhiṣṭhira imagined. It presents a portrait of Diśā as a woman who is similar to a man in being independent as well as in in forthrightly expressing desire and proposing marriage. She is also his intellectual superior, since it is she who mystifies him and teaches him. Like Sulabhā, she has the last word in the dialogue.

On the other hand, at various points in the narrative, Diśā says (as Bhīṣma does elsewhere) that women desire sexual union above all else and will destroy the family in their search for it. This might seem to confirm Yudhiṣṭhira's initial statement that women are innately disordered. Then again, Aṣṭāvakra is clearly just as susceptible to desire as Diśā, perhaps more so, because it is unclear whether she is playing a part in order to test him or whether she really desires him. While her inner being remains obscure, the narrative unambiguously tells us that Aṣṭāvakra is so carried away by pleasure induced by different women that he loses track of time on more than one occasion. This shows that men and women are more alike than different. The only indisputable conclusion is Diśā's statement that sexual desire is not easy for anyone to overcome. If this is the case, and if men are not innately superior to women in self-restraint, then Suprabhā, who is described at the outset as full of virtues (*guṇa*), excellent conduct and manners, would appear to be a fit partner in *dharma* for Aṣṭāvakra.

Since Aṣṭāvakra is described as filled with joy when he marries Sulabhā, the text inscribes pleasure as an aspect of *dharma* into its vision of marriage. Yudhiṣṭhira's earlier distinctions between the *dharma* of sex, the *dharma* of reproduction, and other types of *dharma* do not emerge as viable. First of all, in the fourfold scheme of the goals of life, *kāma* (desire, including sexual desire) precedes *mokṣa*. This can be interpreted to mean that the fulfillment of desire in accordance with *dharma* is a precondition for the achievement of *mokṣa*. Therefore, the *dharma* of sexual delight may be connected to other kinds of *dharma*. Second, Yudhiṣṭhira's formulation unrealistically separates producing a child from raising it. While reproducing merely requires a sexual act, raising a child requires a complex involvement with *dharma*.

Parenting as Joint *Dharma* in Marriage

The complexity of the *dharma* of marriage in relation to a child emerges in a passage in the *Rāmāyaṇa*[36] where Daśaratha reflects on his life as he prepares to abdicate the throne in favor of his eldest son, Rāma. In this moment of retirement, he assesses his past and considers the future embodied in his child. He tells Rāma that he is ready to give up the throne because he has enjoyed all the pleasures he desired, given alms abundantly, studied the scriptures, performed many *yajñas*, and obtained an incomparable son—Rāma—as a result (2.4.12–13). He characterizes the activities he has thus far enumerated as payments of five types of debt: to the Gods, the *ṛṣi*s, the ancestors, *brāhmans*, and oneself (2.4.14). This would mean that *yajña*s (ritual offerings) pay one's debt to the Gods, scriptural study pays one's debt to *ṛṣis* (sages), reproduction pays one's debt to ancestors, alms-giving pays one's debt to *Brāhmans*, and worldly enjoyment pays the debt to oneself (*ātma-ṛna*).

Ātma-ṛna—or debt to the self—is an important notion. It is in accordance with the idea that *kāma* and *artha*, based upon *dharma*, are necessary steps toward *mokṣa*. Striving for *mokṣa* is part of the debt one owes oneself but so too are happiness and satisfaction in the material world. Daśaratha's having lived a fulfilled life prepares him to give up earthly pleasures.

The notion of the debt one owes to oneself integrates the ideas of the *dharma* of sex, the *dharma* of reproduction, and the joint fulfillment of *dharma* in marriage. Yudhiṣṭhira's question wrongly posed the three as alternatives whereas in fact they go together (although marriage for those who cannot reproduce may fulfill the *dharma* of sex and other types of *dharma* in the absence of reproduction). Within marriage, each partner pays the debt to the self, which in the scheme outlined above is a prerequisite for liberation.

The text employs a lovely trope to express the idea of joint fulfillment of *dharma* in marriage and parenthood. Daśaratha's satisfaction in Rāma's beauty and virtues is said to be like the satisfaction of seeing oneself in a mirror when one is well dressed and ornamented (2.3.38). The child is the younger and more perfect version of the parent. But that is not the last word. In the next verse, Daśaratha says, "O son, you are equal to (*sadṛśyāṃ sadṛśaḥ*) my oldest wife" (2.3.39). In Daśaratha's eyes Rāma's goodness consists in being as good as Kauśalyā—he measures up to her. The child is thus a two-way mirror. In Rāma, Daśaratha sees his own best self and also the superior qualities of his wife.

The commonsensical trope of the child as the mirror of both parents reaches toward the ideas of likeness and equality. The child does not mirror the superiority of the father and the inferiority of the mother—or, to use Yudhiṣṭhira's term—the supposedly more disordered nature of the mother. Rather, in the child the mixed natures of both are inextricably blended. Marriage is not just for reproduction (because that can occur outside marriage too) but for raising a child together, and this joint enterprise involves partners capable of sharing *dharma*. Raising a child together does not, of course, require producing it together, as is clear from many cases of adopted children, such as Sītā (who was found and adopted by her father) and Kṛṣṇa (who was raised by adoptive parents).

Knowledge and Interpretation

The complexity of these texts arises from the way they acknowledge and demonstrate how individuals interpret philosophical concepts like *dharma* differently, depending upon their perceptions of reality, and also that the same individual may interpret it differently in different contexts. As Jonardon Ganeri points out, the tradition of reasoning about laws in the scriptures proceeds from case to case, citing precedent and recognizing local norms.[37] One may add that Hindu law, even the codified law in India today, acknowledges the importance of local community custom in certain matters (e.g., which ceremony constitutes a valid Hindu wedding) (2012: 49–54).

This does not mean that all interpretations are equally valid. Not all perceptions are correct, and a valid interpretation depends on accurate knowledge. On the one hand, both Sulabhā and Diśā demonstrate that Janaka's and Aṣṭāvakra's interpretation of a woman's *dharma* as requiring her to be under the control of a man is incorrect. On the other hand, Diśā presents Aṣṭāvakra with options, and it seems that more than one option might be in accordance with *dharma*. For instance, if he yielded to her request for sexual relations he would have obeyed a scriptural injunction. In deciding not to yield, he exercises restraint and remains satisfied with what he has (his fiancée). The second choice may be better than the first, but it is not clear that the first choice would have been entirely wrong either. Similarly, marriage for desire and affection may be valid and so may marriage for reproduction. In both cases, however, the sweeping generalization that a woman must always be under the control of her father, her husband, or her son, falls apart under scrutiny, both because it is based on false ontological premises and also because it does not take into account a woman's choice.

Elsewhere, other women are represented as choosing rather aggressively to adhere to the dictum that fathers must control daughters, even though they appear aware of other ways of doing things. For example, in the *Rāmāyaṇa*, Kuśanābha's hundred daughters scornfully reject the overtures of Vāyu—the wind god—who offers them immortality and eternal youth if they marry him.

They declare that they will never choose their own spouses because that is their father's job. Angered, Vāyu blows through their bodies in a way that cripples them, turning them into hunchbacks.[38] When they complain to their father about this, he surprisingly launches into a panegyric of the virtue of *kṣamā*, saying that they were right to forgive Vāyu. *Kṣamā* may be defined as encompassing forgiveness, tolerance, patience, and endurance but is not directly translatable. Kuśanābha states that *kṣamā* is an ornament to both women and men but is very hard to practice. *Kṣamā* is alms as well as truth and *yajña*, he says; it is also fame, *dharma*, and the foundation of the universe (1.33.6–9).

Here, the same incident evokes two different interpretations of *dharma*. The daughters stick to a conventional idea of their *dharma* and complain to their father against Vāyu. There is no indication in the text that they forgive Vāyu. We might expect a conventional father, as their supposed protector, to wish for vengeance. Instead, he interprets the women's non-retaliation as a sign of forgiveness and tolerance, which implies that they really required no protection because they had the power to retaliate against Vāyu but chose not to do so. Most importantly, he praises *kṣamā* not as a feminine virtue appropriate to women but as a universal virtue and the ornament of both genders (*alaṅkāro hi nārīṇāṃ kṣamā tu puruṣasya vā* 1.33.7). Forgiveness and forbearance are praised as producing merit equal to that produced by performing sacrificial rituals and giving alms.

Kuśanābha says that the universe is founded on *kṣamā*. From the root *kṣa*—which means earth—*kṣamā* is often ascribed to the earth because she endures the misdeeds of living beings. The universe being founded on *kṣamā* also suggests that life cannot go on without everyone to some extent enduring, tolerating, and forgiving the misdeeds of others. The *Śānti Parva*, in its discussion of self-restraint as the highest good, elevates the importance of *kṣamā*, because it is a necessary precondition for the overcoming of greed and anger (12.152–4).[39] It is noteworthy that although the discussion of this virtue occurs in a dialogic philosophical context in the *Mahābhārata* and in an eminently "mythological" kind of story in the *Rāmāyaṇa*, both reach similar ethical conclusions with regard to its place in human *dharma*.

The type of ungendered *dharma* that Sulabhā and Diśā advocate, or that Daśaratha expounds, applies equally to both women and men. But the epics also depict individual women and men putting forward different interpretations of gendered *dharma* and making different choices for themselves in relation to it. Thus, while Diśā insists that she is self-ruled (*svatantraṃ*), Kuśanābha's daughters insist that they are not self-ruled (*svacchanda*) (1.33.3), even though their father shows no interest in the issue of protection and simply expounds on the matter of *kṣamā*.

The crippling of Kuśanābha's daughters dramatizes the relationship of gender to disability, which is also at play in Aṣṭāvakra and Diśā's story.

Gender and Disability

Old age, ugliness, and physical disability are aspects of the body that (like gender) are temporary and do not modify the self. Yet they function as handicaps, not only in society but also at extraterrestrial levels. Kuśanābha's daughters defy a deity in their attempt to act according to their *dharma* as they see it. The result is that their vulnerability takes the form of a physical disability. Similarly, Aṣṭāvakra too becomes disabled when he flouts the father–son hierarchy. While he is in the womb, he corrects his father, who is mispronouncing Vedic texts. His father takes offence and curses him. Born a posthumous child, Aṣṭāvakra's privilege as a male is countered by his fatherlessness and his disability.

The story of Aṣṭāvakra and Diśā nowhere mentions Aṣṭāvakra's disability though this is the characteristic by which he is most commonly identified, inscribed as it is into his name, which means "bent in eight places." In earlier work, I have suggested that the disability associated with Aṣṭāvakra makes him especially available as a catalyst for texts that set out to examine the nature of special vulnerabilities, such as those related to gender, sexuality, and caste.[40] These texts include the *Aṣṭāvakra Gīta* with its radically uncompromising nondualism that discards gender. This text also explicitly discards *varṇāśrama-dharma* or what is now known as caste: "You are neither a *varṇa*, such as Brāhmaṇa, nor do you belong to an *āśrama*, nor are you perceived by the senses. You are non-dual, formless and witness of the universe (Thus contemplating, be happy)" (Mukerjee, 1971, 31–2).

Conclusion

A wide spectrum of female agency and conduct emerges in the *Mahābhārata*. This spectrum is based on the Indian philosophical premises that define the Self as either genderless or dual-gendered. For this reason, the female characters here discussed cannot be dismissed simply as unconventional or as mavericks, as one scholar terms Sulabhā (Shah, 1995: 68).[41] The range of unconventional women and men, the relationships between them, and the range of approaches toward different situations in Hindu narratives suggest that no sweeping generalization is possible about Hindu philosophical approaches to womanhood or gender. The texts themselves undercut tendencies to make such generalizations. Bhīṣma himself represents not one consistent view but a panorama of views. He states that women should never be independent and should be kept under control, but he also says that it is impossible to protect them and that men have to learn to defer to them.

The narratives and dialogues relating to women who are unconventional are not just entertaining stories. They are based on major philosophical premises. It is for this reason that they create a matrix within which Hindu society has been able, and still is able, to accommodate a range of female behaviors, including political, religious, and professional leadership by women who are married, single, and widowed. While such women often face resistance and violence, they also garner widespread support. This is not evidence, as some would have it, of the chaotic nature of Hindu thought but rather of philosophical breadth capacious enough to enable a range of positions and debates.

Notes

1 Andrew J. Nicholson, *Unifying Hinduism: Philosophy and Identity in Indian Intellectual History* (New York: Columbia University Press, 2010), 74–5, 148.

2 I have discussed some aspects of this dialogue in earlier work. See: Ruth Vanita, "The Self Is Not Gendered: Sulabhā's Debate with King Janaka," *NWSA Journal* 15(2) (Summer 2003), 76–93.

3 Given its remarkable brilliance, this dialogue has been little studied. James L. Fitzgerald, "Nun Befuddles King, Shows Karmayoga Does Not Work: Sulabhā's Refutation of King Janaka at MBh 12.308," *Journal of Indian Philosophy* 30(6) (2002): 641–77, and Nicholas Sutton, "An Exposition of Early Saṃkhya, A Rejection of the Bhagavad-Gītā and Critique of the Role of Women in Hindu Society: The Sulabhā–Janaka–Saṃvāda," *Annals of the Bhandarkar Oriental Research Institute* 80 (1999): 53–65 focus mainly on the question of *karma yoga* versus *saṃnyāsa*, noting also Sulabhā's unconventionality. Arti Dhand, *Woman as Fire, Woman as Sage: Sexual Ideology in the Mahābhārata* (Albany: State University of New York Press, 2008), does not cover any new ground in her discussion (89–90). Sumedha Vidyalankar, in her study specifically of the *Śānti Parva*, in *Mahābhārata mein Santi Parva ka Alochnatmak Adhyayan [A Critical Study of Śānti Parva in Mahābhārata]* (Delhi: Eastern Book Linkers, 1984), fails to discuss Sulabhā.

4 Mario Piantelli, "King Janaka as a Male Chauvinistic Pig in the Mahābhārata," in Alessandro Monti, ed., *Hindu Masculinities across the Ages: Updating the Past* (Turin: L'Harmattan Italia, 2002) briefly mentions the Diśā–Aṣṭāvakra dialogue and suggests that Diśā and Sulabhā may be manifestations of the same Goddess (I see no evidence of Goddesses being involved). He also suggests that Sulabhā's yogic union with Janaka may be the catalyst for his liberation. Dhand (2008) mentions Aṣṭāvakra's asceticism in a couple of lines without any analysis of the dialogue with Diśā (81). I examined some aspects of this dialogue in an earlier essay, Ruth Vanita, "Full of God: Aṣṭāvakra and Ideas of Justice in Hindu Texts," *Religions of South Asia* 3(2) (2009), 167–81.

5 The *Śānti Parva*, in which the Sulabhā–Janaka debate occurs, also contains about one third of the precepts of the *Mānavadharmaśastra*, repeated in near-identical form.

This dictum continues to be cited widely both in scholarly and non-scholarly forums without sufficient attention to its contestation in the epics and elsewhere, for instance, Sanjay K. Gautam, *Foucault and the Kamasutra: The Courtesan, the Dandy, and the Birth of Arts Erotica as Theater in India* (Chicago: Chicago University Press, 2016) builds his entire argument around the opposition between the supposed position of women in what he terms Brahmanical law, exemplified by this dictum, and the excluded courtesans who inhabit an aestheticized erotic realm.

6 Brian Black and Laurie Patton, eds., *Dialogue in Early South Asian Religions: Hindu, Buddhist and Jain Traditions* (Farnham, Surrey: Ashgate, 2015), Introduction, 1.

7 I do not use the term soteriology, implying as it does salvation and the intervention of a savior.

8 *Chāṇḍogya Upaniṣad* with the commentary of Śrī Śaṅkarācārya (Calcutta: Advaita Ashrama, 1997), p. 422. Translation mine.

9 *Śvetāśvatara Upaniṣad*, ed. Swami Tyagisnanada (Mylapore, Madras: Sri Rāmakrishna Math, 1949), translation mine.

10 *Aṣṭāvakragītā*, ed. Radhakamal Mukherjee (Delhi: Motilal Banarsidass, 1971), p. 128, translation mine.

11 The metaphor of the body as clothing to be assumed at birth and discarded at death is widely known because of its famous deployment in the Bhagavad Gītā.

12 Ruth Vanita, *Love's Rite: Same-Sex Marriage in India and the West* (New Delhi: Penguin Books, 2005).

13 The tradition of Hindu women seeking liberation by renouncing the world rather than simply serving their husbands has ancient roots and continues into the modern world. See Lynn Teskey Denton, *Female Ascetics in Hinduism* (Albany: SUNY Press, 2004).

14 *Na caiṣāmapyayo rajaṃllakṣyate prabhavo na ca/*
avasthāyāmavasthāyāṃ dīpasyevārciṣo gatiḥ//
Sukthankar XV, 1723.

15 *Tasyāpyevaṃprabhāvasya sadaśvasyeva dhāvataḥ/*
Ajastraṃ sarvalokasya kaḥ kuto vā na vā kutaḥ//
Sukthankar, XV, 1723.

16 *Tasyāpyevaṃprabhāvasya sadaśvasyeva dhāvataḥ/*
Asastraṃ sarvalokasya kaḥ kuto vā na vā kutaḥ//
Kasyedaṃ kasya vā neda. ̦kuto vedaṃ na vā kutaḥ/
*Saṃbandhaḥ ko 'sti bhūtānāṃ svairapyavayavairiha//*Sukthankar XV, 1723.

17 *Ātmanyevātmanātmānaṃ yathā tvam anupaśyasi/*
Evamevātmanātmānaṃ anyasmin kiṃ na paśyasi//
Yadyātmani parasmiṃśca samatamadhyavasyasi/
*Atha māṃ kāsi kasyeti kimarthaṃ anupṛcchasi//Idaṃ me syād idaṃ neti dvaṇdvair muktasya maithila/Kāsi kasya kuto veti vacane kiṃ prayojanam//*Sukthankar, XV, 1725.

18 *Varṇāśramapṛthaktve ca dṛṣṭārthasyāpṛthaktvinaḥ/*
Nānyadanyaditi jñātvā nānyadanyatpravartate//
Sukthankar, XV, 1730.

19 *Sulabhā tvasya dharmeṣu mukto neti sasaṃśayā/*
Sattvaṃ sattvena yogajñā praviveśo mahīpate//
Netrābhyāṃ netrayorasya raśmīnsaṃyojya raśmibhiḥ
*Sā sma saṃcodayiṣyantaṃ yogabandhairabandha ha//*Sukthankar, XV, 1706.

20 *Na pāṇibhyāṃ na bāhubhyāṃ pādorubhyāṃ na cānadha/*
Na gātrāvayavairanyaiḥ spṛśāmi tvā narādhipa//
Sukthankar, XV, 1729.

21 *Yathā puṣkaraparṇasthaṃ jalaṃ tatparṇasaṃsthitam/*
Tiṣṭhatyaspṛśatī tadvattvayi vatsyāmi maithila//
Sukthankar, XV, 1730.

22 *Asaktaḥ padmapatrastho jalabinduryathā calaḥ/*
Evameva śarīre 'syā nivatsyāmi samāhitaḥ//
Sukthankar, XVII, 260.

23 Bhīṣma says that Vipula is the only man who has ever succeeded in protecting a woman. He then makes some self-contradictory statements, instructing Yudhiṣṭhira to always protect women but also stating that no one in the three worlds is capable of protecting them. Good women will restrain themselves and bad women cannot be restrained. The only way to protect them, he suggests, is to distinguish good women from bad. Also, men should not be attached to women or jealous with regard to them.

24 *Saṃdehaḥ sumahāneṣa viruddha iti me matiḥ/*
Iha yaḥ sahadharmo vai pretyāyaṃ vihitaḥ kva nu//
Sukthankar, XVII, 156.

25 *Yāṃ yāmapaśyatkanyāṃ sa sā sā tasya mano 'harat/*

Nāśakruvaddhārayituṃ mano 'thāsyāvasīdati//
Sukthankar, XVII, 163.

26 This last statement is the same one that Bhīṣma elaborates on later, in *Anuśāsana Parva* 2:38, where he agrees with Yudhiṣṭhira that women are faithless and will have sex with any man.

27 *Atharṣirabhisaṃprekṣya striyaṃ tāṃ jarayānvitām/*
Cintāṃ paramikāṃ bheje saṃtapta iva cābhavat/
Sukthankar, XVII, 167.

28 *Yadyadaṅgaṃ hi so 'paśyattasyā viprarṣabhastadā/*
Nāramattatra tatrāsya dṛṣṭī rūpaparājitā//
Sukthankar, XVII, 167.

29 *Śayyāsanamalaṃkāramannapānamanārthayatām/*
Durvāgbhāva.ˌratiṃ caiva dadau strībhyaḥ prajāpatiḥ//
Sukthankar, XVII, 257.

30 In this section, Bhīṣma explains the difference between good and bad women with a curious narrative wherein originally all humans, including women, were good, but the gods, afraid that humans would attain to divinity, asked Brahma to intervene, whereupon he created another set of women who pursued desire (*kāma*) and were in turn pursued by men who thus yielded to desire and anger (*krodha*) (13.40.1–14).

31 *Sā tadā tena vipreṇa tathā dhṛtyā nivartitā/*
Svatantrāsmītyuvācainaṃˌna dharmacchalamasti te//
Sukthankar, XVII, 169.

32 *Bādhate maithunaṃ vipra mama bhaktiṃ ca paśya vai/*
Adharmaṃ prāpsyase vipra yanmāṃ tvaṃ nābhinandasi//
Sukthankar, XVII, 169.

33 *Yadi vā doṣajātaṃ tvaṃ paradāreṣu paśyasi/*
Ātmānaṃ sparśayāmyadya pāṇiṃ gṛhṇīṣva me dvija//
Sukthankar, XVII, 169.

34 *Yathā mama tathā tubhyaṃ yathā tava tathā mama/*
Jijñāseyamṛṣestasya vighnaḥ satyaṃ nu kiṃ bhavet//
Sukthankar, XVII, 170.

35 Diśā is referred to throughout simply as *woman* (*strī*).

36 All references are to Vālmīki-Rāmāyaṇa.

37 Jonardon Ganeri, *Identity as Reasoned Choice: A South Asian Perspective on the Reach and Resources of Public and Practical Reason in Shaping Individual Identities* (New York: Continuum, 2012), 49–54.

38 Sally Sutherland, "Seduction, Counter Seduction, and Sexual Role Models: Bedroom Politics and the Indian Epics," *Journal of Indian Philosophy* 20(2) (1992), 243–51, mentions this episode (247) but does not comment on it.

39 See also Ganeri's discussion of this in *Identity as Reasoned Choice*, 146–7.

40 See Vanita (2009).

41 Shalini Shah, *The Making of Womanhood: Gender Relations in the Mahabharata* (Delhi: Manohar Publications, 1995), 68.

References

Aristotle (1925). *The Nicomachean Ethics*, D. Ross (ed.). Oxford: Oxford University Press.

Black, B., and L. Patton (eds.) (2015). *Dialogue in Early South Asian Religions: Hindu, Buddhist and Jain Traditions*. Farnham, Surrey: Ashgate.

Gambhirananda, S. (1997). *Chāṇḍogya Upaniṣad: With the Commentary of Śrī Śaṅkarācārya*. Calcutta: Advaita Ashrama.

Ganeri, J. (2012). *Identity as Reasoned Choice: A South Asian Perspective on the Reach and Resources of Public and Practical Reason in Shaping Individual Identities*. New York: Continuum.

Jalan, M. (1969). *Śrīmad Vālmīki-Rāmāyaṇa*, Part-I, II, III. Gorakhpur: Gita Press.

Mukerjee, R. (ed.) (1971). *Āṣṭāvakragītā*. Delhi: Motilal Banarsidass.

Nicholson, A. (2010). *Unifying Hinduism: Philosophy and Identity in Indian Intellectual History*. New York: Columbia University Press.

Shah, S. (1995). *The Making of Womanhood: Gender Relations in the Mahabharata*. Delhi: Manohar Publications.

Sukthankar, V. S., S. K. Belvalkar, P. L. Vaidya, et al. (eds.) (1933). *The Mahābhārata: For the First Time Critically Edited*. Poona: Bhandarkar Oriental Research Institute.

Sutherland, S. (1992). Seduction, Counter Seduction, and Sexual Role Models: Bedroom Politics and the Indian Epics. *Journal of Indian Philosophy* 20(2): 243–51.

Tyagisnanada, S. (ed.) (1949). *Śvetāśvatara Upaniṣad*. Mylapore, Madras: Sri Ramakrishna Math.

Vanita, R. (2005). *Love's Rite: Same-Sex Marriage in India and the West*. New Delhi: Penguin Books.

14

The Vision of the Transcendent One: Feminist Hermeneutics and Feminine Symbolism in the Sikh Scripture

Nikky-Guninder Kaur Singh

The literary critic Hans-Georg Gadamer claimed that there is no way that "the objectivity of the meaning to be understood" can ever be separated from the "subjectivity of the reader" (1989: 311). As is the case in most religious traditions, it is the male elites who have had the privilege of interpreting Sikh scripture—the *Guru Granth Sahib* (GGS). We also know that the cognitive and the practical are not different dimensions. Rather, interpretation, understanding, and application constitute a singular hermeneutic process (Gadamer 1989: 309). Since male subjectivity produced Sikh scriptural hermeneutics, it has resulted in male-dominated identity formations, social relations, and power structures. Because of this one-sided approach, the egalitarian and liberating theological, ethical, and aesthetic currents of the sacred text have neither been fully understood nor put in practice. The GGS continues to be the center of Sikh private and public life; it is the core of their religious and moral values; it is the sovereign presiding at all their ceremonies and celebrations. The 25 million Sikhs worldwide rely on its existential power. Indeed Sikh "subjectivity" is born and sustained by the GGS. It is detrimental that the text meant for society as a whole has been taken over by the male gender in its meaning as well as in its praxis.

We begin this chapter by considering some of the post-Guru historical circumstances that led to male-centered interpretations of the scriptural text and consequently shaped practices in Sikh life. The focus is on the feminine symbolism in the poetics of the GGS and its empowering theological imaginary. We also discuss how Sikh praxis deviated from the Gurus' ideal of gender equality and fell back to the practices of the same sociocultural norms that dominated their milieu.

Historical Context

Early on, we hear exegetes and commentators reverse the progressive message of the GGS. In his ethical manual, Chaupa Singh—a tutor and aide of the Tenth Guru—dictates a Sikh woman's primary mode of religiosity as her worship of her husband: She is to "know her husband as god" (*apne bharte nu karta janai*; *The Chaupa Singh Rahit-Nama*, 556); she is to "keep fasts for the sake of her husband" (*patibratu rakhe*, 567).[1] The ideals and practices of the first Sikh community established by the founder Guru Nanak in Kartarpur (1469–1539)—where men and women recited enchanting sacred verse, cooked, and ate together—were soon overturned. Instead, segregation and discrimination were stipulated: Women may listen to but are prohibited from reading the GGS in public (*The Chaupa Singh Rahit-Nama*: 538).

The glamorous regime of Maharaja Ranjit Singh (1799–1839) brought great splendor to the Sikhs but along with it, pernicious values and norms for women. With the elaboration of pomp and ceremony at his royal court, formal ritual and ceremonial discarded by the Gurus entered into the Sikh way of life. The customs of *purdah* and *satī* performed by women from elite Muslim and Hindu families, respectively, began to be emulated by the upper echelons of the Sikh society. British colonialism provided yet another oppressive layer, which produced a "hyper-masculine" culture. Punjab came under the Raj in 1849, and the imperial masters so admired the "martial" character and strong physique of Sikh men that they recruited them in disproportionately large numbers to serve in the British army. A vigorous new patriarchal discourse with its patriotism and paternalism was thereby attached to the "Brotherhood of the Khalsa."

That drive continues on. With the Green Revolution and the industrious spirit of its people, postcolonial Punjab became the breadbasket of India. Today, it is in the ferment of globalization. Contemporary economic and technological priorities have made the patriarchal compulsion for sons even stronger. Parents regard sons as their social security and financial insurance, and as religious functionaries who will eventually perform their funeral rites. Sons are deemed essential for carrying on of the family name, property, and land. With the combination of ancient patriarchal values and new globalization, the gender disparity is deteriorating at an alarming rate. Thus, in spite of the recent economic boom and better laws to protect women and girls, the proportion of baby girls is declining rapidly. The selective abortion of females (through technological means such as amniocentesis) has only reinforced the devaluation of girls and further entrenched gender prejudices. Since immigrant Sikhs maintain transnational ties with their families and friends in Punjab, the customs and values from home are quickly exported to diasporic communities across the globe (Fair 1996). Women are held responsible to preserve the honor (*izzat*) of their fathers and brothers. Parents with daughters are severely pressurized by dowry demands—be it cash, jewelry, furniture, cars, or property.

The post-9/11 era has produced new complications. Valerie Kaur, a third-generation Sikh American activist, poignantly captures the gravity of the contemporary situation in this extract from the *Huffington Post*:

> It took me nearly a decade after 9/11 even to begin talking about women again. After the terrorist attacks, we women tacitly agreed to put our issues on hold. We needed to protect our men first—our brothers and husbands and sons whose turbans and dark skin marked them as primary targets for hate in the years after 9/11. This was a mistake. As we waited (and are still waiting) for the discrimination to pass over us, some of the cultural dysfunctions in our community worsened. Women and girls are always the first casualties within minority communities under siege . . . When riots and massacre swept Punjab during the 1947 Partition of India, some Sikh men poisoned their daughters before letting them fall into the hands of Muslim rioters. Today in America, while many Sikh families champion education and freedom for sons and daughters alike, others have tightened control over women and girls in the 9/11 decade. In the worst anecdotes, domestic violence is an outlet for men who bear racism on the street, intermarriage an act of betrayal, and honor killings an actual threat. (Kaur 2012)

The Sikh community is beginning to recognize the problems it faces. Men and women have started taking steps toward gender justice. Campaigns geared specifically against female feticide are being initiated, and political leaders and NGOs are forging important infrastructures for the protection, welfare, education, and employment of girls and women. Women writers, artists, poets, and film directors are trying to raise social awareness. Along with these important steps, I strongly feel that there must be the disclosure of feminist possibilities permeating Sikh scripture. The sacred verse so central to Sikh life has the power to reach the deeply unconscious self, the template of real change. The transcendent lyrics have the potential to open up a vast egalitarian horizon free from sexism, classism, and racism. But they need to be retrieved!

The Poetics of Feminine Symbolism

The need for a feminist hermeneutics that will balance the masculine is urgent. The GGS is an enormously rich reservoir upon which a whole range of readers can feed. For several years now, I have been studying, interpreting, and translating it from my feminist subjectivity—that of a Sikh academic woman living in the twenty-first century in the United States—and I find the text most empowering. My selfhood is certainly conditioned by my experiences, both lived and imagined, and by my sociocultural context. And it has been shaped by my sacred text. I grew up in a Sikh home hearing the melodies of the GGS. I may not have understood the actual words at that time, but they did seep into my being. When I first began to study the text, I did so in male habits and patterns I had imbibed. In my undergraduate thesis, I envisioned an all-powerful male God and translated and analyzed the scriptural verses in the masculine gender (Kaur 1981). Feminist epiphany came during graduate school at the American Academy of Religion conference in Chicago where I first heard Mary Daly, Judith Plaskow, Rosemary Ruether, Carol Christ, Rita Gross, and Naomi Goldenberg. Whatever these thinkers said, and however they said it, changed me. I started to explore my heritage from my "female" perspective and have been doing so ever since. The writings of South Asian, womanist, and European feminists have further helped me craft my feminist lenses.

But so entrenched is the "masculinist" in Sikh life that the mainstream rejects a "feminist" approach as a Western gimmick, and in scholarly circles, it is reduced to a tangential lexicon. In reality though, it basically entails understanding the sacred verse in its expansive and inclusive imagery and using that understanding in everyday practices to empower both Sikh men and women in their private and public lives. The scriptural material itself mandates and inspires new hermeneutic possibilities, evoking Gadamer's advice: Every text "must be understood at every moment, in every concrete situation, in a new and different way." (1989: 311). When the existing patriarchal exegesis is contested, we open up a horizon that nurtures the fullness of being human. In this essay, the contesting will be staged in the following four arenas: Theological Imaginary, Spiritual Embodiment, Identity Construction, and Performative Agency.

Theological Imaginary

The challenge here is to break the hold of masculine assumptions in the perception of the Divine that have been shaped by exegetes, scholars, and translators of the GGS (GGS scripture). The fundamental Sikh theological expression is *Ikk Onkar*—at the very outset of the volume, and it is reiterated in its 1,430 portfolio pages. This unique and expansive configuration by the first Guru spells out the infinity of the singular Divine. There is no gender specification, and yet it has been structured and shaped into a male god—its vastness is reduced to an exclusionary concept and an intimidating male symbol. The colonial machine reinforced an omnipotent lordly "God," which has ruptured the intimate relationship between humans and the Divine at the heart of Sikh scripture. In his work, Arvind Mandair exposes how the specter of the West made the indigenous Sikh ideologues psychologically receptive to its categories and polarizations (Mandair 2009). Over the years, scholars have imposed an Abrahamic monotheistic conception on the Gurus' pluralistic and inclusive One. Androcentric interpretations by Sikhs and Westerners have destroyed the elemental modality of *Ikk Onkar*.

A change in the lens reveals the Sikh theological construct with the potential of the radical "metapatriarchal journey" proposed by the feminist philosopher Mary Daly—to exorcise an internalized father—God in his various manifestations and incarnations (Daly 1978). As the inclusive numeral, "One" shatters the dominance of male imagery, it creates a space for the Divine to be experienced in other new and important ways. Logically, it does not matter how the Divine is understood in human terms—the One is totally transcendent and beyond all categories. But in the poetry of the Gurus, both female and male dimensions run parallel. The Divine is identified in both genders: "Itself male, itself is female" (GGS: 1020).[2] Thus, we receive a balanced perspective, which is crucial for mental and spiritual health.

Moreover, the GGS regularly turns attention to the primal home—the mother's body, the ontological base of every person. In particular, it honors the maternal space as a social utopia in which the fetus is free from hegemonic designations of class, caste, and name: "In the dwelling of the womb, there is neither name nor caste" (GGS: 324). The Sikh Gurus were acutely aware of their oppressive patrilineal and patricentered North Indian society in which the family name, caste, and profession came down through birth. So, the mother's pregnant body is envisioned as free from "isms" and social hegemonies. Here the fetus is nurtured by *her* life-giving uterus—it is not suffocated by the father's name, class, or professional ties.

But subsequent commentators of Sikh scripture simply deem it unnecessary to remember *her* body or our origins, and so the unique emphasis of the Sikh Gurus on the divine constitution of female physiology and of our integrated subjectivity has been lost. For instance, the GGS explicitly affirms that the Divine permeates both the heart and the womb (*ghati ghati vartai udari majhare*—[It pervades every heart and flourishes in the womb] GGS: 1026). Eminent scholars like G. S. Talib and Gopal Singh register the heart (*ghat*) but utterly ignore the womb (*udar*) in Guru Nanak's feminist sensibility.[3] The particular female organ even gets altered into a generic "stomach"[4] or "belly."[5] The radical vision of the Gurus and their invigorating overtures thus remain unseen, unheard. Their womb-respecting, birth-oriented glimpses and melodies need to be remembered so that their lingering can make each of us more wholesome and our world a better place.

The seriousness with which the GGS takes women's genealogy is quite remarkable. It celebrates the various natural female processes, including the mother's milk, which is acknowledged as full of biological and spiritual nutrients. Even the recitation of divine name is succulently experienced as milk in the mouth. The language of the Gurus joins in with the words of contemporary French feminist scholar Hélène Cixous: "Voice: milk that could go on forever. Found again. The lost mother/bitter-lost. Eternity: is voice mixed with milk" (Cixous and Clément 1986: 98). Her milk is a biological necessity, keeping us from dying. So is the divine word (*bani*). By pouring the two together, the Sikh Gurus make knowledge essential for everybody—upper class and lower, *brahmin* and *śūdra*. The textuality of the GGS lies in its physical sensuality—in drinking the words as though they were the mother's life-giving milk. Furthermore, the mother is identified with *mati*, wisdom, which is the quintessential characteristic of Sikh epistemology: *mātā mati pitā saṅtokh* (mother is wisdom; father, contentment). Wisdom (*mati*) is also connected with truth (*saca*). As I have elsewhere pointed out, "The nexus between wisdom and woman is metaphorically established," but scholars have not paid attention to such details (Singh 1993: 69–71).

Though the maternal imaginary in the GGS is palpably reclaimed, it is not a matter of religious deification, because "she" is not idolized into some distant goddess—an object of worship. It is when the Divine is genuinely imagined as Mother that her positive characteristics begin to filter the mind and ignite respect for mothers, sisters, daughters, and wives. Thus, an authentic subjectivity is born. Women are regarded as life-and-blood individuals who partake in the qualities and powers of the divine One. They are thanked for their creating and nurturing.

It is critical, however, that the "mother" not to be viewed as the only female symbol for the Divine either. Sikh scripture offers countless ways of imagining and experiencing the infinite One. Even in one short hymn, Guru Nanak imagines the Divine as the bride in her wedding dress, as the groom on the nuptial bed, as the fisherman and the fish, as the waters and the trap, as the weight holding the net, as well as the lost ruby swallowed by the fish! (GGS: 23). In a speedy tempo, his similes and paradoxes free the mind from narrow walls.

Male is not the only way to imagine the Divine. Motherhood therefore is one aspect of womanhood, and surely all women are not mothers and may choose not to be mothers. With the singular stress on the maternal paradigm, woman's creative powers can be misconstrued as an automatic and mandatory process.

The "mother" symbol from the GGS must not be abused to make women into reproductive machines to beget sons! It is important that we do not equate the maternal potential with physical conception or limit the maternal to the domestic world. As Luce Irigaray says, it is not necessary that women give birth to children; they can give birth to many other things such as "love, desire, language, art, social things, political things, religious things" (1993: 18). The "mother" as a Sikh theological principle reveals the potential to create—physically, intellectually, emotionally, politically, and spiritually. It shatters the gender roles that assign production to men and reproduction to women. Conferring a sense of reality on women's creativity, it enables everybody to cultivate meaningful relationships with their past and future generations and with their geological and cosmic community.

We also find a distinct Sikh articulation of the feminine principle in, for instance, Guru Gobind Singh's (1666–1708) compositions on Durgā—whose name is a juxtaposition of the two Sanskrit verbal roots *dur* (meaning "difficult") and *gam* ("to reach"). As I have noted extensively in my book *The Feminine Principle in the Sikh Transcendent,* Guru Gobind Singh represents a unique blend of both martial and devotional elements. Living as he did during times of great suppression against the Sikhs, the Guru realized that he would have to stir his people out of the passivity they had forcibly adopted and rally them to action and revolution. Durgā—a goddess from the Hindu pantheon impressed upon his imagination. The *Purānic* story of her titanic battle against the demons is retold by Guru Gobind Singh in his ornate Braj compositions, the *Candi Caritra* poems, and in his Punjabi work, *Var Durgā Ki*, commonly known as *Candi di Var*. Even his *Akal Ustat*, a hymn written in praise of the Timeless One, contains a panegyric to the prowess of the invincible goddess. The Sikh Guru was very attracted to *her*, the kinetic energy of the Divine.[6] Without her, no creation, and without her, the male gods would have lost to the demons. The goddess legitimizes the war against injustice. In his poems, the Sikh Guru recalls the classical Indian myth recorded in the *Devī Māhātmya* and amplifies the warrior role of the female protagonist with all his artistic zest and fire. Her heroic imagery depicts her both as a beautiful and valorous independent woman. She is one of the only autonomously operating—for example, unmarried—goddesses among millions in the Hindu pantheon of gods.

It is imperative to note that Guru Gobind Singh *does not* treat Durgā as the Supreme Divine principle. That is, he does not worship her in the same way as she has been traditionally worshipped in the Hindu religion *as* a deity. Rather, the Guru was very clear that he was singularly devoted to the *Ikk Onkar*—the One, Transcendent God eulogized by his predecessor Gurus. Therefore, although the Guru references Durgā throughout his writings, this practice of referencing should be seen as a type of devotion to a *mythical* and *literary* figure—one he felt particularly capable of inspiring a martial sentiment in his oppressed peoples. Guru Gobind Singh found inspiration from the fearless image of Durgā, but he was dedicated to the traditional Transcendent One (*Ikk Onkar*) consistent to the Sikh notion of the Divine. He reinforced Guru Nanak's vision of the Divine: the One is never born; the One does not become incarnate. The Sikh faith does not postulate any *avatar* or incarnate being coequal or co-powerful with the Transcendent One and thereby worthy of human worship.

Given his emphasis on *recalling* rather than *worshipping* the figure of Durgā, what specific purpose does this figure serve in the thought of Guru Gobind Singh and among the Sikh society of his time? For one, his deliberate decision to draw on Durgā underscores the Guru's egalitarianism. Specifically, his choice of Durgā means unequivocal acknowledgment of woman's power in society. As mentioned, Durgā is unique among the Hindu goddesses in that she is not associated with any consort—she operates alone and manages to single-handedly achieve victories in various narratives, such as the *Mārkaṇḍeya Purāṇa*. She is, therefore, not merely an inspiring force with respect to the subjugated Sikhs of the Guru's time, galvanizing them to arise and fight for justice, but also a role model for the status of *women* within these larger subjugated societies. The choice of Durgā was deliberate and explicitly expresses Guru Gobind Singh's belief in the equal societal position of women in the Sikh community:

> It was the full independence of Durgā's character, her ability to challenge and quell evil, her power to embrace all of life—birth and death, creation and destruction—that attracted the imagination of Gurū Gobind Singh. Gurū Gobind Singh's choice displays a singular awareness of the intrinsic importance of the female. (Singh 1993: 130)

Durgā represents *energy* and *fury*—the embodiment of martial valor and virility. She is a creator and a conqueror, the Great Mother but also a lethal destroyer. She is the feminine incarnation of both the *śṛṇgāra* and *raudra rasas*—the aesthetic elements of the erotic and the martial, respectively. Such a depiction of the feminine clearly countervails against the traditional depiction of women as meek and submissive; it subverts their societal goal of *patidharma*—their devotion to the husband and dutiful servitude toward him and his family. As David Kinsley observes,

> In many respects, Durga violates the model of the Hindu woman. She is not submissive, she is not subordinated to a male deity, she does not perform household duties, and she excels at what is traditionally a male function—fighting in battle. As an independent warrior who can hold her own against any male on the battlefield, she reverses the normal role for females and therefore stands outside normal society. (1988: 5)

For sure, Durgā is feminine and beautiful and simultaneously overflows with "masculine" martial prowess and fierceness; she fluidly blends superficially antipodean qualities together into a seamless harmony.

The Guru even went as far as to symbolize her by use of the imagery of a *sword*—variously known as *kirpān*, *sarabloh*, *khaṛag*, *bhagautī*, *khaṇḍā*, *tegh*. The sword, like Durgā for the gods, was to be invoked in self-defense and only as a last resort:

> When the matter is past all other remedy
> It is all lawful to take the sword in hand. (Zafarnama, verse 22)

The sword is one of the "Five Ks," the five items of faith worn by Sikh men and women. Associated with Durgā, the sword is uniquely *feminized*. In his compositions such as *Caṇḍī dī Vār*, Guru Gobind Singh's Durgā is metaphorically symbolized as a sword—embodying the light of consciousness and intelligence, as its pierces through the darkness of nescience. Through his fabulous literary techniques, the Guru incites us to imagine a woman's body, drawing us to her strong female hand. We can see *her* flesh, *her* fingers as the source of his sword:

> *kripan pan dhariyam*
> *koror pap tariyam* (Bacitar Natak I: 47)
> The sword in hand
> Crores of sins crossed over.

These literary examples reveal Guru Gobind Singh's intriguing imaginary. The Guru made Durgā the subject of his compositions because she exemplified the power of women—a power he felt had been overlooked by the prevailing patriarchal structures. Furthermore, She embodied traits that would be necessary for the survival of the oppressed Sikh community—martial valor, virility, and strength. Guru Gobind Singh's remythologizing of the goddess unleashes traits and energies that the poet and his readers, both men and women, could identify with and carry out into their own lives. The Tenth Guru realized that the only way of rejuvenating his society was contingent on the actions of both men and women. Male paradigms needed to be balanced by female paradigms. The goddess Durgā is a powerful and active heroine, but she is by no means an object of *pūjā, yajña, tapas, or bhakti* as in the case of conventional Hindu scripture and practice.[7] The fact that Guru Gobind Singh was able to imagine a female hand holding the sword is a vital signifier that he could confidently see the instrument held in the hands of women in his own society. In fact, Sikh history records the case of Mai Bhago who fought valiantly with the Guru. She was from the Amritsar district of the Punjab. When she saw how some Sikhs of her area had fled from helping the Guru in Anandpur, she chided them for their pusillanimity. Mai Bhago led them back to fight for the Guru, and she herself fought in the battle that took place in Muktsar on December 19, 1705.[8] During the period of Sikh persecutions that followed the Guru's death, women not only took care of their families but also fought courageously. The period is replete with the heroic deeds and sacrifices of Sikh men and women like Mai Bhago. The Guru who remembered the mythic woman warrior could have a valorous Mai Bhago by his side.

Spiritual Embodiment and Issues in Purity

The contest here entails reversing the persistent mind–body dualism. Feminist scholars have shown us the terrible consequences of this bipartite framework and its drastic corollaries on the devaluing of our bodies, of our life on earth, and of female gender and sexuality.[9] Centuries-old taboos against the body in the patriarchal milieu of the Punjab have only been reinforced through the Cartesian dichotomy from the colonial experience. These thick patriarchal lenses have blinded Sikhs from recognizing the liberalism of their Gurus in which the male is not antithetical to the female, the spiritual is no different from the physical, and woman's bodies are good in every which way.

The Gurus were male, but they connected with the female at a very deep level. Woman is not "body" below the spirit, a hindrance in the spiritual goal. Rather, she is the one who has the sensitivity and longing for the Divine and opens the way to the transcendent. The male poets put on her dress and her jewels, they perform her jobs, they emulate her feelings, and they think with her. Indeed, they are the "men who are capable of becoming woman" and carry us into Cixous' vast elsewhere (Cixous and Clément 1986). In their case, the human does not stand for the male but actually includes both male and female. The language of the Sikh Gurus is truly gender-inclusive, for they experience the divine from her female presence with their own bodies. They shatter gender essentialism, for theirs is not a symbolic grammar in which the female is masked and oppressed. Theirs is a transcendent mode of existence actualized in *her corporeality in its full emotional resonance.* A profound human–divine intimacy is at the heart of the sacred text:

dhan saci sanguti
hari sang suti (GGS: 843)
[The woman abides in Truth
Intimately locked in the divine embrace]

Here we encounter a woman whose sexuality is healthy and wholesome. She is the scriptural model who incarnates physical beauty and spiritual awakening, and she can rapturously make love with her Divine lover. Sikh scripture provides many such powerful images that overturn fears of intimacy prevalent in our culture and inspire us to enter exciting new horizons with all of our human faculties. In the context of the translation process, Gayatri Spivak has suggested a surrendering to the original text that is "more erotic than ethical" (1993: 185), and interestingly in the Sikh verse, we have a woman who is morally refined, erotically locked in the arms of her Lover—her surrender at once erotic and ethical.

The GGS underscores the spiritual horizon as embodied experience. Its pervasive bridal symbol continuously evokes a sensuous and palpable union with the Infinite One. The Groom (*sahu*) is known as *agam* (infinite), *agocaru* (unfathomable), and *ajoni* (unborn). He is utterly metaphysical and beyond all sense perception. The bride perceives and proclaims the infiniteness of her Groom: "O my Beloved, Your limits I cannot fathom." She is perplexed and wonders how she is going to "see" her True Groom when "He has no color, no garb, no form" (GGS: 945). Ultimately, it is the bride who succeeds in creating proximity to the distant Groom. She is the one to chart out the way that will make the Transcendent accessible to human experience. She addresses the impersonal Being in most personal terms: "O my handsome, unfathomable Beloved"; "my Beloved is the most delicious inebriation." For her, "my loved Groom isn't far at all" (GGS: 1197). She praises him lavishly:

My Beloved is utterly glorious, brilliantly crimson,
Compassionate, beneficent, beloved, enticer of the hearts,
Overflowing with *rasa*, like the *lala* flower. (GGS: 1331)

Of course some feminists may object to the longing bride as a model. They might see an inherent dualism in the relation between the bride and her Groom, and the role of the bride seeking her Beloved may be viewed as restrictive and stifling. In this case, we must remember that it emerged in Sikh literature at a point in time and space when the Indian woman was humiliatingly subjugated. So, to see *her* as the paragon of physical and spiritual refinement, and hear *her* desire being expressed, is significant. The symbol has to be fully understood and not simplistically read as though women must be dependent on their husbands. That would be a grave distortion. The Granth Sahibian bride is dependent only upon the Divine One, and men, women, and the entire cosmos share this dependence. The Sikh scriptural message is not the subjugation of the female to the male, for her Groom is beyond gender. Rather, it is the rising of the individual spirit toward the Absolute. The rich variety of GGS images reveals the complexity and dignity of the female experience, which can loosen the grip of masculine symbols upon the contemporary imagination.

The basic assumption underlying the Sikh holy writ is that *her* body is good. It condemns taboos surrounding menstruation and postpartum pollution. To date, our society is horrified at the sight of women's blood—whether it is her monthly period or the blood that accompanies every birth. Considered a private, shameful process, menstruation is equated with being ill or weak. Because of their menstrual periods, women are barred from religious services. As feminist scholars have been reminding us, the disdain for this natural feminine phenomenon has contributed to the low status of women. The Sikh Gurus were aware of the sexism prevalent in their society and denounced taboos against women. The fear of the gaze, touch, and speech of a menstruating woman had been internalized by Indian society for centuries. These deeply rooted negative attitudes to women have seeped into all of India's religious traditions.

The GGS radically dispels conventional taboos against female pollution, menstruation, and sexuality. Menstrual bleeding is regarded as an essential, natural process. Life itself begins with it. The first Guru reprimands those who stigmatize the garment stained with menstrual blood as polluted (GGS: 140). Many scriptural verses celebrate the female body, and they affirm the centrality of menstrual blood in the creative process: "From mother's blood and father's semen" is created the human form (GGS: 1022). More generally, in the GGS, female figures have positive characteristics. They possess knowledge, they are morally and spiritually refined, they are beautiful, and they exist as palpable models for the human–divine nexus. As friends, companions, lovers, and brides, they are embedded in a web of intimate relationships. Women in the roles of sister, mother, and sister-in-law are also quintessential to Sikh epistemology and spirituality. But male hermeneutics has deflected attention away from the positive accounts of women and their place in the GGS.

A feminist understanding of the Gurus' lyrics boldly subverts patriarchal assumptions and brings into focus empowering female paradigms. It reverses what Judith Fetterly diagnosed as "*immasculation* of women by men."[10] The scriptural verses incite both men and women readers to celebrate their vital *tan* (body)-*man* (mind/heart) conjunction. Our bodies are the home of the infinite One. Our flesh is the source for attaining religious wisdom. "Whatever lies in paradise beyond can be found in the body here—*jo brahmande soi pinde*," proclaims the GGS, loud and clear (GGS: 695). The body is our marvelous possession. The lingering effect of such passages produces an emotional strength. It raises social consciousness and energizes readers to challenge inequality and injustice. The Sikh sacred text has the potential to make the splintered self whole again and thus create pathways for men and women alike to gain their authentic subjectivity.

Construction of Sikh Identity and Feminine Connotations

Sikh men and women wear the five Ks as symbols of their religious identity (the uncut hair, the comb, the sword, the bracelet, and the underpants).[11] Yet, from the traditional codifiers of the ethical manuals to contemporary theoreticians, these five items of faith have been interpreted entirely in male terms. As the Western scholar Brian Axel says, "Within a peculiar, yet seemingly quite banal, logic of signification, 'Sikh' and 'Sikhs' have come to signify Sikh men." (2001: 45). Axel righty observes that Sikh identity has been blatantly monopolized by the male gender, for it is the Sikh man, with beard and turban, who is "positioned on book covers, as frontispieces, and within texts—to stand in for all Sikhs" (2001: 45).

By contesting the conventional understanding of the hair, the comb, the sword, the bracelet, and the underwear, we recognize their spiritual horizon. As I see it, the personal identity of the Sikhs is constructed from the transcendent textures of the GGS (Singh 2005: Chapter 4). It was in a period of intense social and political oppression that the Tenth Guru created the Khalsa and gave them their external identifications—the five Ks. As I read it, these are constructed from the spiritual meaning derived from the holy book, the GGS. "Meaning," according to psychoanalyst Nancy Chodorow, "is an inextricable mixture of the sociocultural and historically contextualized on the one hand and the personally psychodynamic psychobiographically contextualized on the other" (Chodorow 1999: 2). The everyday articles from Guru Gobind Singh's culture—something so simple and common as a comb, a bracelet, a sword, long hair, underwear—had great personal meaning for him because they were laden with spirituality in a text that constituted his psychodynamic and psychobiographic being. The Tenth Sikh Guru grew up on the sacred utterances of his predecessors, which formed the core of his daily routine.

Each of the five Ks ontologically draws upon the female accoutrements enshrined in the GGS. Her hair is neatly braided (GGS: 558), and *her* braids are held together by embroidered tassels (GGS: 937). The long hair of women is an expression of the sanctification of the human personality in the Sikh holy writ. She embodies the central scriptural message that the relationship between the individual and the Divine is tightly braided by following her example of love and tenacity. Furthermore, the image of the brutally shorn hair during Babur's invasion recounted by Guru Nanak in his *Babur-vani* hymns must have been absorbed by his ninth successor. What was violated had to be restored. Guru Gobind Singh reacts to the political repression in his own times by reconstructing tragic memories into triumphant hopes. His people evermore were to keep their hair long, untouched by any scissors.

Similarly, the comb receives its religious significance from the sacred text. We can see the comb in her hands as "the woman with patience gets her braid knotted" (GGS: 359). Another verse from the GGS further qualifies, "It is with Truth that the woman braids her hair" (GGS: 54). Profoundly captured, Truth is the woman's hands holding her long hair and with the help of her comb, weaving the different strands together. The *kangha* (comb) is not an antithesis to the *kesha* (hair)—there is a synchronicity, a close relationship between them. Both, together, release, redesign, and retrieve infinite human potential. The comb is the instrument for attending to oneself, and so combing the hair becomes a self-reflective process, which leads to a life of beauty, imagination, and Truth for both men and women.

The third K—*kirpān* (sword)—is not only worn on the body of the Sikhs, it is mentally evoked in *Ardās* (prayer), and it is physiologically partaken both in the *amrit* sipped by the Khalsa and in the *karah prashad* eaten by the Sikh congregation. *Amrit* is prepared by churning the waters with a double-edged sword accompanied by the recitation of sacred verses; *karah prashad*, the warm and delicious Sikh sacrament, is not distributed to the congregation until it is sanctified by her touch. The sword exerts tremendous influence in the daily life of the Sikh community. The prototype for this K of the Sikhs is distinctly found in the GGS, where the sword is made up of *gur gianu*, literally "divine wisdom" (GGS: 235, 574, 983, 1072). Importantly, the paradigmatic person utilizing the sword in the GGS is a woman. The female subject heroically fights against her inner propensities: "By taking up the sword of knowledge, she fights against her mind and merges with herself" (GGS: 1022). Not only does she know how to wield the powerful sword but she also triumphs over her hostile opponents. She is a crucial model in Sikh epistemology. By following the way *she* carries and uses her sword, men and women alike can get to know the unknowable One.

The fourth K, the steel *kara* (bracelet), also evokes the female ornaments and the mode of dressing up treasured in the GGS. Worn by men and women, it is but another endorsement of the scriptural expression of spirituality through women's activities and embellishments. Like the sword, its material substance is the Divine. As Guru Nanak says, "By wearing the bracelet created by the Creator, consciousness is held steadily" (GGS: 359). Like the shorn hair, the bracelets made of ivory (*dand khand*) worn by the newlywed brides were also broken during Babur's invasion, recorded Guru Nanak. Years later, Guru Gobind Singh took the delicate ivory bracelets from his culture and gave them a new syntax—he converted them into a steel/iron bracelet to be courageously worn forever. The bracelets symbolizing a bride's transitory phase from daughter to wife were made into the *kara* to be worn by both men and women, from birth to death. And, wearers of the *kara* were to be equal and free to enter a profession of their choice.

Finally, the *kacha* (underpants) too is modeled on the metaphysical garments worn by the female figure in the GGS. Not those "who take off their clothes and go naked like Digambaras" (GGS: 1169), but she who "wears the clothes of Love" (GGS: 54) is prized in the Sikh sacred text. The GGS exalts her who "wears the clothes of Love" (GGS: 54) and presents *her* as the paradigm to be emulated by both men and women. Sadly though, these scriptural notes are rarely recognized in the five Ks, and their powerful multivalency has yet to be absorbed.

The Question of Performative Agency

The vital female subjectivity in the GGS is not only marginalized and overturned in its interpretation and translation but is also lost in its worship. Gadamer rightly reminds us that "application is neither a subsequent nor merely an occasional part of the phenomenon of understanding, but co-determines it as a whole from the beginning" (1989: 324). Sikhism has no priesthood, and nowhere in scripture are men delegated to be the sole custodians of their sacred text and leaders in worship, and yet women are tacitly discouraged from conducting public ceremonies. Women do play an active role in devotional practices at home, but when it comes to leading worship in *gurdwaras*, it is primarily the men.

In *Sikhism Today*, Jagbir Jhutti-Johal gives a snapshot of women's exclusion in religious service at the central place of Sikh worship—the Golden Temple:

> Here Sikh women are not allowed to read from the Guru Granth Sahib Sahib, play *kirtan* or perform any *sewa* in the sanctum sanctorum (main prayer room). These *sewas* are "reserved" for men only. (Jhutti-Johal 2011: 47–8).

Jhutti-Johal also cites the widely publicized discriminatory case from 2003, when two Sikh women were not allowed to even touch the palanquin carrying the GGS during its evening ritual. Likewise, Opinderjit Takhar in her case study at a *gurdwara* in the United Kingdom, describes taboos preventing women from cooking meals and preparing *karah prashad* during their menstrual period (Takhar 2005: 49–50).

Something is definitely out of joint here! Women are barred from touching or coming close to the very text that gives them so much space. How could modern women be victims of the very codes of pollution that their revered text rejected centuries earlier? It is essential that Sikhs—men and women—access their scriptural Guru directly. There is no established intermediary, no proxy. The circulating fears and phobias relayed via patriarchal hermeneutics have to end. Both men and women need to enter the hermeneutic process of the text they ardently revere. They must question the sexist codes that are being produced by hegemonic discourses and social practices. The biases and prejudices that block the ears and eyes have to be cleared away so that the sacred lyrics can make their way inside. Only then will the Gurus' message become an automatic reflex in everyday attitudes, actions, and performances.

Concluding Thoughts

In conclusion, I want to return to Valerie Kaur's article in the *Huffington Post*, since it highlights the subtle ways in which the stereotype of female invisibility, subservient passivity, and self-sacrificial altruism is getting worse in contemporary Sikh life. Women therefore have to work really hard to rid themselves of the false consciousness they have been bred upon for centuries. They should derive strength from the fact that their Gurus' teachings are intended for them—not to go against them! Living in a patriarchal society, the Gurus empathized with their situation and tried to create a window of opportunity through which women could achieve liberty, equality, and sorority. Sikh women should know how lucky they are to have their spiritual legacy. Equipped *with* their revered text, they must come out from their kitchens and homes and disrupt the sexist patterns in both domestic and public spheres.

Notes

This essay expands on my ideas expressed in a recent article for the *Oxford Handbook of Sikh Studies* (Oxford University Press). It is a revised version of my earlier essay, "Contesting Subjectivities: Feminist Hermeneutics of Sikh Scripture." In Reilley N. and Scriver S. (eds.) (2014) in *Religion, Gender, and the Public Sphere*, New York: Routledge. Also, some ideas have been taken from earlier work, *The Feminine Principle in the Sikh Vision of the Transcendent* (Cambridge University Press, 1993).

1 Dated between 1740 and 1765, "no existing rahit-mama carries us nearer to the time of the Guru Gobind Singh than this work." W. H. McLeod in his introduction to his translation and edition of the text (1987: 10).

2 See in particular Chapter 4, entitled *Durgā Recalled: Transition from Mythos to Ethos.*

3 All quotations from the standard Guru Granth Sahib (GGS) refer to the original standard text with its 1,430 pages. All translations are mine unless specified otherwise.

4 See Talib (1987: 2098): "In each being's heart pervasive." See also Singh (1965: 979): "and he pervaded the hearts of all."

5 See *Sabdarath Sri Guru Granth Sahib* (1964: 1026).

6 According to Eck, "Nourishing, enabling, kindling, breathing, moving in life and in death—this is Shakti" (1993: 137).

7 Throughout the *Mārkaṇḍeya Purāṇa*, the goddess is extolled as the source of boons both material and spiritual. An example: "When praised with flowers, incense, perfumes, and the like, She grants wealth, sons, an auspicious mind, the pathway to *dharma*" (12.38). See Coburn (1991: 82).

8 See Singh (1992: 323–4) entry on "Mai Bhago."

9 See, for example, Jantzen (1999).

10 This misogynistic principle teaches women to think like men and accept male values as the norm. But rather than impart virile power to women, the immasculation process leaves women powerless. See Judith Fetterley's excellent work (1991).

11 The five items all beginning with the letter "k" are *keśa* (uncut hair), *kangha* (comb tucked in the hair), *kara* (bracelet), *kirpan* (sword), and *kacha* (underpants).

References

Axel, Brian (2001). *The Nation's Tortured Body: Violence, Representation, and the Formation of a Sikh "Diaspora."* Durham, NC: Duke University Press.

Chodorow, Nancy (1999). *The Power of Feelings: Personal Meaning in Psychoanalysis, Gender, and Culture*. New Haven, CT: Yale University Press.

Cixous, H., and C. Clément (1986). *The Newly Born Woman*. Translated by B. Wing. Minneapolis: University of Minnesota Press.

Coburn, Thomas (1991). *Encountering the Goddess: A Translation of the Devi-Mahatmya and a Study of its Interpretation*. New York: SUNY Press.

Daly, Mary (1978). *Gyn-Ecology: The Metaethics of Radical Feminism*. Boston, MA: Beacon Press.

Eck, Diana (1993). *Encountering God: A Spiritual Journey from Benares to Bozeman*. Boston, MA: Beacon Press.

Fair, C. C. (1996). Female Foeticide among Vancouver Sikhs: Recontextualizing Sex Selection in the North American Diaspora. *International Journal of Punjab Studies* 3(1): 1–44.

Fetterley, Judith (1991). "Introduction on the Politics of Literature." In Robyn Warhol-Down and Diane Herndl (eds.), *Feminisms: An Anthology of Literary Theory and Criticism* (pp. 492–501). New Brunswick, NJ: Rutgers University Press.

Gadamer, Hans-Georg (1989). *Truth and Method*. New York: Crossroad.

Irigaray, L. (1993). *Sexes and Genealogies*. Translated by G. Gill. New York: Columbia University Press.

Jantzen, Grace (1999). *Becoming Divine: Towards a Feminist Philosophy of Religion*. Bloomington: Indiana University Press.

Jhutti-Johal, Jagbir (2011). *Sikhism Today*. New York: Continuum.

Kaur, Gunidar (1981). *The Guru Granth Sahib: Its Physics and Metaphysics*. New Delhi: Sterling.

Kaur, Valerie (2012). "10 Sikh Women You Should Know and Why You Should Know Them." *Huffington Post*, March 22. Accessed December 15, 2012, from http://www.huffingtonpost.com/valerie-kaur/10-sikh-women-you-should-know_b_1353700.html.

Mandair, Arvind (2009). *Religion and the Specter of the West: Sikhism, India, Post-Coloniality, and the Politics of Translation*. New York: Columbia University Press.

McLeod, W. H. (ed. and trans.). (1987). *The Chaupa Singh Rahit-Nama*. Dunedin: University of Otago Press.

Sabdarath Sri Guru Granth Sahib Sahib, 4th edn. (1964). Amritsar: Shromani Gudwara Prabandhak Committee.

Singh, Gopal (1965). *Sri Guru Granth Sahib: English Version*. New York: Taplinger.

Singh, Harbans (1992). *The Encyclopaedia of Sikhism* (pp. 323–4). Patiala: Punjabi University.

Singh, Nikky-Guninder Kaur (1993). *The Feminine Principle in the Sikh Vision of the Transcendent*. Cambridge: Cambridge University Press.

Singh, Nikky-Guninder Kaur (2005). *The Birth of the Khalsa: A Feminist Re-Memory of Sikh Identity*. Albany: State University of New York Press.

Spivak, Gayatri Chakravorty (1993). "The Politics of Translation." In Gayatri Chakravorty Spivak (ed.), *Outside in the Teaching Machine*. New York: Routledge.

Takhar, Opinderjit Kaur (2005). *Sikh Identity: An Exploration of Groups among Sikhs*. Burlington, VT: Ashgate.

Talib, G. S. (1987). *Sri Guru Granth Sahib: In English Translation*. Patiala: Punjabi University.

Index